BOOKS

NORWEGIAN
VOCABULARY

ENGLISH-
NORWEGIAN

The most useful words
To expand your lexicon and sharpen
your language skills

9000 words

Norwegian vocabulary for English speakers - 9000 words
By Andrey Taranov

T&P Books vocabularies are intended for helping you learn, memorize and review foreign words. The dictionary is divided into themes, covering all major spheres of everyday activities, business, science, culture, etc.

The process of learning words using T&P Books' theme-based dictionaries gives you the following advantages:

- Correctly grouped source information predetermines success at subsequent stages of word memorization
- Availability of words derived from the same root allowing memorization of word units (rather than separate words)
- Small units of words facilitate the process of establishing associative links needed for consolidation of vocabulary
- Level of language knowledge can be estimated by the number of learned words

T&P Books Publishing
www.tpbooks.com

ISBN: 978-1-78492-011-1

This book is also available in E-book formats.
Please visit www.tpbooks.com or the major online bookstores.

NORWEGIAN VOCABULARY
for English speakers

T&P Books vocabularies are intended to help you learn, memorize, and review foreign words. The vocabulary contains over 9000 commonly used words arranged thematically.

- Vocabulary contains the most commonly used words
- Recommended as an addition to any language course
- Meets the needs of beginners and advanced learners of foreign languages
- Convenient for daily use, revision sessions, and self-testing activities
- Allows you to assess your vocabulary

Special features of the vocabulary

- Words are organized according to their meaning, not alphabetically
- Words are presented in three columns to facilitate the reviewing and self-testing processes
- Words in groups are divided into small blocks to facilitate the learning process
- The vocabulary offers a convenient and simple transcription of each foreign word

The vocabulary has 256 topics including:

Basic Concepts, Numbers, Colors, Months, Seasons, Units of Measurement, Clothing & Accessories, Food & Nutrition, Restaurant, Family Members, Relatives, Character, Feelings, Emotions, Diseases, City, Town, Sightseeing, Shopping, Money, House, Home, Office, Working in the Office, Import & Export, Marketing, Job Search, Sports, Education, Computer, Internet, Tools, Nature, Countries, Nationalities and more ...

T&P BOOKS' THEME-BASED DICTIONARIES

The Correct System for Memorizing Foreign Words

Acquiring vocabulary is one of the most important elements of learning a foreign language, because words allow us to express our thoughts, ask questions, and provide answers. An inadequate vocabulary can impede communication with a foreigner and make it difficult to understand a book or movie well.

The pace of activity in all spheres of modern life, including the learning of modern languages, has increased. Today, we need to memorize large amounts of information (grammar rules, foreign words, etc.) within a short period. However, this does not need to be difficult. All you need to do is to choose the right training materials, learn a few special techniques, and develop your individual training system.

Having a system is critical to the process of language learning. Many people fail to succeed in this regard; they cannot master a foreign language because they fail to follow a system comprised of selecting materials, organizing lessons, arranging new words to be learned, and so on. The lack of a system causes confusion and eventually, lowers self-confidence.

T&P Books' theme-based dictionaries can be included in the list of elements needed for creating an effective system for learning foreign words. These dictionaries were specially developed for learning purposes and are meant to help students effectively memorize words and expand their vocabulary.

Generally speaking, the process of learning words consists of three main elements:

- Reception (creation or acquisition) of a training material, such as a word list
- Work aimed at memorizing new words
- Work aimed at reviewing the learned words, such as self-testing

All three elements are equally important since they determine the quality of work and the final result. All three processes require certain skills and a well-thought-out approach.

New words are often encountered quite randomly when learning a foreign language and it may be difficult to include them all in a unified list. As a result, these words remain written on scraps of paper, in book margins, textbooks, and so on. In order to systematize such words, we have to create and continually update a "book of new words." A paper notebook, a netbook, or a tablet PC can be used for these purposes.

This "book of new words" will be your personal, unique list of words. However, it will only contain the words that you came across during the learning process. For example, you might have written down the words "Sunday," "Tuesday," and "Friday." However, there are additional words for days of the week, for example, "Saturday," that are missing, and your list of words would be incomplete. Using a theme dictionary, in addition to the "book of new words," is a reasonable solution to this problem.

The theme-based dictionary may serve as the basis for expanding your vocabulary.

It will be your big "book of new words" containing the most frequently used words of a foreign language already included. There are quite a few theme-based dictionaries available, and you should ensure that you make the right choice in order to get the maximum benefit from your purchase.

Therefore, we suggest using theme-based dictionaries from T&P Books Publishing as an aid to learning foreign words. Our books are specially developed for effective use in the sphere of vocabulary systematization, expansion and review.

Theme-based dictionaries are not a magical solution to learning new words. However, they can serve as your main database to aid foreign-language acquisition. Apart from theme dictionaries, you can have copybooks for writing down new words, flash cards, glossaries for various texts, as well as other resources; however, a good theme dictionary will always remain your primary collection of words.

T&P Books' theme-based dictionaries are specialty books that contain the most frequently used words in a language.

The main characteristic of such dictionaries is the division of words into themes. For example, the *City* theme contains the words "street," "crossroads," "square," "fountain," and so on. The *Talking* theme might contain words like "to talk," "to ask," "question," and "answer".

All the words in a theme are divided into smaller units, each comprising 3–5 words. Such an arrangement improves the perception of words and makes the learning process less tiresome. Each unit contains a selection of words with similar meanings or identical roots. This allows you to learn words in small groups and establish other associative links that have a positive effect on memorization.

The words on each page are placed in three columns: a word in your native language, its translation, and its transcription. Such positioning allows for the use of techniques for effective memorization. After closing the translation column, you can flip through and review foreign words, and vice versa. "This is an easy and convenient method of review – one that we recommend you do often."

Our theme-based dictionaries contain transcriptions for all the foreign words. Unfortunately, none of the existing transcriptions are able to convey the exact nuances of foreign pronunciation. That is why we recommend using the transcriptions only as a supplementary learning aid. Correct pronunciation can only be acquired with the help of sound. Therefore our collection includes audio theme-based dictionaries.

The process of learning words using T&P Books' theme-based dictionaries gives you the following advantages:

- You have correctly grouped source information, which predetermines your success at subsequent stages of word memorization
- Availability of words derived from the same root (lazy, lazily, lazybones), allowing you to memorize word units instead of separate words
- Small units of words facilitate the process of establishing associative links needed for consolidation of vocabulary
- You can estimate the number of learned words and hence your level of language knowledge
- The dictionary allows for the creation of an effective and high-quality revision process
- You can revise certain themes several times, modifying the revision methods and techniques
- Audio versions of the dictionaries help you to work out the pronunciation of words and develop your skills of auditory word perception

The T&P Books' theme-based dictionaries are offered in several variants differing in the number of words: 1.500, 3.000, 5.000, 7.000, and 9.000 words. There are also dictionaries containing 15,000 words for some language combinations. Your choice of dictionary will depend on your knowledge level and goals.

We sincerely believe that our dictionaries will become your trusty assistant in learning foreign languages and will allow you to easily acquire the necessary vocabulary.

TABLE OF CONTENTS

MISCELLANEOUS

MAIN 500 VERBS

PRONUNCIATION GUIDE

Letter	Norwegian example	T&P phonetic alphabet	English example
Aa	plass	[ɑ], [ɑ:]	bath, to pass
Bb	bøtte, albue	[b]	baby, book
Cc [1]	centimeter	[s]	city, boss
Cc [2]	Canada	[k]	clock, kiss
Dd	radius	[d]	day, doctor
Ee	rett	[e:]	longer than in bell
Ee [3]	begå	[ɛ]	man, bad
Ff	fattig	[f]	face, food
Gg [4]	golf	[g]	game, gold
Gg [5]	gyllen	[j]	yes, New York
Gg [6]	regnbue	[ŋ]	English, ring
Hh	hektar	[h]	humor
Ii	kilometer	[ɪ], [i]	tin, see
Kk	konge	[k]	clock, kiss
Kk [7]	kirke	[h]	humor
Jj	fjerde	[j]	yes, New York
kj	bikkje	[h]	humor
Ll	halvår	[l]	lace, people
Mm	middag	[m]	magic, milk
Nn	november	[n]	name, normal
ng	id_langt	[ŋ]	English, ring
Oo [8]	honning	[ɔ]	bottle, doctor
Oo [9]	fot, krone	[u]	book
Pp	plomme	[p]	pencil, private
Qq	sequoia	[k]	clock, kiss
Rr	sverge	[r]	rice, radio
Ss	appelsin	[s]	city, boss
sk [10]	skikk, skyte	[ʃ]	machine, shark
Tt	stør, torsk	[t]	tourist, trip
Uu	brudd	[y]	fuel, tuna
Vv	kraftverk	[v]	very, river
Ww	webside	[v]	very, river
Xx	mexicaner	[ks]	box, taxi
Yy	nytte	[ɪ], [i]	tin, see
Zz [11]	New Zealand	[s]	star, cats
Ææ	vær, stær	[æ]	chess, man

Letter	Norwegian example	T&P phonetic alphabet	English example
Øø	ørn, gjø	[ø]	eternal, church
Åå	gås, værhår	[oː]	fall, bomb

Comments

[1] before **e**, **i**
[2] elsewhere
[3] unstressed
[4] before **a**, **o**, **u**, **å**
[5] before **i** and **y**
[6] in combination **gn**
[7] before **i** and **y**
[8] before two consonants
[9] before one consonant
[10] before **i** and **y**
[11] in loanwords only

ABBREVIATIONS
used in the vocabulary

English abbreviations

ab.	-	about
adj	-	adjective
adv	-	adverb
anim.	-	animate
as adj	-	attributive noun used as adjective
e.g.	-	for example
etc.	-	et cetera
fam.	-	familiar
fem.	-	feminine
form.	-	formal
inanim.	-	inanimate
masc.	-	masculine
math	-	mathematics
mil.	-	military
n	-	noun
pl	-	plural
pron.	-	pronoun
sb	-	somebody
sing.	-	singular
sth	-	something
v aux	-	auxiliary verb
vi	-	intransitive verb
vi, vt	-	intransitive, transitive verb
vt	-	transitive verb

Norwegian abbreviations

f	-	feminine noun
f pl	-	feminine plural
m	-	masculine noun
m pl	-	masculine plural
m/f	-	masculine, neuter
m/f pl	-	masculine/feminine plural
m/f/n	-	masculine/feminine/neuter

m/n	-	masculine, feminine
n	-	neuter
n pl	-	neuter plural
pl	-	plural

BASIC CONCEPTS

Basic concepts. Part 1

1. Pronouns

I, me	**jeg**	['jæj]
you	**du**	[dʉ]
he	**han**	['hɑn]
she	**hun**	['hʉn]
it	**det, den**	['de], ['den]
we	**vi**	['vi]
you (to a group)	**dere**	['derə]
they	**de**	['de]

2. Greetings. Salutations. Farewells

Hello! (fam.)	**Hei!**	['hæj]
Hello! (form.)	**Hallo! God dag!**	[hɑ'lʊ], [gʊ 'dɑ]
Good morning!	**God morn!**	[gʊ 'mɔːn]
Good afternoon!	**God dag!**	[gʊ'dɑ]
Good evening!	**God kveld!**	[gʊ 'kvɛl]
to say hello	**å hilse**	[ɔ 'hilsə]
Hi! (hello)	**Hei!**	['hæj]
greeting (n)	**hilsen** (m)	['hilsən]
to greet (vt)	**å hilse**	[ɔ 'hilsə]
How are you? (form.)	**Hvordan står det til?**	['vʊːdɑn stoːr de til]
How are you? (fam.)	**Hvordan går det?**	['vʊːdɑn gor de]
What's new?	**Hva nytt?**	[vɑ 'nʏt]
Goodbye! (form.)	**Ha det bra!**	[hɑ de 'brɑ]
Bye! (fam.)	**Ha det!**	[hɑ 'de]
See you soon!	**Vi ses!**	[vi sɛs]
Farewell!	**Farvel!**	[far'vɛl]
to say goodbye	**å si farvel**	[ɔ 'si far'vɛl]
So long!	**Ha det!**	[hɑ 'de]
Thank you!	**Takk!**	['tɑk]
Thank you very much!	**Tusen takk!**	['tʉsən tɑk]

You're welcome	Bare hyggelig	['bɑrə 'hʏgeli]
Don't mention it!	Ikke noe å takke for!	['ikə 'nʊe ɔ 'takə fɔr]
It was nothing	Ingen årsak!	['iŋən 'oːʂak]

Excuse me! (fam.)	Unnskyld, …	['ʉnˌʂyl …]
Excuse me! (form.)	Unnskyld meg, …	['ʉnˌʂyl me …]
to excuse (forgive)	å unnskylde	[ɔ 'ʉnˌʂylə]

to apologize (vi)	å unnskylde seg	[ɔ 'ʉnˌʂylə sæj]
My apologies	Jeg ber om unnskyldning	[jæj ber ɔm 'ʉnˌʂyldniŋ]
I'm sorry!	Unnskyld!	['ʉnˌʂyl]

to forgive (vt)	å tilgi	[ɔ 'tilˌji]
It's okay! (that's all right)	Ikke noe problem	['ikə 'nʊe prʊ'blem]
please (adv)	vær så snill	['vær ʂɔ 'snil]

Don't forget!	Ikke glem!	['ikə 'glem]
Certainly!	Selvfølgelig!	[sɛl'følgəli]
Of course not!	Selvfølgelig ikke!	[sɛl'følgəli 'ikə]

| Okay! (I agree) | OK! Enig! | [ɔ'kɛj], ['ɛni] |
| That's enough! | Det er nok! | [de ær 'nɔk] |

3. How to address

Excuse me, …	Unnskyld, …	['ʉnˌʂyl …]
mister, sir	Herr	['hær]
ma'am	Fru	['frʉ]
miss	Frøken	['frøkən]

young man	unge mann	['ʉŋə ˌman]
young man (little boy, kid)	guttunge	['gʉtˌʉŋə]
miss (little girl)	frøken	['frøkən]

4. Cardinal numbers. Part 1

0 zero	null	['nʉl]
1 one	en	['en]
2 two	to	['tʊ]
3 three	tre	['tre]
4 four	fire	['fire]

5 five	fem	['fɛm]
6 six	seks	['sɛks]
7 seven	sju	['ʂʉ]
8 eight	åtte	['ɔtə]
9 nine	ni	['ni]

10 ten	ti	['ti]
11 eleven	elleve	['ɛlvə]
12 twelve	tolv	['tɔl]
13 thirteen	tretten	['trɛtən]
14 fourteen	fjorten	['fjɔːʈən]
15 fifteen	femten	['fɛmtən]
16 sixteen	seksten	['sæjstən]
17 seventeen	sytten	['sʏtən]
18 eighteen	atten	['ɑtən]
19 nineteen	nitten	['nitən]
20 twenty	tjue	['çʉe]
21 twenty-one	tjueen	['çʉe en]
22 twenty-two	tjueto	['çʉe tʊ]
23 twenty-three	tjuetre	['çʉe tre]
30 thirty	tretti	['trɛti]
31 thirty-one	trettien	['trɛti en]
32 thirty-two	trettito	['trɛti tʊ]
33 thirty-three	trettitre	['trɛti tre]
40 forty	førti	['fœːʈi]
41 forty-one	førtien	['fœːʈi en]
42 forty-two	førtito	['fœːʈi tʊ]
43 forty-three	førtitre	['fœːʈi tre]
50 fifty	femti	['fɛmti]
51 fifty-one	femtien	['fɛmti en]
52 fifty-two	femtito	['fɛmti tʊ]
53 fifty-three	femtitre	['fɛmti tre]
60 sixty	seksti	['sɛksti]
61 sixty-one	sekstien	['sɛksti en]
62 sixty-two	sekstito	['sɛksti tʊ]
63 sixty-three	sekstitre	['sɛksti tre]
70 seventy	sytti	['sʏti]
71 seventy-one	syttien	['sʏti en]
72 seventy-two	syttito	['sʏti tʊ]
73 seventy-three	syttitre	['sʏti tre]
80 eighty	åtti	['ɔti]
81 eighty-one	åttien	['ɔti en]
82 eighty-two	åttito	['ɔti tʊ]
83 eighty-three	åttitre	['ɔti tre]
90 ninety	nitti	['niti]
91 ninety-one	nittien	['niti en]
92 ninety-two	nittito	['niti tʊ]
93 ninety-three	nittitre	['niti tre]

5. Cardinal numbers. Part 2

100 one hundred	**hundre**	['hʉndrə]
200 two hundred	**to hundre**	['tʊ ˌhʉndrə]
300 three hundred	**tre hundre**	['tre ˌhʉndrə]
400 four hundred	**fire hundre**	['fire ˌhʉndrə]
500 five hundred	**fem hundre**	['fɛm ˌhʉndrə]
600 six hundred	**seks hundre**	['sɛks ˌhʉndrə]
700 seven hundred	**syv hundre**	['syv ˌhʉndrə]
800 eight hundred	**åtte hundre**	['ɔtə ˌhʉndrə]
900 nine hundred	**ni hundre**	['ni ˌhʉndrə]
1000 one thousand	**tusen**	['tʉsən]
2000 two thousand	**to tusen**	['tʊ ˌtʉsən]
3000 three thousand	**tre tusen**	['tre ˌtʉsən]
10000 ten thousand	**ti tusen**	['ti ˌtʉsən]
one hundred thousand	**hundre tusen**	['hʉndrə ˌtʉsən]
million	**million** (m)	[mi'ljun]
billion	**milliard** (m)	[mi'lja:d]

6. Ordinal numbers

first (adj)	**første**	['fœʂtə]
second (adj)	**annen**	['ɑnən]
third (adj)	**tredje**	['trɛdjə]
fourth (adj)	**fjerde**	['fjærə]
fifth (adj)	**femte**	['fɛmtə]
sixth (adj)	**sjette**	['ʂɛtə]
seventh (adj)	**sjuende**	['ʂʉenə]
eighth (adj)	**åttende**	['ɔtenə]
ninth (adj)	**niende**	['nienə]
tenth (adj)	**tiende**	['tienə]

7. Numbers. Fractions

fraction	**brøk** (m)	['brøk]
one half	**en halv**	[en 'hal]
one third	**en tredjedel**	[en 'trɛdjəˌdel]
one quarter	**en fjerdedel**	[en 'fjærəˌdel]
one eighth	**en åttendedel**	[en 'ɔtenəˌdel]
one tenth	**en tiendedel**	[en 'tienəˌdel]
two thirds	**to tredjedeler**	['tʊ 'trɛdjəˌdelər]
three quarters	**tre fjerdedeler**	['tre 'fjærˌdelər]

8. Numbers. Basic operations

subtraction	**subtraksjon** (m)	[sʉbtrak'ʂʉn]
to subtract (vi, vt)	**å subtrahere**	[ɔ 'sʉbtraˌherə]
division	**divisjon** (m)	[divi'ʂʉn]
to divide (vt)	**å dividere**	[ɔ divi'derə]
addition	**addisjon** (m)	[adi'ʂʉn]
to add up (vt)	**å addere**	[ɔ a'derə]
to add (vi, vt)	**å addere**	[ɔ a'derə]
multiplication	**multiplikasjon** (m)	[mʉltiplika'ʂʉn]
to multiply (vt)	**å multiplisere**	[ɔ mʉltipli'serə]

9. Numbers. Miscellaneous

digit, figure	**siffer** (n)	['sifər]
number	**tall** (n)	['tal]
numeral	**tallord** (n)	['talˌuːr]
minus sign	**minus** (n)	['minʉs]
plus sign	**pluss** (n)	['plʉs]
formula	**formel** (m)	['fɔrməl]
calculation	**beregning** (m/f)	[be'rɛjniŋ]
to count (vi, vt)	**å telle**	[ɔ 'tɛlə]
to count up	**å telle opp**	[ɔ 'tɛlə ɔp]
to compare (vt)	**å sammenlikne**	[ɔ 'samənˌliknə]
How much?	**Hvor mye?**	[vʉr 'mye]
How many?	**Hvor mange?**	[vʉr 'maŋə]
sum, total	**sum** (m)	['sʉm]
result	**resultat** (n)	[resʉl'tat]
remainder	**rest** (m)	['rɛst]
a few (e.g., ~ years ago)	**noen**	['nʉən]
few (I have ~ friends)	**få, ikke mange**	['fɔ], ['ikə ˌmaŋə]
a little (~ tired)	**lite**	['litə]
the rest	**rest** (m)	['rɛst]
one and a half	**halvannen**	[hal'anən]
dozen	**dusin** (n)	[dʉ'sin]
in half (adv)	**i 2 halvdeler**	[i tʉ hal'delər]
equally (evenly)	**jevnt**	['jɛvnt]
half	**halvdel** (m)	['haldel]
time (three ~s)	**gang** (m)	['gaŋ]

10. The most important verbs. Part 1

to advise (vt)	**å råde**	[ɔ 'rɔːdə]
to agree (say yes)	**å samtykke**	[ɔ 'sɑmˌtʏkə]

to answer (vi, vt)	**å svare**	[ɔ 'svarə]
to apologize (vi)	**å unnskylde seg**	[ɔ 'ʉnˌsylə sæj]
to arrive (vi)	**å ankomme**	[ɔ 'anˌkomə]
to ask (~ oneself)	**å spørre**	[ɔ 'spørə]
to ask (~ sb to do sth)	**å be**	[ɔ 'be]
to be (vi)	**å være**	[ɔ 'værə]
to be afraid	**å frykte**	[ɔ 'frʏktə]
to be hungry	**å være sulten**	[ɔ 'værə 'sʉltən]
to be interested in ...	**å interessere seg**	[ɔ intərə'serə sæj]
to be needed	**å være behøv**	[ɔ 'værə bə'høv]
to be surprised	**å bli forundret**	[ɔ 'bli fɔ'rʉndrət]
to be thirsty	**å være tørst**	[ɔ 'værə 'tœʂt]
to begin (vt)	**å begynne**	[ɔ be'jinə]
to belong to ...	**å tilhøre ...**	[ɔ 'tilˌhørə ...]
to boast (vi)	**å prale**	[ɔ 'pralə]
to break (split into pieces)	**å bryte**	[ɔ 'brʏtə]
to call (~ for help)	**å tilkalle**	[ɔ 'tilˌkalə]
can (v aux)	**å kunne**	[ɔ 'kʉnə]
to catch (vt)	**å fange**	[ɔ 'faŋə]
to change (vt)	**å endre**	[ɔ 'ɛndrə]
to choose (select)	**å velge**	[ɔ 'vɛlgə]
to come down (the stairs)	**å gå ned**	[ɔ 'gɔ ne]
to compare (vt)	**å sammenlikne**	[ɔ 'samənˌliknə]
to complain (vi, vt)	**å klage**	[ɔ 'klagə]
to confuse (mix up)	**å forveksle**	[ɔ fɔr'vɛkslə]
to continue (vt)	**å fortsette**	[ɔ 'fɔrtˌsɛtə]
to control (vt)	**å kontrollere**	[ɔ kʉntrɔ'lerə]
to cook (dinner)	**å lage**	[ɔ 'lagə]
to cost (vt)	**å koste**	[ɔ 'kɔstə]
to count (add up)	**å telle**	[ɔ 'tɛlə]
to count on ...	**å regne med ...**	[ɔ 'rɛjnə me ...]
to create (vt)	**å opprette**	[ɔ 'ɔpˌrɛtə]
to cry (weep)	**å gråte**	[ɔ 'groːtə]

11. The most important verbs. Part 2

to deceive (vi, vt)	**å fuske**	[ɔ 'fʉskə]
to decorate (tree, street)	**å pryde**	[ɔ 'prʏdə]
to defend (a country, etc.)	**å forsvare**	[ɔ fɔ'ʂvarə]
to demand (request firmly)	**å kreve**	[ɔ 'krevə]
to dig (vt)	**å grave**	[ɔ 'gravə]
to discuss (vt)	**å diskutere**	[ɔ diskʉ'terə]
to do (vt)	**å gjøre**	[ɔ 'jørə]

to doubt (have doubts)	å tvile	[ɔ 'tvilə]
to drop (let fall)	å tappe	[ɔ 'tapə]
to enter (room, house, etc.)	å komme inn	[ɔ 'kɔmə in]
to excuse (forgive)	å unnskylde	[ɔ 'ʉn,sylə]
to exist (vi)	å eksistere	[ɔ ɛksi'sterə]
to expect (foresee)	å forutse	[ɔ 'fɔrʉt,sə]
to explain (vt)	å forklare	[ɔ for'klɑrə]
to fall (vi)	å falle	[ɔ 'fɑlə]
to find (vt)	å finne	[ɔ 'finə]
to finish (vt)	å slutte	[ɔ 'ʂlʉtə]
to fly (vi)	å fly	[ɔ 'fly]
to follow … (come after)	å følge etter …	[ɔ 'følə 'ɛtər …]
to forget (vi, vt)	å glemme	[ɔ 'glemə]
to forgive (vt)	å tilgi	[ɔ 'til,ji]
to give (vt)	å gi	[ɔ 'ji]
to give a hint	å gi et vink	[ɔ 'ji et 'vink]
to go (on foot)	å gå	[ɔ 'gɔ]
to go for a swim	å bade	[ɔ 'bɑdə]
to go out (for dinner, etc.)	å gå ut	[ɔ 'gɔ ʉt]
to guess (the answer)	å gjette	[ɔ 'jɛtə]
to have (vt)	å ha	[ɔ 'hɑ]
to have breakfast	å spise frokost	[ɔ 'spisə ,frʉkɔst]
to have dinner	å spise middag	[ɔ 'spisə 'mi,dɑ]
to have lunch	å spise lunsj	[ɔ 'spisə ,lʉnʂ]
to hear (vt)	å høre	[ɔ 'hørə]
to help (vt)	å hjelpe	[ɔ 'jɛlpə]
to hide (vt)	å gjemme	[ɔ 'jɛmə]
to hope (vi, vt)	å håpe	[ɔ 'ho:pə]
to hunt (vi, vt)	å jage	[ɔ 'jɑgə]
to hurry (vi)	å skynde seg	[ɔ 'ʂynə sæj]

12. The most important verbs. Part 3

to inform (vt)	å informere	[ɔ infor'merə]
to insist (vi, vt)	å insistere	[ɔ insi'sterə]
to insult (vt)	å fornærme	[ɔ fɔ:'nærmə]
to invite (vt)	å innby, å invitere	[ɔ 'inby], [ɔ invi'terə]
to joke (vi)	å spøke	[ɔ 'spøkə]
to keep (vt)	å beholde	[ɔ be'hɔlə]
to keep silent	å tie	[ɔ 'tie]
to kill (vt)	å døde, å myrde	[ɔ 'dødə], [ɔ 'mʏ:də]
to know (ɛb)	å kjenne	[ɔ 'çɛnə]

to know (sth)	å vite	[ɔ 'viːtə]
to laugh (vi)	å le, å skratte	[ɔ 'leː], [ɔ 'skrɑtə]
to liberate (city, etc.)	å befri	[ɔ beˈfriː]
to like (I like ...)	å like	[ɔ 'liːkə]
to look for ... (search)	å søke ...	[ɔ 'søːkə ...]
to love (sb)	å elske	[ɔ 'ɛlskə]
to make a mistake	å gjøre feil	[ɔ 'jøːrə ˌfæjl]
to manage, to run	å styre, å lede	[ɔ 'styːrə], [ɔ 'leːdə]
to mean (signify)	å bety	[ɔ 'beːty]
to mention (talk about)	å omtale, å nevne	[ɔ 'ɔmˌtɑlə], [ɔ 'nɛvnə]
to miss (school, etc.)	å skulke	[ɔ 'skʉlkə]
to notice (see)	å bemerke	[ɔ beˈmærkə]
to object (vi, vt)	å innvende	[ɔ 'inˌvɛnə]
to observe (see)	å observere	[ɔ ɔbsɛrˈveːrə]
to open (vt)	å åpne	[ɔ 'ɔpnə]
to order (meal, etc.)	å bestille	[ɔ beˈstilə]
to order (mil.)	å beordre	[ɔ beˈɔrdrə]
to own (possess)	å besidde, å eie	[ɔ bɛˈsidə], [ɔ 'æjə]
to participate (vi)	å delta	[ɔ 'dɛltɑ]
to pay (vi, vt)	å betale	[ɔ beˈtɑlə]
to permit (vt)	å tillate	[ɔ 'tiˌlɑtə]
to plan (vt)	å planlegge	[ɔ 'plɑnˌlegə]
to play (children)	å leke	[ɔ 'leːkə]
to pray (vi, vt)	å be	[ɔ 'beː]
to prefer (vt)	å foretrekke	[ɔ 'fɔrəˌtrɛkə]
to promise (vt)	å love	[ɔ 'lɔvə]
to pronounce (vt)	å uttale	[ɔ 'ʉtˌtɑlə]
to propose (vt)	å foreslå	[ɔ 'fɔrəˌslɔ]
to punish (vt)	å straffe	[ɔ 'strɑfə]

13. The most important verbs. Part 4

to read (vi, vt)	å lese	[ɔ 'leːsə]
to recommend (vt)	å anbefale	[ɔ 'ɑnbeˌfɑlə]
to refuse (vi, vt)	å vegre seg	[ɔ 'vɛgrə sæj]
to regret (be sorry)	å beklage	[ɔ beˈklɑgə]
to rent (sth from sb)	å leie	[ɔ 'læjə]
to repeat (say again)	å gjenta	[ɔ 'jɛntɑ]
to reserve, to book	å reservere	[ɔ resɛrˈveːrə]
to run (vi)	å løpe	[ɔ 'løpə]
to save (rescue)	å redde	[ɔ 'rɛdə]
to say (~ thank you)	å si	[ɔ 'siː]
to scold (vt)	å skjelle	[ɔ 'ʃɛːlə]
to see (vt)	å se	[ɔ 'seː]

to sell (vt)	**å selge**	[ɔ 'sɛlə]
to send (vt)	**å sende**	[ɔ 'sɛnə]
to shoot (vi)	**å skyte**	[ɔ 'ʂytə]
to shout (vi)	**å skrike**	[ɔ 'skrikə]
to show (vt)	**å vise**	[ɔ 'visə]
to sign (document)	**å underskrive**	[ɔ 'ʉnəˌskrivə]
to sit down (vi)	**å sette seg**	[ɔ 'sɛtə sæj]
to smile (vi)	**å smile**	[ɔ 'smilə]
to speak (vi, vt)	**å tale**	[ɔ 'talə]
to steal (money, etc.)	**å stjele**	[ɔ 'stjelə]
to stop (for pause, etc.)	**å stoppe**	[ɔ 'stɔpə]
to stop (please ~ calling me)	**å slutte**	[ɔ 'ʂlʉtə]
to study (vt)	**å studere**	[ɔ stʉ'derə]
to swim (vi)	**å svømme**	[ɔ 'svœmə]
to take (vt)	**å ta**	[ɔ 'ta]
to think (vi, vt)	**å tenke**	[ɔ 'tɛnkə]
to threaten (vt)	**å true**	[ɔ 'trʉə]
to touch (with hands)	**å røre**	[ɔ 'rørə]
to translate (vt)	**å oversette**	[ɔ 'ɔvəˌsɛtə]
to trust (vt)	**å stole på**	[ɔ 'stʉlə pɔ]
to try (attempt)	**å prøve**	[ɔ 'prøvə]
to turn (e.g., ~ left)	**å svinge**	[ɔ 'sviɲə]
to underestimate (vt)	**å undervurdere**	[ɔ 'ʉnərvʉːˌḍerə]
to understand (vt)	**å forstå**	[ɔ fɔ'ʂtɔ]
to unite (vt)	**å forene**	[ɔ fɔ'renə]
to wait (vt)	**å vente**	[ɔ 'vɛntə]
to want (wish, desire)	**å ville**	[ɔ 'vilə]
to warn (vt)	**å varsle**	[ɔ 'vɑʂlə]
to work (vi)	**å arbeide**	[ɔ 'arˌbæjdə]
to write (vt)	**å skrive**	[ɔ 'skrivə]
to write down	**å skrive ned**	[ɔ 'skrivə ne]

14. Colors

color	**farge** (m)	['fɑrgə]
shade (tint)	**nyanse** (m)	[ny'ɑnse]
hue	**fargetone** (m)	['fɑrgəˌtʉnə]
rainbow	**regnbue** (m)	['ræjnˌbʉːə]
white (adj)	**hvit**	['vit]
black (adj)	**svart**	['svɑːt]
gray (adj)	**grå**	['grɔ]
green (adj)	**grønn**	['grœn]

yellow (adj)	**gul**	['gʉl]
red (adj)	**rød**	['rø]
blue (adj)	**blå**	['blɔ]
light blue (adj)	**lyseblå**	['lysəˌblɔ]
pink (adj)	**rosa**	['rɔsɑ]
orange (adj)	**oransje**	[ɔ'rɑnʂɛ]
violet (adj)	**fiolett**	[fiʊ'løt]
brown (adj)	**brun**	['brʉn]
golden (adj)	**gullgul**	['gʉl]
silvery (adj)	**sølv-**	['søl-]
beige (adj)	**beige**	['bɛːʂ]
cream (adj)	**kremfarget**	['krɛmˌfɑrgət]
turquoise (adj)	**turkis**	[tʉr'kis]
cherry red (adj)	**kirsebærrød**	['çiʂəbærˌrød]
lilac (adj)	**lilla**	['lilɑ]
crimson (adj)	**karminrød**	['kɑrmʊ'sinˌrød]
light (adj)	**lys**	['lys]
dark (adj)	**mørk**	['mœrk]
bright, vivid (adj)	**klar**	['klɑr]
colored (pencils)	**farge-**	['fɑrgə-]
color (e.g., ~ film)	**farge-**	['fɑrgə-]
black-and-white (adj)	**svart-hvit**	['svɑːʈ vit]
plain (one-colored)	**ensfarget**	['ɛnsˌfɑrgət]
multicolored (adj)	**mangefarget**	['mɑnəˌfɑrgət]

15. Questions

Who?	**Hvem?**	['vɛm]
What?	**Hva?**	['vɑ]
Where? (at, in)	**Hvor?**	['vʊr]
Where (to)?	**Hvorhen?**	['vʊrhen]
From where?	**Hvorfra?**	['vʊrfrɑ]
When?	**Når?**	[nɔr]
Why? (What for?)	**Hvorfor?**	['vʊrfʊr]
Why? (~ are you crying?)	**Hvorfor?**	['vʊrfʊr]
What for?	**Hvorfor?**	['vʊrfʊr]
How? (in what way)	**Hvordan?**	['vʊːdɑn]
What? (What kind of ...?)	**Hvilken?**	['vilkən]
Which?	**Hvilken?**	['vilkən]
To whom?	**Til hvem?**	[til 'vɛm]
About whom?	**Om hvem?**	[ɔm 'vɛm]
About what?	**Om hva?**	[ɔm 'vɑ]
With whom?	**Med hvem?**	[me 'vɛm]

How many?	Hvor mange?	[vʊr 'maŋə]
How much?	Hvor mye?	[vʊr 'mye]
Whose?	Hvis?	['vis]

16. Prepositions

with (accompanied by)	med	[me]
without	uten	['ʉtən]
to (indicating direction)	til	['til]
about (talking ~ ...)	om	['ɔm]
before (in time)	før	['før]
in front of ...	foran, framfor	['fɔran], ['framfɔr]

under (beneath, below)	under	['ʉnər]
above (over)	over	['ɔvər]
on (atop)	på	['pɔ]
from (off, out of)	fra	['fra]
of (made from)	av	[aː]

| in (e.g., ~ ten minutes) | om | ['ɔm] |
| over (across the top of) | over | ['ɔvər] |

17. Function words. Adverbs. Part 1

Where? (at, in)	Hvor?	['vʊr]
here (adv)	her	['hɛr]
there (adv)	der	['dɛr]

| somewhere (to be) | et sted | [et 'sted] |
| nowhere (not anywhere) | ingensteds | ['iŋən,stɛts] |

| by (near, beside) | ved | ['ve] |
| by the window | ved vinduet | [ve 'vindʉə] |

Where (to)?	Hvorhen?	['vʊrhen]
here (e.g., come ~!)	hit	['hit]
there (e.g., to go ~)	dit	['dit]
from here (adv)	herfra	['hɛr,fra]
from there (adv)	derfra	['dɛr,fra]

| close (adv) | nær | ['nær] |
| far (adv) | langt | ['laŋt] |

near (e.g., ~ Paris)	nær	['nær]
nearby (adv)	i nærheten	[i 'nær,hetən]
not far (adv)	ikke langt	['ikə 'laŋt]
left (adj)	venstre	['vɛnstrə]
on the left	til venstre	[til 'vɛnstrə]

to the left	**til venstre**	[til 'vɛnstrə]
right (adj)	**høyre**	['højrə]
on the right	**til høyre**	[til 'højrə]
to the right	**til høyre**	[til 'højrə]
in front (adv)	**foran**	['fɔran]
front (as adj)	**fremre**	['frɛmrə]
ahead (the kids ran ~)	**fram**	['fram]
behind (adv)	**bakom**	['bakɔm]
from behind	**bakfra**	['bak͵fra]
back (towards the rear)	**tilbake**	[til'bakə]
middle	**midt** (m)	['mit]
in the middle	**i midten**	[i 'mitən]
at the side	**fra siden**	[fra 'sidən]
everywhere (adv)	**overalt**	[ɔvər'alt]
around (in all directions)	**rundt omkring**	['rʉnt ɔm'kriŋ]
from inside	**innefra**	['inə͵fra]
somewhere (to go)	**et sted**	[et 'sted]
straight (directly)	**rett, direkte**	['rɛt], ['di'rɛktə]
back (e.g., come ~)	**tilbake**	[til'bakə]
from anywhere	**et eller annet steds fra**	[et 'elər ͵aːnt 'stɛts fra]
from somewhere	**et eller annet steds fra**	[et 'elər ͵aːnt 'stɛts fra]
firstly (adv)	**for det første**	[fɔr de 'fœʂtə]
secondly (adv)	**for det annet**	[fɔr de 'aːnt]
thirdly (adv)	**for det tredje**	[fɔr de 'trɛdje]
suddenly (adv)	**plutselig**	['plʉtseli]
at first (in the beginning)	**i begynnelsen**	[i be'jinəlsən]
for the first time	**for første gang**	[fɔr 'fœʂtə ͵gaŋ]
long before ...	**lenge før ...**	['leŋə 'før ...]
anew (over again)	**på nytt**	[pɔ 'nʏt]
for good (adv)	**for godt**	[fɔr 'gɔt]
never (adv)	**aldri**	['aldri]
again (adv)	**igjen**	[i'jɛn]
now (adv)	**nå**	['nɔ]
often (adv)	**ofte**	['ɔftə]
then (adv)	**da**	['da]
urgently (quickly)	**omgående**	['ɔm͵gɔːnə]
usually (adv)	**vanligvis**	['vanli͵vis]
by the way, ...	**forresten, ...**	[fɔ'rɛstən ...]
possible (that is ~)	**mulig, kanskje**	['mʉli], ['kanʂə]
probably (adv)	**sannsynligvis**	[san'sʏnli͵vis]
maybe (adv)	**kanskje**	['kanʂə]
besides ...	**dessuten, ...**	[des'ʉtən ...]

that's why ...	**derfor ...**	['dɛrfor ...]
in spite of ...	**på tross av ...**	['pɔ 'trɔs ɑː ...]
thanks to ...	**takket være ...**	['takət ˌværə ...]

what (pron.)	**hva**	['vɑ]
that (conj.)	**at**	[ɑt]
something	**noe**	['nʊe]
anything (something)	**noe**	['nʊe]
nothing	**ingenting**	['iŋəntiŋ]

who (pron.)	**hvem**	['vɛm]
someone	**noen**	['nʊən]
somebody	**noen**	['nʊən]

nobody	**ingen**	['iŋən]
nowhere (a voyage to ~)	**ingensteds**	['iŋənˌstɛts]
nobody's	**ingens**	['iŋəns]
somebody's	**noens**	['nʊəns]

so (I'm ~ glad)	**så**	['sɔː]
also (as well)	**også**	['ɔsɔ]
too (as well)	**også**	['ɔsɔ]

18. Function words. Adverbs. Part 2

Why?	**Hvorfor?**	['vʊrfʊr]
for some reason	**av en eller annen grunn**	[ɑː en elər 'ɑnən ˌgrʉn]
because ...	**fordi ...**	[fɔ'di ...]
for some purpose	**av en eller annen grunn**	[ɑː en elər 'ɑnən ˌgrʉn]

and	**og**	['ɔ]
or	**eller**	['elər]
but	**men**	['men]
for (e.g., ~ me)	**for, til**	[fɔr], [til]

too (~ many people)	**for, altfor**	['fɔr], ['altfɔr]
only (exclusively)	**bare**	['bɑrə]
exactly (adv)	**presis, eksakt**	[prɛ'sis], [ɛk'sɑkt]
about (more or less)	**cirka**	['sirkɑ]

approximately (adv)	**omtrent**	[ɔm'trɛnt]
approximate (adj)	**omtrentlig**	[ɔm'trɛntli]
almost (adv)	**nesten**	['nɛstən]
the rest	**rest** (m)	['rɛst]

the other (second)	**den annen**	[den 'ɑnən]
other (different)	**andre**	['ɑndrə]
each (adj)	**hver**	['vɛr]
any (no matter which)	**hvilken som helst**	['vilkən sɔm 'hɛlst]
many, much (a lot of)	**mye**	['mye]

many people	**mange**	['maŋə]
all (everyone)	**alle**	['alə]
in return for …	**til gjengjeld for …**	[til 'jɛnjɛl for …]
in exchange (adv)	**istedenfor**	[i'steden‚for]
by hand (made)	**for hånd**	[for 'hon]
hardly (negative opinion)	**neppe**	['nepə]
probably (adv)	**sannsynligvis**	[san'sʏnli‚vis]
on purpose (intentionally)	**med vilje**	[me 'viljə]
by accident (adv)	**tilfeldigvis**	[til'fɛldivis]
very (adv)	**meget**	['megət]
for example (adv)	**for eksempel**	[for ɛk'sɛmpəl]
between	**mellom**	['mɛlɔm]
among	**blant**	['blant]
so much (such a lot)	**så mye**	['sɔ: myə]
especially (adv)	**særlig**	['sæ:li̩]

Basic concepts. Part 2

19. Weekdays

Monday	**mandag** (m)	['manˌda]
Tuesday	**tirsdag** (m)	['tiʂˌda]
Wednesday	**onsdag** (m)	['ʊnsˌda]
Thursday	**torsdag** (m)	['tɔʂˌda]
Friday	**fredag** (m)	['frɛˌda]
Saturday	**lørdag** (m)	['lørˌda]
Sunday	**søndag** (m)	['sønˌda]
today (adv)	**i dag**	[i 'da]
tomorrow (adv)	**i morgen**	[i 'mɔːən]
the day after tomorrow	**i overmorgen**	[i 'ɔvərˌmɔːən]
yesterday (adv)	**i går**	[i 'gor]
the day before yesterday	**i forgårs**	[i 'forˌgɔʂ]
day	**dag** (m)	['da]
working day	**arbeidsdag** (m)	['arbæjdsˌda]
public holiday	**festdag** (m)	['fɛstˌda]
day off	**fridag** (m)	['friˌda]
weekend	**ukeslutt** (m), **helg** (f)	['ʉkəˌslʉt], ['hɛlg]
all day long	**hele dagen**	['helə 'dagən]
the next day (adv)	**neste dag**	['nɛstə ˌda]
two days ago	**for to dager siden**	[for tʉ 'dagər ˌsidən]
the day before	**dagen før**	['dagən 'før]
daily (adj)	**daglig**	['dagli]
every day (adv)	**hver dag**	['vɛr da]
week	**uke** (m/f)	['ʉkə]
last week (adv)	**siste uke**	['sistə 'ʉkə]
next week (adv)	**i neste uke**	[i 'nɛstə 'ʉkə]
weekly (adj)	**ukentlig**	['ʉkəntli]
every week (adv)	**hver uke**	['vɛr 'ʉkə]
twice a week	**to ganger per uke**	['tʉ 'gaŋər per 'ʉkə]
every Tuesday	**hver tirsdag**	['vɛr 'tiʂda]

20. Hours. Day and night

morning	**morgen** (m)	['mɔːən]
in the morning	**om morgenen**	[ɔm 'mɔːenən]
noon, midday	**middag** (m)	['miˌda]

in the afternoon	om ettermiddagen	[ɔm 'ɛtər͵midagən]
evening	kveld (m)	['kvɛl]
in the evening	om kvelden	[ɔm 'kvɛlən]
night	natt (m/f)	['nat]
at night	om natta	[ɔm 'nata]
midnight	midnatt (m/f)	['mid͵nat]

second	sekund (m/n)	[se'kʉn]
minute	minutt (n)	[mi'nʉt]
hour	time (m)	['timə]
half an hour	halvtime (m)	['hal͵timə]
a quarter-hour	kvarter (n)	[kvɑːʈer]
fifteen minutes	femten minutter	['fɛmtən mi'nʉtər]
24 hours	døgn (n)	['døjn]

sunrise	soloppgang (m)	['sʉlɔp͵gɑŋ]
dawn	daggry (n)	['dɑg͵gry]
early morning	tidlig morgen (m)	['tili 'mɔːən]
sunset	solnedgang (m)	['sʉlned͵gɑŋ]

early in the morning	tidlig om morgenen	['tili ɔm 'mɔːenən]
this morning	i morges	[i 'mɔrəs]
tomorrow morning	i morgen tidlig	[i 'mɔːən 'tili]
this afternoon	i formiddag	[i 'fɔrmi͵da]
in the afternoon	om ettermiddagen	[ɔm 'ɛtər͵midagən]
tomorrow afternoon	i morgen ettermiddag	[i 'mɔːən 'ɛtər͵mida]
tonight (this evening)	i kveld	[i 'kvɛl]
tomorrow night	i morgen kveld	[i 'mɔːən ͵kvɛl]

at 3 o'clock sharp	presis klokka tre	[prɛ'sis 'klɔka tre]
about 4 o'clock	ved fire-tiden	[ve 'fire ͵tidən]
by 12 o'clock	innen klokken tolv	['inən 'klɔkən tɔl]

in 20 minutes	om tjue minutter	[ɔm 'çʉə mi'nʉtər]
in an hour	om en time	[ɔm en 'timə]
on time (adv)	i tide	[i 'tidə]

a quarter of …	kvart på …	['kvaːʈ pɔ …]
within an hour	innen en time	['inən en 'timə]
every 15 minutes	hvert kvarter	['vɛːʈ kvaː'ʈer]
round the clock	døgnet rundt	['døjne ͵rʉnt]

21. Months. Seasons

January	januar (m)	['janʉ͵ar]
February	februar (m)	['febrʉ͵ar]
March	mars (m)	['maʂ]
April	april (m)	[a'pril]
May	mai (m)	['maj]
June	juni (m)	['jʉni]

July	juli (m)	['jɵli]
August	august (m)	[aʊ'gʊst]
September	september (m)	[sep'tɛmbər]
October	oktober (m)	[ɔk'tʊbər]
November	november (m)	[nʊ'vɛmbər]
December	desember (m)	[de'sɛmbər]

spring	vår (m)	['voːr]
in spring	om våren	[ɔm 'voːrən]
spring (as adj)	vår-, vårlig	['voːr-], ['voːli]

summer	sommer (m)	['sɔmər]
in summer	om sommeren	[ɔm 'sɔmerən]
summer (as adj)	sommer-	['sɔmər-]

fall	høst (m)	['høst]
in fall	om høsten	[ɔm 'høstən]
fall (as adj)	høst-, høstlig	['høst-], ['høstli]

winter	vinter (m)	['vintər]
in winter	om vinteren	[ɔm 'vinterən]
winter (as adj)	vinter-	['vintər-]

month	måned (m)	['moːnət]
this month	denne måneden	['dɛnə 'moːnedən]
next month	neste måned	['nɛstə 'moːnət]
last month	forrige måned	['fɔriə ˌmoːnət]

a month ago	for en måned siden	[fɔr en 'moːnət ˌsidən]
in a month (a month later)	om en måned	[ɔm en 'moːnət]
in 2 months (2 months later)	om to måneder	[ɔm 'tʊ 'moːnedər]
the whole month	en hel måned	[en 'hel 'moːnət]
all month long	hele måned	['helə 'moːnət]

monthly (~ magazine)	månedlig	['moːnədli]
monthly (adv)	månedligt	['moːnedlət]
every month	hver måned	[ˌvɛr 'moːnət]
twice a month	to ganger per måned	['tʊ 'gɑŋər per 'moːnət]

year	år (n)	['ɔr]
this year	i år	[i 'oːr]
next year	neste år	['nɛstə ˌoːr]
last year	i fjor	[i 'fjɔr]

a year ago	for et år siden	[fɔr et 'oːr ˌsidən]
in a year	om et år	[ɔm et 'oːr]
in two years	om to år	[ɔm 'tʊ 'oːr]

the whole year	hele året	['helə 'oːrə]
all year long	hele året	['helə 'oːrə]
every year	hvert år	['vɛːʈ 'oːr]

annual (adj)	**årlig**	['o:li]
annually (adv)	**årlig, hvert år**	['o:li], ['vɛ:t 'ɔr]
4 times a year	**fire ganger per år**	['fire 'gaŋər per 'o:r]
date (e.g., today's ~)	**dato** (m)	['datʊ]
date (e.g., ~ of birth)	**dato** (m)	['datʊ]
calendar	**kalender** (m)	[ka'lendər]
half a year	**halvår** (n)	['hal‚o:r]
six months	**halvår** (n)	['hal‚o:r]
season (summer, etc.)	**årstid** (m/f)	['o:ʂ‚tid]
century	**århundre** (n)	['ɔr‚hʉndrə]

22. Time. Miscellaneous

time	**tid** (m/f)	['tid]
moment	**øyeblikk** (n)	['øjə‚blik]
instant (n)	**øyeblikk** (n)	['øjə‚blik]
instant (adj)	**øyeblikkelig**	['øjə‚blikəli]
lapse (of time)	**tidsavsnitt** (n)	['tids‚afsnit]
life	**liv** (n)	['liv]
eternity	**evighet** (m)	['ɛvi‚het]
epoch	**epoke** (m)	[ɛ'pʊkə]
era	**æra** (m)	['ærɑ]
cycle	**syklus** (m)	['syklʉs]
period	**periode** (m)	[pæri'ʊdə]
term (short-~)	**sikt** (m)	['sikt]
the future	**framtid** (m/f)	['fram‚tid]
future (as adj)	**framtidig, fremtidig**	['fram‚tidi], ['frɛm‚tidi]
next time	**neste gang**	['nɛstə ‚gaŋ]
the past	**fortid** (m/f)	['fɔ:‚tid]
past (recent)	**forrige**	['fɔriə]
last time	**siste gang**	['sistə ‚gaŋ]
later (adv)	**senere**	['senerə]
after (prep.)	**etterpå**	['ɛtər‚pɔ]
nowadays (adv)	**for nærværende**	[for 'nær‚værnə]
now (adv)	**nå**	['nɔ]
immediately (adv)	**umiddelbart**	['ʉmidəl‚ba:t]
soon (adv)	**snart**	['snɑ:t]
in advance (beforehand)	**på forhånd**	[pɔ 'fo:r‚hɔn]
a long time ago	**for lenge siden**	[for 'leŋə ‚sidən]
recently (adv)	**nylig**	['nyli]
destiny	**skjebne** (m)	['ʂɛbnə]
memories (childhood ~)	**minner** (n pl)	['minər]
archives	**arkiv** (n)	[ar'kiv]
during ...	**under ...**	['ʉnər ...]

long, a long time (adv)	lenge	['leŋə]
not long (adv)	ikke lenge	['ikə 'leŋə]
early (in the morning)	tidlig	['tili]
late (not early)	sent	['sɛnt]

forever (for good)	for alltid	[fɔr 'al,tid]
to start (begin)	å begynne	[ɔ be'jinə]
to postpone (vt)	å utsette	[ɔ 'ʉt,sɛtə]

at the same time	samtidig	['sam,tidi]
permanently (adv)	alltid, stadig	['al,tid], ['stadi]
constant (noise, pain)	konstant	[kʊn'stant]
temporary (adj)	midlertidig, temporær	['midlə,tidi], ['tɛmpɔ,rær]
sometimes (adv)	av og til	['av ɔ ,til]
rarely (adv)	sjelden	['ʂɛlən]
often (adv)	ofte	['ɔftə]

23. Opposites

| rich (adj) | rik | ['rik] |
| poor (adj) | fattig | ['fati] |

| ill, sick (adj) | syk | ['syk] |
| well (not sick) | frisk | ['frisk] |

| big (adj) | stor | ['stʊr] |
| small (adj) | liten | ['litən] |

| quickly (adv) | fort | ['fʊːt] |
| slowly (adv) | langsomt | ['laŋsɔmt] |

| fast (adj) | hurtig | ['hø:ʈi] |
| slow (adj) | langsom | ['laŋsɔm] |

| glad (adj) | glad | ['gla] |
| sad (adj) | sørgmodig | [sør'mʊdi] |

| together (adv) | sammen | ['samən] |
| separately (adv) | separat | [sepa'rat] |

| aloud (to read) | høyt | ['højt] |
| silently (to oneself) | for seg selv | [fɔr sæj 'sɛl] |

| tall (adj) | høy | ['høj] |
| low (adj) | lav | ['lav] |

| deep (adj) | dyp | ['dyp] |
| shallow (adj) | grunn | ['grʉn] |

| yes | ja | ['ja] |

no	**nei**	['næj]
distant (in space)	**fjern**	['fjæːn]
nearby (adj)	**nær**	['nær]
far (adv)	**langt**	['lɑŋt]
nearby (adv)	**i nærheten**	[i 'nær‚hetən]
long (adj)	**lang**	['lɑŋ]
short (adj)	**kort**	['kʊːt]
good (kindhearted)	**god**	['gʊ]
evil (adj)	**ond**	['ʊn]
married (adj)	**gift**	['jift]
single (adj)	**ugift**	[ʉː'jift]
to forbid (vt)	**å forby**	[ɔ fɔr'by]
to permit (vt)	**å tillate**	[ɔ 'ti‚lɑtə]
end	**slutt** (m)	['ʂlʉt]
beginning	**begynnelse** (m)	[be'jinəlsə]
left (adj)	**venstre**	['vɛnstrə]
right (adj)	**høyre**	['højrə]
first (adj)	**første**	['fœʂtə]
last (adj)	**sist**	['sist]
crime	**forbrytelse** (m)	[fɔr'brytəlsə]
punishment	**straff** (m)	['strɑf]
to order (vt)	**å beordre**	[ɔ be'ɔrdrə]
to obey (vi, vt)	**å underordne seg**	[ɔ 'ʉnər‚ɔrdnə sæj]
straight (adj)	**rett**	['rɛt]
curved (adj)	**kroket**	['krɔkət]
paradise	**paradis** (n)	['pɑrɑ‚dis]
hell	**helvete** (n)	['hɛlvetə]
to be born	**å fødes**	[ɔ 'fødə]
to die (vi)	**å dø**	[ɔ 'dø]
strong (adj)	**sterk**	['stærk]
weak (adj)	**svak**	['svɑk]
old (adj)	**gammel**	['gɑməl]
young (adj)	**ung**	['ʉŋ]
old (adj)	**gammel**	['gɑməl]
new (adj)	**ny**	['ny]

hard (adj)	hard	['hɑr]
soft (adj)	bløt	['bløt]
warm (tepid)	varm	['vɑrm]
cold (adj)	kald	['kɑl]
fat (adj)	tykk	['tʏk]
thin (adj)	tynn	['tʏn]
narrow (adj)	smal	['smɑl]
wide (adj)	bred	['bre]
good (adj)	bra	['brɑ]
bad (adj)	dårlig	['doːli]
brave (adj)	tapper	['tɑpər]
cowardly (adj)	feig	['fæjg]

24. Lines and shapes

square	kvadrat (n)	[kvɑ'drɑt]
square (as adj)	kvadratisk	[kvɑ'drɑtisk]
circle	sirkel (m)	['sirkəl]
round (adj)	rund	['rʉn]
triangle	trekant (m)	['treˌkɑnt]
triangular (adj)	trekantet	['treˌkɑntət]
oval	oval (m)	[ʊ'vɑl]
oval (as adj)	oval	[ʊ'vɑl]
rectangle	rektangel (n)	['rɛkˌtɑŋəl]
rectangular (adj)	rettvinklet	['rɛtˌvinklət]
pyramid	pyramide (m)	[pyrɑ'midə]
rhombus	rombe (m)	['rʊmbə]
trapezoid	trapes (m/n)	[trɑ'pes]
cube	kube, terning (m)	['kʉbə], ['tæːŋiŋ]
prism	prisme (n)	['prismə]
circumference	omkrets (m)	['ɔmˌkrɛts]
sphere	sfære (m)	['sfærə]
ball (solid sphere)	kule (m/f)	['kʉːlə]
diameter	diameter (m)	['diɑˌmetər]
radius	radius (m)	['rɑdiʉs]
perimeter (circle's ~)	perimeter (n)	[peri'metər]
center	midtpunkt (n)	['mitˌpʉnkt]
horizontal (adj)	horisontal	[hʊrisɔn'tɑl]
vertical (adj)	loddrett, lodd-	['lɔdˌrɛt], ['lɔd-]
parallel (n)	parallell (m)	[pɑrɑ'lel]
parallel (as adj)	parallell	[pɑrɑ'lel]

line	**linje** (m)	['linjə]
stroke	**strek** (m)	['strɛk]
straight line	**rett linje** (m/f)	['rɛt 'linjə]
curve (curved line)	**kurve** (m)	['kʉrvə]
thin (line, etc.)	**tynn**	['tʏn]
contour (outline)	**kontur** (m)	[kʊn'tʉr]

intersection	**skjæringspunkt** (n)	['særiŋsˌpʉnkt]
right angle	**rett vinkel** (m)	['rɛt 'vinkəl]
segment	**segment** (n)	[seg'mɛnt]
sector	**sektor** (m)	['sɛktʊr]
side (of triangle)	**side** (m/f)	['sidə]
angle	**vinkel** (m)	['vinkəl]

25. Units of measurement

weight	**vekt** (m)	['vɛkt]
length	**lengde** (m/f)	['leŋdə]
width	**bredde** (m)	['brɛdə]
height	**høyde** (m)	['højdə]
depth	**dybde** (m)	['dʏbdə]
volume	**volum** (n)	[vɔ'lʉm]
area	**areal** (n)	[ˌare'al]

gram	**gram** (n)	['gram]
milligram	**milligram** (n)	['miliˌgram]
kilogram	**kilogram** (n)	['çiluˌgram]
ton	**tonn** (m/n)	['tɔn]
pound	**pund** (n)	['pʉn]
ounce	**unse** (m)	['ʉnsə]

meter	**meter** (m)	['metər]
millimeter	**millimeter** (m)	['miliˌmetər]
centimeter	**centimeter** (m)	['sɛntiˌmetər]
kilometer	**kilometer** (m)	['çiluˌmetər]
mile	**mil** (m/f)	['mil]

inch	**tomme** (m)	['tɔmə]
foot	**fot** (m)	['fʊt]
yard	**yard** (m)	['jaːrd]

square meter	**kvadratmeter** (m)	[kva'dratˌmetər]
hectare	**hektar** (n)	['hɛktar]

liter	**liter** (m)	['litər]
degree	**grad** (m)	['grad]
volt	**volt** (m)	['vɔlt]
ampere	**ampere** (m)	[am'pɛr]
horsepower	**hestekraft** (m/f)	['hɛstəˌkraft]
quantity	**mengde** (m)	['mɛŋdə]

a little bit of ...	få ...	['fɔ ...]
half	halvdel (m)	['haldel]
dozen	dusin (n)	[dʉ'sin]
piece (item)	stykke (n)	['stʏkə]
size	størrelse (m)	['stœrəlsə]
scale (map ~)	målestokk (m)	['mo:lə‚stɔk]
minimal (adj)	minimal	[mini'mal]
the smallest (adj)	minste	['minstə]
medium (adj)	middel-	['midəl-]
maximal (adj)	maksimal	[maksi'mal]
the largest (adj)	største	['stœʂtə]

26. Containers

canning jar (glass ~)	glaskrukke (m/f)	['glas‚krʉkə]
can	boks (m)	['bɔks]
bucket	bøtte (m/f)	['bœtə]
barrel	tønne (m)	['tœnə]
wash basin (e.g., plastic ~)	vaskefat (n)	['vaskə‚fat]
tank (100L water ~)	tank (m)	['tank]
hip flask	lommelerke (m/f)	['lʊmə‚lærkə]
jerrycan	bensinkanne (m/f)	[bɛn'sin‚kanə]
tank (e.g., tank car)	tank (m)	['tank]
mug	krus (n)	['krʉs]
cup (of coffee, etc.)	kopp (m)	['kɔp]
saucer	tefat (n)	['te‚fat]
glass (tumbler)	glass (n)	['glas]
wine glass	vinglass (n)	['vin‚glas]
stock pot (soup pot)	gryte (m/f)	['grytə]
bottle (~ of wine)	flaske (m)	['flaskə]
neck (of the bottle, etc.)	flaskehals (m)	['flaskə‚hals]
carafe (decanter)	karaffel (m)	[ka'rafəl]
pitcher	mugge (m/f)	['mʉgə]
vessel (container)	beholder (m)	[be'hɔlər]
pot (crock, stoneware ~)	pott, potte (m)	['pɔt], ['pɔtə]
vase	vase (m)	['vasə]
bottle (perfume ~)	flakong (m)	[fla'kɔŋ]
vial, small bottle	flaske (m/f)	['flaskə]
tube (of toothpaste)	tube (m)	['tʉbə]
sack (bag)	sekk (m)	['sɛk]
bag (paper ~, plastic ~)	pose (m)	['pʊsə]
pack (of cigarettes, etc.)	pakke (m/f)	['pakə]

box (e.g., shoebox)	eske (m/f)	['ɛskə]
crate	kasse (m/f)	['kasə]
basket	kurv (m)	['kʉrv]

27. Materials

material	materiale (n)	[materi'alə]
wood (n)	tre (n)	['trɛ]
wood-, wooden (adj)	tre-, av tre	['trɛ-], [ɑ: 'trɛ]

| glass (n) | glass (n) | ['glɑs] |
| glass (as adj) | glass- | ['glɑs-] |

| stone (n) | stein (m) | ['stæjn] |
| stone (as adj) | stein- | ['stæjn-] |

| plastic (n) | plast (m) | ['plɑst] |
| plastic (as adj) | plast- | ['plɑst-] |

| rubber (n) | gummi (m) | ['gʉmi] |
| rubber (as adj) | gummi- | ['gʉmi-] |

| cloth, fabric (n) | tøy (n) | ['tøj] |
| fabric (as adj) | tøy- | ['tøj-] |

| paper (n) | papir (n) | [pɑ'pir] |
| paper (as adj) | papir- | [pɑ'pir-] |

| cardboard (n) | papp, kartong (m) | ['pɑp], [kɑ:'ʈɔŋ] |
| cardboard (as adj) | papp-, kartong- | ['pɑp-], [kɑ:'ʈɔŋ-] |

polyethylene	polyetylen (n)	['pʉlyɛtyˌlen]
cellophane	cellofan (m)	[sɛlu'fɑn]
linoleum	linoleum (m)	[li'nɔleum]
plywood	kryssfiner (m)	['krʏsfiˌnɛr]

porcelain (n)	porselen (n)	[pɔṣə'len]
porcelain (as adj)	porselens-	[pɔṣə'lens-]
clay (n)	leir (n)	['læjr]
clay (as adj)	leir-	['læjr-]
ceramic (n)	keramikk (m)	[çerɑ'mik]
ceramic (as adj)	keramisk	[çe'rɑmisk]

28. Metals

metal (n)	metall (n)	[me'tɑl]
metal (as adj)	metall-	[me'tɑl-]
alloy (n)	legering (m/f)	[le'geriŋ]

gold (n)	**gull** (n)	['gʉl]
gold, golden (adj)	**av gull, gull-**	[ɑ: 'gʉl], ['gʉl-]
silver (n)	**sølv** (n)	['søl]
silver (as adj)	**sølv-, av sølv**	['søl-], [ɑ: 'søl]
iron (n)	**jern** (n)	['jæːɳ]
iron-, made of iron (adj)	**jern-**	['jæːɳ-]
steel (n)	**stål** (n)	['stɔl]
steel (as adj)	**stål-**	['stɔl-]
copper (n)	**kobber** (n)	['kɔbər]
copper (as adj)	**kobber-**	['kɔbər-]
aluminum (n)	**aluminium** (n)	[ɑlu'minium]
aluminum (as adj)	**aluminium-**	[ɑlu'minium-]
bronze (n)	**bronse** (m)	['brɔnsə]
bronze (as adj)	**bronse-**	['brɔnsə-]
brass	**messing** (m)	['mɛsiŋ]
nickel	**nikkel** (m)	['nikəl]
platinum	**platina** (m/n)	['plɑtinɑ]
mercury	**kvikksølv** (n)	['kvikˌsøl]
tin	**tinn** (n)	['tin]
lead	**bly** (n)	['bly]
zinc	**sink** (m/n)	['sink]

HUMAN BEING

Human being. The body

29. Humans. Basic concepts

human being	menneske (n)	['mɛnəskə]
man (adult male)	mann (m)	['man]
woman	kvinne (m/f)	['kvinə]
child	barn (n)	['bɑːn]
girl	jente (m/f)	['jɛntə]
boy	gutt (m)	['gʉt]
teenager	tenåring (m)	['tɛnoːriŋ]
old man	eldre mann (m)	['ɛldrə ˌman]
old woman	eldre kvinne (m/f)	['ɛldrə ˌkvinə]

30. Human anatomy

organism (body)	organisme (m)	[ɔrgɑ'nismə]
heart	hjerte (n)	['jæːtə]
blood	blod (n)	['blʉ]
artery	arterie (m)	[ɑː'ʈeriə]
vein	vene (m)	['veːnə]
brain	hjerne (m)	['jæːŋə]
nerve	nerve (m)	['nærvə]
nerves	nerver (m pl)	['nærvər]
vertebra	ryggvirvel (m)	['rʏgˌvirvəl]
spine (backbone)	ryggrad (m)	['rʏgˌrɑd]
stomach (organ)	magesekk (m)	['mɑgəˌsɛk]
intestines, bowels	innvoller, tarmer (m pl)	['inˌvɔlər], ['tɑrmər]
intestine (e.g., large ~)	tarm (m)	['tɑrm]
liver	lever (m)	['levər]
kidney	nyre (m/n)	['nyrə]
bone	bein (n)	['bæjn]
skeleton	skjelett (n)	[ʂe'let]
rib	ribbein (n)	['ribˌbæjn]
skull	hodeskalle (m)	['hʉdəˌskɑlə]
muscle	muskel (m)	['mʉskəl]
biceps	biceps (m)	['bisɛps]

triceps	**triceps** (m)	['trisɛps]
tendon	**sene** (m/f)	['se:nə]
joint	**ledd** (n)	['led]
lungs	**lunger** (m pl)	['lʉŋər]
genitals	**kjønnsorganer** (n pl)	['çœns‚ɔr'ɡɑnər]
skin	**hud** (m/f)	['hʉd]

31. Head

head	**hode** (n)	['hʊdə]
face	**ansikt** (n)	['ɑnsikt]
nose	**nese** (m/f)	['nese]
mouth	**munn** (m)	['mʉn]

eye	**øye** (n)	['øjə]
eyes	**øyne** (n pl)	['øjnə]
pupil	**pupill** (m)	[pʉ'pil]
eyebrow	**øyenbryn** (n)	['øjən‚bryn]
eyelash	**øyenvipp** (m)	['øjən‚vip]
eyelid	**øyelokk** (m)	['øjə‚lɔk]

tongue	**tunge** (m/f)	['tʉŋə]
tooth	**tann** (m/f)	['tɑn]
lips	**lepper** (m/f pl)	['lepər]
cheekbones	**kinnbein** (n pl)	['çin‚bæjn]
gum	**tannkjøtt** (n)	['tɑn‚çœt]
palate	**gane** (m)	['ɡɑnə]

nostrils	**nesebor** (n pl)	['nesə‚bʊr]
chin	**hake** (m/f)	['hɑkə]
jaw	**kjeve** (m)	['çɛvə]
cheek	**kinn** (n)	['çin]

forehead	**panne** (m/f)	['pɑnə]
temple	**tinning** (m)	['tiniŋ]
ear	**øre** (n)	['ørə]
back of the head	**bakhode** (n)	['bɑk‚hʊdə]
neck	**hals** (m)	['hɑls]
throat	**strupe, hals** (m)	['strʉpə], ['hɑls]

hair	**hår** (n pl)	['hɔr]
hairstyle	**frisyre** (m)	[fri'syrə]
haircut	**hårfasong** (m)	['hoːrfɑ‚sɔŋ]
wig	**parykk** (m)	[pɑ'rʏk]

mustache	**mustasje** (m)	[mʉ'stɑʂə]
beard	**skjegg** (n)	['ʂɛɡ]
to have (a beard, etc.)	**å ha**	[ɔ 'hɑ]
braid	**flette** (m/f)	['fletə]
sideburns	**bakkenbarter** (pl)	['bɑkən‚bɑːţər]

red-haired (adj)	rødhåret	['rø‚ho:rət]
gray (hair)	grå	['grɔ]
bald (adj)	skallet	['skɑlət]
bald patch	skallet flekk (m)	['skɑlət ‚flek]

| ponytail | hestehale (m) | ['hɛstə‚hɑlə] |
| bangs | pannelugg (m) | ['pɑnə‚lʉg] |

32. Human body

hand	hånd (m/f)	['hɔn]
arm	arm (m)	['ɑrm]
finger	finger (m)	['fiŋər]
toe	tå (m/f)	['tɔ]
thumb	tommel (m)	['tɔməl]
little finger	lillefinger (m)	['lilə‚fiŋər]
nail	negl (m)	['nɛjl]

fist	knyttneve (m)	['knʏt‚nevə]
palm	håndflate (m/f)	['hɔn‚flɑtə]
wrist	håndledd (n)	['hɔn‚led]
forearm	underarm (m)	['ʉnər‚ɑrm]
elbow	albue (m)	['ɑl‚bʉə]
shoulder	skulder (m)	['skʉldər]

leg	bein (n)	['bæjn]
foot	fot (m)	['fʊt]
knee	kne (n)	['knɛ]
calf (part of leg)	legg (m)	['leg]
hip	hofte (m)	['hɔftə]
heel	hæl (m)	['hæl]

body	kropp (m)	['krɔp]
stomach	mage (m)	['mɑgə]
chest	bryst (n)	['brʏst]
breast	bryst (n)	['brʏst]
flank	side (m/f)	['sidə]
back	rygg (m)	['rʏg]
lower back	korsrygg (m)	['kɔːʂ‚rʏg]
waist	liv (n), midje (m/f)	['liv], ['midjə]

navel (belly button)	navle (m)	['nɑvlə]
buttocks	rumpeballer (m pl)	['rʉmpə‚bɑlər]
bottom	bak (m)	['bɑk]

beauty mark	føflekk (m)	['fø‚flek]
birthmark (café au lait spot)	fødselsmerke (n)	['føtsəls‚mærke]
tattoo	tatovering (m/f)	[tɑtʊ'vɛriŋ]
scar	arr (n)	['ɑr]

Clothing & Accessories

33. Outerwear. Coats

clothes	klær (n)	['klær]
outerwear	yttertøy (n)	['ytə‚tøj]
winter clothing	vinterklær (n pl)	['vintər‚klær]
coat (overcoat)	frakk (m), kåpe (m/f)	['frɑk], ['ko:pə]
fur coat	pels (m), pelskåpe (m/f)	['pɛls], ['pɛls‚ko:pə]
fur jacket	pelsjakke (m/f)	['pɛls‚jakə]
down coat	dunjakke (m/f)	['dʉn‚jakə]
jacket (e.g., leather ~)	jakke (m/f)	['jakə]
raincoat (trenchcoat, etc.)	regnfrakk (m)	['ræjn‚frɑk]
waterproof (adj)	vanntett	['vɑn‚tɛt]

34. Men's & women's clothing

shirt (button shirt)	skjorte (m/f)	['ʂœ:ʈə]
pants	bukse (m)	['bʉksə]
jeans	jeans (m)	['dʒins]
suit jacket	dressjakke (m/f)	['drɛs‚jakə]
suit	dress (m)	['drɛs]
dress (frock)	kjole (m)	['çulə]
skirt	skjørt (n)	['ʂø:t]
blouse	bluse (m)	['blʉsə]
knitted jacket (cardigan, etc.)	strikket trøye (m/f)	['strikə 'trøjə]
jacket (of woman's suit)	blazer (m)	['blæsər]
t-shirt	T-skjorte (m/f)	['te‚ʂœ:ʈə]
shorts (short trousers)	shorts (m)	['ʂɔ:ʈs]
tracksuit	treningsdrakt (m/f)	['treniŋs‚drɑkt]
bathrobe	badekåpe (m/f)	['bɑdə‚ko:pə]
pajamas	pyjamas (m)	[py'ʂɑmɑs]
sweater	sweater (m)	['svɛtər]
pullover	pullover (m)	[pʉ'lɔvər]
vest	vest (m)	['vɛst]
tailcoat	livkjole (m)	['liv‚çulə]
tuxedo	smoking (m)	['smɔkiŋ]

uniform	uniform (m)	[ɵni'fɔrm]
workwear	arbeidsklær (n pl)	['arbæjds͵klær]
overalls	kjeledress, overall (m)	['çelə͵drɛs], ['ɔvɛr͵ɔl]
coat (e.g., doctor's smock)	kittel (m)	['çitəl]

35. Clothing. Underwear

underwear	undertøy (n)	['ɵnə͵tøj]
boxers, briefs	underbukse (m/f)	['ɵnər͵bɵksə]
panties	truse (m/f)	['trɵsə]
undershirt (A-shirt)	undertrøye (m/f)	['ɵnə͵trøjə]
socks	sokker (m pl)	['sɔkər]
nightgown	nattkjole (m)	['nat͵çulə]
bra	behå (m)	['be͵hɔ]
knee highs (knee-high socks)	knestrømper (m/f pl)	['knɛ͵strømpər]
pantyhose	strømpebukse (m/f)	['strømpə͵bɵksə]
stockings (thigh highs)	strømper (m/f pl)	['strømpər]
bathing suit	badedrakt (m/f)	['badə͵drakt]

36. Headwear

hat	hatt (m)	['hat]
fedora	hatt (m)	['hat]
baseball cap	baseball cap (m)	['bɛjsbɔl kɛp]
flatcap	sikspens (m)	['sikspens]
beret	alpelue, baskerlue (m/f)	['alpə͵lɵə], ['baskə͵lɵə]
hood	hette (m/f)	['hɛtə]
panama hat	panamahatt (m)	['panama͵hat]
knit cap (knitted hat)	strikket lue (m/f)	['strikə͵lɵə]
headscarf	skaut (n)	['skaʊt]
women's hat	hatt (m)	['hat]
hard hat	hjelm (m)	['jɛlm]
garrison cap	båtlue (m/f)	['bɔt͵lɵə]
helmet	hjelm (m)	['jɛlm]
derby	bowlerhatt, skalk (m)	['bouler͵hat], ['skalk]
top hat	flosshatt (m)	['flɔs͵hat]

37. Footwear

| footwear | skotøy (n) | ['skʊtøj] |
| shoes (men's shoes) | skor (m pl) | ['skʊr] |

shoes (women's shoes)	**pumps** (m pl)	['pʉmps]
boots (e.g., cowboy ~)	**støvler** (m pl)	['støvlər]
slippers	**tøfler** (m pl)	['tøflər]
tennis shoes (e.g., Nike ~)	**tennissko** (m pl)	['tɛnisˌskʉ]
sneakers	**canvas sko** (m pl)	['kanvas ˌskʉ]
(e.g., Converse ~)		
sandals	**sandaler** (m pl)	[san'dalər]
cobbler (shoe repairer)	**skomaker** (m)	['skʉˌmakər]
heel	**hæl** (m)	['hæl]
pair (of shoes)	**par** (n)	['par]
shoestring	**skolisse** (m/f)	['skʉˌlisə]
to lace (vt)	**å snøre**	[ɔ 'snørə]
shoehorn	**skohorn** (n)	['skʉˌhuːŋ]
shoe polish	**skokrem** (m)	['skʉˌkrɛm]

38. Textile. Fabrics

cotton (n)	**bomull** (m/f)	['bʉˌmʉl]
cotton (as adj)	**bomulls-**	['bʉˌmʉls-]
flax (n)	**lin** (n)	['lin]
flax (as adj)	**lin-**	['lin-]
silk (n)	**silke** (m)	['silkə]
silk (as adj)	**silke-**	['silkə-]
wool (n)	**ull** (m/f)	['ʉl]
wool (as adj)	**ull-, av ull**	['ʉl-], ['aː ʉl]
velvet	**fløyel** (m)	['fløjəl]
suede	**semsket skinn** (n)	['sɛmsket ˌʃin]
corduroy	**kordfløyel** (m/n)	['kɔːɖˌfløjəl]
nylon (n)	**nylon** (n)	['nyˌlɔn]
nylon (as adj)	**nylon-**	['nyˌlɔn-]
polyester (n)	**polyester** (m)	[pʉly'ɛstər]
polyester (as adj)	**polyester-**	[pʉly'ɛstər-]
leather (n)	**lær, skinn** (n)	['lær], ['ʃin]
leather (as adj)	**lær-, av lær**	['lær-], ['aː lær]
fur (n)	**pels** (m)	['pɛls]
fur (e.g., ~ coat)	**pels-**	['pɛls-]

39. Personal accessories

gloves	**hansker** (m pl)	['hanskər]
mittens	**votter** (m pl)	['votər]

scarf (muffler)	skjerf (n)	['ṣærf]
glasses (eyeglasses)	briller (m pl)	['brilər]
frame (eyeglass ~)	innfatning (m/f)	['in‚fɑtniŋ]
umbrella	paraply (m)	[pɑrɑ'ply]
walking stick	stokk (m)	['stɔk]
hairbrush	hårbørste (m)	['hɔr‚bœṣtə]
fan	vifte (m/f)	['viftə]

tie (necktie)	slips (n)	['slips]
bow tie	sløyfe (m/f)	['ṣløjfə]
suspenders	bukseseler (m pl)	['bʉksə'selər]
handkerchief	lommetørkle (n)	['lʊmə‚tœrklə]

comb	kam (m)	['kɑm]
barrette	hårspenne (m/f/n)	['hɔːr‚spɛnə]
hairpin	hårnål (m/f)	['hɔːr‚nɔl]
buckle	spenne (m/f/n)	['spɛnə]

| belt | belte (m) | ['bɛltə] |
| shoulder strap | skulderreim, rem (m/f) | ['skʉldə‚ræjm], ['rem] |

bag (handbag)	veske (m/f)	['vɛskə]
purse	håndveske (m/f)	['hɔn‚vɛskə]
backpack	ryggsekk (m)	['rʏg‚sɛk]

40. Clothing. Miscellaneous

fashion	mote (m)	['mʊtə]
in vogue (adj)	moteriktig	['mʊtə‚rikti]
fashion designer	moteskaper (m)	['mʊtə‚skɑpər]

collar	krage (m)	['krɑgə]
pocket	lomme (m/f)	['lʊmə]
pocket (as adj)	lomme-	['lʊmə-]
sleeve	erme (n)	['ærmə]
hanging loop	hempe (m)	['hɛmpə]
fly (on trousers)	gylf, buksesmekk (m)	['gylf], ['bʉksə‚smɛk]

zipper (fastener)	glidelås (m/n)	['glidə‚lɔs]
fastener	hekte (m/f), knepping (m)	['hɛktə], ['knɛpiŋ]
button	knapp (m)	['knɑp]
buttonhole	klapphull (n)	['klɑp‚hʉl]
to come off (ab. button)	å falle av	[ɔ 'fɑlə ɑː]

to sew (vi, vt)	å sy	[ɔ 'sy]
to embroider (vi, vt)	å brodere	[ɔ brʊ'derə]
embroidery	broderi (n)	[brʊde'ri]
sewing needle	synål (m/f)	['sy‚nɔl]
thread	tråd (m)	['trɔ]
seam	søm (m)	['søm]

to get dirty (vi)	**å skitne seg til**	['ʂitnə sæj til]
stain (mark, spot)	**flekk** (m)	['flek]
to crease, crumple (vi)	**å bli skrukkete**	[ɔ 'bli 'skrʉketə]
to tear, to rip (vt)	**å rive**	[ɔ 'rivə]
clothes moth	**møll** (m/n)	['møl]

41. Personal care. Cosmetics

toothpaste	**tannpasta** (m)	['tan,pasta]
toothbrush	**tannbørste** (m)	['tan,bœʂtə]
to brush one's teeth	**å pusse tennene**	[ɔ 'pʉsə 'tɛnənə]
razor	**høvel** (m)	['høvəl]
shaving cream	**barberkrem** (m)	[bar'bɛrˌkrɛm]
to shave (vi)	**å barbere seg**	[ɔ bar'berə sæj]
soap	**såpe** (m/f)	['soːpə]
shampoo	**sjampo** (m)	['ʂamˌpʊ]
scissors	**saks** (m/f)	['saks]
nail file	**neglefil** (m/f)	['nɛjləˌfil]
nail clippers	**negleklipper** (m)	['nɛjləˌklipər]
tweezers	**pinsett** (m)	[pin'sɛt]
cosmetics	**kosmetikk** (m)	[kʊsme'tik]
face mask	**ansiktsmaske** (m/f)	['ansiktsˌmaskə]
manicure	**manikyr** (m)	[mani'kyr]
to have a manicure	**å få manikyr**	[ɔ 'fɔ mani'kyr]
pedicure	**pedikyr** (m)	[pedi'kyr]
make-up bag	**sminkeveske** (m/f)	['sminkəˌvɛskə]
face powder	**pudder** (n)	['pʉdər]
powder compact	**pudderdåse** (m)	['pʉdərˌdoːsə]
blusher	**rouge** (m)	['ruːʂ]
perfume (bottled)	**parfyme** (m)	[par'fymə]
toilet water (lotion)	**eau de toilette** (m)	['ɔː də twa'let]
lotion	**lotion** (m)	['loʊʂɛn]
cologne	**eau do cologne** (m)	['ɔː də kɔ'lɔn]
eyeshadow	**øyeskygge** (m)	['øjeˌsygə]
eyeliner	**eyeliner** (m)	['aːjˌlajnər]
mascara	**maskara** (m)	[ma'skara]
lipstick	**leppestift** (m)	['lepəˌstift]
nail polish, enamel	**neglelakk** (m)	['nɛjləˌlak]
hair spray	**hårlakk** (m)	['hoːrˌlak]
deodorant	**deodorant** (m)	[deudʊ'rant]
cream	**krem** (m)	['krɛm]
face cream	**ansiktskrem** (m)	['ansiktsˌkrɛm]

hand cream	håndkrem (m)	['hɔnˌkrɛm]
anti-wrinkle cream	antirynkekrem (m)	[anti'rʏnkəˌkrɛm]
day cream	dagkrem (m)	['dɑgˌkrɛm]
night cream	nattkrem (m)	['natˌkrɛm]
day (as adj)	dag-	['dɑg-]
night (as adj)	natt-	['nat-]

tampon	tampong (m)	[tam'pɔŋ]
toilet paper (toilet roll)	toalettpapir (n)	[tʊɑ'let pɑ'pir]
hair dryer	hårføner (m)	['hoːrˌfønər]

42. Jewelry

jewelry	smykker (n pl)	['smʏkər]
precious (e.g., ~ stone)	edel-	['ɛdəl-]
hallmark stamp	stempel (n)	['stɛmpəl]

ring	ring (m)	['riŋ]
wedding ring	giftering (m)	['jiftəˌriŋ]
bracelet	armbånd (n)	['armˌbɔn]

earrings	øreringer (m pl)	['ørəˌriŋər]
necklace (~ of pearls)	halssmykke (n)	['halsˌsmʏkə]
crown	krone (m/f)	['krʊnə]
bead necklace	perlekjede (m/n)	['pærləˌçɛːdə]

diamond	diamant (m)	[diɑ'mant]
emerald	smaragd (m)	[smɑ'rɑgd]
ruby	rubin (m)	[rʉ'bin]
sapphire	safir (m)	[sɑ'fir]
pearl	perler (m pl)	['pærlər]
amber	rav (n)	['rɑv]

43. Watches. Clocks

watch (wristwatch)	armbåndsur (n)	['ɑrmbɔnsˌʉr]
dial	urskive (m/f)	['ʉːˌʂivə]
hand (of clock, watch)	viser (m)	['visər]
metal watch band	armbånd (n)	['armˌbɔn]
watch strap	rem (m/f)	['rem]

battery	batteri (n)	[batɛ'ri]
to be dead (battery)	å bli utladet	[ɔ 'bli 'ʉtˌlɑdət]
to change a battery	å skifte batteriene	[ɔ ˌʂiftə batɛ'rienə]
to run fast	å gå for fort	[ɔ 'gɔ fɔ 'fɔːt]
to run slow	å gå for sakte	[ɔ 'gɔ fɔ 'sɑktə]
wall clock	veggur (n)	['vɛgˌʉr]
hourglass	timeglass (n)	['timəˌglɑs]

sundial	**solur** (n)	['sʊlˌʉr]
alarm clock	**vekkerklokka** (m/f)	['vɛkərˌklɔka]
watchmaker	**urmaker** (m)	['ʉrˌmakər]
to repair (vt)	**å reparere**	[ɔ repaˈrerə]

Food. Nutricion

44. Food

meat	kjøtt (n)	['çœt]
chicken	høne (m/f)	['hønə]
Rock Cornish hen (poussin)	kylling (m)	['çyliŋ]
duck	and (m/f)	['ɑn]
goose	gås (m/f)	['gɔs]
game	vilt (n)	['vilt]
turkey	kalkun (m)	[kɑl'kʉn]
pork	svinekjøtt (n)	['svinə,çœt]
veal	kalvekjøtt (n)	['kɑlvə,çœt]
lamb	fårekjøtt (n)	['fo:rə,çœt]
beef	oksekjøtt (n)	['ɔksə,çœt]
rabbit	kanin (m)	[kɑ'nin]
sausage (bologna, pepperoni, etc.)	pølse (m/f)	['pølsə]
vienna sausage (frankfurter)	wienerpølse (m/f)	['vinər,pølsə]
bacon	bacon (n)	['bɛjkən]
ham	skinke (m)	['ʂinkə]
gammon	skinke (m)	['ʂinkə]
pâté	pate, paté (m)	[pɑ'te]
liver	lever (m)	['levər]
hamburger (ground beef)	kjøttfarse (m)	['çœt,farʂə]
tongue	tunge (m/f)	['tʉŋə]
egg	egg (n)	['ɛg]
eggs	egg (n pl)	['ɛg]
egg white	eggehvite (m)	['ɛgə,vitə]
egg yolk	plomme (m/f)	['plʊmə]
fish	fisk (m)	['fisk]
seafood	sjømat (m)	['ʂø,mɑt]
crustaceans	krepsdyr (n pl)	['krɛps,dyr]
caviar	kaviar (m)	['kɑvi,ɑr]
crab	krabbe (m)	['krɑbə]
shrimp	reke (m/f)	['rekə]
oyster	østers (m)	['østəs]
spiny lobster	langust (m)	[lɑŋ'gʉst]

octopus	**blekksprut** (m)	['blek‚sprʉt]
squid	**blekksprut** (m)	['blek‚sprʉt]
sturgeon	**stør** (m)	['stør]
salmon	**laks** (m)	['lɑks]
halibut	**kveite** (m/f)	['kvæjtə]
cod	**torsk** (m)	['toʂk]
mackerel	**makrell** (m)	[mɑ'krɛl]
tuna	**tunfisk** (m)	['tʉn‚fisk]
eel	**ål** (m)	['ɔl]
trout	**ørret** (m)	['øret]
sardine	**sardin** (m)	[sɑ:'ɖin]
pike	**gjedde** (m/f)	['jɛdə]
herring	**sild** (m/f)	['sil]
bread	**brød** (n)	['brø]
cheese	**ost** (m)	['ʊst]
sugar	**sukker** (n)	['sʉkər]
salt	**salt** (n)	['sɑlt]
rice	**ris** (m)	['ris]
pasta (macaroni)	**pasta, makaroni** (m)	['pɑsta], [mɑkɑ'rʊni]
noodles	**nudler** (m pl)	['nʉdlər]
butter	**smør** (n)	['smør]
vegetable oil	**vegetabilsk olje** (m)	[vegeta'bilsk ‚ɔljə]
sunflower oil	**solsikkeolje** (m)	['sʊlsikə‚ɔljə]
margarine	**margarin** (m)	[mɑrgɑ'rin]
olives	**olivener** (m pl)	[ʊ'livenər]
olive oil	**olivenolje** (m)	[ʊ'livən‚ɔljə]
milk	**melk** (m/f)	['mɛlk]
condensed milk	**kondensert melk** (m/f)	[kʊndən'se:ʈ ‚mɛlk]
yogurt	**jogurt** (m)	['jɔgʉ:ʈ]
sour cream	**rømme, syrnet fløte** (m)	['rœmə], ['sy:ŋet 'fløtə]
cream (of milk)	**fløte** (m)	['fløtə]
mayonnaise	**majones** (m)	[mɑjɔ'nɛs」
buttercream	**krem** (m)	['krɛm]
cereal grains (wheat, etc.)	**gryn** (n)	['gryn]
flour	**mel** (n)	['mel]
canned food	**hermetikk** (m)	[hɛrme'tik]
cornflakes	**cornflakes** (m)	['kɔ:ɳ‚flejks]
honey	**honning** (m)	['hɔniŋ]
jam	**syltetøy** (n)	['syltə‚tøj]
chewing gum	**tyggegummi** (m)	['tygə‚gʉmi]

45. Drinks

water	vann (n)	['van]
drinking water	drikkevann (n)	['drikə,van]
mineral water	mineralvann (n)	[minə'ral,van]
still (adj)	uten kullsyre	['ʉtən kʉl'syrə]
carbonated (adj)	kullsyret	[kʉl'syrət]
sparkling (adj)	med kullsyre	[me kʉl'syrə]
ice	is (m)	['is]
with ice	med is	[me 'is]
non-alcoholic (adj)	alkoholfri	['alkʉhʉl,fri]
soft drink	alkoholfri drikk (m)	['alkʉhʉl,fri drik]
refreshing drink	leskedrikk (m)	['leskə,drik]
lemonade	limonade (m)	[limɔ'nadə]
liquors	rusdrikker (m pl)	['rʉs,drikər]
wine	vin (m)	['vin]
white wine	hvitvin (m)	['vit,vin]
red wine	rødvin (m)	['rø,vin]
liqueur	likør (m)	[li'kør]
champagne	champagne (m)	[ʂam'panjə]
vermouth	vermut (m)	['værmʉt]
whiskey	whisky (m)	['viski]
vodka	vodka (m)	['vɔdka]
gin	gin (m)	['dʒin]
cognac	konjakk (m)	['kunjak]
rum	rom (m)	['rʊm]
coffee	kaffe (m)	['kafə]
black coffee	svart kaffe (m)	['svaːʈ 'kafə]
coffee with milk	kaffe (m) med melk	['kafə me 'mɛlk]
cappuccino	cappuccino (m)	[kapʊ'tʃinɔ]
instant coffee	pulverkaffe (m)	['pʉlvər,kafə]
milk	melk (m/f)	['mɛlk]
cocktail	cocktail (m)	['kɔk,tɛjl]
milkshake	milkshake (m)	['milk,ʂɛjk]
juice	jus, juice (m)	['dʒʉs]
tomato juice	tomatjuice (m)	[tʊ'mat,dʒʉs]
orange juice	appelsinjuice (m)	[apel'sin,dʒʉs]
freshly squeezed juice	nypresset juice (m)	['ny,prɛsə 'dʒʉs]
beer	øl (m/n)	['øl]
light beer	lettøl (n)	['let,øl]
dark beer	mørkt øl (n)	['mœrkt,øl]
tea	te (m)	['te]

| black tea | **svart te** (m) | ['svɑːt ˌte] |
| green tea | **grønn te** (m) | ['grœn ˌte] |

46. Vegetables

| vegetables | **grønnsaker** (m pl) | ['grœnˌsɑkər] |
| greens | **grønnsaker** (m pl) | ['grœnˌsɑkər] |

tomato	**tomat** (m)	[tʉ'mɑt]
cucumber	**agurk** (m)	[ɑ'gʉrk]
carrot	**gulrot** (m/f)	['gʉlˌrʊt]
potato	**potet** (m/f)	[pʉ'tet]
onion	**løk** (m)	['løk]
garlic	**hvitløk** (m)	['vitˌløk]

cabbage	**kål** (m)	['kɔl]
cauliflower	**blomkål** (m)	['blɔmˌkɔl]
Brussels sprouts	**rosenkål** (m)	['rʊsənˌkɔl]
broccoli	**brokkoli** (m)	['brɔkɔli]

beetroot	**rødbete** (m/f)	['røˌbetə]
eggplant	**aubergine** (m)	[ɔbɛr'ʂin]
zucchini	**squash** (m)	['skvɔʂ]
pumpkin	**gresskar** (n)	['grɛskɑr]
turnip	**nepe** (m/f)	['nepə]

parsley	**persille** (m/f)	[pæ'ʂilə]
dill	**dill** (m)	['dil]
lettuce	**salat** (m)	[sɑ'lɑt]
celery	**selleri** (m/n)	[sɛleˌri]
asparagus	**asparges** (m)	[ɑ'spɑrʂəs]
spinach	**spinat** (m)	[spi'nɑt]

pea	**erter** (m pl)	['æːʈər]
beans	**bønner** (m/f pl)	['bœnər]
corn (maize)	**mais** (m)	['mɑis]
kidney bean	**bønne** (m/f)	['bœnə]

bell pepper	**pepper** (m)	['pɛpər]
radish	**reddik** (m)	['rɛdik]
artichoke	**artisjokk** (m)	[ˌɑːʈi'ʂɔk]

47. Fruits. Nuts

fruit	**frukt** (m/f)	['frʉkt]
apple	**eple** (n)	['ɛplə]
pear	**pære** (m/f)	['pærə]
lemon	**sitron** (m)	[si'trʉn]

| orange | appelsin (m) | [apel'sin] |
| strawberry (garden ~) | jordbær (n) | ['ju:r,bær] |

mandarin	mandarin (m)	[manda'rin]
plum	plomme (m/f)	['plʊmə]
peach	fersken (m)	['fæʂkən]
apricot	aprikos (m)	[apri'kʊs]
raspberry	bringebær (n)	['briŋə,bær]
pineapple	ananas (m)	['ananas]

banana	banan (m)	[ba'nan]
watermelon	vannmelon (m)	['vanme,lʊn]
grape	drue (m)	['drʉə]
sour cherry	kirsebær (n)	['çiʂə,bær]
sweet cherry	morell (m)	[mʊ'rɛl]
melon	melon (m)	[me'lun]

grapefruit	grapefrukt (m/f)	['grɛjp,frʉkt]
avocado	avokado (m)	[avo'kadɔ]
papaya	papaya (m)	[pa'paja]
mango	mango (m)	['maŋu]
pomegranate	granateple (n)	[gra'nat,ɛplə]

redcurrant	rips (m)	['rips]
blackcurrant	solbær (n)	['sʊl,bær]
gooseberry	stikkelsbær (n)	['stikəls,bær]
bilberry	blåbær (n)	['blo,bær]
blackberry	bjørnebær (m)	['bjœ:nə,bær]

raisin	rosin (m)	[rʊ'sin]
fig	fiken (m)	['fikən]
date	daddel (m)	['dadəl]

peanut	jordnøtt (m)	['ju:r,nœt]
almond	mandel (m)	['mandəl]
walnut	valnøtt (m/f)	['val,nœt]
hazelnut	hasselnøtt (m/f)	['hasəl,nœt]
coconut	kokosnøtt (m/f)	['kʊkʊs,nœt]
pistachios	pistasier (m pl)	[pi'staʂiər]

48. Bread. Candy

bakers' confectionery (pastry)	bakevarer (m/f pl)	['bakə,varər]
bread	brød (n)	['brø]
cookies	kjeks (m)	['çɛks]

chocolate (n)	sjokolade (m)	[ʂʊkʊ'ladə]
chocolate (as adj)	sjokolade-	[ʂʊkʊ'ladə-]
candy (wrapped)	sukkertøy (n), karamell (m)	['sʉkə:ʈøj], [kara'mɛl]

cake (e.g., cupcake)	kake (m/f)	['kɑkə]
cake (e.g., birthday ~)	bløtkake (m/f)	['bløtˌkɑkə]
pie (e.g., apple ~)	pai (m)	['pɑj]
filling (for cake, pie)	fyll (m/n)	['fʏl]
jam (whole fruit jam)	syltetøy (n)	['sʏltəˌtøj]
marmalade	marmelade (m)	[marme'lɑdə]
waffles	vaffel (m)	['vɑfəl]
ice-cream	iskrem (m)	['iskrɛm]
pudding	pudding (m)	['pʉdiŋ]

49. Cooked dishes

course, dish	rett (m)	['rɛt]
cuisine	kjøkken (n)	['çœkən]
recipe	oppskrift (m)	['ɔpˌskrift]
portion	porsjon (m)	[pɔ'ʂʉn]
salad	salat (m)	[sɑ'lɑt]
soup	suppe (m/f)	['sʉpə]
clear soup (broth)	buljong (m)	[bu'ljɔŋ]
sandwich (bread)	smørbrød (n)	['smørˌbrø]
fried eggs	speilegg (n)	['spæjlˌɛg]
hamburger (beefburger)	hamburger (m)	['hɑmbʉrgər]
beefsteak	biff (m)	['bif]
side dish	tilbehør (n)	['tilbəˌhør]
spaghetti	spagetti (m)	[spɑ'gɛti]
mashed potatoes	potetmos (m)	[pʉ'tetˌmʊs]
pizza	pizza (m)	['pitsɑ]
porridge (oatmeal, etc.)	grøt (m)	['grøt]
omelet	omelett (m)	[ɔmə'let]
boiled (e.g., ~ beef)	kokt	['kʊkt]
smoked (adj)	røkt	['røkt]
fried (adj)	stekt	['stɛkt]
dried (adj)	tørket	['tœrkət]
frozen (adj)	frossen, dypfryst	['frɔsən], ['dypˌfrʏst]
pickled (adj)	syltet	['sʏltət]
sweet (sugary)	søt	['søt]
salty (adj)	salt	['salt]
cold (adj)	kald	['kɑl]
hot (adj)	het, varm	['het], ['vɑrm]
bitter (adj)	bitter	['bitər]
tasty (adj)	lekker	['lekər]
to cook in boiling water	å koke	[ɔ 'kɔkə]

to cook (dinner)	å lage	[ɔ 'lagə]
to fry (vt)	å steke	[ɔ 'stekə]
to heat up (food)	å varme opp	[ɔ 'varmə ɔp]
to salt (vt)	å salte	[ɔ 'saltə]
to pepper (vt)	å pepre	[ɔ 'pɛprə]
to grate (vt)	å rive	[ɔ 'rivə]
peel (n)	skall (n)	['skal]
to peel (vt)	å skrelle	[ɔ 'skrɛlə]

50. Spices

salt	salt (n)	['salt]
salty (adj)	salt	['salt]
to salt (vt)	å salte	[ɔ 'saltə]
black pepper	svart pepper (m)	['svaːʈ 'pɛpər]
red pepper (milled ~)	rød pepper (m)	['rø 'pɛpər]
mustard	sennep (m)	['sɛnəp]
horseradish	pepperrot (m/f)	['pɛpərˌrʊt]
condiment	krydder (n)	['krʏdər]
spice	krydder (n)	['krʏdər]
sauce	saus (m)	['saʊs]
vinegar	eddik (m)	['ɛdik]
anise	anis (m)	['anis]
basil	basilik (m)	[basi'lik]
cloves	nellik (m)	['nɛlik]
ginger	ingefær (m)	['iŋəˌfær]
coriander	koriander (m)	[kʊri'andər]
cinnamon	kanel (m)	[ka'nel]
sesame	sesam (m)	['sesam]
bay leaf	laurbærblad (n)	['laʊrbærˌbla]
paprika	paprika (m)	['paprika]
caraway	karve, kummin (m)	['karvə], ['kʉmin]
saffron	safran (m)	[sa'fran]

51. Meals

food	mat (m)	['mat]
to eat (vi, vt)	å spise	[ɔ 'spisə]
breakfast	frokost (m)	['frʊkɔst]
to have breakfast	å spise frokost	[ɔ 'spisə ˌfrʊkɔst]
lunch	lunsj, lunch (m)	['lʉnʂ]
to have lunch	å spise lunsj	[ɔ 'spisə ˌlʉnʂ]

dinner	middag (m)	['mi̩da]
to have dinner	å spise middag	[ɔ 'spisə 'mi̩da]
appetite	appetitt (m)	[apeˈtit]
Enjoy your meal!	God appetitt!	['gʊ apeˈtit]
to open (~ a bottle)	å åpne	[ɔ 'ɔpnə]
to spill (liquid)	å spille	[ɔ 'spilə]
to spill out (vi)	å bli spilt	[ɔ 'bli 'spilt]
to boil (vi)	å koke	[ɔ 'kʊkə]
to boil (vt)	å koke	[ɔ 'kʊkə]
boiled (~ water)	kokt	['kʊkt]
to chill, cool down (vt)	å svalne	[ɔ 'svalnə]
to chill (vi)	å avkjøles	[ɔ 'av̩çœləs]
taste, flavor	smak (m)	['smak]
aftertaste	bismak (m)	['bismak]
to slim down (lose weight)	å være på diet	[ɔ 'værə pɔ di'et]
diet	diett (m)	[di'et]
vitamin	vitamin (n)	[vita'min]
calorie	kalori (m)	[kalʊ'ri]
vegetarian (n)	vegetarianer (m)	[vegetari'anər]
vegetarian (adj)	vegetarisk	[vege'tarisk]
fats (nutrient)	fett (n)	['fɛt]
proteins	proteiner (n pl)	[prɔte'inər]
carbohydrates	kullhydrater (n pl)	['kʉlhy̩dratər]
slice (of lemon, ham)	skive (m/f)	['ʂivə]
piece (of cake, pie)	stykke (n)	['stʏkə]
crumb	smule (m)	['smʉlə]
(of bread, cake, etc.)		

52. Table setting

spoon	skje (m)	['ʂe]
knife	kniv (m)	['kniv]
fork	gaffel (m)	['gafəl]
cup (e.g., coffee ~)	kopp (m)	['kɔp]
plate (dinner ~)	tallerken (m)	[ta'lærkən]
saucer	tefat (n)	['te̩fat]
napkin (on table)	serviett (m)	[sɛrvi'ɛt]
toothpick	tannpirker (m)	['tan̩pirkər]

53. Restaurant

| restaurant | restaurant (m) | [rɛstʊ'raŋ] |
| coffee house | kafé, kaffebar (m) | [ka'fe], ['kɑfə̩bar] |

pub, bar	**bar** (m)	['bɑr]
tearoom	**tesalong** (m)	['tesɑˌlɔŋ]
waiter	**servitør** (m)	['særvi'tør]
waitress	**servitrise** (m/f)	[særvi'trisə]
bartender	**bartender** (m)	['bɑːˌtɛndər]
menu	**meny** (m)	[me'ny]
wine list	**vinkart** (n)	['vinˌkɑːt]
to book a table	**å reservere bord**	[ɔ resɛr'verə 'bʊr]
course, dish	**rett** (m)	['rɛt]
to order (meal)	**å bestille**	[ɔ be'stilə]
to make an order	**å bestille**	[ɔ be'stilə]
aperitif	**aperitiff** (m)	[ɑperi'tif]
appetizer	**forrett** (m)	['fɔrɛt]
dessert	**dessert** (m)	[de'sɛːr]
check	**regning** (m/f)	['rɛjniŋ]
to pay the check	**å betale regningen**	[ɔ be'talə 'rɛjniŋən]
to give change	**å gi tilbake veksel**	[ɔ ji til'bɑkə 'vɛksəl]
tip	**driks** (m)	['driks]

Family, relatives and friends

54. Personal information. Forms

name (first name)	**navn** (n)	['navn]
surname (last name)	**etternavn** (n)	['ɛtəˌŋavn]
date of birth	**fødselsdato** (m)	['føtsəlsˌdatʉ]
place of birth	**fødested** (n)	['fødəˌsted]
nationality	**nasjonalitet** (m)	[naʂʉnali'tet]
place of residence	**bosted** (n)	['bʉˌsted]
country	**land** (n)	['lan]
profession (occupation)	**yrke** (n), **profesjon** (m)	['yrkə], [prʉfe'ʂʉn]
gender, sex	**kjønn** (n)	['çœn]
height	**høyde** (m)	['højdə]
weight	**vekt** (m)	['vɛkt]

55. Family members. Relatives

mother	**mor** (m/f)	['mʉr]
father	**far** (m)	['far]
son	**sønn** (m)	['sœn]
daughter	**datter** (m/f)	['datər]
younger daughter	**yngste datter** (m/f)	['yŋstə 'datər]
younger son	**yngste sønn** (m)	['yŋstə 'sœn]
eldest daughter	**eldste datter** (m/f)	['ɛlstə 'datər]
eldest son	**eldste sønn** (m)	['ɛlstə 'sœn]
brother	**bror** (m)	['brʉr]
elder brother	**eldre bror** (m)	['ɛldrə ˌbrʉr]
younger brother	**lillobror** (m)	['liləˌbrʉr]
sister	**søster** (m/f)	['søstər]
elder sister	**eldre søster** (m/f)	['ɛldrə ˌsøstər]
younger sister	**lillesøster** (m/f)	['liləˌsøstər]
cousin (masc.)	**fetter** (m/f)	['fɛtər]
cousin (fem.)	**kusine** (m)	[kʉ'sinə]
mom, mommy	**mamma** (m)	['mama]
dad, daddy	**pappa** (m)	['papa]
parents	**foreldre** (pl)	[for'ɛldrə]
child	**barn** (n)	['baːŋ]
children	**barn** (n pl)	['baːŋ]

grandmother	bestemor (m)	['bɛstə‚mʊr]
grandfather	bestefar (m)	['bɛstə‚far]
grandson	barnebarn (n)	['bɑːnə‚bɑːŋ]
granddaughter	barnebarn (n)	['bɑːnə‚bɑːŋ]
grandchildren	barnebarn (n pl)	['bɑːnə‚bɑːŋ]

uncle	onkel (m)	['ʊnkəl]
aunt	tante (m/f)	['tɑntə]
nephew	nevø (m)	[ne'vø]
niece	niese (m/f)	[ni'esə]

mother-in-law (wife's mother)	svigermor (m/f)	['sviɡər‚mʊr]
father-in-law (husband's father)	svigerfar (m)	['sviɡər‚far]
son-in-law (daughter's husband)	svigersønn (m)	['sviɡər‚sœn]
stepmother	stemor (m/f)	['ste‚mʊr]
stepfather	stefar (m)	['ste‚far]
infant	brystbarn (n)	['brʏst‚bɑːŋ]
baby (infant)	spedbarn (n)	['spe‚bɑːŋ]
little boy, kid	lite barn (n)	['litə 'bɑːŋ]

wife	kone (m/f)	['kʊnə]
husband	mann (m)	['mɑn]
spouse (husband)	ektemann (m)	['ɛktə‚mɑn]
spouse (wife)	hustru (m)	['hʉstrʉ]

married (masc.)	gift	['jift]
married (fem.)	gift	['jift]
single (unmarried)	ugift	[ʉ:'jift]
bachelor	ungkar (m)	['ʉŋ‚kar]
divorced (masc.)	fraskilt	['fra‚silt]
widow	enke (m)	['ɛnkə]
widower	enkemann (m)	['ɛnkə‚mɑn]

relative	slektning (m)	['slɛktniŋ]
close relative	nær slektning (m)	['nær 'slɛktniŋ]
distant relative	fjern slektning (m)	['fjæːŋ 'slɛktniŋ]
relatives	slektninger (m pl)	['slɛktniŋər]

orphan (boy or girl)	foreldreløst barn (n)	[fɔr'ɛldrəløst ‚bɑːŋ]
guardian (of a minor)	formynder (m)	['fɔr‚mʏnər]
to adopt (a boy)	å adoptere	[ɔ adɔp'terə]
to adopt (a girl)	å adoptere	[ɔ adɔp'terə]

56. Friends. Coworkers

| friend (masc.) | venn (m) | ['vɛn] |
| friend (fem.) | venninne (m/f) | [vɛ'ninə] |

friendship	vennskap (n)	['vɛnˌskap]
to be friends	å være venner	[ɔ 'værə 'vɛnər]
buddy (masc.)	venn (m)	['vɛn]
buddy (fem.)	venninne (m/f)	[vɛ'ninə]
partner	partner (m)	['pɑːʈnər]
chief (boss)	sjef (m)	['ʂɛf]
superior (n)	overordnet (m)	['ɔvərˌɔrdnet]
owner, proprietor	eier (m)	['æjər]
subordinate (n)	underordnet (m)	['ʉnərˌɔrdnet]
colleague	kollega (m)	[kʊ'lega]
acquaintance (person)	bekjent (m)	[be'çɛnt]
fellow traveler	medpassasjer (m)	['meˌpasa'ʂɛr]
classmate	klassekamerat (m)	['klasəˌkamə'raːt]
neighbor (masc.)	nabo (m)	['nabʊ]
neighbor (fem.)	nabo (m)	['nabʊ]
neighbors	naboer (m pl)	['nabʊər]

57. Man. Woman

woman	kvinne (m/f)	['kvinə]
girl (young woman)	jente (m/f)	['jɛntə]
bride	brud (m/f)	['brʉd]
beautiful (adj)	vakker	['vakər]
tall (adj)	høy	['høj]
slender (adj)	slank	['ʂlank]
short (adj)	liten av vekst	['litən ɑ 'vɛkst]
blonde (n)	blondine (m)	[blɔn'dinə]
brunette (n)	brunette (m)	[brʉ'nɛtə]
ladies' (adj)	dame-	['damə-]
virgin (girl)	jomfru (m/f)	['ʉmfrʉ]
pregnant (adj)	gravid	[grɑ'vid]
man (adult male)	mann (m)	['man]
blond (n)	blond mann (m)	['blɔn ˌman]
brunet (n)	mørkhåret mann (m)	['mœrkˌhoːret man]
tall (adj)	høy	['høj]
short (adj)	liten av vekst	['litən ɑ 'vɛkst]
rude (rough)	grov	['grɔv]
stocky (adj)	undersetsig	['ʉnəˌsɛtsi]
robust (adj)	robust	[rʊ'bʉst]
strong (adj)	sterk	['stærk]
strength	kraft, styrke (m)	['kraft], ['styrkə]

stout, fat (adj)	**tykk**	['tʏk]
swarthy (adj)	**mørkhudet**	['mœrkˌhʉdət]
slender (well-built)	**slank**	['ṣlɑnk]
elegant (adj)	**elegant**	[ɛle'gɑnt]

58. Age

age	**alder** (m)	['ɑldər]
youth (young age)	**ungdom** (m)	['ʉŋˌdɔm]
young (adj)	**ung**	['ʉŋ]
younger (adj)	**yngre**	['ʏŋrə]
older (adj)	**eldre**	['ɛldrə]
young man	**unge mann** (m)	['ʉŋə ˌmɑn]
teenager	**tenåring** (m)	['tɛnoːriŋ]
guy, fellow	**kar** (m)	['kɑr]
old man	**gammel mann** (m)	['gɑməl ˌmɑn]
old woman	**gammel kvinne** (m/f)	['gɑməl ˌkvinə]
adult (adj)	**voksen**	['vɔksən]
middle-aged (adj)	**middelaldrende**	['midəlˌɑldrɛnə]
elderly (adj)	**eldre**	['ɛldrə]
old (adj)	**gammel**	['gɑməl]
retirement	**pensjon** (m)	[pɑn'ṣʉn]
to retire (from job)	**å gå av med pensjon**	[ɔ 'gɔ ɑ: me pɑn'ṣʉn]
retiree	**pensjonist** (m)	[pɑnṣʉ'nist]

59. Children

child	**barn** (n)	['bɑːɳ]
children	**barn** (n pl)	['bɑːɳ]
twins	**tvillinger** (m pl)	['tviliŋər]
cradle	**vogge** (m/f)	['vɔgə]
rattle	**rangle** (m/f)	['rɑŋlə]
diaper	**bleie** (m/f)	['blæjə]
pacifier	**smokk** (m)	['smʊk]
baby carriage	**barnevogn** (m/f)	['bɑːnəˌvɔŋn]
kindergarten	**barnehage** (m)	['bɑːnəˌhɑgə]
babysitter	**babysitter** (m)	['bɛbyˌsitər]
childhood	**barndom** (m)	['bɑːɳˌdɔm]
doll	**dukke** (m/f)	['dʉkə]
toy	**leketøy** (n)	['lekəˌtøj]

construction set (toy)	**byggesett** (n)	['bʏɡəˌsɛt]
well-bred (adj)	**veloppdragen**	['velˌɔp'dragən]
ill-bred (adj)	**uoppdragen**	[ʉop'dragən]
spoiled (adj)	**bortskjemt**	['bʉːʦɛmt]
to be naughty	**å være stygg**	[ɔ 'værə 'stʏɡ]
mischievous (adj)	**skøyeraktig**	['skøjəˌrakti]
mischievousness	**skøyeraktighet** (m)	['skøjəˌraktihet]
mischievous child	**skøyer** (m)	['skøjər]
obedient (adj)	**lydig**	['lydi]
disobedient (adj)	**ulydig**	[ʉ'lydi]
docile (adj)	**føyelig**	['føjli]
clever (smart)	**klok**	['klʊk]
child prodigy	**vidunderbarn** (n)	['vidˌʉndərˌbaːɳ]

60. Married couples. Family life

to kiss (vt)	**å kysse**	[ɔ 'çʏsə]
to kiss (vi)	**å kysse hverandre**	[ɔ 'çʏsə ˌverandrə]
family (n)	**familie** (m)	[fɑ'miliə]
family (as adj)	**familie-**	[fɑ'miliə-]
couple	**par** (n)	['pɑr]
marriage (state)	**ekteskap** (n)	['ɛktəˌskɑp]
hearth (home)	**hjemmets arne** (m)	['jɛmeʦ 'ɑːɳə]
dynasty	**dynasti** (n)	[dinɑs'ti]
date	**stevnemøte** (n)	['stɛvnəˌmøtə]
kiss	**kyss** (n)	['çʏs]
love (for sb)	**kjærlighet** (m)	['çæː[iˌhet]
to love (sb)	**å elske**	[ɔ 'ɛlskə]
beloved	**elskling**	['ɛlskliŋ]
tenderness	**ømhet** (m)	['ømˌhet]
tender (affectionate)	**øm**	['øm]
faithfulness	**troskap** (m)	['trʊˌskɑp]
faithful (adj)	**trofast**	['trʊfast]
care (attention)	**omsorg** (m)	['ɔmˌsɔrg]
caring (~ father)	**omsorgsfull**	['ɔmˌsɔrgsfʉl]
newlyweds	**nygifte** (n)	['nyˌjiftə]
honeymoon	**hvetebrødsdager** (m pl)	['vetɛbrøsˌdagər]
to get married (ab. woman)	**å gifte seg**	[ɔ 'jiftə sæj]
to get married (ab. man)	**å gifte seg**	[ɔ 'jiftə sæj]
wedding	**bryllup** (n)	['brʏlʉp]
golden wedding	**gullbryllup** (n)	['gulˌbrʏlup]

anniversary	årsdag (m)	['oːʂˌda]
lover (masc.)	elsker (m)	['ɛlskər]
mistress (lover)	elskerinne (m/f)	['ɛlskəˌrinə]

adultery	utroskap (m)	['ʉˌtrɔskap]
to cheat on …	å være utro	[ɔ 'værə 'ʉˌtrʊ]
(commit adultery)		

jealous (adj)	sjalu	[ʂɑ'lʉː]
to be jealous	å være sjalu	[ɔ 'værə ʂa'lʉː]
divorce	skilsmisse (m)	['ʂilsˌmisə]
to divorce (vi)	å skille seg	[ɔ 'ʂilə sæj]

to quarrel (vi)	å krangle	[ɔ 'kraŋlə]
to be reconciled	å forsone seg	[ɔ fɔ'ʂʊnə sæj]
(after an argument)		
together (adv)	sammen	['samən]
sex	sex (m)	['sɛks]

happiness	lykke (m/f)	['lʏkə]
happy (adj)	lykkelig	['lʏkəli]
misfortune (accident)	ulykke (m/f)	['ʉˌlʏkə]
unhappy (adj)	ulykkelig	['ʉˌlʏkəli]

Character. Feelings. Emotions

61. Feelings. Emotions

feeling (emotion)	følelse (m)	['følelse]
feelings	følelser (m pl)	['følelser]
to feel (vt)	å kjenne	[ɔ 'çɛnə]
hunger	sult (m)	['sʉlt]
to be hungry	å være sulten	[ɔ 'værə 'sʉltən]
thirst	tørst (m)	['tœʂt]
to be thirsty	å være tørst	[ɔ 'værə 'tœʂt]
sleepiness	søvnighet (m)	['sœvni̩het]
to feel sleepy	å være søvnig	[ɔ 'værə 'sœvni]
tiredness	tretthet (m)	['trɛt̩het]
tired (adj)	trett	['trɛt]
to get tired	å bli trett	[ɔ 'bli 'trɛt]
mood (humor)	humør (n)	[hʉ'mør]
boredom	kjedsomhet (m/f)	['çɛdsom̩het]
to be bored	å kjede seg	[ɔ 'çedə sæj]
seclusion	avsondrethet (m/f)	['ɑfsɔndrɛt̩het]
to seclude oneself	å isolere seg	[ɔ isʉ'lerə sæj]
to worry (make anxious)	å bekymre, å uroe	[ɔ be'çymrə], [ɔ 'ʉːrʊə]
to be worried	å bekymre seg	[ɔ be'çymrə sæj]
worrying (n)	bekymring (m/f)	[be'çymriŋ]
anxiety	uro (m/f)	['ʉrʊ]
preoccupied (adj)	bekymret	[be'çymrət]
to be nervous	å være nervøs	[ɔ 'værə nær'vøs]
to panic (vi)	å få panikk	[ɔ 'fɔ pɑ'nik]
hope	håp (n)	['hɔp]
to hope (vi, vt)	å håpe	[ɔ 'hoːpə]
certainty	sikkerhet (m/f)	['sikər̩het]
certain, sure (adj)	sikker	['sikər]
uncertainty	usikkerhet (m)	['ʉsikər̩het]
uncertain (adj)	usikker	['ʉ̩sikər]
drunk (adj)	beruset, full	[be'rʉsət], ['fʉl]
sober (adj)	edru	['ɛdrʉ]
weak (adj)	svak	['svɑk]
happy (adj)	lykkelig	['lykəli]
to scare (vt)	å skremme	[ɔ 'skrɛmə]

| fury (madness) | raseri (n) | [rɑsɛ'ri] |
| rage (fury) | raseri (n) | [rɑsɛ'ri] |

depression	depresjon (m)	[dɛpre'ʂʊn]
discomfort (unease)	ubehag (n)	['ʉbeˌhɑg]
comfort	komfort (m)	[kʊm'fɔːr]
to regret (be sorry)	å beklage	[ɔ be'klɑgə]
regret	beklagelse (m)	[be'klɑgəlsə]
bad luck	uhell (n)	['ʉˌhɛl]
sadness	sorg (m/f)	['sɔr]

shame (remorse)	skam (m/f)	['skɑm]
gladness	glede (m/f)	['gledə]
enthusiasm, zeal	entusiasme (m)	[ɛntʉsi'ɑsmə]
enthusiast	entusiast (m)	[ɛntʉsi'ɑst]
to show enthusiasm	å vise entusiasme	[ɔ 'visə ɛntʉsi'ɑsmə]

62. Character. Personality

character	karakter (m)	[kɑrɑk'ter]
character flaw	karakterbrist (m/f)	[kɑrɑk'terˌbrist]
mind	sinn (n)	['sin]
reason	forstand (m)	[fɔ'ʂtɑn]

conscience	samvittighet (m)	[sɑm'vitiˌhet]
habit (custom)	vane (m)	['vɑnə]
ability (talent)	evne (m/f)	['ɛvnə]
can (e.g., ~ swim)	å kunne	[ɔ 'kʉnə]

patient (adj)	tålmodig	[tɔl'mʊdi]
impatient (adj)	utålmodig	['ʉtɔlˌmʊdi]
curious (inquisitive)	nysgjerrig	['nyˌsæri]
curiosity	nysgjerrighet (m)	['nyˌsæriˌhet]

modesty	beskjedenhet (m)	[be'ʂedenˌhet]
modest (adj)	beskjeden	[be'ʂedən]
immodest (adj)	ubeskjeden	['ʉbeˌʂedən]

laziness	lathet (m)	['lɑtˌhet]
lazy (adj)	doven	['dʊvən]
lazy person (masc.)	dovendyr (n)	['dʊvənˌdyr]

cunning (n)	list (m/f)	['list]
cunning (as adj)	listig	['listi]
distrust	mistro (m/f)	['misˌtrɔ]
distrustful (adj)	mistroende	['misˌtrʊenə]

generosity	gavmildhet (m)	['gɑvmilˌhet]
generous (adj)	generøs	[ʂenə'røs]
talented (adj)	talentfull	[tɑ'lentˌfʉl]

talent	**talent** (n)	[tɑ'lent]
courageous (adj)	**modig**	['mʊdi]
courage	**mot** (n)	['mʊt]
honest (adj)	**ærlig**	['æːli]
honesty	**ærlighet** (m)	['æːli,het]

careful (cautious)	**forsiktig**	[fɔ'ʂikti]
brave (courageous)	**modig**	['mʊdi]
serious (adj)	**alvorlig**	[al'vɔːli]
strict (severe, stern)	**streng**	['strɛŋ]

decisive (adj)	**besluttsom**	[be'ʂlʉt,sɔm]
indecisive (adj)	**ubesluttsom**	[ʉbe'ʂlʉt,sɔm]
shy, timid (adj)	**forsagt**	['fɔ,ʂakt]
shyness, timidity	**forsagthet** (m)	['fɔʂakt,het]

confidence (trust)	**tillit** (m)	['tilit]
to believe (trust)	**å tro**	[ɔ 'trʊ]
trusting (credulous)	**tillitsfull**	['tilits,fʉl]

sincerely (adv)	**oppriktig**	[ɔp'rikti]
sincere (adj)	**oppriktig**	[ɔp'rikti]
sincerity	**oppriktighet** (m)	[ɔp'rikti,het]
open (person)	**åpen**	['ɔpən]

calm (adj)	**stille**	['stilə]
frank (sincere)	**oppriktig**	[ɔp'rikti]
naïve (adj)	**naiv**	[nɑ'iv]
absent-minded (adj)	**forstrødd**	['fʊ,strød]
funny (odd)	**morsom**	['mʊʂɔm]

greed	**grådighet** (m)	['groːdi,het]
greedy (adj)	**grådig**	['groːdi]
stingy (adj)	**gjerrig**	['jæri]
evil (adj)	**ond**	['ʊn]
stubborn (adj)	**hårdnakket**	['hɔːr,nakət]
unpleasant (adj)	**ubehagelig**	[ʉbe'hageli]

selfish person (masc.)	**egoist** (m)	[ɛgʊ'ist]
selfish (adj)	**egoistisk**	[ɛgʊ'istisk]
coward	**feiging** (m)	['fæjgiŋ]
cowardly (adj)	**feig**	['fæjg]

63. Sleep. Dreams

to sleep (vi)	**å sove**	[ɔ 'sɔvə]
sleep, sleeping	**søvn** (m)	['sœvn]
dream	**drøm** (m)	['drøm]
to dream (in sleep)	**å drømme**	[ɔ 'drœmə]
sleepy (adj)	**søvnig**	['sœvni]

bed	seng (m/f)	['sɛŋ]
mattress	madrass (m)	[ma'dras]
blanket (comforter)	dyne (m/f)	['dynə]
pillow	pute (m/f)	['pʉtə]
sheet	laken (n)	['lakən]

insomnia	søvnløshet (m)	['sœvnløsˌhet]
sleepless (adj)	søvnløs	['sœvnˌløs]
sleeping pill	sovetablett (n)	['soveˌtab'let]
to take a sleeping pill	å ta en sovetablett	[ɔ 'ta en 'soveˌtab'let]

to feel sleepy	å være søvnig	[ɔ 'værə 'sœvni]
to yawn (vi)	å gjespe	[ɔ 'jɛspə]
to go to bed	å gå til sengs	[ɔ 'gɔ til 'sɛŋs]
to make up the bed	å re opp sengen	[ɔ 're ɔp 'sɛŋən]
to fall asleep	å falle i søvn	[ɔ 'falə i 'sœvn]

nightmare	mareritt (n)	['marəˌrit]
snore, snoring	snork (m)	['snɔrk]
to snore (vi)	å snorke	[ɔ 'snɔrkə]

alarm clock	vekkerklokka (m/f)	['vɛkərˌklɔka]
to wake (vt)	å vekke	[ɔ 'vɛkə]
to wake up	å våkne	[ɔ 'vɔknə]
to get up (vi)	å stå opp	[ɔ 'stɔ: ɔp]
to wash up (wash face)	å vaske seg	[ɔ 'vaskə sæj]

64. Humour. Laughter. Gladness

humor (wit, fun)	humor (m/n)	['hʉmʊr]
sense of humor	sans (m) for humor	['sans fɔr 'hʉmʊr]
to enjoy oneself	å more seg	[ɔ 'mʊrə sæj]
cheerful (merry)	glad, munter	['gla], ['mʉntər]
merriment (gaiety)	munterhet (m)	['mʉntərˌhet]

smile	smil (m/n)	['smil]
to smile (vi)	å smile	[ɔ 'smilə]
to start laughing	å begynne å skratte	[ɔ be'jinə ɔ 'skratə]
to laugh (vi)	å le, å skratte	[ɔ 'le], [ɔ 'skratə]
laugh, laughter	latter (m), skratt (m/n)	['latər], ['skrat]

anecdote	anekdote (m)	[anek'dotə]
funny (anecdote, etc.)	morsom	['mʉʂɔm]
funny (odd)	morsom	['mʉʂɔm]

to joke (vi)	å spøke	[ɔ 'spøkə]
joke (verbal)	skjemt, spøk (m)	['ʂɛmt], ['spøk]
joy (emotion)	glede (m/f)	['gledə]
to rejoice (vi)	å glede seg	[ɔ 'gledə sæj]
joyful (adj)	glad	['gla]

65. Discussion, conversation. Part 1

communication	**kommunikasjon** (m)	[kʉmʉnikə'ʂʊn]
to communicate	**å kommunisere**	[ɔ kʉmʉni'serə]
conversation	**samtale** (m)	['sam‚talə]
dialog	**dialog** (m)	[dia'lɔg]
discussion (discourse)	**diskusjon** (m)	[diskʉ'ʂʊn]
dispute (debate)	**debatt** (m)	[de'bat]
to dispute	**å diskutere**	[ɔ diskʉ'terə]
interlocutor	**samtalepartner** (m)	['sam‚talə 'pɑːʈnər]
topic (theme)	**emne** (n)	['ɛmnə]
point of view	**synspunkt** (n)	['sʏns‚pʉnt]
opinion (point of view)	**mening** (m/f)	['meniŋ]
speech (talk)	**tale** (m)	['talə]
discussion (of report, etc.)	**diskusjon** (m)	[diskʉ'ʂʊn]
to discuss (vt)	**å drøfte, å diskutere**	[ɔ 'drœftə], [ɔ diskʉ'terə]
talk (conversation)	**samtale** (m)	['sam‚talə]
to talk (to chat)	**å snakke, å samtale**	[ɔ 'snɑkə], [ɔ 'sam‚talə]
meeting	**møte** (n)	['møtə]
to meet (vi, vt)	**å møtes**	[ɔ 'møtəs]
proverb	**ordspråk** (n)	['uːr‚sprɔk]
saying	**ordstev** (n)	['uːr‚stev]
riddle (poser)	**gåte** (m)	['goːtə]
to pose a riddle	**å utgjøre en gåte**	[ɔ ʉt'jørə en 'goːtə]
password	**passord** (n)	['pɑs‚uːr]
secret	**hemmelighet** (m/f)	['hɛməli‚het]
oath (vow)	**ed** (m)	['ɛd]
to swear (an oath)	**å sverge**	[ɔ 'sværgə]
promise	**løfte** (n), **loven** (m)	['lœftə], ['lɔvən]
to promise (vt)	**å love**	[ɔ 'lɔvə]
advice (counsel)	**råd** (n)	['rɔd]
to advise (vt)	**å råde**	[ɔ 'roːdə]
to follow one's advice	**å følge råd**	[ɔ 'følə 'roːd]
to listen to … (obey)	**å adlyde**	[ɔ 'ad‚lydə]
news	**nyhet** (m)	['nyhet]
sensation (news)	**sensasjon** (m)	[sɛnsa'ʂʊn]
information (data)	**opplysninger** (m/f pl)	['ɔp‚lʏsniŋər]
conclusion (decision)	**slutning** (m)	['ʂlʉtniŋ]
voice	**røst** (m/f), **stemme** (m)	['røst], ['stɛmə]
compliment	**kompliment** (m)	[kʊmpli'maŋ]
kind (nice)	**elskverdig**	[ɛlsk'værdi]
word	**ord** (n)	['uːr]
phrase	**frase** (m)	['frɑsə]

answer	svar (n)	['svɑr]
truth	sannhet (m)	['sɑn‚het]
lie	løgn (m/f)	['løjn]

thought	tanke (m)	['tɑnkə]
idea (inspiration)	ide (m)	[i'de]
fantasy	fantasi (m)	[fɑntɑ'si]

66. Discussion, conversation. Part 2

respected (adj)	respektert	[rɛspɛk'tɛːt]
to respect (vt)	å respektere	[ɔ rɛspɛk'terə]
respect	respekt (m)	[rɛ'spɛkt]
Dear ... (letter)	Kjære ...	['çærə ...]

to introduce (sb to sb)	å introdusere	[ɔ introdʉ'serə]
to make acquaintance	å stifte bekjentskap med ...	[ɔ 'stiftə be'çɛn‚skɑp me ...]
intention	hensikt (m)	['hɛn‚sikt]
to intend (have in mind)	å ha til hensikt	[ɔ 'hɑ til 'hɛn‚sikt]
wish	ønske (n)	['ønskə]
to wish (~ good luck)	å ønske	[ɔ 'ønskə]

surprise (astonishment)	overraskelse (m/f)	['ɔvə‚rɑskəlsə]
to surprise (amaze)	å forundre	[ɔ fɔ'rʉndrə]
to be surprised	å bli forundret	[ɔ 'bli fɔ'rʉndrət]

to give (vt)	å gi	[ɔ 'ji]
to take (get hold of)	å ta	[ɔ 'tɑ]
to give back	å gi tilbake	[ɔ 'ji til'bɑkə]
to return (give back)	å returnere	[ɔ retʉr'nerə]

to apologize (vi)	å unnskylde seg	[ɔ 'ʉn‚sylə sæj]
apology	unnskyldning (m/f)	['ʉn‚syldniŋ]
to forgive (vt)	å tilgi	[ɔ 'til‚ji]

to talk (speak)	å tale	[ɔ 'tɑlə]
to listen (vi)	å lye, å lytte	[ɔ 'lyə], [ɔ 'lʏtə]
to hear out	å høre på	[ɔ 'hørə pɔ]
to understand (vt)	å forstå	[ɔ fɔ'ʂtɔ]

to show (to display)	å vise	[ɔ 'visə]
to look at ...	å se på ...	[ɔ 'se pɔ ...]
to call (yell for sb)	å kalle	[ɔ 'kɑlə]
to distract (disturb)	å distrahere	[ɔ distrɑ'erə]
to disturb (vt)	å forstyrre	[ɔ fɔ'ʂtʏrə]
to pass (to hand sth)	å rekke	[ɔ 'rɛkə]

| demand (request) | begjæring (m/f) | [be'jæriŋ] |
| to request (ask) | å be, å bede | [ɔ 'be], [ɔ 'bedə] |

demand (firm request)	**krav** (n)	['krɑv]
to demand (request firmly)	**å kreve**	[ɔ 'krevə]
to tease (call names)	**å erte**	[ɔ 'ɛːʈə]
to mock (make fun of)	**å håne**	[ɔ 'hoːnə]
mockery, derision	**hån** (m)	['hɔn]
nickname	**kallenavn, tilnavn** (n)	['kalə,nɑvn], ['til,nɑvn]
insinuation	**insinuasjon** (m)	[insinʉɑ'ʂʊn]
to insinuate (imply)	**å insinuere**	[ɔ insinʉ'erə]
to mean (vt)	**å bety**	[ɔ 'bety]
description	**beskrivelse** (m)	[be'skrivəlsə]
to describe (vt)	**å beskrive**	[ɔ be'skrivə]
praise (compliments)	**ros** (m)	['rʊs]
to praise (vt)	**å rose, å berømme**	[ɔ 'rʊsə], [ɔ be'rœmə]
disappointment	**skuffelse** (m)	['skʉfəlsə]
to disappoint (vt)	**å skuffe**	[ɔ 'skʉfə]
to be disappointed	**å bli skuffet**	[ɔ 'bli 'skʉfət]
supposition	**antagelse** (m)	[ɑn'tɑgəlsə]
to suppose (assume)	**å anta, å formode**	[ɔ 'an,tɑ], [ɔ fɔr'mʊdə]
warning (caution)	**advarsel** (m)	['ɑd,vɑʂəl]
to warn (vt)	**å advare**	[ɔ 'ɑd,vɑrə]

67. Discussion, conversation. Part 3

to talk into (convince)	**å overtale**	[ɔ 'ɔvə,tɑlə]
to calm down (vt)	**å berolige**	[ɔ be'rʊliə]
silence (~ is golden)	**taushet** (m)	['tɑʊs,het]
to be silent (not speaking)	**å tie**	[ɔ 'tie]
to whisper (vi, vt)	**å hviske**	[ɔ 'viskə]
whisper	**hvisking** (m/f)	['viskiŋ]
frankly, sincerely (adv)	**oppriktig**	[ɔp'rikti]
in my opinion …	**etter min mening …**	['ɛtər min 'meniŋ …]
detail (of the story)	**detalj** (m)	[de'tɑlj]
detailed (adj)	**detaljert**	[deta'ljɛːt]
in detail (adv)	**i detaljer**	[i de'taljer]
hint, clue	**vink** (n)	['vink]
to give a hint	**å gi et vink**	[ɔ 'ji et 'vink]
look (glance)	**blikk** (n)	['blik]
to have a look	**å kaste et blikk**	[ɔ 'kastə et 'blik]
fixed (look)	**stiv**	['stiv]
to blink (vi)	**å blinke**	[ɔ 'blinkə]

to wink (vi)	**å blinke**	[ɔ 'blinkə]
to nod (in assent)	**å nikke**	[ɔ 'nikə]
sigh	**sukk** (n)	['sʉk]
to sigh (vi)	**å sukke**	[ɔ 'sʉkə]
to shudder (vi)	**å gyse**	[ɔ 'jisə]
gesture	**gest** (m)	['gɛst]
to touch (one's arm, etc.)	**å røre**	[ɔ 'rørə]
to seize	**å gripe**	[ɔ 'gripə]
(e.g., ~ by the arm)		
to tap (on the shoulder)	**å klappe**	[ɔ 'klɑpə]
Look out!	**Pass på!**	['pɑs 'pɔ]
Really?	**Virkelig?**	['virkəli]
Are you sure?	**Er du sikker?**	[ɛr dʉ 'sikər]
Good luck!	**Lykke til!**	['lʏkə til]
I see!	**Jeg forstår!**	['jæ fɔ'ʂtoːr]
What a pity!	**Det var synd!**	[de vɑr 'sʏn]

68. Agreement. Refusal

consent	**samtykke** (n)	['sɑm‚tʏkə]
to consent (vi)	**å samtykke**	[ɔ 'sɑm‚tʏkə]
approval	**godkjennelse** (m)	['gʉ‚çɛnəlsə]
to approve (vt)	**å godkjenne**	[ɔ 'gʉ‚çɛnə]
refusal	**avslag** (n)	['ɑf‚slɑg]
to refuse (vi, vt)	**å vegre seg**	[ɔ 'vɛgrə sæj]
Great!	**Det er fint!**	['de ær 'fint]
All right!	**Godt!**	['gɔt]
Okay! (I agree)	**OK! Enig!**	[ɔ'kɛj], ['ɛni]
forbidden (adj)	**forbudt**	[fɔr'bʉt]
it's forbidden	**det er forbudt**	[de ær fɔr'bʉt]
it's impossible	**det er umulig**	[de ær ʉ'mʉli]
incorrect (adj)	**uriktig, ikke riktig**	['ʉ‚rikti], ['ikə ‚rikti]
to reject (~ a demand)	**å avslå**	[ɔ 'ɑf‚slɔ]
to support (cause, idea)	**å støtte**	[ɔ 'stœtə]
to accept (~ an apology)	**å akseptere**	[ɔ ɑksɛp'terə]
to confirm (vt)	**å bekrefte**	[ɔ be'krɛftə]
confirmation	**bekreftelse** (m)	[be'krɛftəlsə]
permission	**tillatelse** (m)	['ti‚lɑtəlsə]
to permit (vt)	**å tillate**	[ɔ 'ti‚lɑtə]
decision	**beslutning** (m)	[be'ʂlʉtniŋ]
to say nothing	**å tie**	[ɔ 'tie]
(hold one's tongue)		
condition (term)	**betingelse** (m)	[be'tiŋəlsə]
excuse (pretext)	**foregivende** (n)	['fɔrə‚jivnə]

| praise (compliments) | ros (m) | ['rʊs] |
| to praise (vt) | å rose, å berømme | [ɔ 'rʊsə], [ɔ be'rœmə] |

69. Success. Good luck. Failure

success	suksess (m)	[sʉk'sɛ]
successfully (adv)	med suksess	[me sʉk'sɛ]
successful (adj)	vellykket	['vel,lʏkət]

luck (good luck)	hell (n), lykke (m/f)	['hɛl], ['lʏkə]
Good luck!	Lykke til!	['lʏkə til]
lucky (e.g., ~ day)	heldig, lykkelig	['hɛldi], ['lʏkəli]
lucky (fortunate)	heldig	['hɛldi]

failure	mislykkelse, fiasko (m)	['mis,lʏkəlsə], [fi'ɑskʊ]
misfortune	uhell (n), utur (m)	['ʉ,hɛl], ['ʉ,tʉr]
bad luck	uhell (n)	['ʉ,hɛl]
unsuccessful (adj)	mislykket	['mis,lʏkət]
catastrophe	katastrofe (m)	[kɑtɑ'strɔfə]

pride	stolthet (m)	['stɔlt,het]
proud (adj)	stolt	['stɔlt]
to be proud	å være stolt	[ɔ 'værə 'stɔlt]

winner	seierherre (m)	['sæjər,hɛrə]
to win (vi)	å seire, å vinne	[ɔ 'sæjrə], [ɔ 'vinə]
to lose (not win)	å tape	[ɔ 'tɑpə]
try	forsøk (n)	['fɔ'ʂøk]
to try (vi)	å prøve, å forsøke	[ɔ 'prøvə], [ɔ fɔ'ʂøkə]
chance (opportunity)	sjanse (m)	['ʂɑnsə]

70. Quarrels. Negative emotions

shout (scream)	skrik (n)	['skrik]
to shout (vi)	å skrike	[ɔ 'skrikə]
to start to cry out	å begynne å skrike	[ɔ be'jinə ɔ 'skrikə]

quarrel	krangel (m)	['krɑŋəl]
to quarrel (vi)	å krangle	[ɔ 'krɑŋlə]
fight (squabble)	skandale (m)	[skɑn'dɑlə]
to make a scene	å gjøre skandale	[ɔ 'jørə skɑn'dɑlə]
conflict	konflikt (m)	[kʊn'flikt]
misunderstanding	misforståelse (m)	[misfɔ'ʂtɔəlsə]

insult	fornærmelse (m)	[fɔ'nærməlsə]
to insult (vt)	å fornærme	[ɔ fɔ'nærmə]
insulted (adj)	fornærmet	[fɔ'nærmət]
resentment	fornærmelse (m)	[fɔ'nærməlsə]

| to offend (vt) | å fornærme | [ɔ fɔːˈŋærmə] |
| to take offense | å bli fornærmet | [ɔ ˈbli fɔːˈŋærmət] |

indignation	forargelse (m)	[fɔˈrɑrgəlsə]
to be indignant	å bli indignert	[ɔ ˈbli indiˈgnɛːt]
complaint	klage (m)	[ˈklɑgə]
to complain (vi, vt)	å klage	[ɔ ˈklɑgə]

apology	unnskyldning (m/f)	[ˈʉnˌʂyldniŋ]
to apologize (vi)	å unnskylde seg	[ɔ ˈʉnˌʂylə sæj]
to beg pardon	å be om forlatelse	[ɔ ˈbe ɔm fɔːˈlɑtəlsə]

criticism	kritikk (m)	[kriˈtik]
to criticize (vt)	å kritisere	[ɔ kritiˈserə]
accusation	anklagelse (m)	[ˈɑnˌklɑgəlsə]
to accuse (vt)	å anklage	[ɔ ˈɑnˌklɑgə]

revenge	hevn (m)	[ˈhɛvn]
to avenge (get revenge)	å hevne	[ɔ ˈhɛvnə]
to pay back	å hevne	[ɔ ˈhɛvnə]

disdain	forakt (m)	[fɔˈrɑkt]
to despise (vt)	å forakte	[ɔ fɔˈrɑktə]
hatred, hate	hat (n)	[ˈhɑt]
to hate (vt)	å hate	[ɔ ˈhɑtə]

nervous (adj)	nervøs	[nærˈvøs]
to be nervous	å være nervøs	[ɔ ˈværə nærˈvøs]
angry (mad)	vred, sint	[ˈvred], [ˈsint]
to make angry	å gjøre sint	[ɔ ˈjørə ˌsint]

humiliation	ydmykelse (m)	[ˈydˌmykəlsə]
to humiliate (vt)	å ydmyke	[ɔ ˈydˌmykə]
to humiliate oneself	å ydmyke seg	[ɔ ˈydˌmykə sæj]

| shock | sjokk (n) | [ˈʂɔk] |
| to shock (vt) | å sjokkere | [ɔ ʂɔˈkerə] |

| trouble (e.g., serious ~) | knipe (m/f) | [ˈknipə] |
| unpleasant (adj) | ubehagelig | [ʉbeˈhɑgeli] |

fear (dread)	redsel, frykt (m)	[ˈrɛtsəl], [ˈfrykt]
terrible (storm, heat)	fryktelig	[ˈfrykteli]
scary (e.g., ~ story)	uhyggelig, skremmende	[ˈʉhygəli], [ˈskrɛmənə]
horror	redsel (m)	[ˈrɛtsəl]
awful (crime, news)	forferdelig	[fɔrˈfærdəli]

to begin to tremble	å begynne å ryste	[ɔ beˈjinə ɔ ˈrystə]
to cry (weep)	å gråte	[ɔ ˈgroːtə]
to start crying	å begynne å gråte	[ɔ beˈjinə ɔ ˈgroːtə]
tear	tåre (m/f)	[ˈtoːrə]
fault	skyld (m/f)	[ˈʂyl]

guilt (feeling)	**skyldfølelse** (m)	[ˈʂylˌføləlsə]
dishonor (disgrace)	**skam, vanære** (m/f)	[ˈskɑm], [ˈvɑnærə]
protest	**protest** (m)	[prʊˈtɛst]
stress	**stress** (m/n)	[ˈstrɛs]
to disturb (vt)	**å forstyrre**	[ɔ fɔˈʂtʏrə]
to be furious	**å være sint**	[ɔ ˈværə ˌsint]
mad, angry (adj)	**vred, sint**	[ˈvred], [ˈsint]
to end (~ a relationship)	**å avbryte**	[ɔ ˈɑvˌbrytə]
to swear (at sb)	**å sverge**	[ɔ ˈsværgə]
to scare (become afraid)	**å bli skremt**	[ɔ ˈbli ˈskrɛmt]
to hit (strike with hand)	**å slå**	[ɔ ˈʂlɔ]
to fight (street fight, etc.)	**å slåss**	[ɔ ˈʂlɔs]
to settle (a conflict)	**å løse**	[ɔ ˈløsə]
discontented (adj)	**misfornøyd, utilfreds**	[ˈmisˌfoːˈnøjd], [ˈʉtilˌfrɛds]
furious (adj)	**rasende**	[ˈrɑsenə]
It's not good!	**Det er ikke bra!**	[de ær ikə ˈbrɑ]
It's bad!	**Det er dårlig!**	[de ær ˈdoːˌli]

Medicine

71. Diseases

sickness	sykdom (m)	['sʏkˌdɔm]
to be sick	å være syk	[ɔ 'værə 'syk]
health	helse (m/f)	['hɛlsə]
runny nose (coryza)	snue (m)	['snʉə]
tonsillitis	angina (m)	[an'ginɑ]
cold (illness)	forkjølelse (m)	[fɔr'çœləlsə]
to catch a cold	å forkjøle seg	[ɔ fɔr'çœlə sæj]
bronchitis	bronkitt (m)	[brɔn'kit]
pneumonia	lungebetennelse (m)	['lʉŋə be'tɛnəlsə]
flu, influenza	influensa (m)	[inflʉ'ɛnsɑ]
nearsighted (adj)	nærsynt	['næˌsʏnt]
farsighted (adj)	langsynt	['laŋsʏnt]
strabismus (crossed eyes)	skjeløydhet (m)	['ʂɛløjdˌhet]
cross-eyed (adj)	skjeløyd	['ʂɛlˌøjd]
cataract	grå stær, katarakt (m)	['grɔ ˌstær], [katɑ'rakt]
glaucoma	glaukom (n)	[glaʉ'kɔm]
stroke	hjerneslag (n)	['jæːŋəˌslag]
heart attack	infarkt (n)	[in'farkt]
myocardial infarction	myokardieinfarkt (n)	['miɔ'kardiə in'farkt]
paralysis	paralyse, lammelse (m)	['pɑrɑ'lyse], ['laməlsə]
to paralyze (vt)	å lamme	[ɔ 'lamə]
allergy	allergi (m)	[alæː'gi]
asthma	astma (m)	['ɑstmɑ]
diabetes	diabetes (m)	[diɑ'betəs]
toothache	tannpine (m/f)	['tanˌpinə]
caries	karies (m)	['kɑries]
diarrhea	diaré (m)	[diɑ'rɛ]
constipation	forstoppelse (m)	[fɔ'ʂtɔpəlsə]
stomach upset	magebesvær (m)	['mɑgəˌbe'svær]
food poisoning	matforgiftning (m/f)	['matˌfɔr'jiftniŋ]
to get food poisoning	å få matforgiftning	[ɔ 'fɔ matˌfɔr'jiftniŋ]
arthritis	artritt (m)	[ɑːˌt'rit]
rickets	rakitt (m)	[rɑ'kit]
rheumatism	revmatisme (m)	[revmɑ'tismə]

atherosclerosis	**arteriosklerose** (m)	[ɑːˈt̪eriʊsklerʊsə]
gastritis	**magekatarr, gastritt** (m)	[ˈmɑgəkɑˌtɑr], [ˌgɑˈstrit]
appendicitis	**appendisitt** (m)	[ɑpɛndiˈsit]
cholecystitis	**galleblærebetennelse** (m)	[ˈgɑləˌblærə beˈtɛnəlsə]
ulcer	**magesår** (n)	[ˈmɑgəˌsɔr]
measles	**meslinger** (m pl)	[ˈmɛsˌliŋər]
rubella (German measles)	**røde hunder** (m pl)	[ˈrødə ˈhʉnər]
jaundice	**gulsott** (m/f)	[ˈgʉlˌsʊt]
hepatitis	**hepatitt** (m)	[hepɑˈtit]
schizophrenia	**schizofreni** (m)	[ʂisʊfreˈni]
rabies (hydrophobia)	**rabies** (m)	[ˈrɑbiəs]
neurosis	**nevrose** (m)	[nevˈrʊsə]
concussion	**hjernerystelse** (m)	[ˈjæːŋəˌrʏstəlsə]
cancer	**kreft, cancer** (m)	[ˈkrɛft], [ˈkɑnsər]
sclerosis	**sklerose** (m)	[skleˈrʊsə]
multiple sclerosis	**multippel sklerose** (m)	[mʉlˈtipəl skleˈrʊsə]
alcoholism	**alkoholisme** (m)	[ɑlkʊhʊˈlismə]
alcoholic (n)	**alkoholiker** (m)	[ɑlkʊˈhʊlikər]
syphilis	**syfilis** (m)	[ˈsyfilis]
AIDS	**AIDS, aids** (m)	[ˈɛjds]
tumor	**svulst, tumor** (m)	[ˈsvʉlst], [tʉˈmʊr]
malignant (adj)	**ondartet, malign**	[ˈʊnˌɑːțət], [mɑˈlign]
benign (adj)	**godartet**	[ˈgʊˌɑːțət]
fever	**feber** (m)	[ˈfebər]
malaria	**malaria** (m)	[mɑˈlɑriɑ]
gangrene	**koldbrann** (m)	[ˈkɔlbrɑn]
seasickness	**sjøsyke** (m)	[ˈʂøˌsykə]
epilepsy	**epilepsi** (m)	[ɛpilepˈsi]
epidemic	**epidemi** (m)	[ɛpideˈmi]
typhus	**tyfus** (m)	[ˈtyfʉs]
tuberculosis	**tuberkulose** (m)	[tubærkʉˈlɔsə]
cholera	**kolera** (m)	[ˈkʊlerɑ]
plague (bubonic ~)	**pest** (m)	[ˈpɛst]

72. Symptoms. Treatments. Part 1

symptom	**symptom** (n)	[sʏmpˈtʊm]
temperature	**temperatur** (m)	[tɛmpərɑˈtʉr]
high temperature (fever)	**høy temperatur** (m)	[ˈhøj tɛmpərɑˈtʉr]
pulse	**puls** (m)	[ˈpʉls]
dizziness (vertigo)	**svimmelhet** (m)	[ˈsviməlˌhet]
hot (adj)	**varm**	[ˈvɑrm]

| shivering | skjelving (m/f) | ['ʂɛlviŋ] |
| pale (e.g., ~ face) | blek | ['blek] |

cough	hoste (m)	['hʊstə]
to cough (vi)	å hoste	[ɔ 'hʊstə]
to sneeze (vi)	å nyse	[ɔ 'nysə]
faint	besvimelse (m)	[bɛ'sviməlsə]
to faint (vi)	å besvime	[ɔ be'svimə]

bruise (hématome)	blåmerke (n)	['blɔˌmærkə]
bump (lump)	bule (m)	['bʉlə]
to bang (bump)	å slå seg	[ɔ 'ʂlɔ sæj]
contusion (bruise)	blåmerke (n)	['blɔˌmærkə]
to get a bruise	å slå seg	[ɔ 'ʂlɔ sæj]

to limp (vi)	å halte	[ɔ 'haltə]
dislocation	forvridning (m)	[fɔr'vridniŋ]
to dislocate (vt)	å forvri	[ɔ fɔr'vri]
fracture	brudd (n), fraktur (m)	['brʉd], [frɑk'tʉr]
to have a fracture	å få brudd	[ɔ 'fɔ 'brʉd]

cut (e.g., paper ~)	skjæresår (n)	['sæːrəˌsɔr]
to cut oneself	å skjære seg	[ɔ 'sæːrə sæj]
bleeding	blødning (m/f)	['blødniŋ]

| burn (injury) | brannsår (n) | ['branˌsɔr] |
| to get burned | å brenne seg | [ɔ 'brɛnə sæj] |

to prick (vt)	å stikke	[ɔ 'stikə]
to prick oneself	å stikke seg	[ɔ 'stikə sæj]
to injure (vt)	å skade	[ɔ 'skadə]
injury	skade (n)	['skadə]
wound	sår (n)	['sɔr]
trauma	traume (m)	['traʊmə]

to be delirious	å snakke i villelse	[ɔ 'snakə i 'viləlsə]
to stutter (vi)	å stamme	[ɔ 'stamə]
sunstroke	solstikk (n)	['sʊlˌstik]

73. Symptoms. Treatments. Part 2

| pain, ache | smerte (m) | ['smæːʈə] |
| splinter (in foot, etc.) | flis (m/f) | ['flis] |

sweat (perspiration)	svette (m)	['svɛtə]
to sweat (perspire)	å svette	[ɔ 'svɛtə]
vomiting	oppkast (n)	['ɔpˌkast]
convulsions	kramper (m pl)	['krampər]
pregnant (adj)	gravid	[gra'vid]
to be born	å fødes	[ɔ 'fødə]

delivery, labor	**fødsel** (m)	['føtsəl]
to deliver (~ a baby)	**å føde**	[ɔ 'fødə]
abortion	**abort** (m)	[a'bɔːt]
breathing, respiration	**åndedrett** (n)	['ɔndəˌdrɛt]
in-breath (inhalation)	**innånding** (m/f)	['inˌɔniŋ]
out-breath (exhalation)	**utånding** (m/f)	['ʉtˌɔndiŋ]
to exhale (breathe out)	**å puste ut**	[ɔ 'pʉstə ʉt]
to inhale (vi)	**å ånde inn**	[ɔ 'ɔndə ˌin]
disabled person	**handikappet person** (m)	['handiˌkapət pæ'ʂʉn]
cripple	**krøpling** (m)	['krøpliŋ]
drug addict	**narkoman** (m)	[narkʊ'man]
deaf (adj)	**døv**	['døv]
mute (adj)	**stum**	['stʉm]
deaf mute (adj)	**døvstum**	['døfˌstʉm]
mad, insane (adj)	**gal**	['gal]
madman (demented person)	**gal mann** (m)	['gal ˌman]
madwoman	**gal kvinne** (m/f)	['gal ˌkvinə]
to go insane	**å bli sinnssyk**	[ɔ 'bli 'sinˌsyk]
gene	**gen** (m)	['gen]
immunity	**immunitet** (m)	[imʉni'tet]
hereditary (adj)	**arvelig**	['arvəli]
congenital (adj)	**medfødt**	['meːˌføt]
virus	**virus** (m)	['virʉs]
microbe	**mikrobe** (m)	[mi'krʊbə]
bacterium	**bakterie** (m)	[bak'teriə]
infection	**infeksjon** (m)	[infɛk'ʂʉn]

74. Symptoms. Treatments. Part 3

hospital	**sykehus** (n)	['sykəˌhʉs]
patient	**pasient** (m)	[pasi'ɛnt]
diagnosis	**diagnose** (m)	[dia'gnʊsə]
cure	**kur** (m)	['kʉr]
medical treatment	**behandling** (m/f)	[be'handliŋ]
to get treatment	**å bli behandlet**	[ɔ 'bli be'handlət]
to treat (~ a patient)	**å behandle**	[ɔ be'handlə]
to nurse (look after)	**å skjøtte**	[ɔ 'ʂøtə]
care (nursing ~)	**sykepleie** (m/f)	['sykəˌplæjə]
operation, surgery	**operasjon** (m)	[ɔpəra'ʂʉn]
to bandage (head, limb)	**å forbinde**	[ɔ for'binə]
bandaging	**forbinding** (m)	[for'biniŋ]

vaccination	vaksinering (m/f)	[vaksi'neriŋ]
to vaccinate (vt)	å vaksinere	[ɔ vaksi'nerə]
injection, shot	injeksjon (m), sprøyte (m/f)	[injɛk'ʂʊn], ['sprøjtə]
to give an injection	å gi en sprøyte	[ɔ 'ji en 'sprøjtə]
attack	anfall (n)	['an͵fal]
amputation	amputasjon (m)	[ampʉta'ʂʊn]
to amputate (vt)	å amputere	[ɔ ampʉ'terə]
coma	koma (m)	['kʊma]
to be in a coma	å ligge i koma	[ɔ 'ligə i 'kʊma]
intensive care	intensivavdeling (m/f)	['inten͵siv 'av͵deliŋ]
to recover (~ from flu)	å bli frisk	[ɔ 'bli 'frisk]
condition (patient's ~)	tilstand (m)	['til͵stan]
consciousness	bevissthet (m)	[be'vist͵het]
memory (faculty)	minne (n),	['minə],
	hukommelse (m)	[hʉ'kɔmǝlsə]
to pull out (tooth)	å trekke ut	[ɔ 'trɛkǝ ʉt]
filling	fylling (m/f)	['fʏliŋ]
to fill (a tooth)	å plombere	[ɔ plʊm'berə]
hypnosis	hypnose (m)	[hʏp'nʊsə]
to hypnotize (vt)	å hypnotisere	[ɔ hʏpnʊti'serə]

75. Doctors

doctor	lege (m)	['legə]
nurse	sykepleierske (m/f)	['sykə͵plæjeʂkə]
personal doctor	personlig lege (m)	[pæ'ʂʊnli 'legə]
dentist	tannlege (m)	['tan͵legə]
eye doctor	øyelege (m)	['øjə͵legə]
internist	terapeut (m)	[tera'pɛut]
surgeon	kirurg (m)	[çi'rʉrg]
psychiatrist	psykiater (m)	[syki'atər]
pediatrician	barnelege (m)	['ba:ṇə͵legə]
psychologist	psykolog (m)	[sykʊ'lɔg]
gynecologist	gynekolog (m)	[gynekʊ'lɔg]
cardiologist	kardiolog (m)	[ka:ɖiʊ'lɔg]

76. Medicine. Drugs. Accessories

medicine, drug	medisin (m)	[medi'sin]
remedy	middel (n)	['midəl]
to prescribe (vt)	å ordinere	[ɔ ɔrdi'nerə]
prescription	resept (m)	[re'sɛpt]

tablet, pill	**tablett** (m)	[tab'let]
ointment	**salve** (m/f)	['salvə]
ampule	**ampulle** (m)	[am'pʉlə]
mixture	**mikstur** (m)	[miks'tʉr]
syrup	**sirup** (m)	['sirʉp]
pill	**pille** (m/f)	['pilə]
powder	**pulver** (n)	['pʉlvər]

gauze bandage	**gasbind** (n)	['gas,bin]
cotton wool	**vatt** (m/n)	['vat]
iodine	**jod** (m/n)	['ʉd]

Band-Aid	**plaster** (n)	['plastər]
eyedropper	**pipette** (m)	[pi'pɛtə]
thermometer	**termometer** (n)	[tɛrmʊ'metər]
syringe	**sprøyte** (m/f)	['sprøjtə]

| wheelchair | **rullestol** (m) | ['rʉlə,stʊl] |
| crutches | **krykker** (m/f pl) | ['krʏkər] |

painkiller	**smertestillende middel** (n)	['smæːtə,stilenə 'midəl]
laxative	**laksativ** (n)	[laksa'tiv]
spirits (ethanol)	**sprit** (m)	['sprit]
medicinal herbs	**legeurter** (m/f pl)	['legə,ʉːtər]
herbal (~ tea)	**urte-**	['ʉːtə-]

77. Smoking. Tobacco products

tobacco	**tobakk** (m)	[tʊ'bak]
cigarette	**sigarett** (m)	[siga'rɛt]
cigar	**sigar** (m)	[si'gar]
pipe	**pipe** (m/f)	['pipə]
pack (of cigarettes)	**pakke** (m/f)	['pakə]

matches	**fyrstikker** (m/f pl)	['fy,stikər]
matchbox	**fyrstikkeske** (m)	['fyʂtik,ɛskə]
lighter	**tenner** (m)	['tɛnər]
ashtray	**askebeger** (n)	['askə,begər]
cigarette case	**sigarettetui** (n)	[siga'rɛt ɛtʉ'i]
cigarette holder	**munnstykke** (n)	['mʉn,stʏkə]
filter (cigarette tip)	**filter** (n)	['filtər]

to smoke (vi, vt)	**å røyke**	[ɔ 'røjkə]
to light a cigarette	**å tenne en sigarett**	[ɔ 'tɛnə en siga'rɛt]
smoking	**røyking, røkning** (m)	['røjkiŋ], ['røkniŋ]
smoker	**røyker** (m)	['røjkər]

stub, butt (of cigarette)	**stump** (m)	['stʉmp]
smoke, fumes	**røyk** (m)	['røjk]
ash	**aske** (m/f)	['askə]

HUMAN HABITAT

City

78. City. Life in the city

city, town	by (m)	['by]
capital city	hovedstad (m)	['hʊvəd‚stɑd]
village	landsby (m)	['lɑns‚by]
city map	bykart (n)	['by‚kɑːt]
downtown	sentrum (n)	['sɛntrum]
suburb	forstad (m)	['fɔ‚ʂtɑd]
suburban (adj)	forstads-	['fɔ‚ʂtɑds-]
outskirts	utkant (m)	['ʉt‚kɑnt]
environs (suburbs)	omegner (m pl)	['ɔm‚æjnər]
city block	kvarter (n)	[kvɑːʈer]
residential block (area)	boligkvarter (n)	['bʊli‚kvɑːʈer]
traffic	trafikk (m)	[trɑ'fik]
traffic lights	trafikklys (n)	[trɑ'fik‚lys]
public transportation	offentlig transport (m)	['ɔfentli trɑns'pɔːʈ]
intersection	veikryss (n)	['væjkrʏs]
crosswalk	fotgjengerovergang (m)	['fʊtˌjɛŋər 'ɔvərˌgɑŋ]
pedestrian underpass	undergang (m)	['ʉnərˌgɑŋ]
to cross (~ the street)	å gå over	[ɔ 'gɔ 'ɔvər]
pedestrian	fotgjenger (m)	['fʊtˌjɛŋər]
sidewalk	fortau (n)	['fɔːˌtɑʉ]
bridge	bro (m/f)	['brʊ]
embankment (river walk)	kai (m/f)	['kɑj]
fountain	fontene (m)	['fʊntnə]
allée (garden walkway)	allé (m)	[ɑ'leː]
park	park (m)	['pɑrk]
boulevard	bulevard (m)	[bule'vɑr]
square	torg (n)	['tɔr]
avenue (wide street)	aveny (m)	[ɑve'ny]
street	gate (m/f)	['gɑtə]
side street	sidegate (m/f)	['sidəˌgɑtə]
dead end	blindgate (m/f)	['blinˌgɑtə]
house	hus (n)	['hʉs]
building	bygning (m/f)	['bʏgniŋ]

skyscraper	skyskraper (m)	[ˈʂyˌskrɑpər]
facade	fasade (m)	[faˈsɑdə]
roof	tak (n)	[ˈtɑk]
window	vindu (n)	[ˈvindʉ]
arch	bue (m)	[ˈbʉːə]
column	søyle (m)	[ˈsøjlə]
corner	hjørne (n)	[ˈjœːɳə]

store window	utstillingsvindu (n)	[ˈʉtˌstiliŋs ˈvindʉ]
signboard (store sign, etc.)	skilt (n)	[ˈʂilt]
poster	plakat (m)	[plaˈkɑt]
advertising poster	reklameplakat (m)	[rɛˈklɑməˌplaˈkɑt]
billboard	reklametavle (m/f)	[rɛˈklɑməˌtɑvlə]

garbage, trash	søppel (m/f/n), avfall (n)	[ˈsœpəl], [ˈɑvˌfɑl]
trashcan (public ~)	søppelkasse (m/f)	[ˈsœpəlˌkɑsə]
to litter (vi)	å kaste søppel	[ɔ ˈkɑstə ˈsœpəl]
garbage dump	søppelfylling (m/f), deponi (n)	[ˈsœpəlˌfʏliŋ], [ˌdepoˈni]

phone booth	telefonboks (m)	[teleˈfʉnˌbɔks]
lamppost	lyktestolpe (m)	[ˈlʏktəˌstɔlpə]
bench (park ~)	benk (m)	[ˈbɛŋk]

police officer	politi (m)	[pʉliˈti]
police	politi (n)	[pʉliˈti]
beggar	tigger (m)	[ˈtigər]
homeless (n)	hjemløs	[ˈjɛmˌløs]

79. Urban institutions

store	forretning, butikk (m)	[fɔˈrɛtniŋ], [bʉˈtik]
drugstore, pharmacy	apotek (n)	[apʉˈtek]
eyeglass store	optikk (m)	[ɔpˈtik]
shopping mall	kjøpesenter (n)	[ˈçœpəˌsɛntər]
supermarket	supermarked (n)	[ˈsʉpəˌmɑrket]

bakery	bakeri (n)	[bɑkeˈri]
baker	baker (m)	[ˈbɑkər]
pastry shop	konditori (n)	[kʉnditoˈri]
grocery store	matbutikk (m)	[ˈmɑtbʉˌtik]
butcher shop	slakterbutikk (m)	[ˈʂlɑktəbʉˌtik]

| produce store | grønnsaksbutikk (m) | [ˈgrœnˌsɑks bʉˈtik] |
| market | marked (n) | [ˈmɑrkəd] |

coffee house	kafé, kaffebar (m)	[kɑˈfe], [ˈkɑfəˌbar]
restaurant	restaurant (m)	[rɛstʉˈrɑŋ]
pub, bar	pub (m)	[ˈpʉb]
pizzeria	pizzeria (m)	[pitsəˈriɑ]

hair salon	frisørsalong (m)	[fri'sør sɑˌlɔŋ]
post office	post (m)	['pɔst]
dry cleaners	renseri (n)	[rɛnse'ri]
photo studio	fotostudio (n)	['fɔtɔˌstʉdiɔ]

shoe store	skobutikk (m)	['skʊˌbʉ'tik]
bookstore	bokhandel (m)	['bʊkˌhandəl]
sporting goods store	idrettsbutikk (m)	['idrɛts bʉ'tik]

clothes repair shop	reparasjon (m) av klær	[repɑrɑ'ʂʊn ɑ: ˌklær]
formal wear rental	leie (m/f) av klær	['læjə ɑ: ˌklær]
video rental store	filmutleie (m/f)	['filmˌʉt'læje]

circus	sirkus (m/n)	['sirkʉs]
zoo	zoo, dyrepark (m)	['sʊ:], [dyrə'park]
movie theater	kino (m)	['çinʊ]
museum	museum (n)	[mʉ'seum]
library	bibliotek (n)	[bibliʊ'tek]

theater	teater (n)	[te'atər]
opera (opera house)	opera (m)	['ʊperɑ]
nightclub	nattklubb (m)	['natˌklʉb]
casino	kasino (n)	[ka'sinʊ]

mosque	moské (m)	[mʊ'ske]
synagogue	synagoge (m)	[synɑ'gʊgə]
cathedral	katedral (m)	[kate'drɑl]

| temple | tempel (n) | ['tɛmpəl] |
| church | kirke (m/f) | ['çirkə] |

college	institutt (n)	[insti'tʉt]
university	universitet (n)	[ʉnivæʂi'tet]
school	skole (m/f)	['skʊlə]

| prefecture | prefektur (n) | [prɛfɛk'tʉr] |
| city hall | rådhus (n) | ['rɔdˌhʉs] |

| hotel | hotell (n) | [hʊ'tɛl] |
| bank | bank (m) | ['bank] |

| embassy | ambassade (m) | [ambɑ'sɑdə] |
| travel agency | reisebyrå (n) | ['ræjsə byˌrɔ] |

| information office | opplysningskontor (n) | [ɔp'lʏsniŋs kʊn'tʊr] |
| currency exchange | vekslingskontor (n) | ['vɛkʂliŋs kʊn'tʊr] |

| subway | tunnelbane, T-bane (m) | ['tʉnəlˌbɑnə], ['tɛːˌbɑnə] |
| hospital | sykehus (n) | ['sykəˌhʉs] |

| gas station | bensinstasjon (m) | [bɛn'sinˌstɑ'ʂʊn] |
| parking lot | parkeringsplass (m) | [par'keriŋsˌplɑs] |

80. Signs

signboard (store sign, etc.)	**skilt** (n)	['ʂilt]
notice (door sign, etc.)	**innskrift** (m/f)	['inˌskrift]
poster	**plakat, poster** (m)	['plaˌkat], ['pɔstər]
direction sign	**veiviser** (m)	['væjˌvisər]
arrow (sign)	**pil** (m/f)	['pil]
caution	**advarsel** (m)	['adˌvaʂəl]
warning sign	**varselskilt** (n)	['vaʂəlˌʂilt]
to warn (vt)	**å varsle**	[ɔ 'vaʂlə]
rest day (weekly ~)	**fridag** (m)	['friˌda]
timetable (schedule)	**rutetabell** (m)	['rʉtəˌta'bɛl]
opening hours	**åpningstider** (m/f pl)	['ɔpniŋsˌtidər]
WELCOME!	**VELKOMMEN!**	['vɛlˌkɔmən]
ENTRANCE	**INNGANG**	['inˌgaŋ]
EXIT	**UTGANG**	['ʉtˌgaŋ]
PUSH	**SKYV**	['ʂyv]
PULL	**TREKK**	['trɛk]
OPEN	**ÅPENT**	['ɔpənt]
CLOSED	**STENGT**	['stɛŋt]
WOMEN	**DAMER**	['damər]
MEN	**HERRER**	['hærər]
DISCOUNTS	**RABATT**	[ra'bat]
SALE	**SALG**	['salg]
NEW!	**NYTT!**	['nʏt]
FREE	**GRATIS**	['gratis]
ATTENTION!	**FORSIKTIG!**	[fʊ'ʂiktə]
NO VACANCIES	**INGEN LEDIGE ROM**	['iŋən 'lediə rʊm]
RESERVED	**RESERVERT**	[resɛr'vɛ:t]
ADMINISTRATION	**ADMINISTRASJON**	[administra'ʂʊn]
STAFF ONLY	**KUN FOR ANSATTE**	['kʉn fɔr an'satə]
BEWARE OF THE DOG!	**VOKT DEM FOR HUNDEN**	['vɔkt dem fɔ 'hʉnən]
NO SMOKING	**RØYKING FORBUDT**	['røjkiŋ fɔr'bʉt]
DO NOT TOUCH!	**IKKE RØR!**	['ikə 'rør]
DANGEROUS	**FARLIG**	['fɑ:li]
DANGER	**FARE**	['farə]
HIGH VOLTAGE	**HØYSPENNING**	['højˌspɛniŋ]
NO SWIMMING!	**BADING FORBUDT**	['badiŋ fɔr'bʉt]
OUT OF ORDER	**I USTAND**	[i 'ʉˌstan]
FLAMMABLE	**BRANNFARLIG**	['branˌfɑ:li]

FORBIDDEN	**FORBUDT**	[fɔr'bʉt]
NO TRESPASSING!	**INGEN INNKJØRING**	['iŋən 'in̩çœriŋ]
WET PAINT	**NYMALT**	['ny̩malt]

81. Urban transportation

bus	**buss** (m)	['bʉs]
streetcar	**trikk** (m)	['trik]
trolley bus	**trolleybuss** (m)	['trɔli̩bʉs]
route (of bus, etc.)	**rute** (m/f)	['rʉtə]
number (e.g., bus ~)	**nummer** (n)	['nʉmər]

to go by ...	**å kjøre med ...**	[ɔ 'çœːrə me ...]
to get on (~ the bus)	**å gå på ...**	[ɔ 'gɔ pɔ ...]
to get off ...	**å gå av ...**	[ɔ 'gɔ ɑː ...]

stop (e.g., bus ~)	**holdeplass** (m)	['hɔlə̩plas]
next stop	**neste holdeplass** (m)	['nɛstə 'hɔlə̩plas]
terminus	**endestasjon** (m)	['ɛnə̩sta'ʂʉn]
schedule	**rutetabell** (m)	['rʉtə̩ta'bɛl]
to wait (vt)	**å vente**	[ɔ 'vɛntə]

| ticket | **billett** (m) | [bi'let] |
| fare | **billettpris** (m) | [bi'let̩pris] |

cashier (ticket seller)	**kasserer** (m)	[ka'serər]
ticket inspection	**billettkontroll** (m)	[bi'let kʉn̩trɔl]
ticket inspector	**billett inspektør** (m)	[bi'let inspɛk'tør]

to be late (for ...)	**å komme for sent**	[ɔ 'kɔmə fɔ'ʂɛnt]
to miss (~ the train, etc.)	**å komme for sent til ...**	[ɔ 'kɔmə fɔ'ʂɛnt til ...]
to be in a hurry	**å skynde seg**	[ɔ 'ʂynə sæj]

taxi, cab	**drosje** (m/f), **taxi** (m)	['drɔʂɛ], ['taksi]
taxi driver	**taxisjåfør** (m)	['taksi ʂɔ'før]
by taxi	**med taxi**	[me 'taksi]
taxi stand	**taxiholdeplass** (m)	['taksi 'hɔlə̩plas]
to call a taxi	**å taxi bestellen**	[ɔ 'taksi be'stɛlən]
to take a taxi	**å ta taxi**	[ɔ 'tɑ ̩taksi]

traffic	**trafikk** (m)	[tra'fik]
traffic jam	**trafikkork** (m)	[tra'fik̩kɔrk]
rush hour	**rushtid** (m/f)	['rʉʂ̩tid]
to park (vi)	**å parkere**	[ɔ par'kerə]
to park (vt)	**å parkere**	[ɔ par'kerə]
parking lot	**parkeringsplass** (m)	[par'keriŋs̩plas]

subway	**tunnelbane, T-bane** (m)	['tʉnəl̩banə], ['tɛː̩banə]
station	**stasjon** (m)	[sta'ʂʉn]
to take the subway	**å kjøre med T-bane**	[ɔ 'çœːrə me 'tɛː̩banə]

| train | tog (n) | ['tɔg] |
| train station | togstasjon (m) | ['tɔg,stɑ'ʂʊn] |

82. Sightseeing

monument	monument (n)	[mɔnʉ'mɛnt]
fortress	festning (m/f)	['fɛstniŋ]
palace	palass (n)	[pɑ'lɑs]
castle	borg (m)	['bɔrg]
tower	tårn (n)	['tɔːŋ]
mausoleum	mausoleum (n)	[mɑʊsʊ'leum]

architecture	arkitektur (m)	[ɑrkitɛk'tʉr]
medieval (adj)	middelalderlig	['midəl,ɑldɛːli]
ancient (adj)	gammel	['gɑməl]
national (adj)	nasjonal	[nɑʂʊ'nɑl]
famous (monument, etc.)	kjent	['çɛnt]

tourist	turist (m)	[tʉ'rist]
guide (person)	guide (m)	['gɑjd]
excursion, sightseeing tour	utflukt (m/f)	['ʉt,flukt]
to show (vt)	å vise	[ɔ 'visə]
to tell (vt)	å fortelle	[ɔ fɔː'tɛlə]

to find (vt)	å finne	[ɔ 'finə]
to get lost (lose one's way)	å gå seg bort	[ɔ 'gɔ sæj 'bʊːt]
map (e.g., subway ~)	kart, linjekart (n)	['kɑːt], ['linjə'kɑːt]
map (e.g., city ~)	kart (n)	['kɑːt]

souvenir, gift	suvenir (m)	[sʉve'nir]
gift shop	suvenirbutikk (m)	[sʉve'nir bʉ'tik]
to take pictures	å fotografere	[ɔ fɔtɔgrɑ'ferə]
to have one's picture taken	å bli fotografert	[ɔ 'bli fɔtɔgrɑ'fɛːt]

83. Shopping

to buy (purchase)	å kjøpe	[ɔ 'çœːpə]
purchase	innkjøp (n)	['in,çœp]
to go shopping	å gå shopping	[ɔ 'gɔ ,ʂɔpiŋ]
shopping	shopping (m)	['ʂɔpiŋ]

| to be open (ab. store) | å være åpen | [ɔ 'værə 'ɔpən] |
| to be closed | å være stengt | [ɔ 'værə 'stɛŋt] |

footwear, shoes	skotøy (n)	['skʊtøj]
clothes, clothing	klær (n)	['klær]
cosmetics	kosmetikk (m)	[kʊsme'tik]
food products	matvarer (m/f pl)	['mɑt,vɑrər]

gift, present	gave (m/f)	['gɑvə]
salesman	forselger (m)	[fɔ'sɛlər]
saleswoman	forselger (m)	[fɔ'sɛlər]

check out, cash desk	kasse (m/f)	['kɑsə]
mirror	speil (n)	['spæjl]
counter (store ~)	disk (m)	['disk]
fitting room	prøverom (n)	['prøvəˌrʊm]

to try on	å prøve	[ɔ 'prøvə]
to fit (ab. dress, etc.)	å passe	[ɔ 'pɑsə]
to like (I like …)	å like	[ɔ 'likə]

price	pris (m)	['pris]
price tag	prislapp (m)	['prisˌlɑp]
to cost (vt)	å koste	[ɔ 'kɔstə]
How much?	Hvor mye?	[vʊr 'mye]
discount	rabatt (m)	[rɑ'bɑt]

inexpensive (adj)	billig	['bili]
cheap (adj)	billig	['bili]
expensive (adj)	dyr	['dyr]
It's expensive	Det er dyrt	[de ær 'dy:t]

rental (n)	utleie (m/f)	['ʉtˌlæje]
to rent (~ a tuxedo)	å leie	[ɔ 'læjə]
credit (trade credit)	kreditt (m)	[krɛ'dit]
on credit (adv)	på kreditt	[pɔ krɛ'dit]

84. Money

money	penger (m pl)	['pɛŋər]
currency exchange	veksling (m/f)	['vɛkʂliŋ]
exchange rate	kurs (m)	['kʉʂ]
ATM	minibank (m)	['miniˌbɑnk]
coin	mynt (m)	['mʏnt]

| dollar | dollar (m) | ['dɔlɑr] |
| euro | euro (m) | ['ɛʉrʊ] |

lira	lira (m)	['lire]
Deutschmark	mark (m/f)	['mɑrk]
franc	franc (m)	['frɑn]
pound sterling	pund sterling (m)	['pʉn stɛ:'liŋ]
yen	yen (m)	['jɛn]

debt	skyld (m/f), gjeld (m)	['ʂyl], ['jɛl]
debtor	skyldner (m)	['ʂylnər]
to lend (money)	å låne ut	[ɔ 'lo:nə ʉt]
to borrow (vi, vt)	å låne	[ɔ 'lo:nə]

bank	bank (m)	['bɑnk]
account	konto (m)	['kɔntʊ]
to deposit (vt)	å sette inn	[ɔ 'sɛtə in]
to deposit into the account	å sette inn på kontoen	[ɔ 'sɛtə in pɔ 'kɔntʊən]
to withdraw (vt)	å ta ut fra kontoen	[ɔ 'tɑ ʉt frɑ 'kɔntʊən]

credit card	kredittkort (n)	[krɛ'dit̚ˌkɔːt̚]
cash	kontanter (m pl)	[kʊn'tɑntər]
check	sjekk (m)	['ʂɛk]
to write a check	å skrive en sjekk	[ɔ 'skrivə en 'ʂɛk]
checkbook	sjekkbok (m/f)	['ʂɛkˌbʊk]

wallet	lommebok (m)	['lʊməˌbʊk]
change purse	pung (m)	['pʉŋ]
safe	safe, seif (m)	['sɛjf]

heir	arving (m)	['ɑrviŋ]
inheritance	arv (m)	['ɑrv]
fortune (wealth)	formue (m)	['fɔrˌmʉə]

lease	leie (m)	['læje]
rent (money)	husleie (m/f)	['hʉsˌlæje]
to rent (sth from sb)	å leie	[ɔ 'læjə]

price	pris (m)	['pris]
cost	kostnad (m)	['kɔstnɑd]
sum	sum (m)	['sʉm]

to spend (vt)	å bruke	[ɔ 'brʉkə]
expenses	utgifter (m/f pl)	['ʉtˌjiftər]
to economize (vi, vt)	å spare	[ɔ 'spɑrə]
economical	sparsom	['spɑʂɔm]

to pay (vi, vt)	å betale	[ɔ be'tɑlə]
payment	betaling (m/f)	[be'tɑliŋ]
change (give the ~)	vekslepenger (pl)	['vɛkʂləˌpɛŋər]

tax	skatt (m)	['skat]
fine	bot (m/f)	['bʊt]
to fine (vt)	å bøtelegge	[ɔ 'bøtəˌlegə]

85. Post. Postal service

post office	post (m)	['pɔst]
mail (letters, etc.)	post (m)	['pɔst]
mailman	postbud (n)	['pɔstˌbʉd]
opening hours	åpningstider (m/f pl)	['ɔpniŋsˌtidər]

| letter | brev (n) | ['brev] |
| registered letter | rekommandert brev (n) | [rɔkʊman'dɛːt̚ ˌbrev] |

postcard	**postkort** (n)	['post,kɔ:t]
telegram	**telegram** (n)	[tele'gram]
package (parcel)	**postpakke** (m/f)	['post,pakə]
money transfer	**pengeoverføring** (m/f)	['pɛŋə 'ɔvər,føriŋ]

to receive (vt)	**å motta**	[ɔ 'mɔta]
to send (vt)	**å sende**	[ɔ 'sɛnə]
sending	**avsending** (m)	['af,sɛniŋ]

address	**adresse** (m)	[a'drɛsə]
ZIP code	**postnummer** (n)	['post,nʉmər]
sender	**avsender** (m)	['af,sɛnər]
receiver	**mottaker** (m)	['mɔt,takər]

name (first name)	**fornavn** (n)	['fɔr,navn]
surname (last name)	**etternavn** (n)	['ɛtə,ŋavn]

postage rate	**tariff** (m)	[ta'rif]
standard (adj)	**vanlig**	['vanli]
economical (adj)	**økonomisk**	[økʉ'nɔmisk]

weight	**vekt** (m)	['vɛkt]
to weigh (~ letters)	**å veie**	[ɔ 'væjə]
envelope	**konvolutt** (m)	[kʉnvʉ'lʉt]
postage stamp	**frimerke** (n)	['fri,mærkə]
to stamp an envelope	**å sette på frimerke**	[ɔ 'sɛtə pɔ 'fri,mærkə]

Dwelling. House. Home

86. House. Dwelling

house	**hus** (n)	['hʉs]
at home (adv)	**hjemme**	['jɛmə]
yard	**gård** (m)	['gɔːr]
fence (iron ~)	**gjerde** (n)	['jærə]
brick (n)	**tegl** (n), **murstein** (m)	['tæjl], ['mʉˌstæjn]
brick (as adj)	**tegl-**	['tæjl-]
stone (n)	**stein** (m)	['stæjn]
stone (as adj)	**stein-**	['stæjn-]
concrete (n)	**betong** (m)	[be'tɔŋ]
concrete (as adj)	**betong-**	[be'tɔŋ-]
new (new-built)	**ny**	['ny]
old (adj)	**gammel**	['gaməl]
decrepit (house)	**falleferdig**	['faləˌfæːɖi]
modern (adj)	**moderne**	[mʊ'dɛːŋə]
multistory (adj)	**fleretasjes-**	['flerɛˌtaʂɛs-]
tall (~ building)	**høy**	['høj]
floor, story	**etasje** (m)	[ɛ'taʂə]
single-story (adj)	**enetasjes**	['ɛnɛˌtaʂɛs]
1st floor	**første etasje** (m)	['fœʂtə ɛ'taʂə]
top floor	**øverste etasje** (m)	['øvəʂtə ɛ'taʂə]
roof	**tak** (n)	['tak]
chimney	**skorstein** (m/f)	['skɔˌstæjn]
roof tiles	**takstein** (m)	['takˌstæjn]
tiled (adj)	**taksteins-**	['takˌstæjns-]
attic (storage place)	**loft** (n)	['lɔft]
window	**vindu** (n)	['vindʉ]
glass	**glass** (n)	['glas]
window ledge	**vinduskarm** (m)	['vindʉsˌkarm]
shutters	**vinduslemmer** (m pl)	['vindʉsˌlemər]
wall	**mur, vegg** (m)	['mʉr], ['vɛg]
balcony	**balkong** (m)	[bal'kɔŋ]
downspout	**nedløpsrør** (n)	['nedløpsˌrør]
upstairs (to be ~)	**oppe**	['ɔpə]
to go upstairs	**å gå ovenpå**	[ɔ 'gɔ 'ɔvənˌpɔ]
to come down (the stairs)	**å gå ned**	[ɔ 'gɔ ne]
to move (to new premises)	**å flytte**	[ɔ 'flʏtə]

87. House. Entrance. Lift

entrance	inngang (m)	['in,gaŋ]
stairs (stairway)	trapp (m/f)	['trap]
steps	trinn (n pl)	['trin]
banister	gelender (n)	[ge'lendər]
lobby (hotel ~)	hall, lobby (m)	['hal], ['lɔbi]
mailbox	postkasse (m/f)	['pɔst,kasə]
garbage can	søppelkasse (m/f)	['sœpəl,kasə]
trash chute	søppelsjakt (m/f)	['sœpəl,sakt]
elevator	heis (m)	['hæjs]
freight elevator	lasteheis (m)	['lastə'hæjs]
elevator cage	heiskorg (m/f)	['hæjs,kɔrg]
to take the elevator	å ta heisen	[ɔ 'ta ,hæjsən]
apartment	leilighet (m/f)	['læjli,het]
residents (~ of a building)	beboere (m pl)	[be'bʊerə]
neighbor (masc.)	nabo (m)	['nabʊ]
neighbor (fem.)	nabo (m)	['nabʊ]
neighbors	naboer (m pl)	['nabʊər]

88. House. Electricity

electricity	elektrisitet (m)	[ɛlektrisi'tet]
light bulb	lyspære (m/f)	['lys,pærə]
switch	strømbryter (m)	['strøm,brytər]
fuse (plug fuse)	sikring (m)	['sikriŋ]
cable, wire (electric ~)	ledning (m)	['ledniŋ]
wiring	ledningsnett (n)	['ledniŋs,nɛt]
electricity meter	elmåler (m)	['ɛl,molər]
readings	avlesninger (m/f pl)	['av,lesniŋər]

89. House. Doors. Locks

door	dør (m/f)	['dœr]
gate (vehicle ~)	grind (m/f), port (m)	['griŋ], ['pɔ:t]
handle, doorknob	dørhåndtak (n)	['dœr,hɔntak]
to unlock (unbolt)	å låse opp	[ɔ 'lo:sə ɔp]
to open (vt)	å åpne	[ɔ 'ɔpnə]
to close (vt)	å lukke	[ɔ 'lʉkə]
key	nøkkel (m)	['nøkəl]
bunch (of keys)	knippe (n)	['knipə]
to creak (door, etc.)	å knirke	[ɔ 'knirkə]

creak	**knirk** (m/n)	['knɪrk]
hinge (door ~)	**hengsel** (m/n)	['hɛŋsel]
doormat	**dørmatte** (m/f)	['dœrˌmatə]
door lock	**dørlås** (m/n)	['dœrˌlɔs]
keyhole	**nøkkelhull** (n)	['nøkəlˌhʉl]
crossbar (sliding bar)	**slå** (m/f)	['ʂlɔ]
door latch	**slå** (m/f)	['ʂlɔ]
padlock	**hengelås** (m/n)	['hɛŋeˌlɔs]
to ring (~ the door bell)	**å ringe**	[ɔ 'rɪŋə]
ringing (sound)	**ringing** (m/f)	['rɪŋɪŋ]
doorbell	**ringeklokke** (m/f)	['rɪŋeˌklɔkə]
doorbell button	**ringeklokke knapp** (m)	['rɪŋeˌklɔkə 'knap]
knock (at the door)	**kakking** (m/f)	['kakɪŋ]
to knock (vi)	**å kakke**	[ɔ 'kakə]
code	**kode** (m)	['kʊdə]
combination lock	**kodelås** (m/n)	['kʊdəˌlɔs]
intercom	**dørtelefon** (m)	['dœrˌtele'fʊn]
number (on the door)	**nummer** (n)	['nʉmər]
doorplate	**dørskilt** (n)	['dœˌʂɪlt]
peephole	**kikhull** (n)	['çikˌhʉl]

90. Country house

village	**landsby** (m)	['lansˌby]
vegetable garden	**kjøkkenhage** (m)	['çœkənˌhagə]
fence	**gjerde** (n)	['jærə]
picket fence	**stakitt** (m/n)	[sta'kit]
wicket gate	**port, stakittport** (m)	['pɔːt], [sta'kitˌpɔːt]
granary	**kornlåve** (m)	['kʊːnˌloːvə]
root cellar	**jordkjeller** (m)	['juːrˌçɛlər]
shed (garden ~)	**skur, skjul** (n)	['skʉr], ['ʂʉl]
well (water)	**brønn** (m)	['brœn]
stove (wood-fired ~)	**ovn** (m)	['ɔvn]
to stoke the stove	**å fyre**	[ɔ 'fyrə]
firewood	**ved** (m)	['ve]
log (firewood)	**vedstykke** (n), **vedskie** (f)	['vɛdˌstʏkə], ['vɛˌʂiə]
veranda	**veranda** (m)	[væ'randa]
deck (terrace)	**terrasse** (m)	[tɛ'rasə]
stoop (front steps)	**yttertrapp** (m/f)	['ytəˌtrap]
swing (hanging seat)	**gynge** (m/f)	['jiŋə]

91. Villa. Mansion

country house	fritidshus (n)	['fritids,hʉs]
villa (seaside ~)	villa (m)	['vila]
wing (~ of a building)	fløy (m)	['fløj]

garden	hage (m)	['hagə]
park	park (m)	['park]
tropical greenhouse	drivhus (n)	['driv,hʉs]
to look after (garden, etc.)	å ta vare	[ɔ 'ta ,varə]

swimming pool	svømmebasseng (n)	['svœmə,ba'sɛŋ]
gym (home gym)	gym (m)	['dʒym]
tennis court	tennisbane (m)	['tɛnis,banə]
home theater (room)	hjemmekino (m)	['jɛmə,çinʉ]
garage	garasje (m)	[ga'raʂə]

private property	privateiendom (m)	[pri'vat 'æjəndɔm]
private land	privat terreng (n)	[pri'vat tɛ'rɛŋ]

warning (caution)	advarsel (m)	['ad,vaʂəl]
warning sign	varselskilt (n)	['vaʂəl,ʂilt]

security	sikkerhet (m/f)	['sikər,het]
security guard	sikkerhetsvakt (m/f)	['sikərhɛts,vakt]
burglar alarm	tyverialarm (m)	[tyve'ri a'larm]

92. Castle. Palace

castle	borg (m)	['bɔrg]
palace	palass (n)	[pa'las]
fortress	festning (m/f)	['fɛstniŋ]

wall (round castle)	mur (m)	['mʉr]
tower	tårn (n)	['tɔ:ŋ]
keep, donjon	kjernetårn (n)	['çæ:ŋə'tɔ:ŋ]

portcullis	fallgitter (n)	['fal,gitər]
underground passage	underjordisk gang (m)	['ʉnər,ju:rdisk 'gaŋ]
moat	vollgrav (m/f)	['vɔl,grav]

chain	kjede (m)	['çɛ:de]
arrow loop	skyteskår (n)	['ʂytə,skɔr]

magnificent (adj)	praktfull	['prakt,fʉl]
majestic (adj)	majestetisk	[maje'stɛtisk]

impregnable (adj)	uinntakelig	[ʉən'takəli]
medieval (adj)	middelalderlig	['midəl,aldɛ:[i]

93. Apartment

apartment	leilighet (m/f)	['læjli̩het]
room	rom (n)	['rʊm]
bedroom	soverom (n)	['sɔvə̩rʊm]
dining room	spisestue (m/f)	['spisə̩stʉə]
living room	dagligstue (m/f)	['dɑgli̩stʉə]
study (home office)	arbeidsrom (n)	['ɑrbæjds̩rʊm]
entry room	entré (m)	[ɑn'trɛː]
bathroom (room with a bath or shower)	bad, baderom (n)	['bɑd], ['bɑdə̩rʊm]
half bath	toalett, WC (n)	[tʊɑ'let], [vɛ'sɛ]
ceiling	tak (n)	['tɑk]
floor	gulv (n)	['gʉlv]
corner	hjørne (n)	['jœːɳə]

94. Apartment. Cleaning

to clean (vi, vt)	å rydde	[ɔ 'rʏdə]
to put away (to stow)	å stue unna	[ɔ 'stʉə 'ʉnɑ]
dust	støv (n)	['støv]
dusty (adj)	støvet	['støvət]
to dust (vt)	å tørke støv	[ɔ 'tœrkə 'støv]
vacuum cleaner	støvsuger (m)	['støf̩sʉgər]
to vacuum (vt)	å støvsuge	[ɔ 'støf̩sʉgə]
to sweep (vi, vt)	å sope, å feie	[ɔ 'sɔpə], [ɔ 'fæjə]
sweepings	søppel (m/f/n)	['sœpəl]
order	orden (m)	['ɔrdən]
disorder, mess	uorden (m)	['ʉːɔrdən]
mop	mopp (m)	['mɔp]
dust cloth	klut (m)	['klʉt]
short broom	feiekost (m)	['fæjə̩kʊst]
dustpan	feiebrett (n)	['fæjə̩brɛt]

95. Furniture. Interior

furniture	møbler (n pl)	['møblər]
table	bord (n)	['bʊr]
chair	stol (m)	['stʊl]
bed	seng (m/f)	['sɛŋ]
couch, sofa	sofa (m)	['sʊfɑ]
armchair	lenestol (m)	['lenə̩stʊl]
bookcase	bokskap (n)	['bʊk̩skɑp]

shelf	hylle (m/f)	['hʏlə]
wardrobe	klesskap (n)	['kleˌskɑp]
coat rack (wall-mounted ~)	knaggbrett (n)	['knɑgˌbrɛt]
coat stand	stumtjener (m)	['stʉmˌtjenər]

| bureau, dresser | kommode (m) | [kʊ'mʊdə] |
| coffee table | kaffebord (n) | ['kɑfəˌbʊr] |

mirror	speil (n)	['spæjl]
carpet	teppe (n)	['tɛpə]
rug, small carpet	lite teppe (n)	['litə 'tɛpə]

fireplace	peis (m), ildsted (n)	['pæjs], ['ilsted]
candle	lys (n)	['lys]
candlestick	lysestake (m)	['lysəˌstɑkə]

drapes	gardiner (m/f pl)	[gɑː'dinər]
wallpaper	tapet (n)	[tɑ'pet]
blinds (jalousie)	persienne (m)	[pæʂi'enə]

table lamp	bordlampe (m/f)	['bʊrˌlampə]
wall lamp (sconce)	vegglampe (m/f)	['vɛgˌlampə]
floor lamp	gulvlampe (m/f)	['gʉlvˌlampə]
chandelier	lysekrone (m/f)	['lysəˌkrʊnə]

leg (of chair, table)	bein (n)	['bæjn]
armrest	armlene (n)	['armˌlenə]
back (backrest)	rygg (m)	['rʏg]
drawer	skuff (m)	['skʉf]

96. Bedding

bedclothes	sengetøy (n)	['sɛŋəˌtøj]
pillow	pute (m/f)	['pʉtə]
pillowcase	putevar, putetrekk (n)	['pʉtəˌvar], ['pʉtəˌtrɛk]
duvet, comforter	dyne (m/f)	['dynə]
sheet	laken (n)	['lɑkən]
bedspread	sengeteppe (n)	['sɛŋəˌtɛpə]

97. Kitchen

kitchen	kjøkken (n)	['çœkən]
gas	gass (m)	['gɑs]
gas stove (range)	gasskomfyr (m)	['gɑs kɔmˌfyr]
electric stove	elektrisk komfyr (m)	[ɛ'lektrisk kɔmˌfyr]
oven	bakeovn (m)	['bɑkəˌovn]
microwave oven	mikrobølgeovn (m)	['mikrʊˌbølgə'ovn]
refrigerator	kjøleskap (n)	['çœləˌskɑp]

freezer	**fryser** (m)	['frysər]
dishwasher	**oppvaskmaskin** (m)	['ɔpvɑsk mɑˌʂin]
meat grinder	**kjøttkvern** (m/f)	['çœtˌkvɛːŋ]
juicer	**juicepresse** (m/f)	['dʒʉsˌprɛsə]
toaster	**brødrister** (m)	['brøˌristər]
mixer	**mikser** (m)	['miksər]
coffee machine	**kaffetrakter** (m)	['kafəˌtraktər]
coffee pot	**kaffekanne** (m/f)	['kafəˌkanə]
coffee grinder	**kaffekvern** (m/f)	['kafəˌkvɛːŋ]
kettle	**tekjele** (m)	['teˌçelə]
teapot	**tekanne** (m/f)	['teˌkanə]
lid	**lokk** (n)	['lɔk]
tea strainer	**tesil** (m)	['teˌsil]
spoon	**skje** (m)	['ʂe]
teaspoon	**teskje** (m)	['teˌʂe]
soup spoon	**spiseskje** (m)	['spisəˌʂɛ]
fork	**gaffel** (m)	['gafəl]
knife	**kniv** (m)	['kniv]
tableware (dishes)	**servise** (n)	[sær'visə]
plate (dinner ~)	**tallerken** (m)	[ta'lærkən]
saucer	**tefat** (n)	['teˌfat]
shot glass	**shotglass** (n)	['ʂɔtˌglas]
glass (tumbler)	**glass** (n)	['glas]
cup	**kopp** (m)	['kɔp]
sugar bowl	**sukkerskål** (m/f)	['sʉkərˌskɔl]
salt shaker	**saltbøsse** (m/f)	['saltˌbøsə]
pepper shaker	**pepperbøsse** (m/f)	['pɛpərˌbøsə]
butter dish	**smørkopp** (m)	['smœrˌkɔp]
stock pot (soup pot)	**gryte** (m/f)	['grytə]
frying pan (skillet)	**steikepanne** (m/f)	['stæjkəˌpanə]
ladle	**sleiv** (m/f)	['ʂlæjv]
colander	**dørslag** (n)	['dœʂlag]
tray (serving ~)	**brett** (n)	['brɛt]
bottle	**flaske** (m)	['flaskə]
jar (glass)	**glasskrukke** (m/f)	['glasˌkrʉkə]
can	**boks** (m)	['bɔks]
bottle opener	**flaskeåpner** (m)	['flaskəˌɔpnər]
can opener	**konservåpner** (m)	['kʉnsəvˌɔpnər]
corkscrew	**korketrekker** (m)	['kɔrkəˌtrɛkər]
filter	**filter** (n)	['filtər]
to filter (vt)	**å filtrere**	[ɔ fil'trerə]
trash, garbage (food waste, etc.)	**søppel** (m/f/n)	['sœpəl]
trash can (kitchen ~)	**søppelbøtte** (m/f)	['ʂœpolˌbœtə]

98. Bathroom

bathroom	bad, baderom (n)	['bɑd], ['bɑdə,rʊm]
water	vann (n)	['vɑn]
faucet	kran (m/f)	['krɑn]
hot water	varmt vann (n)	['vɑrmt ˌvɑn]
cold water	kaldt vann (n)	['kɑlt vɑn]
toothpaste	tannpasta (m)	['tɑnˌpɑstɑ]
to brush one's teeth	å pusse tennene	[ɔ 'pʉsə 'tɛnənə]
toothbrush	tannbørste (m)	['tɑnˌbœʂtə]
to shave (vi)	å barbere seg	[ɔ bɑr'berə sæj]
shaving foam	barberskum (n)	[bɑr'bɛˌskʊm]
razor	høvel (m)	['høvəl]
to wash (one's hands, etc.)	å vaske	[ɔ 'vɑskə]
to take a bath	å vaske seg	[ɔ 'vɑskə sæj]
shower	dusj (m)	['dʉʂ]
to take a shower	å ta en dusj	[ɔ 'tɑ en 'dʉʂ]
bathtub	badekar (n)	['bɑdəˌkɑr]
toilet (toilet bowl)	toalettstol (m)	[tʊɑ'letˌstʊl]
sink (washbasin)	vaskeservant (m)	['vɑskəˌsɛr'vɑnt]
soap	såpe (m/f)	['soːpə]
soap dish	såpeskål (m/f)	['soːpəˌskɔl]
sponge	svamp (m)	['svɑmp]
shampoo	sjampo (m)	['ʂɑmˌpʊ]
towel	håndkle (n)	['hɔnˌkle]
bathrobe	badekåpe (m/f)	['bɑdəˌkoːpə]
laundry (process)	vask (m)	['vɑsk]
washing machine	vaskemaskin (m)	['vɑskə mɑˌʂin]
to do the laundry	å vaske tøy	[ɔ 'vɑskə 'tøj]
laundry detergent	vaskepulver (n)	['vɑskəˌpʉlvər]

99. Household appliances

TV set	TV (m), TV-apparat (n)	['teːvɛ], ['tɛvɛ ɑpɑ'rɑt]
tape recorder	båndopptaker (m)	['bɔnˌɔptɑkər]
VCR (video recorder)	video (m)	['videʊ]
radio	radio (m)	['rɑdiʊ]
player (CD, MP3, etc.)	spiller (m)	['spilər]
video projector	videoprojektor (m)	['videʊ prɔ'jɛktɔr] •
home movie theater	hjemmekino (m)	['jɛməˌçinʊ]
DVD player	DVD-spiller (m)	[deve'de ˌspilər]

| amplifier | **forsterker** (m) | [fɔ'ʂtærkər] |
| video game console | **spillkonsoll** (m) | ['spil kʊn'sɔl] |

video camera	**videokamera** (n)	['videʊ ˌkamera]
camera (photo)	**kamera** (n)	['kamera]
digital camera	**digitalkamera** (n)	[digi'tal ˌkamera]

vacuum cleaner	**støvsuger** (m)	['støfˌsʉgər]
iron (e.g., steam ~)	**strykejern** (n)	['strykəˌjæːŋ]
ironing board	**strykebrett** (n)	['strykəˌbrɛt]

telephone	**telefon** (m)	[tele'fʊn]
cell phone	**mobiltelefon** (m)	[mʊ'bil tele'fʊn]
typewriter	**skrivemaskin** (m)	['skrivə maˌʂin]
sewing machine	**symaskin** (m)	['siːmaˌʂin]

microphone	**mikrofon** (m)	[mikrʊ'fʊn]
headphones	**hodetelefoner** (n pl)	['hɔdəteleˌfʊnər]
remote control (TV)	**fjernkontroll** (m)	['fjæːŋ kʊn'trɔl]

CD, compact disc	**CD-rom** (m)	['sɛdɛˌrʊm]
cassette, tape	**kassett** (m)	[ka'sɛt]
vinyl record	**plate, skive** (m/f)	['platə], ['ʂivə]

renovations	**renovering** (m/f)	[renʊ'veriŋ]
to renovate (vt)	**å renovere**	[ɔ renʊ'verə]
to repair, to fix (vt)	**å reparere**	[ɔ repa'rerə]
to put in order	**å bringe orden**	[ɔ 'briŋə 'ɔrdən]
to redo (do again)	**å gjøre om**	[ɔ 'jørə ɔm]

paint	**maling** (m/f)	['maliŋ]
to paint (~ a wall)	**å male**	[ɔ 'malə]
house painter	**maler** (m)	['malər]
paintbrush	**pensel** (m)	['pɛnsəl]
whitewash	**kalkmaling** (m/f)	['kalkˌmaliŋ]
to whitewash (vt)	**å hvitmale**	[ɔ 'vitˌmalə]

wallpaper	**tapet** (n)	[ta'pet]
to wallpaper (vt)	**å tapetsere**	[ɔ tapet'serə]
varnish	**ferniss** (m)	['fæːˌɲis]
to varnish (vt)	**å lakkere**	[ɔ la'kerə]

| water | **vann** (n) | ['van] |
| hot water | **varmt vann** (n) | ['varmt ˌvan] |

| cold water | **kaldt vann** (n) | ['kalt van] |
| faucet | **kran** (m/f) | ['kran] |

drop (of water)	**dråpe** (m)	['dro:pə]
to drip (vi)	**å dryppe**	[ɔ 'drʏpə]
to leak (ab. pipe)	**å lekke**	[ɔ 'lekə]
leak (pipe ~)	**lekk** (m)	['lek]
puddle	**pøl, pytt** (m)	['pøl], ['pʏt]

pipe	**rør** (n)	['rør]
valve (e.g., ball ~)	**ventil** (m)	[vɛn'til]
to be clogged up	**å bli tilstoppet**	[ɔ 'bli til'stɔpət]

tools	**verktøy** (n pl)	['værk,tøj]
adjustable wrench	**skiftenøkkel** (m)	['ʂiftə,nøkəl]
to unscrew (lid, filter, etc.)	**å skru ut**	[ɔ 'skrʉ ʉt]
to screw (tighten)	**å skru fast**	[ɔ 'skrʉ 'fast]

to unclog (vt)	**å rense**	[ɔ 'rɛnsə]
plumber	**rørlegger** (m)	['rør,legər]
basement	**kjeller** (m)	['çɛlər]
sewerage (system)	**avløp** (n)	['av,løp]

102. Fire. Conflagration

fire (accident)	**ild** (m)	['il]
flame	**flamme** (m)	['flamə]
spark	**gnist** (m)	['gnist]
smoke (from fire)	**røyk** (m)	['røjk]
torch (flaming stick)	**fakkel** (m)	['fakəl]
campfire	**bål** (n)	['bɔl]

gas, gasoline	**bensin** (m)	[bɛn'sin]
kerosene (type of fuel)	**parafin** (m)	[para'fin]
flammable (adj)	**brennbar**	['brɛn,bar]
explosive (adj)	**eksplosiv**	['ɛksplu,siv]
NO SMOKING	**RØYKING FORBUDT**	['røjkiŋ for'bʉt]

safety	**sikkerhet** (m/f)	['sikər,het]
danger	**fare** (m)	['farə]
dangerous (adj)	**farlig**	['fa:li]

to catch fire	**å ta fyr**	[ɔ 'ta ,fyr]
explosion	**eksplosjon** (m)	[ɛksplu'ʂun]
to set fire	**å sette fyr**	[ɔ 'sɛtə ,fyr]
arsonist	**brannstifter** (m)	['bran,stiftər]
arson	**brannstiftelse** (m)	['bran,stiftəlsə]

| to blaze (vi) | **å flamme** | [ɔ 'flamə] |
| to burn (be on fire) | **å brenne** | [ɔ 'brɛnə] |

to burn down	å brenne ned	[ɔ 'brɛnə ne]
to call the fire department	å ringe bransvesenet	[ɔ 'riŋə 'brans‚vesənə]
firefighter, fireman	brannmann (m)	['bran‚man]
fire truck	brannbil (m)	['bran‚bil]
fire department	brannkorps (n)	['bran‚kɔrps]
fire truck ladder	teleskopstige (m)	['tele'skʊp‚stiːə]

fire hose	slange (m)	['şlaŋə]
fire extinguisher	brannslukker (n)	['bran‚şlʉkər]
helmet	hjelm (m)	['jɛlm]
siren	sirene (m/f)	[si'renə]

to cry (for help)	å skrike	[ɔ 'skrikə]
to call for help	å rope på hjelp	[ɔ 'rʊpə pɔ 'jɛlp]
rescuer	redningsmann (m)	['rɛdniŋs‚man]
to rescue (vt)	å redde	[ɔ 'rɛdə]

to arrive (vi)	å ankomme	[ɔ 'an‚kɔmə]
to extinguish (vt)	å slokke	[ɔ 'şløkə]
water	vann (n)	['van]
sand	sand (m)	['san]

ruins (destruction)	ruiner (m pl)	[rʉ'inər]
to collapse (building, etc.)	å falle sammen	[ɔ 'falə 'samən]
to fall down (vi)	å styrte ned	[ɔ 'styːţə ne]
to cave in (ceiling, floor)	å styrte inn	[ɔ 'styːţə in]

| piece of debris | del (m) | ['del] |
| ash | aske (m/f) | ['askə] |

| to suffocate (die) | å kveles | [ɔ 'kveləs] |
| to be killed (perish) | å omkomme | [ɔ 'ɔm‚kɔmə] |

HUMAN ACTIVITIES

Job. Business. Part 1

103. Office. Working in the office

office (company ~)	**kontor** (n)	[kʊn'tʊr]
office (of director, etc.)	**kontor** (n)	[kʊn'tʊr]
reception desk	**resepsjon** (m)	[resɛp'ʂʊn]
secretary	**sekretær** (m)	[sɛkrə'tær]
secretary (fem.)	**sekretær** (m)	[sɛkrə'tær]
director	**direktør** (m)	[dirɛk'tør]
manager	**manager** (m)	['mɛnidʒər]
accountant	**regnskapsfører** (m)	['rɛjnskaps,førər]
employee	**ansatt** (n)	['an,sat]
furniture	**møbler** (n pl)	['møblər]
desk	**bord** (n)	['bʊr]
desk chair	**arbeidsstol** (m)	['arbæjds,stʊl]
drawer unit	**skuffeseksjon** (m)	['skʉfə,sɛk'ʂʊn]
coat stand	**stumtjener** (m)	['stʉm,tjenər]
computer	**datamaskin** (m)	['data ma,ʂin]
printer	**skriver** (m)	['skrivər]
fax machine	**faks** (m)	['faks]
photocopier	**kopimaskin** (m)	[kʊ'pi ma,ʂin]
paper	**papir** (n)	[pa'pir]
office supplies	**kontorartikler** (m pl)	[kʊn'tʊr ɑ:'ʈiklər]
mouse pad	**musematte** (m/f)	['mʉsə,matə]
sheet (of paper)	**ark** (n)	['ark]
binder	**mappe** (m/f)	['mapə]
catalog	**katalog** (m)	[kata'lɔg]
phone directory	**telefonkatalog** (m)	[tele'fʊn kata'lɔg]
documentation	**dokumentasjon** (m)	[dɔkʉmɛnta'ʂʊn]
brochure (e.g., 12 pages ~)	**brosjyre** (m)	[brɔ'ʂyrə]
leaflet (promotional ~)	**reklameblad** (n)	[rɛ'klamə,bla]
sample	**prøve** (m)	['prøvə]
training meeting	**trening** (m/f)	['treniŋ]
meeting (of managers)	**møte** (n)	['møtə]
lunch time	**lunsj pause** (m)	['lʉnʂ ,paʊsə]

to make a copy	å lage en kopi	[ɔ 'lagə en ku'pi]
to make multiple copies	å kopiere	[ɔ ku'pjerə]
to receive a fax	å motta faks	[ɔ 'mɔta ˌfaks]
to send a fax	å sende faks	[ɔ 'sɛnə ˌfaks]
to call (by phone)	å ringe	[ɔ 'riŋə]
to answer (vt)	å svare	[ɔ 'svarə]
to put through	å sætte over til ...	[ɔ 'sætə 'ɔvər til ...]
to arrange, to set up	å arrangere	[ɔ araŋ'şerə]
to demonstrate (vt)	å demonstrere	[ɔ demɔn'strerə]
to be absent	å være fraværende	[ɔ 'værə 'fraˌværənə]
absence	fravær (n)	['fraˌvær]

104. Business processes. Part 1

business	bedrift, handel (m)	[be'drift], ['handəl]
occupation	yrke (n)	['yrkə]
firm	firma (n)	['firma]
company	foretak (n)	['fɔrəˌtak]
corporation	korporasjon (m)	[kurpura'şun]
enterprise	foretak (n)	['fɔrəˌtak]
agency	agentur (n)	[agɛn'tʉr]
agreement (contract)	avtale (m)	['avˌtalə]
contract	kontrakt (m)	[kun'trakt]
deal	avtale (m)	['avˌtalə]
order (to place an ~)	bestilling (m)	[be'stiliŋ]
terms (of the contract)	vilkår (n)	['vilˌkɔːr]
wholesale (adv)	en gros	[ɛn 'grɔ]
wholesale (adj)	engros-	[ɛŋ'grɔ-]
wholesale (n)	engroshandel (m)	[ɛŋ'grɔˌhandəl]
retail (adj)	detalj-	[de'talj-]
retail (n)	detaljhandel (m)	[de'taljˌhandəl]
competitor	konkurrent (m)	[kunkʉ'rɛnt]
competition	konkurranse (m)	[kunkʉ'ransə]
to compete (vi)	å konkurrere	[ɔ kunkʉ'rerə]
partner (associate)	partner (m)	['paːʈnər]
partnership	partnerskap (n)	['paːʈnəˌşkap]
crisis	krise (m/f)	['krisə]
bankruptcy	fallitt (m)	[fa'lit]
to go bankrupt	å gå konkurs	[ɔ gɔ kɔn'kʉş]
difficulty	vanskelighet (m)	['vanskəliˌhet]
problem	problem (n)	[prʉ'blem]
catastrophe	katastrofe (m)	[kata'strɔfə]
economy	økonomi (m)	[økunʉ'mi]

economic (~ growth)	**økonomisk**	[økʉ'nɔmisk]
economic recession	**økonomisk nedgang** (m)	[økʉ'nɔmisk 'nedˌgɑŋ]
goal (aim)	**mål** (n)	['mol]
task	**oppgave** (m/f)	['ɔpˌgɑvə]
to trade (vi)	**å handle**	[ɔ 'hɑndlə]
network (distribution ~)	**nettverk** (n)	['nɛtˌværk]
inventory (stock)	**lager** (n)	['lɑgər]
range (assortment)	**sortiment** (n)	[sɔːʈi'mɛn]
leader (leading company)	**leder** (m)	['ledər]
large (~ company)	**stor**	['stʉr]
monopoly	**monopol** (n)	[mʉnʉ'pɔl]
theory	**teori** (m)	[teʉ'ri]
practice	**praksis** (m)	['prɑksis]
experience (in my ~)	**erfaring** (m/f)	[ær'fɑriŋ]
trend (tendency)	**tendens** (m)	[tɛn'dɛns]
development	**utvikling** (m/f)	['ʉtˌvikliŋ]

105. Business processes. Part 2

profit (foregone ~)	**utbytte** (n), **fordel** (m)	['ʉtˌbʏtə], ['fɔːdel]
profitable (~ deal)	**fordelaktig**	[fɔːdəl'ɑkti]
delegation (group)	**delegasjon** (m)	[delegɑ'ʂʉn]
salary	**lønn** (m/f)	['lœn]
to correct (an error)	**å rette**	[ɔ 'rɛtə]
business trip	**forretningsreise** (m/f)	[fɔ'rɛtniŋsˌræjsə]
commission	**provisjon** (m)	[prʉvi'ʂʉn]
to control (vt)	**å kontrollere**	[ɔ kʉntrɔ'lerə]
conference	**konferanse** (m)	[kʉnfə'rɑnsə]
license	**lisens** (m)	[li'sɛns]
reliable (~ partner)	**pålitelig**	[pɔ'liteli]
initiative (undertaking)	**initiativ** (n)	[initsiɑ'tiv]
norm (standard)	**norm** (m)	['nɔrm]
circumstance	**omstendighet** (m)	[ɔm'stɛndiˌhet]
duty (of employee)	**plikt** (m/f)	['plikt]
organization (company)	**organisasjon** (m)	[ɔrgɑnisɑ'ʂʉn]
organization (process)	**organisering** (m)	[ɔrgɑni'seriŋ]
organized (adj)	**organisert**	[ɔrgɑni'sɛːʈ]
cancellation	**avlysning** (m/f)	['ɑvˌlʏsniŋ]
to cancel (call off)	**å avlyse, å annullere**	[ɔ 'ɑvˌlʏsə], [ɔ ɑnʉ'lerə]
report (official ~)	**rapport** (m)	[rɑ'pɔːʈ]
patent	**patent** (n)	[pɑ'tɛnt]
to patent (obtain patent)	**å patentere**	[ɔ pɑten'terə]

to plan (vt)	**å planlegge**	[ɔ ˈplanˌlegə]
bonus (money)	**gratiale** (n)	[gratsiˈɑːlə]
professional (adj)	**professionel**	[prʊˈfɛsjɔˌnɛl]
procedure	**prosedyre** (m)	[prʊseˈdyrə]
to examine (contract, etc.)	**å undersøke**	[ɔ ˈʉnəˌsøkə]
calculation	**beregning** (m/f)	[beˈrɛjniŋ]
reputation	**rykte** (n)	[ˈrʏktə]
risk	**risiko** (m)	[ˈrisikʊ]
to manage, to run	**å styre, å lede**	[ɔ ˈstyrə], [ɔ ˈledə]
information	**opplysninger** (m/f pl)	[ˈɔpˌlʏsniŋər]
property	**eiendom** (m)	[ˈæjənˌdɔm]
union	**forbund** (n)	[ˈforˌbʉn]
life insurance	**livsforsikring** (m/f)	[ˈlifsfɔˌşikriŋ]
to insure (vt)	**å forsikre**	[ɔ fɔˈşikrə]
insurance	**forsikring** (m/f)	[fɔˈşikriŋ]
auction (~ sale)	**auksjon** (m)	[aʊkˈşʊn]
to notify (inform)	**å underrette**	[ɔ ˈʉnəˌrɛtə]
management (process)	**ledelse** (m)	[ˈledəlsə]
service (~ industry)	**tjeneste** (m)	[ˈtjenɛstə]
forum	**forum** (n)	[ˈfɔrum]
to function (vi)	**å fungere**	[ɔ fʉˈŋerə]
stage (phase)	**etappe** (m)	[eˈtapə]
legal (~ services)	**juridisk**	[jʉˈridisk]
lawyer (legal advisor)	**jurist** (m)	[jʉˈrist]

106. Production. Works

plant	**verk** (n)	[ˈværk]
factory	**fabrikk** (m)	[faˈbrik]
workshop	**verkstad** (m)	[ˈværkˌstad]
works, production site	**produksjonsplass** (m)	[prʊdʊkˈşʊns ˌplas]
industry (manufacturing)	**industri** (m)	[indʉˈstri]
industrial (adj)	**industriell**	[indʉstriˈɛl]
heavy industry	**tungindustri** (m)	[ˈtʉŋ ˌindʉˈstri]
light industry	**lettindustri** (m)	[ˈletˌindʉˈstri]
products	**produksjon** (m)	[prʊdʊkˈşʊn]
to produce (vt)	**å produsere**	[ɔ prʊdʉˈserə]
raw materials	**råstoffer** (n pl)	[ˈrɔˌstofər]
foreman (construction ~)	**formann, bas** (m)	[ˈfɔrman], [ˈbas]
workers team (crew)	**arbeidslag** (n)	[ˈarbæjdsˌlag]
worker	**arbeider** (m)	[ˈarˌbæjdər]
working day	**arbeidsdag** (m)	[ˈarbæjdsˌda]

pause (rest break)	hvilepause (m)	['vilə‚pause]
meeting	møte (n)	['møtə]
to discuss (vt)	å drøfte, å diskutere	[ɔ 'drœftə], [ɔ diskʉ'terə]
plan	plan (m)	['plɑn]
to fulfill the plan	å oppfylle planen	[ɔ 'ɔp‚fʏlə 'plɑnən]
rate of output	produksjonsmål (n)	[prʉdʉk'ʂʉns ‚mol]
quality	kvalitet (m)	[kvɑli'tɛt]
control (checking)	kontroll (m)	[kʉn'trɔl]
quality control	kvalitetskontroll (m)	[kvɑli'tɛt kʉn'trɔl]
workplace safety	arbeidervern (n)	['ɑrbæjdər‚væː‚ɳ]
discipline	disiplin (m)	[disip'lin]
violation	brudd (n)	['brʉd]
(of safety rules, etc.)		
to violate (rules)	å bryte	[ɔ 'brytə]
strike	streik (m)	['stræjk]
striker	streiker (m)	['stræjkər]
to be on strike	å streike	[ɔ 'stræjkə]
labor union	fagforening (m/f)	['fɑgfɔ‚reniŋ]
to invent (machine, etc.)	å oppfinne	[ɔ 'ɔp‚finə]
invention	oppfinnelse (m)	['ɔp‚finəlsə]
research	forskning (m)	['fɔːʂkniŋ]
to improve (make better)	å forbedre	[ɔ fɔr'bɛdrə]
technology	teknologi (m)	[tɛknʉlʉ'gi]
technical drawing	teknisk tegning (m/f)	['tɛknisk ‚tæjniŋ]
load, cargo	last (m/f)	['lɑst]
loader (person)	lastearbeider (m)	['lɑstə'ɑr‚bæjdər]
to load (vehicle, etc.)	å laste	[ɔ 'lɑstə]
loading (process)	lasting (m/f)	['lɑstiŋ]
to unload (vi, vt)	å lesse av	[ɔ 'lesə ɑː]
unloading	avlessing (m/f)	['ɑv‚lesiŋ]
transportation	transport (m)	[trɑns'pɔːt]
transportation company	transportfirma (n)	[trɑns'pɔːt ‚firmɑ]
to transport (vt)	å transportere	[ɔ trɑnspɔː'ʈerə]
freight car	godsvogn (m/f)	['gʉts‚vɔŋn]
tank (e.g., oil ~)	tank (m)	['tɑnk]
truck	lastebil (m)	['lɑstə‚bil]
machine tool	verktøymaskin (m)	['værktøj mɑ‚ʂin]
mechanism	mekanisme (m)	[mekɑ'nismə]
industrial waste	industrielt avfall (n)	[indʉstri'ɛlt 'ɑv‚fɑl]
packing (process)	pakning (m/f)	['pɑkniŋ]
to pack (vt)	å pakke	[ɔ 'pɑkə]

107. Contract. Agreement

contract	**kontrakt** (m)	[kʊn'trɑkt]
agreement	**avtale** (m)	['ɑv,tɑlə]
addendum	**tillegg, bilag** (n)	['ti,leg], ['bi,lɑg]
to sign a contract	**å inngå kontrakt**	[ɔ 'in,gɔ kʊn'trɑkt]
signature	**underskrift** (m/f)	['ʉnə,skrift]
to sign (vt)	**å underskrive**	[ɔ 'ʉnə,skrivə]
seal (stamp)	**stempel** (n)	['stɛmpəl]
subject of contract	**kontraktens gjenstand** (m)	[kʊn'trɑktəns 'jɛn,stɑn]
clause	**klausul** (m)	[klɑʊ'sʉl]
parties (in contract)	**parter** (m pl)	['pɑːtər]
legal address	**juridisk adresse** (m/f)	[jʉ'ridisk ɑ'drɛsə]
to violate the contract	**å bryte kontrakten**	[ɔ 'brytə kʊn'trɑktən]
commitment (obligation)	**forpliktelse** (m)	[fɔr'pliktəlsə]
responsibility	**ansvar** (n)	['ɑn,svɑr]
force majeure	**force majeure** (m)	[,fɔrs mɑ'ʒøːr]
dispute	**tvist** (m)	['tvist]
penalties	**straffeavgifter** (m pl)	['strɑfə ɑv'jiftər]

108. Import & Export

import	**import** (m)	[im'pɔːt]
importer	**importør** (m)	[impɔ:'tør]
to import (vt)	**å importere**	[ɔ impɔ:'terə]
import (as adj.)	**import-**	[im'pɔːt-]
export (exportation)	**eksport** (m)	[ɛks'pɔːt]
exporter	**eksportør** (m)	[ɛkspɔ:'tør]
to export (vi, vt)	**å eksportere**	[ɔ ɛkspɔ:'terə]
export (as adj.)	**eksport-**	[ɛks'pɔːt-]
goods (merchandise)	**vare** (m/f)	['vɑrə]
consignment, lot	**parti** (n)	[pɑː'ti]
weight	**vekt** (m)	['vɛkt]
volume	**volum** (n)	[vɔ'lʉm]
cubic meter	**kubikkmeter** (m)	[kʉ'bik,metər]
manufacturer	**produsent** (m)	[prʊdʉ'sɛnt]
transportation company	**transportfirma** (n)	[trɑns'pɔ:t ,firmɑ]
container	**container** (m)	[kɔn'tɛjnər]
border	**grense** (m/f)	['grɛnsə]
customs	**toll** (m)	['tɔl]
customs duty	**tollavgift** (m)	['tɔl ɑv'jift]

customs officer	**tollbetjent** (m)	['tɔlbeˌtjɛnt]
smuggling	**smugling** (m/f)	['smʉgliŋ]
contraband (smuggled goods)	**smuglergods** (n)	['smʉgləˌgʊts]

109. Finances

stock (share)	**aksje** (m)	['akʂə]
bond (certificate)	**obligasjon** (m)	[ɔbliga'ʂʊn]
promissory note	**veksel** (m)	['vɛksəl]

| stock exchange | **børs** (m) | ['bœʂ] |
| stock price | **aksjekurs** (m) | ['akʂəˌkʉʂ] |

| to go down (become cheaper) | **å gå ned** | [ɔ 'gɔ ne] |
| to go up (become more expensive) | **å gå opp** | [ɔ 'gɔ ɔp] |

share	**andel** (m)	['anˌdel]
controlling interest	**aksjemajoritet** (m)	['akʂəˌmajɔri'tet]
investment	**investering** (m/f)	[inve'steriŋ]
to invest (vt)	**å investere**	[ɔ inve'sterə]
percent	**prosent** (m)	[prʊ'sɛnt]
interest (on investment)	**rente** (m/f)	['rɛntə]
profit	**profitt** (m), **fortjeneste** (m/f)	[prɔ'fit], [fɔː'tjenɛstə]
profitable (adj)	**profitabel**	[profi'tabəl]
tax	**skatt** (m)	['skat]

currency (foreign ~)	**valuta** (m)	[va'lʉta]
national (adj)	**nasjonal**	[naʂʊ'nal]
exchange (currency ~)	**veksling** (m/f)	['vɛkʂliŋ]

| accountant | **regnskapsfører** (m) | ['rɛjnskapsˌførər] |
| accounting | **bokføring** (m/f) | ['bʊk'føriŋ] |

bankruptcy	**fallitt** (m)	[fa'lit]
collapse, crash	**krakk** (n)	['krak]
ruin	**ruin** (m)	[rʉ'in]
to be ruined (financially)	**å ruinere seg**	[ɔ rʉi'nerə sæj]
inflation	**inflasjon** (m)	[infla'ʂʊn]
devaluation	**devaluering** (m)	[devalʉ'eriŋ]

capital	**kapital** (m)	[kapi'tal]
income	**inntekt** (m/f), **innkomst** (m)	['inˌtɛkt], ['inˌkɔmst]
turnover	**omsetning** (m/f)	['ɔmˌsɛtniŋ]
resources	**ressurser** (m pl)	[re'sʉʂər]
monetary resources	**pengemidler** (m pl)	['pɛŋəˌmidlər]
overhead	**faste utgifter** (m/f pl)	['fastə 'ʉtˌjiftər]
to reduce (expenses)	**å redusere**	[ɔ redʉ'serə]

110. Marketing

marketing	**markedsføring** (m/f)	['markəds,føriŋ]
market	**marked** (n)	['markəd]
market segment	**markedssegment** (n)	['markəds seg'mɛnt]
product	**produkt** (n)	[prʊ'dʉkt]
goods (merchandise)	**vare** (m/f)	['varə]
brand	**merkenavn** (n)	['mærkə,navn]
trademark	**varemerke** (n)	['varə,mærkə]
logotype	**firmamerke** (n)	['firma,mærkə]
logo	**logo** (m)	['lugʊ]
demand	**etterspørsel** (m)	['ɛtə,spœsəl]
supply	**tilbud** (n)	['til,bʉd]
need	**behov** (n)	[be'hʊv]
consumer	**forbruker** (m)	[fɔr'brʉkər]
analysis	**analyse** (m)	[ana'lysə]
to analyze (vt)	**å analysere**	[ɔ analy'serə]
positioning	**posisjonering** (m/f)	[pʊsiʂʊ'neriŋ]
to position (vt)	**å posisjonere**	[ɔ pʊsiʂʊ'nerə]
price	**pris** (m)	['pris]
pricing policy	**prispolitikk** (m)	['pris pʊli'tik]
price formation	**prisdannelse** (m)	['pris,danəlsə]

111. Advertising

advertising	**reklame** (m)	[rɛ'klamə]
to advertise (vt)	**å reklamere**	[ɔ rɛkla'merə]
budget	**budsjett** (n)	[bʉd'ʂɛt]
ad, advertisement	**annonse** (m)	[a'nɔnsə]
TV advertising	**TV-reklame** (m)	['tɛvɛ rɛ'klamə]
radio advertising	**radioreklame** (m)	['radiʊ rɛ'klamə]
outdoor advertising	**utendørsreklame** (m)	['ʉtən,dœʂ rɛ'klamə]
mass media	**massemedier** (n pl)	['masə,mediər]
periodical (n)	**tidsskrift** (n)	['tid,skrift]
image (public appearance)	**image** (m)	['imidʒ]
slogan	**slogan** (n)	['slɔgan]
motto (maxim)	**motto** (n)	['mɔtʊ]
campaign	**kampanje** (m)	[kam'panjə]
advertising campaign	**reklamekampanje** (m)	[rɛ'klamə kam'panjə]
target group	**målgruppe** (m/f)	['moːl,grʉpə]
business card	**visittkort** (n)	[vi'sit,kɔːt]

leaflet (promotional ~)	**reklameblad** (n)	[rɛ'klɑmə‚blɑ]
brochure	**brosjyre** (m)	[brɔ'ʂyrə]
(e.g., 12 pages ~)		
pamphlet	**folder** (m)	['fɔlər]
newsletter	**nyhetsbrev** (n)	['nyhets‚brev]
signboard (store sign, etc.)	**skilt** (n)	['ʂilt]
poster	**plakat, poster** (m)	['plɑ‚kɑt], ['pɔstər]
billboard	**reklameskilt** (m/f)	[rɛ'klɑmə‚ʂilt]

112. Banking

bank	**bank** (m)	['bɑnk]
branch (of bank, etc.)	**avdeling** (m)	['ɑv‚deliŋ]
bank clerk, consultant	**konsulent** (m)	[kʊnsʉ'lent]
manager (director)	**forstander** (m)	[fɔ'ʂtɑndər]
bank account	**bankkonto** (m)	['bɑnk‚kɔntʊ]
account number	**kontonummer** (n)	['kɔntʊ‚nʉmər]
checking account	**sjekkonto** (m)	['ʂɛk‚kɔntʊ]
savings account	**sparekonto** (m)	['spɑrə‚kɔntʊ]
to open an account	**å åpne en konto**	[ɔ 'ɔpnə en 'kɔntʊ]
to close the account	**å lukke kontoen**	[ɔ 'lʉkə 'kɔntʊən]
to deposit into the account	**å sette inn på kontoen**	[ɔ 'sɛtə in pɔ 'kɔntʊən]
to withdraw (vt)	**å ta ut fra kontoen**	[ɔ 'tɑ ʉt frɑ 'kɔntʊən]
deposit	**innskudd** (n)	['in‚skʉd]
to make a deposit	**å sette inn**	[ɔ 'sɛtə in]
wire transfer	**overføring** (m/f)	['ɔvər‚føriŋ]
to wire, to transfer	**å overføre**	[ɔ 'ɔvər‚førə]
sum	**sum** (m)	['sʉm]
How much?	**Hvor mye?**	[vʊr 'mye]
signature	**underskrift** (m/f)	['ʉnə‚skrift]
to sign (vt)	**å underskrive**	[ɔ 'ʉnə‚skrivə]
credit card	**kredittkort** (n)	[krɛ'dit‚kɔːt]
code (PIN code)	**kode** (m)	['kʊdə]
credit card number	**kreditkortnummer** (n)	[krɛ'dit‚kɔːʈ 'nʉmər]
ATM	**minibank** (m)	['mini‚bɑnk]
check	**sjekk** (m)	['ʂɛk]
to write a check	**å skrive en sjekk**	[ɔ 'skrivə en 'ʂɛk]
checkbook	**sjekkbok** (m/f)	['ʂɛk‚bʊk]
loan (bank ~)	**lån** (n)	['lɔn]
to apply for a loan	**å søke om lån**	[ɔ ‚søkə ɔm 'lɔn]

to get a loan	å få lån	[ɔ 'fɔ 'lɔn]
to give a loan	å gi lån	[ɔ 'ji 'lɔn]
guarantee	garanti (m)	[gɑrɑn'ti]

113. Telephone. Phone conversation

telephone	telefon (m)	[tele'fʉn]
cell phone	mobiltelefon (m)	[mʉ'bil tele'fʉn]
answering machine	telefonsvarer (m)	[tele'fʉn‚svɑrər]

| to call (by phone) | å ringe | [ɔ 'riŋə] |
| phone call | telefonsamtale (m) | [tele'fʉn 'sɑm‚tɑlə] |

to dial a number	å slå et nummer	[ɔ 'ʂlɔ et 'nʉmər]
Hello!	Hallo!	[hɑ'lʉ]
to ask (vt)	å spørre	[ɔ 'spørə]
to answer (vi, vt)	å svare	[ɔ 'svɑrə]

to hear (vt)	å høre	[ɔ 'hørə]
well (adv)	godt	['gɔt]
not well (adv)	dårlig	['doːli]
noises (interference)	støy (m)	['støj]

receiver	telefonrør (n)	[tele'fʉn‚rør]
to pick up (~ the phone)	å ta telefonen	[ɔ 'tɑ tele'fʉnən]
to hang up (~ the phone)	å legge på røret	[ɔ 'legə pɔ 'rørə]

busy (engaged)	opptatt	['ɔp‚tɑt]
to ring (ab. phone)	å ringe	[ɔ 'riŋə]
telephone book	telefonkatalog (m)	[tele'fʉn kɑtɑ'lɔg]

local (adj)	lokal-	[lɔ'kɑl-]
local call	lokalsamtale (m)	[lɔ'kɑl 'sɑm‚tɑlə]
long distance (~ call)	riks-	['riks-]
long-distance call	rikssamtale (m)	['riks 'sɑm‚tɑlə]
international (adj)	internasjonal	['intɛːnɑʂʉ‚nɑl]
international call	internasjonal samtale (m)	['intɛːnɑʂʉ‚nɑl 'sɑm‚tɑlə]

114. Cell phone

cell phone	mobiltelefon (m)	[mʉ'bil tele'fʉn]
display	skjerm (m)	['ʂærm]
button	knapp (m)	['knɑp]
SIM card	SIM-kort (n)	['sim‚kɔːt]

battery	batteri (n)	[bɑtɛ'ri]
to be dead (battery)	å bli utladet	[ɔ 'bli 'ʉt‚lɑdət]
charger	lader (m)	['lɑdər]

menu	meny (m)	[me'ny]
settings	innstillinger (m/f pl)	['in‚stiliŋər]
tune (melody)	melodi (m)	[melɔ'di]
to select (vt)	å velge	[ɔ 'vɛlgə]

calculator	regnemaskin (m)	['rɛjnə ma‚sin]
voice mail	telefonsvarer (m)	[tele'fʉn‚svarər]
alarm clock	vekkerklokka (m/f)	['vɛkər‚klɔka]
contacts	kontakter (m pl)	[kʉn'taktər]

| SMS (text message) | SMS-beskjed (m) | [ɛsɛm'ɛs bɛ‚ʂɛ] |
| subscriber | abonnent (m) | [abɔ'nɛnt] |

115. Stationery

| ballpoint pen | kulepenn (m) | ['kʉːlə‚pɛn] |
| fountain pen | fyllepenn (m) | ['fʏlə‚pɛn] |

pencil	blyant (m)	['bly‚ant]
highlighter	merkepenn (m)	['mærkə‚pɛn]
felt-tip pen	tusjpenn (m)	['tʉʂ‚pɛn]

| notepad | notatbok (m/f) | [nʉ'tat‚bʉk] |
| agenda (diary) | dagbok (m/f) | ['dag‚bʉk] |

ruler	linjal (m)	[li'njal]
calculator	regnemaskin (m)	['rɛjnə ma‚sin]
eraser	viskelær (n)	['viskə‚lær]
thumbtack	tegnestift (m)	['tæjnə‚stift]
paper clip	binders (m)	['bindɛʂ]

glue	lim (n)	['lim]
stapler	stiftemaskin (m)	['stiftə ma‚sin]
hole punch	hullemaskin (m)	['hʉlə ma‚sin]
pencil sharpener	blyantspisser (m)	['blyant‚spisər]

116. Various kinds of documents

account (report)	rapport (m)	[ra'pɔːt]
agreement	avtale (m)	['av‚talə]
application form	søknadsskjema (n)	['søknads‚ʂema]
authentic (adj)	ekte	['ɛktə]
badge (identity tag)	badge (n)	['bædʒ]
business card	visittkort (n)	[vi'sit‚kɔːt]

certificate (~ of quality)	sertifikat (n)	[sæː‚ţifi'kat]
check (e.g., draw a ~)	sjekk (m)	['ʂɛk]
check (in restaurant)	regning (m/f)	['rɛjniŋ]

constitution	**grunnlov** (m)	['grʉnˌlɔv]
contract (agreement)	**avtale** (m)	['avˌtɑlə]
copy	**kopi** (m)	[kʉ'pi]
copy (of contract, etc.)	**eksemplar** (n)	[ɛksɛm'plɑr]
customs declaration	**tolldeklarasjon** (m)	['tɔldɛklɑrɑˌʂʉn]
document	**dokument** (n)	[dɔkʉ'mɛnt]
driver's license	**førerkort** (n)	['førərˌkɔːt]
addendum	**tillegg, bilag** (n)	['tiˌleg], ['biˌlɑg]
form	**skjema** (n)	['ʂema]
ID card (e.g., FBI ~)	**legitimasjon** (m)	[legitimɑ'ʂʉn]
inquiry (request)	**forespørsel** (m)	['forəˌspœʂəl]
invitation card	**invitasjonskort** (n)	[invitɑ'ʂʉnsˌkɔːt]
invoice	**faktura** (m)	[fɑk'tʉrɑ]
law	**lov** (m)	['lɔv]
letter (mail)	**brev** (n)	['brev]
letterhead	**brevpapir** (n)	['brevˌpa'pir]
list (of names, etc.)	**liste** (m/f)	['listə]
manuscript	**manuskript** (n)	[mɑnʉ'skript]
newsletter	**nyhetsbrev** (n)	['nyhetsˌbrev]
note (short letter)	**lapp, seddel** (m)	['lɑp], ['sɛdəl]
pass (for worker, visitor)	**adgangskort** (n)	['ɑdgɑŋsˌkɔːt]
passport	**pass** (n)	['pɑs]
permit	**tillatelse** (m)	['tiˌlɑtəlsə]
résumé	**CV** (m/n)	['sɛvɛ]
debt note, IOU	**skyldbrev, gjeldsbrev** (m/f)	['ʂylˌbrev], ['jɛlˌbrev]
receipt (for purchase)	**kvittering** (m/f)	[kvi'tɜriŋ]
sales slip, receipt	**kassalapp** (m)	['kɑsaˌlɑp]
report (mil.)	**rapport** (m)	[rɑ'pɔːt]
to show (ID, etc.)	**å vise**	[ɔ 'visə]
to sign (vt)	**å underskrive**	[ɔ 'ʉnəˌskrivə]
signature	**underskrift** (m/f)	['ʉnəˌskrift]
seal (stamp)	**stempel** (n)	['stɛmpəl]
text	**tekst** (m/f)	['tɛkst]
ticket (for entry)	**billett** (m)	[bi'let]
to cross out	**å stryke ut**	[ɔ 'strykə ʉt]
to fill out (~ a form)	**å utfylle**	[ɔ 'ʉtˌfʏlə]
waybill (shipping invoice)	**fraktbrev** (n)	['frɑktˌbrev]
will (testament)	**testament** (n)	[tɛstɑ'mɛnt]

117. Kinds of business

accounting services	**bokføringstjenester** (m pl)	['bʊkˌføriŋs 'tjenɛstər]
advertising	**reklame** (m)	[rɾ'klɑmə]

advertising agency	reklamebyrå (n)	[rɛ'klamə byˌro]
air-conditioners	klimaanlegg (n pl)	['klima'anˌleg]
airline	flyselskap (n)	['flysəlˌskap]
alcoholic beverages	alkoholholdige drikke (m pl)	[alkʊ'hʊlˌhɔldiə 'drikə]
antiques (antique dealers)	antikviteter (m pl)	[antikvi'tetər]
art gallery (contemporary ~)	kunstgalleri (n)	['kʉnst gale'ri]
audit services	revisjonstjenester (m pl)	[revi'ʂʊnsˌtjenɛstər]
banking industry	bankvirksomhet (m/f)	['bankˌvirksɔmhet]
bar	bar (m)	['bar]
beauty parlor	skjønnhetssalong (m)	['ʂønhɛts sa'lɔŋ]
bookstore	bokhandel (m)	['bʊkˌhandəl]
brewery	bryggeri (n)	[brʏge'ri]
business center	forretningssenter (n)	[fɔ'rɛtniŋsˌsɛntər]
business school	handelsskole (m)	['handɛlsˌskʊlə]
casino	kasino (n)	[ka'sinʊ]
construction	byggeri (m/f)	[bʏgə'ri]
consulting	konsulenttjenester (m pl)	[kʊnsu'lent ˌtjenɛstər]
dental clinic	tannklinik (m)	['tankli'nik]
design	design (m)	['desɑjn]
drugstore, pharmacy	apotek (n)	[apʊ'tek]
dry cleaners	renseri (n)	[rɛnse'ri]
employment agency	rekrutteringsbyrå (n)	['rekrʉˌteriŋs byˌro]
financial services	finansielle tjenester (m pl)	[finan'sielə ˌtjenɛstər]
food products	matvarer (m/f pl)	['matˌvarər]
funeral home	begravelsesbyrå (n)	[be'gravəlsəs byˌro]
furniture (e.g., house ~)	møbler (n pl)	['møblər]
clothing, garment	klær (n)	['klær]
hotel	hotell (n)	[hʊ'tɛl]
ice-cream	iskrem (m)	['iskrɛm]
industry (manufacturing)	industri (m)	[indʉ'stri]
insurance	forsikring (m/f)	[fɔ'ʂikriŋ]
Internet	Internett	['intəˌŋɛt]
investments (finance)	investering (m/f)	[inve'steriŋ]
jeweler	juveler (m)	[jʉ'velər]
jewelry	smykker (n pl)	['smʏkər]
laundry (shop)	vaskeri (n)	[vaske'ri]
legal advisor	juridisk rådgiver (m pl)	[jʉ'ridisk 'rɔdˌjivər]
light industry	lettindustri (m)	['letˌindʉ'stri]
magazine	magasin, tidsskrift (n)	[maga'sin], ['tidˌskrift]
mail-order selling	postordresalg (m)	['pɔstˌɔrdrə'salg]
medicine	medisin (m)	[medi'sin]
movie theater	kino (m)	['çinʊ]

museum	museum (n)	[mʉ'seum]
news agency	nyhetsbyrå (n)	['nyhets by‚ro]
newspaper	avis (m/f)	[ɑ'vis]
nightclub	nattklubb (m)	['nɑt‚klʉb]

oil (petroleum)	olje (m)	['ɔljə]
courier services	budtjeneste (m)	[bʉd'tjenɛstə]
pharmaceutics	legemidler (pl)	['legə'midlər]
printing (industry)	trykkeri (n)	[trʏkə'ri]
publishing house	forlag (n)	['fɔ:‚lɑg]

radio (~ station)	radio (m)	['rɑdiʉ]
real estate	fast eiendom (m)	[‚fɑst 'æjən‚dɔm]
restaurant	restaurant (m)	[rɛstʉ'rɑn]

security company	sikkerhetsselskap (n)	['sikərhɛts 'sel‚skɑp]
sports	sport, idrett (m)	['spɔ:t], ['idrɛt]
stock exchange	børs (m)	['bœʂ]
store	forretning, butikk (m)	[fɔ'rɛtniŋ], [bʉ'tik]
supermarket	supermarked (n)	['sʉpə‚market]
swimming pool (public ~)	svømmebasseng (n)	['svœmə‚bɑ'sɛŋ]

tailor shop	skredderi (n)	[skrɛdə'ri]
television	televisjon (m)	['televi‚ʂʉn]
theater	teater (n)	[te'ɑtər]
trade (commerce)	handel (m)	['hɑndəl]
transportation	transport (m)	[trɑns'pɔ:t]
travel	turisme (m)	[tʉ'rismə]

veterinarian	dyrlege, veterinær (m)	['dyr‚legə], [vetəri'nær]
warehouse	lager (n)	['lɑgər]
waste collection	avfallstømming (m/f)	['ɑvfɑls‚tømiŋ]

Job. Business. Part 2

118. Show. Exhibition

exhibition, show	messe (m/f)	['mɛsə]
trade show	varemesse (m/f)	['varə,mɛsə]
participation	deltagelse (m)	['del,tagəlsə]
to participate (vi)	å delta	[ɔ 'dɛlta]
participant (exhibitor)	deltaker (m)	['del,takər]
director	direktør (m)	[dirɛk'tør]
organizers' office	arrangørkontor (m)	[araŋ'ṣør kʉn'tʊr]
organizer	arrangør (m)	[araŋ'ṣør]
to organize (vt)	å organisere	[ɔ ɔrgani'serə]
participation form	påmeldingsskjema (n)	['pɔmeliŋs,ṣɛma]
to fill out (vt)	å utfylle	[ɔ 'ʉt,fʏlə]
details	detaljer (m pl)	[de'taljər]
information	informasjon (m)	[infɔrma'ṣʊn]
price (cost, rate)	pris (m)	['pris]
including	inklusive	['inklʉ,sivə]
to include (vt)	å inkludere	[ɔ inklʉ'derə]
to pay (vi, vt)	å betale	[ɔ be'talə]
registration fee	registreringsavgift (m/f)	[rɛgi'strɛriŋs av'jift]
entrance	inngang (m)	['in,gaŋ]
pavilion, hall	paviljong (m)	[pavi'ljɔŋ]
to register (vt)	å registrere	[ɔ regi'strerə]
badge (identity tag)	badge (n)	['bædʒ]
booth, stand	messestand (m)	['mɛsə,stan]
to reserve, to book	å reservere	[ɔ resɛr'verə]
display case	glassmonter (m)	['glas,mɔntər]
spotlight	lampe (m/f), spotlys (n)	['lampə], ['spɔt,lys]
design	design (m)	['desɑjn]
to place (put, set)	å plassere	[ɔ pla'serə]
to be placed	å bli plasseret	[ɔ 'bli pla'serət]
distributor	distributør (m)	[distribʉ'tør]
supplier	leverandør (m)	[levəran'dør]
to supply (vt)	å levere	[ɔ le'verə]
country	land (n)	['lan]
foreign (adj)	utenlandsk	['ʉtən,lansk]

product	**produkt** (n)	[prʊ'dʉkt]
association	**forening** (m/f)	[fɔ'reniŋ]
conference hall	**konferansesal** (m)	[kʊnfə'ransə͵sɑl]
congress	**kongress** (m)	[kʊn'grɛs]
contest (competition)	**tevling** (m)	['tɛvliŋ]
visitor (attendee)	**besøkende** (m)	[be'søkenə]
to visit (attend)	**å besøke**	[ɔ be'søkə]
customer	**kunde** (m)	['kʉndə]

119. Mass Media

newspaper	**avis** (m/f)	[ɑ'vis]
magazine	**magasin, tidsskrift** (n)	[mɑgɑ'sin], ['tid͵skrift]
press (printed media)	**presse** (m/f)	['prɛsə]
radio	**radio** (m)	['rɑdiʊ]
radio station	**radiostasjon** (m)	['rɑdiʊ͵stɑ'ʂʊn]
television	**televisjon** (m)	['televi͵ʂʊn]
presenter, host	**programleder** (m)	[prʊ'grɑm͵ledər]
newscaster	**nyhetsoppleser** (m)	['nyhets'ɔp͵lesər]
commentator	**kommentator** (m)	[kʊmən'tɑtʊr]
journalist	**journalist** (m)	[ʂu:ŋɑ'list]
correspondent (reporter)	**korrespondent** (m)	[kʉrespɔn'dɛnt]
press photographer	**pressefotograf** (m)	['prɛsə fɔtʊ'grɑf]
reporter	**reporter** (m)	[re'pɔːtər]
editor	**redaktør** (m)	[rɛdɑk'tør]
editor-in-chief	**sjefredaktør** (m)	['ʂɛf rɛdɑk'tør]
to subscribe (to …)	**å abonnere**	[ɔ abɔ'nerə]
subscription	**abonnement** (n)	[abɔnə'mɑŋ]
subscriber	**abonnent** (m)	[abɔ'nɛnt]
to read (vi, vt)	**å lese**	[ɔ 'lesə]
reader	**leser** (m)	['lesər]
circulation (of newspaper)	**opplag** (n)	['ɔp͵lɑg]
monthly (adj)	**månedlig**	['moːnədli]
weekly (adj)	**ukentlig**	['ʉkəntli]
issue (edition)	**nummer** (n)	['nʉmər]
new (~ issue)	**ny, fersk**	['ny], ['fæʂk]
headline	**overskrift** (m)	['ɔvə͵skrift]
short article	**notis** (m)	[nʊ'tis]
column (regular article)	**rubrikk** (m)	[rʉ'brik]
article	**artikkel** (m)	[ɑː'ʈikəl]
page	**side** (m/f)	['sidə]
reportage, report	**reportasje** (m)	[repɔː'ʈɑʂə]
event (happening)	**hendelse** (m)	['hɛndəlsə]

sensation (news)	sensasjon (m)	[sɛnsɑ'ʂʊn]
scandal	skandale (m)	[skɑn'dɑlə]
scandalous (adj)	skandaløs	[skɑndɑ'løs]
great (~ scandal)	stor	['stʊr]

show (e.g., cooking ~)	program (n)	[prʊ'grɑm]
interview	intervju (n)	[intə'vjʉː]
live broadcast	direktesending (m/f)	[di'rɛktə‚sɛniŋ]
channel	kanal (m)	[kɑ'nɑl]

120. Agriculture

agriculture	landbruk (n)	['lɑn‚brʉk]
peasant (masc.)	bonde (m)	['bɔnə]
peasant (fem.)	bondekone (m/f)	['bɔnə‚kʉnə]
farmer	gårdbruker, bonde (m)	['gɔːr‚brʉkər], ['bɔnə]

| tractor (farm ~) | traktor (m) | ['trɑktʊr] |
| combine, harvester | skurtresker (m) | ['skʉː‚trɛskər] |

plow	plog (m)	['plug]
to plow (vi, vt)	å pløye	[ɔ 'pløjə]
plowland	pløyemark (m/f)	['pløjə‚mɑrk]
furrow (in field)	fure (m)	['fʉrə]

to sow (vi, vt)	å så	[ɔ 'sɔ]
seeder	såmaskin (m)	['soːmɑ‚ʂin]
sowing (process)	såing (m/f)	['soːiŋ]

| scythe | ljå (m) | ['ljoː] |
| to mow, to scythe | å meie, å slå | [ɔ 'mæjə], [ɔ 'slɔ] |

| spade (tool) | spade (m) | ['spɑdə] |
| to till (vt) | å grave | [ɔ 'grɑvə] |

hoe	hakke (m/f)	['hɑkə]
to hoe, to weed	å hakke	[ɔ 'hɑkə]
weed (plant)	ugras (n)	[ʉ'grɑs]

watering can	vannkanne (f)	['vɑn‚kɑnə]
to water (plants)	å vanne	[ɔ 'vɑnə]
watering (act)	vanning (m/f)	['vɑniŋ]

| pitchfork | greip (m) | ['græjp] |
| rake | rive (m/f) | ['rivə] |

fertilizer	gjødsel (m/f)	['jøtsəl]
to fertilize (vt)	å gjødsle	[ɔ 'jøtslə]
manure (fertilizer)	møkk (m/f)	['møk]
field	åker (m)	['oːker]

meadow	eng (m/f)	['ɛŋ]
vegetable garden	kjøkkenhage (m)	['çœkən,hagə]
orchard (e.g., apple ~)	frukthage (m)	['frʉkt,hagə]
to graze (vt)	å beite	[ɔ 'bæjtə]
herder (herdsman)	gjeter, hyrde (m)	['jetər], ['hʏrdə]
pasture	beite (n), beitemark (m/f)	['bæjtə], ['bæjtə,mɑrk]
cattle breeding	husdyrhold (n)	['hʉsdyr,hɔl]
sheep farming	sauehold (n)	['saʉə,hɔl]
plantation	plantasje (m)	[plɑn'taʂə]
row (garden bed ~s)	rad (m/f)	['rɑd]
hothouse	drivhus (n)	['driv,hʉs]
drought (lack of rain)	tørke (m/f)	['tœrkə]
dry (~ summer)	tørr	['tœr]
grain	korn (n)	['kʉːn]
cereal crops	cerealer (n pl)	[sere'alər]
to harvest, to gather	å høste	[ɔ 'høstə]
miller (person)	møller (m)	['mølər]
mill (e.g., gristmill)	mølle (m/f)	['mølə]
to grind (grain)	å male	[ɔ 'malə]
flour	mel (n)	['mel]
straw	halm (m)	['halm]

121. Building. Building process

construction site	byggeplass (m)	['bʏɡə,plɑs]
to build (vt)	å bygge	[ɔ 'bʏɡə]
construction worker	bygningsarbeider (m)	['bʏɡniŋs 'ɑr,bæjər]
project	prosjekt (n)	[prʉ'ʂɛkt]
architect	arkitekt (m)	[ɑrki'tɛkt]
worker	arbeider (m)	['ɑr,bæjdər]
foundation (of a building)	fundament (n)	[fʉndɑ'mɛnt]
roof	tak (n)	['tɑk]
foundation pile	pæl (m)	['pæl]
wall	mur, vegg (m)	['mʉr], ['vɛɡ]
reinforcing bars	armeringsjern (n)	[ɑr'meriŋs'jæːn]
scaffolding	stillas (n)	[sti'lɑs]
concrete	betong (m)	[be'tɔŋ]
granite	granitt (m)	[grɑ'nit]
stone	stein (m)	['stæjn]
brick	tegl (n), murstein (m)	['tæjl], ['mʉ,ʂtæjn]

sand	**sand** (m)	['san]
cement	**sement** (m)	[se'mɛnt]
plaster (for walls)	**puss** (m)	['pʉs]
to plaster (vt)	**å pusse**	[ɔ 'pʉsə]
paint	**maling** (m/f)	['maliŋ]
to paint (~ a wall)	**å male**	[ɔ 'malə]
barrel	**tønne** (m)	['tœnə]
crane	**heisekran** (m/f)	['hæjsə͵kran]
to lift, to hoist (vt)	**å løfte**	[ɔ 'lœftə]
to lower (vt)	**å heise ned**	[ɔ 'hæjsə ne]
bulldozer	**bulldoser** (m)	['bʉl͵dʉsər]
excavator	**gravemaskin** (m)	['gravə ma'şin]
scoop, bucket	**skuffe** (m/f)	['skʉfə]
to dig (excavate)	**å grave**	[ɔ 'gravə]
hard hat	**hjelm** (m)	['jɛlm]

122. Science. Research. Scientists

science	**vitenskap** (m)	['vitən͵skap]
scientific (adj)	**vitenskapelig**	['vitən͵skapəli]
scientist	**vitenskapsmann** (m)	['vitən͵skaps man]
theory	**teori** (m)	[teʉ'ri]
axiom	**aksiom** (n)	[aksi'ɔm]
analysis	**analyse** (m)	[ana'lysə]
to analyze (vt)	**å analysere**	[ɔ analy'serə]
argument (strong ~)	**argument** (n)	[argʉ'mɛnt]
substance (matter)	**stoff** (n), **substans** (m)	['stɔf], [sʉb'stans]
hypothesis	**hypotese** (m)	[hypʉ'tesə]
dilemma	**dilemma** (n)	[di'lema]
dissertation	**avhandling** (m/f)	['av͵handliŋ]
dogma	**dogme** (n)	['dɔgmə]
doctrine	**doktrine** (m)	[dɔk'trinə]
research	**forskning** (m)	['fɔːşkniŋ]
to research (vt)	**å forske**	[ɔ 'fɔːşkə]
tests (laboratory ~)	**test** (m), **prøve** (m/f)	['tɛst], ['prøve]
laboratory	**laboratorium** (n)	[labʉra'tɔrium]
method	**metode** (m)	[me'tʉdə]
molecule	**molekyl** (n)	[mʉle'kyl]
monitoring	**overvåking** (m/f)	['ɔver͵vɔkiŋ]
discovery (act, event)	**oppdagelse** (m)	['ɔp͵dagəlsə]
postulate	**postulat** (n)	[postʉ'lat]
principle	**prinsipp** (n)	[prin'sip]
forecast	**prognose** (m)	[prʉg'nʉsə]

to forecast (vt)	**å prognostisere**	[ɔ prʊgnʊsti'serə]
synthesis	**syntese** (m)	[sʏn'tesə]
trend (tendency)	**tendens** (m)	[tɛn'dɛns]
theorem	**teorem** (n)	[teʊ'rɛm]
teachings	**lære** (m/f pl)	['lærə]
fact	**faktum** (n)	['fɑktum]
expedition	**ekspedisjon** (m)	[ɛkspedi'ʂʊn]
experiment	**eksperiment** (n)	[ɛksperi'mɛnt]
academician	**akademiker** (m)	[ɑkɑ'demikər]
bachelor (e.g., ~ of Arts)	**bachelor** (m)	['batʂɛlɔr]
doctor (PhD)	**doktor** (m)	['dɔktʊr]
Associate Professor	**dosent** (m)	[dʊ'sɛnt]
Master (e.g., ~ of Arts)	**magister** (m)	[mɑ'gistər]
professor	**professor** (m)	[prʊ'fɛsʊr]

Professions and occupations

123. Job search. Dismissal

job	arbeid (n), jobb (m)	['arbæj], ['job]
staff (work force)	ansatte (pl)	['an‚satə]
personnel	personale (n)	[pæʂʉ'nalə]
career	karriere (m)	[kari'ɛrə]
prospects (chances)	utsikter (m pl)	['ʉt‚siktər]
skills (mastery)	mesterskap (n)	['mɛstæ‚ʂkap]
selection (screening)	utvelgelse (m)	['ʉt‚vɛlgəlsə]
employment agency	rekrutteringsbyrå (n)	['rekrʉ‚teriŋgs by‚ro]
résumé	CV (m/n)	['sɛvɛ]
job interview	jobbintervju (n)	['job ‚intər'vjʉ]
vacancy, opening	vakanse (m)	['vakansə]
salary, pay	lønn (m/f)	['lœn]
fixed salary	fastlønn (m/f)	['fast‚lœn]
pay, compensation	betaling (m/f)	[be'taliŋ]
position (job)	stilling (m/f)	['stiliŋ]
duty (of employee)	plikt (m/f)	['plikt]
range of duties	arbeidsplikter (m/f pl)	['arbæjds‚pliktər]
busy (I'm ~)	opptatt	['ɔp‚tat]
to fire (dismiss)	å avskjedige	[ɔ 'af‚ʂedigə]
dismissal	avskjedigelse (m)	['afʂe‚digəlsə]
unemployment	arbeidsløshet (m)	['arbæjdsløs‚het]
unemployed (n)	arbeidsløs (m)	['arbæjds‚løs]
retirement	pensjon (m)	[pan'ʂun]
to retire (from job)	å gå av med pensjon	[ɔ 'gɔ a: me pan'ʂun]

124. Business people

director	direktør (m)	[dirɛk'tør]
manager (director)	forstander (m)	[fo'ʂtandər]
boss	boss (m)	['bɔs]
superior	overordnet (m)	['ɔvər‚ɔrdnet]
superiors	overordnede (pl)	['ɔvər‚ɔrdnedə]
president	president (m)	[prɛsi'dɛnt]

chairman	styreformann (m)	['styrə,fɔrman]
deputy (substitute)	stedfortreder (m)	['stedfɔ:‚tredər]
assistant	assistent (m)	[ɑsi'stɛnt]
secretary	sekretær (m)	[sɛkrə'tær]
personal assistant	privatsekretær (m)	[pri'vɑt sɛkrə'tær]

businessman	forretningsmann (m)	[fɔ'rɛtniŋs‚man]
entrepreneur	entreprenør (m)	[ɛntreprə'nør]
founder	grunnlegger (m)	['grʉn‚legər]
to found (vt)	å grunnlegge, å stifte	[ɔ 'grʉn‚legə], [ɔ 'stiftə]

incorporator	stifter (m)	['stiftər]
partner	partner (m)	['pɑ:tnər]
stockholder	aksjonær (m)	[ɑkʂʊ'nær]

millionaire	millionær (m)	[milju'nær]
billionaire	milliardær (m)	[milja:'dær]
owner, proprietor	eier (m)	['æjər]
landowner	jordeier (m)	['ju:r‚æjər]

client	kunde (m)	['kʉndə]
regular client	fast kunde (m)	[‚fɑst 'kʉndə]
buyer (customer)	kjøper (m)	['çœ:pər]
visitor	besøkende (m)	[be'søkenə]

professional (n)	yrkesmann (m)	['yrkəs‚man]
expert	ekspert (m)	[ɛks'pæ:t]
specialist	spesialist (m)	[spesia'list]

| banker | bankier (m) | [banki'e] |
| broker | mekler, megler (m) | ['mɛklər] |

cashier, teller	kasserer (m)	[ka'serər]
accountant	regnskapsfører (m)	['rɛjnskɑps‚førər]
security guard	sikkerhetsvakt (m/f)	['sikərhɛts‚vakt]

investor	investor (m)	[in'vɛstʊr]
debtor	skyldner (m)	['ʂylnər]
creditor	kreditor (m)	['krɛditʊr]
borrower	låntaker (m)	['lɔn‚takər]

| importer | importør (m) | [impɔ:'tør] |
| exporter | eksportør (m) | [ɛkspɔ:'tør] |

manufacturer	produsent (m)	[prʊdʉ'sɛnt]
distributor	distributør (m)	[distribʉ'tør]
middleman	mellommann (m)	['mɛlɔ‚man]

consultant	konsulent (m)	[kʊnsʉ'lent]
sales representative	representant (m)	[represɛn'tant]
agent	agent (m)	[a'gɛnt]
insurance agent	forsikringsagent (m)	[fɔ'ʂikriŋs a'gɛnt]

125. Service professions

cook	kokk (m)	['kʊk]
chef (kitchen chef)	sjefkokk (m)	['ʂɛf,kʊk]
baker	baker (m)	['bɑkər]
bartender	bartender (m)	['bɑː,tɛndər]
waiter	servitør (m)	['særvi'tør]
waitress	servitrise (m/f)	[særvi'trisə]
lawyer, attorney	advokat (m)	[ɑdvʊ'kɑt]
lawyer (legal expert)	jurist (m)	[jʉ'rist]
notary	notar (m)	[nʊ'tɑr]
electrician	elektriker (m)	[ɛ'lektrikər]
plumber	rørlegger (m)	['rør,legər]
carpenter	tømmermann (m)	['tœmər,mɑn]
masseur	massør (m)	[mɑ'sør]
masseuse	massøse (m)	[mɑ'søsə]
doctor	lege (m)	['legə]
taxi driver	taxisjåfør (m)	['tɑksi ʂɔ'før]
driver	sjåfør (m)	[ʂɔ'før]
delivery man	bud (n)	['bʉd]
chambermaid	stuepike (m/f)	['stʉə,pikə]
security guard	sikkerhetsvakt (m/f)	['sikərhɛts,vɑkt]
flight attendant (fem.)	flyvertinne (m/f)	[flyvɛ:'ʈinə]
schoolteacher	lærer (m)	['lærər]
librarian	bibliotekar (m)	[bibliʊ'tekɑr]
translator	oversetter (m)	['ɔvə,sɛtər]
interpreter	tolk (m)	['tɔlk]
guide	guide (m)	['gɑjd]
hairdresser	frisør (m)	[fri'sør]
mailman	postbud (n)	['pɔst,bʉd]
salesman (store staff)	forselger (m)	[fɔ'ʂɛlər]
gardener	gartner (m)	['gɑːʈnər]
domestic servant	tjener (m)	['tjenər]
maid (female servant)	tjenestepike (m/f)	['tjenɛstə,pikə]
cleaner (cleaning lady)	vaskedame (m/f)	['vɑskə,dɑmə]

126. Military professions and ranks

private	menig (m)	['meni]
sergeant	sersjant (m)	[sær'ʂɑnt]

| lieutenant | løytnant (m) | ['løjt‚nɑnt] |
| captain | kaptein (m) | [kɑp'tæjn] |

major	major (m)	[mɑ'jɔr]
colonel	oberst (m)	['ʊbɛʂt]
general	general (m)	[gene'rɑl]
marshal	marskalk (m)	['mɑrʂɑl]
admiral	admiral (m)	[ɑdmi'rɑl]

military (n)	militær (m)	[mili'tær]
soldier	soldat (m)	[sʊl'dɑt]
officer	offiser (m)	[ɔfi'sɛr]
commander	befalshaver (m)	[be'fɑls‚hɑvər]

border guard	grensevakt (m/f)	['grɛnsə‚vɑkt]
radio operator	radiooperatør (m)	['rɑdiʊ ʊpəra'tør]
scout (searcher)	oppklaringssoldat (m)	['ɔp‚klɑriŋ sʊl'dɑt]
pioneer (sapper)	pioner (m)	[piʊ'ner]
marksman	skytter (m)	['ʂytər]
navigator	styrmann (m)	['styr‚mɑn]

127. Officials. Priests

| king | konge (m) | ['kʊŋə] |
| queen | dronning (m/f) | ['drɔniŋ] |

| prince | prins (m) | ['prins] |
| princess | prinsesse (m/f) | [prin'sɛsə] |

| czar | tsar (m) | ['tsɑr] |
| czarina | tsarina (m) | [tsɑ'rinɑ] |

president	president (m)	[prɛsi'dɛnt]
Secretary (minister)	minister (m)	[mi'nistər]
prime minister	statsminister (m)	['stɑts mi'nistər]
senator	senator (m)	[se'nɑtʊr]

diplomat	diplomat (m)	[diplʊ'mɑt]
consul	konsul (m)	['kʊn‚sʉl]
ambassador	ambassadør (m)	[ɑmbɑsɑ'dør]
counsilor (diplomatic officer)	rådgiver (m)	['rɔdˌjivər]

official, functionary (civil servant)	embetsmann (m)	['ɛmbets‚mɑn]
prefect	prefekt (m)	[prɛ'fɛkt]
mayor	borgermester (m)	[bɔrgər'mɛstər]
judge	dommer (m)	['dɔmər]
prosecutor (e.g., district attorney)	anklager (m)	['ɑn‚klɑgər]

missionary	misjonær (m)	[miʂʊˈnær]
monk	munk (m)	[ˈmʉnk]
abbot	abbed (m)	[ˈɑbed]
rabbi	rabbiner (m)	[rɑˈbinər]

vizier	vesir (m)	[vɛˈsir]
shah	sjah (m)	[ˈʂɑ]
sheikh	sjeik (m)	[ˈʂæjk]

128. Agricultural professions

beekeeper	birøkter (m)	[ˈbiˌrøktər]
herder, shepherd	gjeter, hyrde (m)	[ˈjetər], [ˈhʏrdə]
agronomist	agronom (m)	[ɑgrʊˈnʊm]
cattle breeder	husdyrholder (m)	[ˈhʉsdyrˌhɔldər]
veterinarian	dyrlege, veterinær (m)	[ˈdyrˌlegə], [vetəriˈnær]

farmer	gårdbruker, bonde (m)	[ˈgɔːrˌbrʉkər], [ˈbɔnə]
winemaker	vinmaker (m)	[ˈvinˌmakər]
zoologist	zoolog (m)	[sʊːˈlɔg]
cowboy	cowboy (m)	[ˈkɑwˌbɔj]

129. Art professions

| actor | skuespiller (m) | [ˈskʉəˌspilər] |
| actress | skuespillerinne (m/f) | [ˈskʉeˌspiləˈrinə] |

| singer (masc.) | sanger (m) | [ˈsɑŋər] |
| singer (fem.) | sangerinne (m/f) | [sɑŋəˈrinə] |

| dancer (masc.) | danser (m) | [ˈdɑnsər] |
| dancer (fem.) | danserinne (m/f) | [dɑnseˈrinə] |

| performer (masc.) | skuespiller (m) | [ˈskʉəˌspilər] |
| performer (fem.) | skuespillerinne (m/f) | [ˈskʉeˌspiləˈrinə] |

musician	musiker (m)	[ˈmʉsikər]
pianist	pianist (m)	[piɑˈnist]
guitar player	gitarspiller (m)	[giˈtarˌspilər]

conductor (orchestra ~)	dirigent (m)	[diriˈgɛnt]
composer	komponist (m)	[kʊmpʊˈnist]
impresario	impresario (m)	[impreˈsariʊ]

film director	regissør (m)	[rɛʂiˈsør]
producer	produsent (m)	[prʊdʉˈsɛnt]
scriptwriter	manusforfatter (m)	[ˈmɑnʉs fɔrˈfatər]
critic	kritiker (m)	[ˈkritikər]

writer	**forfatter** (m)	[fɔr'fatər]
poet	**poet, dikter** (m)	['pɔɛt], ['diktər]
sculptor	**skulptør** (m)	[skʉlp'tør]
artist (painter)	**kunstner** (m)	['kʉnstnər]

juggler	**sjonglør** (m)	[ʂɔɲ'lør]
clown	**klovn** (m)	['klɔvn]
acrobat	**akrobat** (m)	[akrʉ'bat]
magician	**tryllekunstner** (m)	['trʏlə,kʉnstnər]

130. Various professions

doctor	**lege** (m)	['legə]
nurse	**sykepleierske** (m/f)	['sykə,plæjeʂkə]
psychiatrist	**psykiater** (m)	[syki'atər]
dentist	**tannlege** (m)	['tan,legə]
surgeon	**kirurg** (m)	[çi'rʉrg]

| astronaut | **astronaut** (m) | [astrʉ'naʉt] |
| astronomer | **astronom** (m) | [astrʉ'nʉm] |

driver (of taxi, etc.)	**fører** (m)	['førər]
engineer (train driver)	**lokfører** (m)	['lʊk,førər]
mechanic	**mekaniker** (m)	[me'kanikər]

miner	**gruvearbeider** (m)	['grʉvə'ar,bæjdər]
worker	**arbeider** (m)	['ar,bæjdər]
locksmith	**låsesmed** (m)	['lo:sə,sme]
joiner (carpenter)	**snekker** (m)	['snɛkər]
turner (lathe machine operator)	**dreier** (m)	['dræjər]
construction worker	**bygningsarbeider** (m)	['bʏgniŋs 'ar,bæjər]
welder	**sveiser** (m)	['svæjsər]

professor (title)	**professor** (m)	[prʉ'fɛsʊr]
architect	**arkitekt** (m)	[arki'tɛkt]
historian	**historiker** (m)	[hi'stʉrikər]
scientist	**vitenskapsmann** (m)	['vitən,skaps man]
physicist	**fysiker** (m)	['fysikər]
chemist (scientist)	**kjemiker** (m)	['çemikər]

archeologist	**arkeolog** (m)	[,arkeʉ'lɔg]
geologist	**geolog** (m)	[geʉ'lɔg]
researcher (scientist)	**forsker** (m)	['fɔʂkər]

| babysitter | **babysitter** (m) | ['bɛby,sitər] |
| teacher, educator | **lærer, pedagog** (m) | ['lærər], [peda'gɔg] |

| editor | **redaktør** (m) | [rɛdak'tør] |
| editor-in-chief | **sjefredaktør** (m) | ['ʂɛf rɛdak'tør] |

| correspondent | korrespondent (m) | [kʊrespɔn'dɛnt] |
| typist (fem.) | maskinskriverske (m) | [ma'ʂin ˌskrivɛʂkə] |

designer	designer (m)	[de'sajnər]
computer expert	dataekspert (m)	['dɑtɑ ɛks'pɛːʈ]
programmer	programmerer (m)	[prʊɡrɑ'merər]
engineer (designer)	ingeniør (m)	[inʂə'njør]

sailor	sjømann (m)	['ʂøˌmɑn]
seaman	matros (m)	[mɑ'trʊs]
rescuer	redningsmann (m)	['rɛdniŋsˌmɑn]

fireman	brannmann (m)	['brɑnˌmɑn]
police officer	politi (m)	[pʊli'ti]
watchman	nattvakt (m)	['nɑtˌvɑkt]
detective	detektiv (m)	[detɛk'tiv]

customs officer	tollbetjent (m)	['tɔlbeˌtjɛnt]
bodyguard	livvakt (m/f)	['livˌvɑkt]
prison guard	fangevokter (m)	['fɑŋəˌvɔktər]
inspector	inspektør (m)	[inspɛk'tør]

sportsman	idrettsmann (m)	['idrɛtsˌmɑn]
trainer, coach	trener (m)	['trenər]
butcher	slakter (m)	['ʂlɑktər]
cobbler (shoe repairer)	skomaker (m)	['skʊˌmɑkər]
merchant	handelsmann (m)	['hɑndəlsˌmɑn]
loader (person)	lastearbeider (m)	['lɑstə'ɑrˌbæjdər]

| fashion designer | moteskaper (m) | ['mʊtəˌskɑpər] |
| model (fem.) | modell (m) | [mʊ'dɛl] |

131. Occupations. Social status

| schoolboy | skolegutt (m) | ['skʊləˌɡʉt] |
| student (college ~) | student (m) | [stʉ'dɛnt] |

philosopher	filosof (m)	[filu'sʊf]
economist	økonom (m)	[økʊ'nʊm]
inventor	oppfinner (m)	['ɔpˌfinər]

unemployed (n)	arbeidsløs (m)	['ɑrbæjdsˌløs]
retiree	pensjonist (m)	[pɑnʂʊ'nist]
spy, secret agent	spion (m)	[spi'un]

prisoner	fange (m)	['fɑŋə]
striker	streiker (m)	['stræjkər]
bureaucrat	byråkrat (m)	[byrɔ'krɑt]
traveler (globetrotter)	reisende (m)	['ræjsenə]
gay, homosexual (n)	homofil (m)	['hʊmʊˌfil]

hacker	hacker (m)	['hakər]
hippie	hippie (m)	['hipi]
bandit	banditt (m)	[ban'dit]
hit man, killer	leiemorder (m)	['læjə͵mʊrdər]
drug addict	narkoman (m)	[narkʊ'man]
drug dealer	narkolanger (m)	['narkɔ͵laŋər]
prostitute (fem.)	prostituert (m)	[prʊstitʉ'eːt]
pimp	hallik (m)	['halik]
sorcerer	trollmann (m)	['trɔl͵man]
sorceress (evil ~)	trollkjerring (m/f)	['trɔl͵çæriŋ]
pirate	pirat, sjørøver (m)	['pi'rat], ['şø͵røvər]
slave	slave (m)	['slavə]
samurai	samurai (m)	[samʉ'raj]
savage (primitive)	villmann (m)	['vil͵man]

Sports

132. Kinds of sports. Sportspersons

sportsman	idrettsmann (m)	['idrɛts‚man]
kind of sports	idrettsgren (m/f)	['idrɛts‚gren]
basketball	basketball (m)	['bɑsketbɑl]
basketball player	basketballspiller (m)	['bɑsketbɑl‚spilər]
baseball	baseball (m)	['bɛjsbɔl]
baseball player	baseballspiller (m)	['bɛjsbɔl‚spilər]
soccer	fotball (m)	['fʊtbɑl]
soccer player	fotballspiller (m)	['fʊtbɑl‚spilər]
goalkeeper	målmann (m)	['moːl‚man]
hockey	ishockey (m)	['is‚hɔki]
hockey player	ishockeyspiller (m)	['is‚hɔki 'spilər]
volleyball	volleyball (m)	['vɔlibɑl]
volleyball player	volleyballspiller (m)	['vɔlibɑl‚spilər]
boxing	boksing (m)	['bɔksiŋ]
boxer	bokser (m)	['bɔksər]
wrestling	bryting (m/f)	['brytiŋ]
wrestler	bryter (m)	['brytər]
karate	karate (m)	[ka'rɑte]
karate fighter	karateutøver (m)	[ka'rɑte 'ʉ‚tøvər]
judo	judo (m)	['jʉdɔ]
judo athlete	judobryter (m)	['jʉdɔ‚brytər]
tennis	tennis (m)	['tɛnis]
tennis player	tennisspiller (m)	['tɛnis‚spilər]
swimming	svømming (m/f)	['svœmiŋ]
swimmer	svømmer (m)	['svœmər]
fencing	fekting (m)	['fɛktiŋ]
fencer	fekter (m)	['fɛktər]
chess	sjakk (m)	['ʂak]
chess player	sjakkspiller (m)	['ʂak‚spilər]

| alpinism | alpinisme (m) | [alpi'nismə] |
| alpinist | alpinist (m) | [alpi'nist] |

| running | løp (n) | ['løp] |
| runner | løper (m) | ['løpər] |

| athletics | friidrett (m) | ['fri: 'iˌdrɛt] |
| athlete | atlet (m) | [at'let] |

| horseback riding | ridesport (m) | ['ridəˌspɔːt] |
| horse rider | rytter (m) | ['rʏtər] |

figure skating	kunstløp (n)	['kʉnstˌløp]
figure skater (masc.)	kunstløper (m)	['kʉnstˌløpər]
figure skater (fem.)	kunstløperske (m/f)	['kʉnstˌløpəşkə]

| powerlifting | vektløfting (m/f) | ['vɛktˌlœftiŋ] |
| powerlifter | vektløfter (m) | ['vɛktˌlœftər] |

| car racing | billøp (m), bilrace (n) | ['bilˌløp], ['bilˌras] |
| racing driver | racerfører (m) | ['resəˌførər] |

| cycling | sykkelsport (m) | ['sʏkəlˌspɔːt] |
| cyclist | syklist (m) | [sʏk'list] |

broad jump	lengdehopp (n pl)	['leŋdəˌhɔp]
pole vault	stavhopp (n)	['stavˌhɔp]
jumper	hopper (m)	['hɔpər]

133. Kinds of sports. Miscellaneous

football	amerikansk fotball (m)	[ameri'kansk 'fʊtbal]
badminton	badminton (m)	['bɛdmintɔn]
biathlon	skiskyting (m/f)	['şiˌşytiŋ]
billiards	biljard (m)	[bil'jaːd]

bobsled	bobsleigh (m)	['bɔbslej]
bodybuilding	kroppsbygging (m/f)	['krɔpsˌbʏgiŋ]
water polo	vannpolo (m)	['vanˌpʊlʊ]
handball	håndball (m)	['hɔnˌbalj]
golf	golf (m)	['gɔlf]

rowing, crew	roing (m/f)	['rʊiŋ]
scuba diving	dykking (m/f)	['dʏkiŋ]
cross-country skiing	langrenn (n), skirenn (n)	['laŋˌrɛn], ['şiˌrɛn]
table tennis (ping-pong)	bordtennis (m)	['bʊrˌtɛnis]

sailing	seiling (m/f)	['sæjliŋ]
rally racing	rally (n)	['rɛli]
rugby	rugby (m)	['rʏgbi]

| snowboarding | snøbrett (n) | ['snø‚brɛt] |
| archery | bueskyting (m/f) | ['bʉːə‚sytiŋ] |

134. Gym

| barbell | vektstang (m/f) | ['vɛkt‚staŋ] |
| dumbbells | manualer (m pl) | ['manʉ‚alər] |

training machine	treningsapparat (n)	['treniŋs apa'rat]
exercise bicycle	trimsykkel (m)	['trim‚sykəl]
treadmill	løpebånd (n)	['løpə‚bɔːn]

horizontal bar	svingstang (m/f)	['sviŋstaŋ]
parallel bars	barre (m)	['barə]
vault (vaulting horse)	hest (m)	['hɛst]
mat (exercise ~)	matte (m/f)	['matə]

jump rope	hoppetau (n)	['hɔpə‚taʉ]
aerobics	aerobic (m)	[aɛ'rɔbik]
yoga	yoga (m)	['jɔga]

135. Hockey

hockey	ishockey (m)	['is‚hɔki]
hockey player	ishockeyspiller (m)	['is‚hɔki 'spilər]
to play hockey	å spille ishockey	[ɔ 'spilə 'is‚hɔki]
ice	is (m)	['is]

puck	puck (m)	['puk]
hockey stick	kølle (m/f)	['kølə]
ice skates	skøyter (m/f pl)	['ʂøjtər]

board (ice hockey rink ~)	vant (n)	['vant]
shot	skudd (n)	['skʉd]
goaltender	målvakt (m/f)	['moːl‚vakt]
goal (score)	mål (n)	['mol]
to score a goal	å score mål	[ɔ 'skɔrə ‚mol]

period	periode (m)	[pæri'ʉdə]
second period	andre periode (m)	['andrə pæri'ʉdə]
substitutes bench	reservebenk (m)	[re'sɛrvə‚bɛnk]

136. Soccer

| soccer | fotball (m) | ['fʉtbal] |
| soccer player | fotballspiller (m) | ['fʉtbal‚spilər] |

to play soccer	å spille fotball	[ɔ 'spilə 'fʊtbal]
major league	øverste liga (m)	['øvəʂtə ˌliga]
soccer club	fotballklubb (m)	['fʊtbalˌklʉb]
coach	trener (m)	['trenər]
owner, proprietor	eier (m)	['æjər]
team	lag (n)	['lag]
team captain	kaptein (m) på laget	[kap'tæjn pɔ 'lage]
player	spiller (m)	['spilər]
substitute	reservespiller (m)	[re'sɛrvəˌspilər]
forward	spiss, angriper (m)	['spis], ['anˌgripər]
center forward	sentral spiss (m)	[sɛn'tral ˌspis]
scorer	målscorer (m)	['mo:lˌskɔrər]
defender, back	forsvarer, back (m)	['fɔˌsvarər], ['bɛk]
midfielder, halfback	midtbanespiller (m)	['mitˌbanə 'spilər]
match	kamp (m)	['kamp]
to meet (vi, vt)	å møtes	[ɔ 'møtəs]
final	finale (m)	[fi'nalə]
semi-final	semifinale (m)	[ˌsemifi'nalə]
championship	mesterskap (n)	['mɛstæˌskap]
period, half	omgang (m)	['ɔmgaŋ]
first period	første omgang (m)	['fœʂtə ˌɔmgaŋ]
half-time	halvtid (m)	['halˌtid]
goal	mål (n)	['mol]
goalkeeper	målmann (m), målvakt (m/f)	['mo:lˌman], ['mo:lˌvakt]
goalpost	stolpe (m)	['stɔlpə]
crossbar	tverrligger (m)	['tvæːˌligər]
net	nett (n)	['nɛt]
to concede a goal	å slippe inn et mål	[ɔ 'ʂlipə in et 'mol]
ball	ball (m)	['bal]
pass	pasning (m/f)	['pasniŋ]
kick	spark (m/n)	['spark]
to kick (~ the ball)	å sparke	[ɔ 'sparkə]
free kick (direct ~)	frispark (m/n)	['friˌspark]
corner kick	hjørnespark (m/n)	['jœːnəˌspark]
attack	angrop (n)	['aŋˌgrɛp]
counterattack	kontring (m/f)	['kɔntriŋ]
combination	kombinasjon (m)	[kʊmbina'ʂʊn]
referee	dommer (m)	['dɔmər]
to blow the whistle	å blåse i fløyte	[ɔ 'blo:sə i 'fløjtə]
whistle (sound)	plystring (m/f)	['plʏstriŋ]
foul, misconduct	brudd (n), forseelse (m)	['brʉd], [fɔ'ʂeəlsə]
to commit a foul	å begå en forseelse	[ɔ be'gɔ en fɔ'ʂeəlsə]
to send off	å utvise	[ɔ 'ʉtˌvisə]
yellow card	gult kort (n)	['gʉlt ˌkɔːʈ]

red card	rødt kort (n)	['røt kɔːt]
disqualification	diskvalifisering (m)	['diskvɑlifiˌseriŋ]
to disqualify (vt)	å diskvalifisere	[ɔ 'diskvɑlifiˌserə]

penalty kick	straffespark (m/n)	['strɑfəˌspɑrk]
wall	mur (m)	['mʉr]
to score (vi, vt)	å score	[ɔ 'skɔrə]
goal (score)	mål (n)	['mol]
to score a goal	å score mål	[ɔ 'skɔrə ˌmol]

substitution	erstatning (m)	['æˌstɑtniŋ]
to replace (a player)	å bytte ut	[ɔ 'bʏtə ʉt]
rules	regler (m pl)	['rɛglər]
tactics	taktikk (m)	[tɑk'tik]

stadium	stadion (m/n)	['stɑdiɔn]
stand (bleachers)	tribune (m)	[tri'bʉnə]
fan, supporter	fan (m)	['fæn]
to shout (vi)	å skrike	[ɔ 'skrikə]

| scoreboard | måltavle (m/f) | ['moːlˌtɑvlə] |
| score | resultat (n) | [resʉl'tɑt] |

defeat	nederlag (n)	['nedəˌlɑg]
to lose (not win)	å tape	[ɔ 'tɑpə]
tie	uavgjort (m)	[ʉːɑv'jɔːt]
to tie (vi)	å spille uavgjort	[ɔ 'spilə ʉːɑv'jɔːt]

| victory | seier (m) | ['sæjər] |
| to win (vi, vt) | å vinne | [ɔ 'vinə] |

champion	mester (m)	['mɛstər]
best (adj)	best	['bɛst]
to congratulate (vt)	å gratulere	[ɔ grɑtʉ'lerə]

commentator	kommentator (m)	[kʊmən'tɑtʊr]
to commentate (vt)	å kommentere	[ɔ kʊmən'terə]
broadcast	sending (m/f)	['sɛniŋ]

137. Alpine skiing

| skis | ski (m/f pl) | ['ʂi] |
| to ski (vi) | å gå på ski | [ɔ 'gɔ pɔ 'ʂi] |

| mountain-ski resort | skisted (n) | ['ʂistəd] |
| ski lift | skiheis (m) | ['ʂiˌhæjs] |

ski poles	skistaver (m pl)	['ʂiˌstɑvər]
slope	skråning (m)	['skrɔniŋ]
slalom	slalåm (m)	['ʂlɑlɔm]

138. Tennis. Golf

golf	**golf** (m)	[ˈgɔlf]
golf club	**golfklubb** (m)	[ˈgɔlfˌklʉb]
golfer	**golfspiller** (m)	[ˈgɔlfˌspilər]
hole	**hull** (n)	[ˈhʉl]
club	**kølle** (m/f)	[ˈkølə]
golf trolley	**golftralle** (m/f)	[ˈgɔlfˌtralə]
tennis	**tennis** (m)	[ˈtɛnis]
tennis court	**tennisbane** (m)	[ˈtɛnisˌbanə]
serve	**serve** (m)	[ˈsɛrv]
to serve (vt)	**å serve**	[ɔ ˈsɛrvə]
racket	**racket** (m)	[ˈrɛket]
net	**nett** (n)	[ˈnɛt]
ball	**ball** (m)	[ˈbal]

139. Chess

chess	**sjakk** (m)	[ˈʂak]
chessmen	**sjakkbrikker** (m/f pl)	[ˈʂakˌbrikər]
chess player	**sjakkspiller** (m)	[ˈʂakˌspilər]
chessboard	**sjakkbrett** (n)	[ˈʂakˌbrɛt]
chessman	**sjakbrikke** (m/f)	[ˈʂakˌbrikə]
White (white pieces)	**hvite brikker** (m/f pl)	[ˈvitə ˌbrikər]
Black (black pieces)	**svarte brikker** (m/f pl)	[ˈsvaːtə ˌbrikər]
pawn	**bonde** (m)	[ˈbɔnə]
bishop	**løper** (m)	[ˈløpər]
knight	**springer** (m)	[ˈspriŋər]
rook	**tårn** (n)	[ˈtɔːɳ]
queen	**dronning** (m/f)	[ˈdrɔniŋ]
king	**konge** (m)	[ˈkʊŋə]
move	**trekk** (n)	[ˈtrɛk]
to move (vi, vt)	**å flytte**	[ɔ ˈflʏtə]
to sacrifice (vt)	**å ofre**	[ʊ ˈʊfrə]
castling	**rokade** (m)	[rʊˈkadə]
check	**sjakk** (m)	[ˈʂak]
checkmate	**matt** (m)	[ˈmat]
chess tournament	**sjakkturnering** (m/f)	[ˈʂak tʉrˌneriŋ]
Grand Master	**stormester** (m)	[ˈstʉrˌmɛstər]
combination	**kombinasjon** (m)	[kʊmbinaˈʂʊn]
game (in chess)	**parti** (n)	[paˈʈi]
checkers	**damspill** (n)	[ˈdamˌspil]

140. Boxing

boxing	**boksing** (m)	['bɔksiŋ]
fight (bout)	**kamp** (m)	['kamp]
boxing match	**boksekamp** (m)	['bɔksə‚kamp]
round (in boxing)	**runde** (m)	['rʉndə]
ring	**ring** (m)	['riŋ]
gong	**gong** (m)	['gɔŋ]
punch	**støt, slag** (n)	['støt], ['ʂlag]
knockdown	**knockdown** (m)	[nɔk'daʊn]
knockout	**knockout** (m)	[nɔk'aʊt]
to knock out	**å slå ut**	[ɔ 'ʂlɔ ʉt]
boxing glove	**boksehanske** (m)	['bɔksə‚hanskə]
referee	**dommer** (m)	['dɔmər]
lightweight	**lettvekt** (m/f)	['let‚vɛkt]
middleweight	**mellomvekt** (m/f)	['mɛlɔm‚vɛkt]
heavyweight	**tungvekt** (m/f)	['tʉŋ‚vɛkt]

141. Sports. Miscellaneous

Olympic Games	**de olympiske leker**	[de u'lʏmpiskə 'lekər]
winner	**seierherre** (m)	['sæjər‚hɛrə]
to be winning	**å vinne, å seire**	[ɔ 'vinə], [ɔ 'sæjrə]
to win (vi)	**å vinne**	[ɔ 'vinə]
leader	**leder** (m)	['ledər]
to lead (vi)	**å lede**	[ɔ 'ledə]
first place	**førsteplass** (m)	['fœʂtə‚plas]
second place	**annenplass** (m)	['anən‚plas]
third place	**tredjeplass** (m)	['trɛdjə‚plas]
medal	**medalje** (m)	[me'daljə]
trophy	**trofé** (m/n)	[trɔ'fe]
prize cup (trophy)	**pokal** (m)	[pɔ'kal]
prize (in game)	**pris** (m)	['pris]
main prize	**hovedpris** (m)	['hʊvəd‚pris]
record	**rekord** (m)	[re'kɔrd]
to set a record	**å sette rekord**	[ɔ 'sɛtə re'kɔrd]
final	**finale** (m)	[fi'nalə]
final (adj)	**finale-**	[fi'nalə-]
champion	**mester** (m)	['mɛstər]
championship	**mesterskap** (n)	['mɛstæ‚skap]

stadium	**stadion** (m/n)	['stɑdiɔn]
stand (bleachers)	**tribune** (m)	[tri'bʉnə]
fan, supporter	**fan** (m)	['fæn]
opponent, rival	**motstander** (m)	['mʊt̩ˌstɑnər]
start (start line)	**start** (m)	['stɑːt]
finish line	**mål** (n), **målstrek** (m)	['moːl], ['moːlˌstrek]
defeat	**nederlag** (n)	['nedəˌlɑg]
to lose (not win)	**å tape**	[ɔ 'tɑpə]
referee	**dommer** (m)	['dɔmər]
jury (judges)	**jury** (m)	['jʉry]
score	**resultat** (n)	[resʉl'tɑt]
tie	**uavgjort** (m)	[ʉːav'jɔːt]
to tie (vi)	**å spille uavgjort**	[ɔ 'spilə ʉːav'jɔːt]
point	**poeng** (n)	[pɔ'ɛŋ]
result (final score)	**resultat** (n)	[resʉl'tɑt]
period	**periode** (m)	[pæri'ʊdə]
half-time	**halvtid** (m)	['hɑlˌtid]
doping	**doping** (m)	['dʊpiŋ]
to penalize (vt)	**å straffe**	[ɔ 'strɑfə]
to disqualify (vt)	**å diskvalifisere**	[ɔ 'diskvɑlifiˌserə]
apparatus	**redskap** (m/n)	['rɛdˌskɑp]
javelin	**spyd** (n)	['spyd]
shot (metal ball)	**kule** (m/f)	['kʉːlə]
ball (snooker, etc.)	**kule** (m/f), **ball** (m)	['kʉːlə], ['bɑl]
aim (target)	**mål** (n)	['mol]
target	**målskive** (m/f)	['moːlˌʂivə]
to shoot (vi)	**å skyte**	[ɔ 'ʂytə]
accurate (~ shot)	**fulltreffer**	['fʉlˌtrɛfər]
trainer, coach	**trener** (m)	['trenər]
to train (sb)	**å trene**	[ɔ 'trenə]
to train (vi)	**å trene**	[ɔ 'trenə]
training	**trening** (m/f)	['treniŋ]
gym	**idrettssal** (m)	['idrɛtsˌsɑl]
exercise (physical)	**øvelse** (m)	['øvəlsə]
warm-up (athlete ~)	**oppvarming** (m/f)	['ɔpˌvɑrmiŋ]

Education

142. School

school	**skole** (m/f)	['skʊlə]
principal (headmaster)	**rektor** (m)	['rektʊr]
pupil (boy)	**elev** (m)	[e'lev]
pupil (girl)	**elev** (m)	[e'lev]
schoolboy	**skolegutt** (m)	['skʊlə‚gʉt]
schoolgirl	**skolepike** (m)	['skʊlə‚pikə]
to teach (sb)	**å undervise**	[ɔ 'ʉnər‚visə]
to learn (language, etc.)	**å lære**	[ɔ 'lærə]
to learn by heart	**å lære utenat**	[ɔ 'lærə 'ʉtənat]
to learn (~ to count, etc.)	**å lære**	[ɔ 'lærə]
to be in school	**å gå på skolen**	[ɔ 'gɔ pɔ 'skʊlən]
to go to school	**å gå på skolen**	[ɔ 'gɔ pɔ 'skʊlən]
alphabet	**alfabet** (n)	[alfɑ'bet]
subject (at school)	**fag** (n)	['fɑg]
classroom	**klasserom** (m/f)	['klɑsə‚rʊm]
lesson	**time** (m)	['timə]
recess	**frikvarter** (n)	['frikvɑːˌʈər]
school bell	**skoleklokke** (m/f)	['skʊlə‚klɔkə]
school desk	**skolepult** (m)	['skʊlə‚pʉlt]
chalkboard	**tavle** (m/f)	['tɑvlə]
grade	**karakter** (m)	[karɑk'ter]
good grade	**god karakter** (m)	['gʊ karɑk'ter]
bad grade	**dårlig karakter** (m)	['dɔː[i karɑk'ter]
to give a grade	**å gi en karakter**	[ɔ 'ji en karɑk'ter]
mistake, error	**feil** (m)	['fæjl]
to make mistakes	**å gjøre feil**	[ɔ 'jørə ˌfæjl]
to correct (an error)	**å rette**	[ɔ 'rɛtə]
cheat sheet	**fuskelapp** (m)	['fʉskə‚lɑp]
homework	**lekser** (m/f pl)	['leksər]
exercise (in education)	**øvelse** (m)	['øvəlsə]
to be present	**å være til stede**	[ɔ 'værə til 'stedə]
to be absent	**å være fraværende**	[ɔ 'værə 'frɑˌværənə]
to miss school	**å skulke skolen**	[ɔ 'skʉlkə 'skʊlən]

to punish (vt)	å straffe	[ɔ 'strafə]
punishment	straff, avstraffelse (m)	['straf], ['af‚strafəlsə]
conduct (behavior)	oppførsel (m)	['ɔp‚fœşəl]

report card	karakterbok (m/f)	[karak'ter‚bʊk]
pencil	blyant (m)	['bly‚ant]
eraser	viskelær (n)	['viskə‚lær]
chalk	kritt (n)	['krit]
pencil case	pennal (n)	[pɛ'nal]

schoolbag	skoleveske (m/f)	['skʊlə‚vɛskə]
pen	penn (m)	['pɛn]
school notebook	skrivebok (m/f)	['skrivə‚bʊk]
textbook	lærebok (m/f)	['lærə‚bʊk]
compasses	passer (m)	['pasər]

| to make technical drawings | å tegne | [ɔ 'tæjnə] |
| technical drawing | teknisk tegning (m/f) | ['tɛknisk ‚tæjniŋ] |

poem	dikt (n)	['dikt]
by heart (adv)	utenat	['ʉtən‚at]
to learn by heart	å lære utenat	[ɔ 'lærə 'ʉtənat]

school vacation	skoleferie (m)	['skʊlə‚fɛriə]
to be on vacation	å være på ferie	[ɔ 'værə pɔ 'fɛriə]
to spend one's vacation	å tilbringe ferien	[ɔ 'til‚briŋə 'fɛriən]

test (written math ~)	prøve (m/f)	['prøvə]
essay (composition)	essay (n)	[ɛ'sɛj]
dictation	diktat (m)	[dik'tat]
exam (examination)	eksamen (m)	[ɛk'samən]
to take an exam	å ta eksamen	[ɔ 'ta ɛk'samən]
experiment (e.g., chemistry ~)	forsøk (n)	['fɔ'şøk]

143. College. University

academy	akademi (n)	[akade'mi]
university	universitet (n)	[ʉnivæşi'tet]
faculty (e.g., ~ of Medicine)	fakultet (n)	[fakʉl'tet]

student (masc.)	student (m)	[stʉ'dɛnt]
student (fem.)	kvinnelig student (m)	['kvinəli stʉ'dɛnt]
lecturer (teacher)	lærer, foreleser (m)	['lærər], ['fʊrə‚lesər]

lecture hall, room	auditorium (n)	[‚aʊdi'tʊrium]
graduate	alumn (m)	[a'lʉmn]
diploma	diplom (n)	[di'plʊm]

dissertation	avhandling (m/f)	['avˌhandliŋ]
study (report)	studie (m)	['stʉdiə]
laboratory	laboratorium (n)	[labʊra'tɔrium]

lecture	forelesning (m)	['fɔrəˌlesniŋ]
coursemate	studiekamerat (m)	['stʉdiə kameˌrat]
scholarship	stipendium (n)	[sti'pɛndium]
academic degree	akademisk grad (m)	[aka'demisk ˌgrad]

144. Sciences. Disciplines

mathematics	matematikk (m)	[matəma'tik]
algebra	algebra (m)	['algəˌbra]
geometry	geometri (m)	[geʉme'tri]

astronomy	astronomi (m)	[astrʊnʊ'mi]
biology	biologi (m)	[biʉlʊ'gi]
geography	geografi (m)	[geʉgra'fi]
geology	geologi (m)	[geʉlʊ'gi]
history	historie (m/f)	[hi'stʊriə]

medicine	medisin (m)	[medi'sin]
pedagogy	pedagogikk (m)	[pedagʉ'gik]
law	rett (m)	['rɛt]

physics	fysikk (m)	[fy'sik]
chemistry	kjemi (m)	[çe'mi]
philosophy	filosofi (m)	[filʉsʊ'fi]
psychology	psykologi (m)	[sikʉlʊ'gi]

145. Writing system. Orthography

grammar	grammatikk (m)	[grama'tik]
vocabulary	ordforråd (n)	['uːrfʊˌrɔd]
phonetics	fonetikk (m)	[fʊne'tik]

noun	substantiv (n)	['sʉbstanˌtiv]
adjective	adjektiv (n)	['adjɛkˌtiv]
verb	verb (n)	['væɾb]
adverb	adverb (n)	[ad'væːb]

pronoun	pronomen (n)	[prʊ'nʊmən]
interjection	interjeksjon (m)	[interjɛk'ʂʊn]
preposition	preposisjon (m)	[prɛpʊsi'ʂʊn]

root	rot (m/f)	['rʊt]
ending	endelse (m)	['ɛnəlsə]
prefix	prefiks (n)	[prɛ'fiks]

syllable	**stavelse** (m)	['stavǝlsǝ]
suffix	**suffiks** (n)	[sʉ'fiks]
stress mark	**betoning** (m), **trykk** (n)	['be'tɔniŋ], ['trʏk]
apostrophe	**apostrof** (m)	[apʊ'strɔf]
period, dot	**punktum** (n)	['pʉnktum]
comma	**komma** (n)	['kɔma]
semicolon	**semikolon** (n)	[ˌsemikʊ'lɔn]
colon	**kolon** (n)	['kʊlɔn]
ellipsis	**tre prikker** (m pl)	['tre 'prikǝr]
question mark	**spørsmålstegn** (n)	['spœşmolsˌtæjn]
exclamation point	**utropstegn** (n)	['ʉtrʊpsˌtæjn]
quotation marks	**anførselstegn** (n pl)	[an'fœşɛlsˌtejn]
in quotation marks	**i anførselstegn**	[i an'fœşɛlsˌtejn]
parenthesis	**parentes** (m)	[parɛn'tes]
in parenthesis	**i parentes**	[i parɛn'tes]
hyphen	**bindestrek** (m)	['binǝˌstrek]
dash	**tankestrek** (m)	['tɑnkǝˌstrek]
space (between words)	**mellomrom** (n)	['mɛlɔmˌrum]
letter	**bokstav** (m)	['bʊkstɑv]
capital letter	**stor bokstav** (m)	['stʊr 'bʊkstɑv]
vowel (n)	**vokal** (m)	[vʊ'kal]
consonant (n)	**konsonant** (m)	[kʊnsʊ'nɑnt]
sentence	**setning** (m)	['sɛtniŋ]
subject	**subjekt** (n)	[sʉb'jɛkt]
predicate	**predikat** (n)	[prɛdi'kɑt]
line	**linje** (m)	['linjǝ]
on a new line	**på ny linje**	[pɔ ny 'linjǝ]
paragraph	**avsnitt** (n)	['afˌsnit]
word	**ord** (n)	['uːr]
group of words	**ordgruppe** (m/f)	['uːrˌgrʉpǝ]
expression	**uttrykk** (n)	['ʉtˌtrʏk]
synonym	**synonym** (n)	[syʉnʊ'nym]
antonym	**antonym** (n)	[antʊ'nym]
rule	**regel** (m)	['rɛgǝl]
exception	**unntak** (n)	['ʉnˌtak]
correct (adj)	**riktig**	['rikti]
conjugation	**bøyning** (m/f)	['bøjniŋ]
declension	**bøyning** (m/f)	['bøjniŋ]
nominal case	**kasus** (m)	['kasʉs]
question	**spørsmål** (n)	['spœşˌmol]

| to underline (vt) | å understreke | [ɔ 'ʉnəˌstrekə] |
| dotted line | prikket linje (m) | ['prikət 'linjə] |

146. Foreign languages

language	språk (n)	['sprɔk]
foreign (adj)	fremmed-	['fremə-]
foreign language	fremmedspråk (n)	['fremedˌsprɔk]
to study (vt)	å studere	[ɔ stʉ'derə]
to learn (language, etc.)	å lære	[ɔ 'lærə]

to read (vi, vt)	å lese	[ɔ 'lesə]
to speak (vi, vt)	å tale	[ɔ 'talə]
to understand (vt)	å forstå	[ɔ fɔ'ʂtɔ]
to write (vt)	å skrive	[ɔ 'skrivə]

fast (adv)	fort	['fʊːt]
slowly (adv)	langsomt	['laŋsɔmt]
fluently (adv)	flytende	['flytnə]

rules	regler (m pl)	['rɛglər]
grammar	grammatikk (m)	[grama'tik]
vocabulary	ordforråd (n)	['uːrfʊˌrɔd]
phonetics	fonetikk (m)	[fʊne'tik]

textbook	lærebok (m/f)	['lærəˌbʊk]
dictionary	ordbok (m/f)	['uːrˌbʊk]
teach-yourself book	lærebok (m/f) for selvstudium	['lærəˌbʊk fɔ 'selˌstʉdium]

| phrasebook | parlør (m) | [pɑː'lør] |

cassette, tape	kassett (m)	[ka'sɛt]
videotape	videokassett (m)	['videʊ ka'sɛt]
CD, compact disc	CD-rom (m)	['sɛdɛˌrʊm]
DVD	DVD (m)	[deve'de]

alphabet	alfabet (n)	[ɑlfɑ'bet]
to spell (vt)	å stave	[ɔ 'stavə]
pronunciation	uttale (m)	['ʉtˌtalə]

accent	aksent (m)	[ak'saŋ]
with an accent	med aksent	[me ak'saŋ]
without an accent	uten aksent	['ʉtən ak'saŋ]

| word | ord (n) | ['uːr] |
| meaning | betydning (m) | [be'tʏdniŋ] |

course (e.g., a French ~)	kurs (n)	['kʉʂ]
to sign up	å anmelde seg	[ɔ 'anˌmɛlə sæj]
teacher	lærer (m)	['lærər]

translation (process)	oversettelse (m)	['ɔvəˌsɛtəlsə]
translation (text, etc.)	oversettelse (m)	['ɔvəˌsɛtəlsə]
translator	oversetter (m)	['ɔvəˌsɛtər]
interpreter	tolk (m)	['tɔlk]
polyglot	polyglott (m)	[pʊlʏ'glɔt]
memory	minne (n),	['minə],
	hukommelse (m)	[hʉ'kɔməlsə]

147. Fairy tale characters

Santa Claus	Julenissen	['jʉləˌnisən]
Cinderella	Askepott	['askəˌpɔt]
mermaid	havfrue (m/f)	['havˌfrʉə]
Neptune	Neptun	[nɛp'tʉn]
magician, wizard	trollmann (m)	['trɔlˌman]
fairy	fe (m)	['fe]
magic (adj)	trylle-	['trʏlə-]
magic wand	tryllestav (m)	['trʏləˌstav]
fairy tale	eventyr (n)	['ɛvənˌtyr]
miracle	mirakel (n)	[mi'rakəl]
dwarf	gnom, dverg (m)	['gnʊm], ['dvɛrg]
to turn into ...	å forvandle seg til ...	[ɔ fɔr'vandlə sæj til ...]
ghost	spøkelse (n)	['spøkəlsə]
phantom	fantom (m)	[fan'tɔm]
monster	monster (n)	['mɔnstər]
dragon	drage (m)	['dragə]
giant	gigant (m)	[gi'gant]

148. Zodiac Signs

Aries	Væren (m)	['værən]
Taurus	Tyren (m)	['tyrən]
Gemini	Tvillingene (m pl)	['tviliŋənə]
Cancer	Krepsen (m)	['krɛpsən]
Leo	Løven (m)	['løvən]
Virgo	Jomfruen (m)	['ʉmfrʉən]
Libra	Vekten (m)	['vɛktən]
Scorpio	Skorpionen	[skɔrpi'ʊnən]
Sagittarius	Skytten (m)	['ʂytən]
Capricorn	Steinbukken (m)	['stæjnˌbʉkən]
Aquarius	Vannmannen (m)	['vanˌmanən]
Pisces	Fiskene (pl)	['fiskenə]
character	karakter (m)	[karak'ter]

character traits	**karaktertrekk** (n pl)	[kɑrɑk'ter͵trɛk]
behavior	**oppførsel** (m)	['ɔp͵fœʂəl]
to tell fortunes	**å spå**	[ɔ 'spɔ]
fortune-teller	**spåkone** (m/f)	['spoː͵kɔnə]
horoscope	**horoskop** (n)	[hʊrʊ'skɔp]

Arts

149. Theater

theater	**teater** (n)	[te'atər]
opera	**opera** (m)	['ʊpera]
operetta	**operette** (m)	[ʊpe'rɛtə]
ballet	**ballett** (m)	[bɑ'let]
theater poster	**plakat** (m)	[plɑ'kat]
troupe	**teatertrupp** (m)	[te'atər,trʊp]
(theatrical company)		
tour	**turné** (m)	[tʉr'ne:]
to be on tour	**å være på turné**	[ɔ 'værə pɔ tʉr'ne:]
to rehearse (vi, vt)	**å repetere**	[ɔ repe'terə]
rehearsal	**repetisjon** (m)	[repeti'ʂʊn]
repertoire	**repertoar** (n)	[repæ:ʈʊ'ar]
performance	**forestilling** (m/f)	['fɔrə,stiliŋ]
theatrical show	**teaterstykke** (n)	[te'atər,stʏkə]
play	**skuespill** (n)	['skʉə,spil]
ticket	**billett** (m)	[bi'let]
box office (ticket booth)	**billettluke** (m/f)	[bi'let,lʉkə]
lobby, foyer	**lobby, foajé** (m)	['lɔbi], [fʊɑ'je]
coat check (cloakroom)	**garderobe** (m)	[gɑ:də'rʊbə]
coat check tag	**garderobemerke** (n)	[gɑ:də'rʊbə 'mærkə]
binoculars	**kikkert** (m)	['çikɛ:t]
usher	**plassanviser** (m)	['plas an,visər]
orchestra seats	**parkett** (m)	[par'kɛt]
balcony	**balkong** (m)	[bɑl'kɔŋ]
dress circle	**første losjerad** (m)	['fœstə ,luʂɛrad]
box	**losje** (m)	['lʊʂə]
row	**rad** (m/f)	['rad]
seat	**plass** (m)	['plʉs]
audience	**publikum** (n)	['pʉblikum]
spectator	**tilskuer** (m)	['til,skʉər]
to clap (vi, vt)	**å klappe**	[ɔ 'klapə]
applause	**applaus** (m)	[a'plaʊs]
ovation	**bifall** (n)	['bi,fal]
stage	**scene** (m)	['se:nə]
curtain	**teppe** (n)	['tɛpə]
scenery	**dekorasjon** (m)	[dekʊrɑ'ʂʊn]

backstage	**kulisser** (m pl)	[kʉˈlisər]
scene (e.g., the last ~)	**scene** (m)	[ˈseːnə]
act	**akt** (m)	[ˈɑkt]
intermission	**mellomakt** (m)	[ˈmɛlɔmˌɑkt]

150. Cinema

actor	**skuespiller** (m)	[ˈskʉəˌspilər]
actress	**skuespillerinne** (m/f)	[ˈskʉəˌspiləˈrinə]
movies (industry)	**filmindustri** (m)	[ˈfilm indʉˈstri]
movie	**film** (m)	[ˈfilm]
episode	**del** (m)	[ˈdel]
detective movie	**kriminalfilm** (m)	[krimiˈnɑlˌfilm]
action movie	**actionfilm** (m)	[ˈɛkʂənˌfilm]
adventure movie	**eventyrfilm** (m)	[ˈɛvəntyrˌfilm]
science fiction movie	**Sci-Fi film** (m)	[ˈsɑjˌfɑj film]
horror movie	**skrekkfilm** (m)	[ˈskrɛkˌfilm]
comedy movie	**komedie** (m)	[ˈkʊˈmediə]
melodrama	**melodrama** (n)	[melɔˈdrɑmɑ]
drama	**drama** (n)	[ˈdrɑmɑ]
fictional movie	**spillefilm** (m)	[ˈspiləˌfilm]
documentary	**dokumentarfilm** (m)	[dɔkʉmɛnˈtɑr ˌfilm]
cartoon	**tegnefilm** (m)	[ˈtæjnəˌfilm]
silent movies	**stumfilm** (m)	[ˈstʉmˌfilm]
role (part)	**rolle** (m/f)	[ˈrɔlə]
leading role	**hovedrolle** (m)	[ˈhʊvədˌrɔle]
to play (vi, vt)	**å spille**	[ɔ ˈspilə]
movie star	**filmstjerne** (m)	[ˈfilmˌstjæːŋə]
well-known (adj)	**kjent**	[ˈçɛnt]
famous (adj)	**berømt**	[beˈrømt]
popular (adj)	**populær**	[pʊpʉˈlær]
script (screenplay)	**manus** (n)	[ˈmɑnʉs]
scriptwriter	**manusforfatter** (m)	[ˈmɑnʉs fɔrˈfɑtər]
movie director	**regissør** (m)	[rɛʂiˈsør]
producer	**produsent** (m)	[prʊdʉˈsɛnt]
assistant	**assistent** (m)	[ɑsiˈstɛnt]
cameraman	**kameramann** (m)	[ˈkɑmerɑˌmɑn]
stuntman	**stuntmann** (m)	[ˈstɑntˌmɑn]
double (stuntman)	**stand-in** (m)	[ˌstɑndˈin]
to shoot a movie	**å spille inn en film**	[ɔ ˈspilə in en ˈfilm]
audition, screen test	**prøve** (m/f)	[ˈprøvə]
shooting	**opptak** (n)	[ˈɔpˌtɑk]

movie crew	filmteam (n)	['film,tim]
movie set	opptaksplass (m)	['ɔptaks,plas]
camera	filmkamera (n)	['film,kamera]
movie theater	kino (m)	['çinʊ]
screen (e.g., big ~)	filmduk (m)	['film,dʉk]
to show a movie	å vise en film	[ɔ 'visə en 'film]
soundtrack	lydspor (n)	['lyd,spʊr]
special effects	spesialeffekter (m pl)	['spesi'al e'fɛktər]
subtitles	undertekster (m/f)	['ʉnə,tɛkstər]
credits	rulletekst (m)	['rʉlə,tɛkst]
translation	oversettelse (m)	['ɔvə,sɛtəlsə]

151. Painting

art	kunst (m)	['kʉnst]
fine arts	de skjønne kunster	[de 'sønə 'kʉnstər]
art gallery	kunstgalleri (n)	['kʉnst gale'ri]
art exhibition	maleriutstilling (m/f)	[,male'ri ʉt,stiliŋ]
painting (art)	malerkunst (m)	['malər,kʉnst]
graphic art	grafikk (m)	[gra'fik]
abstract art	abstrakt kunst (m)	[ab'strakt 'kʉnst]
impressionism	impresjonisme (m)	[imprɛsʊ'nisme]
picture (painting)	maleri (m/f)	[,male'ri]
drawing	tegning (m/f)	['tæjniŋ]
poster	plakat, poster (m)	['pla,kat], ['postər]
illustration (picture)	illustrasjon (m)	[ilʉstra'sʉn]
miniature	miniatyr (m)	[minia'tyr]
copy (of painting, etc.)	kopi (m)	[kʊ'pi]
reproduction	reproduksjon (m)	[reprʊdʉk'sʉn]
mosaic	mosaikk (m)	[mʊsa'ik]
stained glass window	glassmaleri (n)	['glas,male'ri]
fresco	freske (m)	['frɛskə]
engraving	gravyr (m)	[gra'vyr]
bust (sculpture)	byste (m)	['bʏstə]
sculpture	skulptur (m)	[skʉlp'tʉr]
statue	statue (m)	['statʉə]
plaster of Paris	gips (m)	['jips]
plaster (as adj)	gips-	['jips-]
portrait	portrett (n)	[pɔ:'trɛt]
self-portrait	selvportrett (n)	['sɛl,pɔ:'trɛt]
landscape painting	landskapsmaleri (n)	['lanskaps,male'ri]
still life	stilleben (n)	['stil,lebən]

| caricature | karikatur (m) | [karika'tʉr] |
| sketch | skisse (m/f) | ['şisə] |

paint	maling (m/f)	['maliŋ]
watercolor paint	akvarell (m)	[akva'rɛl]
oil (paint)	olje (m)	['ɔljə]
pencil	blyant (m)	['bly,ant]
India ink	tusj (m/n)	['tʉş]
charcoal	kull (n)	['kʉl]

| to draw (vi, vt) | å tegne | [ɔ 'tæjnə] |
| to paint (vi, vt) | å male | [ɔ 'malə] |

to pose (vi)	å posere	[ɔ pɔ'serə]
artist's model (masc.)	modell (m)	[mʊ'dɛl]
artist's model (fem.)	modell (m)	[mʊ'dɛl]

artist (painter)	kunstner (m)	['kʉnstnər]
work of art	kunstverk (n)	['kʉnst,værk]
masterpiece	mesterverk (n)	['mɛstɛr,værk]
studio (artist's workroom)	atelier (n)	[ate'lje]

canvas (cloth)	kanvas (m/n), lerret (n)	['kanvas], ['leret]
easel	staffeli (n)	[stafe'li]
palette	palett (m)	[pa'let]

frame (picture ~, etc.)	ramme (m/f)	['ramə]
restoration	restaurering (m)	[rɛstaʊ'reriŋ]
to restore (vt)	å restaurere	[ɔ rɛstaʊ'rerə]

152. Literature & Poetry

literature	litteratur (m)	[litəra'tʉr]
author (writer)	forfatter (m)	[fɔr'fatər]
pseudonym	pseudonym (n)	[sewdʊ'nym]

book	bok (m/f)	['bʊk]
volume	bind (n)	['bin]
table of contents	innholdsfortegnelse (m)	['inhɔls fɔ:'tæjnəlsə]
page	side (m/f)	['sidə]
main character	hovedperson (m)	['hʊvəd pæ'şʊn]
autograph	autograf (m)	[aʊtʊ'graf]

short story	novelle (m/f)	[nʊ'vɛlə]
story (novella)	kortroman (m)	['kʊ:ţ rʊ,man]
novel	roman (m)	[rʊ'man]
work (writing)	verk (n)	['værk]
fable	fabel (m)	['fabəl]
detective novel	kriminalroman (m)	[krimi'nal rʊ,man]
poem (verse)	dikt (n)	['dikt]

poetry	**poesi** (m)	[pɔɛ'si]
poem (epic, ballad)	**epos** (n)	['ɛpɔs]
poet	**poet, dikter** (m)	['pɔɛt], ['diktər]
fiction	**skjønnlitteratur** (m)	['ʂøn litera'tʉr]
science fiction	**science fiction** (m)	['sajəns ˌfikʂn]
adventures	**eventyr** (n pl)	['ɛvənˌtyr]
educational literature	**undervisnings-litteratur** (m)	['ʉnərˌvisniŋs litera'tʉr]
children's literature	**barnelitteratur** (m)	['bɑːŋə litera'tʉr]

153. Circus

circus	**sirkus** (m/n)	['sirkʉs]
traveling circus	**ambulerende sirkus** (n)	['ɑmbʉˌlerɛnə 'sirkʉs]
program	**program** (n)	[prʉ'grɑm]
performance	**forestilling** (m/f)	['fɔrəˌstiliŋ]
act (circus ~)	**nummer** (n)	['nʉmər]
circus ring	**manesje, arena** (m)	[mɑ'neʂə], [ɑ'renɑ]
pantomime (act)	**pantomime** (m)	[pɑntʉ'mimə]
clown	**klovn** (m)	['klɔvn]
acrobat	**akrobat** (m)	[ɑkrʉ'bɑt]
acrobatics	**akrobatikk** (m)	[ɑkrʉbɑ'tik]
gymnast	**gymnast** (m)	[gʏm'nɑst]
gymnastics	**gymnastikk** (m)	[gʏmnɑ'stik]
somersault	**salto** (m)	['sɑltʉ]
athlete (strongman)	**atlet** (m)	[ɑt'let]
tamer (e.g., lion ~)	**dyretemmer** (m)	['dyrɛˌtɛmər]
rider (circus horse ~)	**rytter** (m)	['rʏtər]
assistant	**assistent** (m)	[ɑsi'stɛnt]
stunt	**trikk, triks** (n)	['trik], ['triks]
magic trick	**trylletriks** (n)	['trʏləˌtriks]
conjurer, magician	**tryllekunstner** (m)	['trʏləˌkʉnstnər]
juggler	**sjonglør** (m)	[ʂɔŋ'lør]
to juggle (vi, vt)	**å sjonglere**	[ɔ 'ʂɔŋˌlɛrə]
animal trainer	**dressør** (m)	[drɛ'sør]
animal training	**dressur** (m)	[drɛ'sʉr]
to train (animals)	**å dressere**	[ɔ drɛ'serə]

154. Music. Pop music

music	**musikk** (m)	[mʉ'sik]
musician	**musiker** (m)	['mʉsikər]

musical instrument	musikkinstrument (n)	[mʉ'sik instrʉ'mɛnt]
to play ...	å spille ...	[ɔ 'spilə ...]
guitar	gitar (m)	['gi,tɑr]
violin	fiolin (m)	[fiʊ'lin]
cello	cello (m)	['sɛlʊ]
double bass	kontrabass (m)	['kʊntra,bɑs]
harp	harpe (m)	['hɑrpə]
piano	piano (n)	[pi'anʊ]
grand piano	flygel (n)	['flygəl]
organ	orgel (n)	['ɔrgəl]
wind instruments	blåseinstrumenter (n pl)	['blo:sə instrʉ'mɛntər]
oboe	obo (m)	[ʊ'bʊ]
saxophone	saksofon (m)	[sɑksʊ'fʊn]
clarinet	klarinett (m)	[klɑri'nɛt]
flute	fløyte (m)	['fløjtə]
trumpet	trompet (m)	[trʊm'pet]
accordion	trekkspill (n)	['trɛk,spil]
drum	tromme (m)	['trʊmə]
duo	duett (m)	[dʉ'ɛt]
trio	trio (m)	['triʊ]
quartet	kvartett (m)	[kva:'tɛt]
choir	kor (n)	['kʊr]
orchestra	orkester (n)	[ɔr'kɛstər]
pop music	popmusikk (m)	['pɔp mʉ'sik]
rock music	rockmusikk (m)	['rɔk mʉ'sik]
rock group	rockeband (n)	['rɔkə,bɛnd]
jazz	jazz (m)	['jas]
idol	idol (n)	[i'dʊl]
admirer, fan	beundrer (m)	[be'ʉndrər]
concert	konsert (m)	[kʊn'sæ:t]
symphony	symfoni (m)	[sʏmfʊ'ni]
composition	komposisjon (m)	[kʊmpʊzi'ʂʊn]
to compose (write)	å komponere	[ɔ kʊmpʊ'nerə]
singing (n)	synging (m/f)	['sʏŋiŋ]
song	sang (m)	['sɑŋ]
tune (melody)	melodi (m)	[melɔ'di]
rhythm	rytme (m)	['rʏtmə]
blues	blues (m)	['blʉs]
sheet music	noter (m pl)	['nʊtər]
baton	taktstokk (m)	['takt,stɔk]
bow	bue, boge (m)	['bʉ:ə], ['bɔgə]
string	streng (m)	['strɛŋ]
case (e.g., guitar ~)	futteral (n), kasse (m/f)	['fʉte'rɑl], ['kɑsə]

Rest. Entertainment. Travel

155. Trip. Travel

tourism, travel	**turisme** (m)	[tʉ'rismə]
tourist	**turist** (m)	[tʉ'rist]
trip, voyage	**reise** (m/f)	['ræjsə]
adventure	**eventyr** (n)	['ɛvən‚tyr]
trip, journey	**tripp** (m)	['trip]
vacation	**ferie** (m)	['fɛriə]
to be on vacation	**å være på ferie**	[ɔ 'værə pɔ 'fɛriə]
rest	**hvile** (m/f)	['vilə]
train	**tog** (n)	['tɔg]
by train	**med tog**	[me 'tɔg]
airplane	**fly** (n)	['fly]
by airplane	**med fly**	[me 'fly]
by car	**med bil**	[me 'bil]
by ship	**med skip**	[me 'ʂip]
luggage	**bagasje** (m)	[bɑ'gɑʂə]
suitcase	**koffert** (m)	['kʊfɛːt]
luggage cart	**bagasjetralle** (m/f)	[bɑ'gɑʂə‚trɑlə]
passport	**pass** (n)	['pɑs]
visa	**visum** (n)	['visʉm]
ticket	**billett** (m)	[bi'let]
air ticket	**flybillett** (m)	['fly bi'let]
guidebook	**reisehåndbok** (m/f)	['ræjsə‚hɔnbʊk]
map (tourist ~)	**kart** (n)	['kɑːt]
area (rural ~)	**område** (n)	['ɔm‚ro:də]
place, site	**sted** (n)	['sted]
exotic (adj)	**eksotisk**	[ɛk'sʊtisk]
amazing (adj)	**forunderlig**	[fɔ'rʉnde:ʃi]
group	**gruppe** (m)	['grʉpə]
excursion, sightseeing tour	**utflukt** (m/f)	['ʉt‚flʉkt]
guide (person)	**guide** (m)	['gɑjd]

156. Hotel

hotel	**hotell** (n)	[hʊ'tɛl]
motel	**motell** (n)	[mʊ'tɛl]

three-star (~ hotel)	**trestjernet**	['treˌstjæːŋə]
five-star	**femstjernet**	['fɛmˌstjæːŋə]
to stay (in a hotel, etc.)	**å bo**	[ɔ 'buː]

room	**rom** (n)	['rʊm]
single room	**enkeltrom** (n)	['ɛnkeltˌrʊm]
double room	**dobbeltrom** (n)	['dɔbeltˌrʊm]
to book a room	**å reservere rom**	[ɔ resɛr'verə 'rʊm]

| half board | **halvpensjon** (m) | ['hɑl panˌʂʊn] |
| full board | **fullpensjon** (m) | ['fʉl panˌʂʊn] |

with bath	**med badekar**	[me 'badəˌkar]
with shower	**med dusj**	[me 'dʉʂ]
satellite television	**satellitt-TV** (m)	[satɛ'lit 'tɛvɛ]
air-conditioner	**klimaanlegg** (n)	['klimɑ'anˌleg]
towel	**håndkle** (n)	['hɔnˌkle]
key	**nøkkel** (m)	['nøkəl]

administrator	**administrator** (m)	[admini'straːtʊr]
chambermaid	**stuepike** (m/f)	['stʉəˌpikə]
porter, bellboy	**pikkolo** (m)	['pikɔlo]
doorman	**portier** (m)	[pɔːˈtje]

restaurant	**restaurant** (m)	[rɛstʊ'rɑŋ]
pub, bar	**bar** (m)	['bar]
breakfast	**frokost** (m)	['frʊkɔst]
dinner	**middag** (m)	['miˌdɑ]
buffet	**buffet** (m)	[bʉ'fɛ]

| lobby | **hall, lobby** (m) | ['hɑl], ['lɔbi] |
| elevator | **heis** (m) | ['hæjs] |

| DO NOT DISTURB | **VENNLIGST IKKE FORSTYRR!** | ['vɛnligt ikə fɔ'ʂtyr] |
| NO SMOKING | **RØYKING FORBUDT** | ['røjkiŋ fɔr'bʉt] |

157. Books. Reading

book	**bok** (m/f)	['bʊk]
author	**forfatter** (m)	[fɔr'fatər]
writer	**forfatter** (m)	[fɔr'fatər]
to write (~ a book)	**å skrive**	[ɔ 'skrivə]

reader	**leser** (m)	['lesər]
to read (vi, vt)	**å lese**	[ɔ 'lesə]
reading (activity)	**lesning** (m/f)	['lesniŋ]

| silently (to oneself) | **for seg selv** | [for sæj 'sɛl] |
| aloud (adv) | **høyt** | ['højt] |

to publish (vt)	å publisere	[ɔ pʉbli'serə]
publishing (process)	publisering (m/f)	[pʉbli'serɪŋ]
publisher	forlegger (m)	['fɔːˌlegər]
publishing house	forlag (n)	['fɔːlɑg]
to come out (be released)	å komme ut	[ɔ 'kɔmə ʉt]
release (of a book)	utgivelse (m)	['ʉtˌjivəlsə]
print run	opplag (n)	['ɔpˌlɑg]
bookstore	bokhandel (m)	['bʉkˌhɑndəl]
library	bibliotek (n)	[biblɪʉ'tek]
story (novella)	kortroman (m)	['kʉːʈ rʉˌmɑn]
short story	novelle (m/f)	[nʉ'vɛlə]
novel	roman (m)	[rʉ'mɑn]
detective novel	kriminalroman (m)	[krimi'nɑl rʉˌmɑn]
memoirs	memoarer (pl)	[memʉ'ɑrər]
legend	legende (m)	[le'gɛndə]
myth	myte (m)	['myːtə]
poetry, poems	dikt (n pl)	['dikt]
autobiography	selvbiografi (m)	['sɛlˌbɪʉgrɑ'fi]
selected works	utvalgte verker (n pl)	['ʉtˌvɑlgtə 'værkər]
science fiction	science fiction (m)	['sɑjəns ˌfikʂn]
title	tittel (m)	['titəl]
introduction	innledning (m)	['inˌlednɪŋ]
title page	tittelblad (n)	['titəlˌblɑ]
chapter	kapitel (n)	[kɑ'pitəl]
extract	utdrag (n)	['ʉtˌdrɑg]
episode	episode (m)	[ɛpi'sʉdə]
plot (storyline)	handling (m/f)	['hɑndlɪŋ]
contents	innhold (n)	['inˌhɔl]
table of contents	innholdsfortegnelse (m)	['inhɔls fɔː'ʈæjnəlsə]
main character	hovedperson (m)	['hʉvəd pæ'ʂʉn]
volume	bind (n)	['bin]
cover	omslag (n)	['ɔmˌslɑg]
binding	bokbind (n)	['bʉkˌbin]
bookmark	bokmerke (n)	['bʉkˌmærkə]
page	side (m/f)	['sidə]
to page through	å bla	[ɔ 'blɑ]
margins	marger (m pl)	['mɑrgər]
annotation (marginal note, etc.)	annotering (n)	[ɑnʉ'tɛrɪŋ]
footnote	anmerkning (m)	['ɑnˌmærknɪŋ]
text	tekst (m/f)	['tɛkst]
type, font	skrift, font (m)	['skrift], ['fɔnt]

misprint, typo	trykkfeil (m)	['trʏkˌfæjl]
translation	oversettelse (m)	['ɔvəˌsɛtəlsə]
to translate (vt)	å oversette	[ɔ 'ɔveˌsɛtə]
original (n)	original (m)	[ɔrigi'nɑl]

famous (adj)	berømt	[be'rømt]
unknown (not famous)	ukjent	['ʉˌçɛnt]
interesting (adj)	interessant	[intere'sɑn]
bestseller	bestselger (m)	['bɛstˌsɛlər]

dictionary	ordbok (m/f)	['uːrˌbʊk]
textbook	lærebok (m/f)	['læʁəˌbʊk]
encyclopedia	encyklopedi (m)	[ɛnsʏklɔpe'di]

158. Hunting. Fishing

hunting	jakt (m/f)	['jakt]
to hunt (vi, vt)	å jage	[ɔ 'jagə]
hunter	jeger (m)	['jɛːgər]
to shoot (vi)	å skyte	[ɔ 'sytə]
rifle	gevær (n)	[ge'vær]
bullet (shell)	patron (m)	[pɑ'trʊn]
shot (lead balls)	hagl (n)	['hɑgl]

steel trap	saks (m/f)	['sɑks]
snare (for birds, etc.)	felle (m/f)	['fɛlə]
to fall into the steel trap	å fanges i felle	[ɔ 'fɑŋəs i 'fɛlə]
to lay a steel trap	å sette opp felle	[ɔ 'sɛtə ɔp 'fɛlə]

poacher	tyvskytter (m)	['tyfˌsytər]
game (in hunting)	vilt (n)	['vilt]
hound dog	jakthund (m)	['jaktˌhʉn]
safari	safari (m)	[sɑ'fɑri]
mounted animal	utstoppet dyr (n)	['ʉtˌstɔpet ˌdyr]

fisherman, angler	fisker (m)	['fiskər]
fishing (angling)	fiske (n)	['fiskə]
to fish (vi)	å fiske	[ɔ 'fiskə]

fishing rod	fiskestang (m/f)	['fiskəˌstɑŋ]
fishing line	fiskesnøre (n)	['fiskəˌsnørə]
hook	krok (m)	['krʊk]
float, bobber	dupp (m)	['dʉp]
bait	agn (m)	['ɑŋn]

to cast a line	å kaste ut	[ɔ 'kɑstə ʉt]
to bite (ab. fish)	å bite	[ɔ 'bitə]
catch (of fish)	fangst (m)	['fɑŋst]
ice-hole	hull (n) i isen	['hʉl i ˌisən]
fishing net	nett (n)	['nɛt]

boat	**båt** (m)	['bɔt]
to net (to fish with a net)	**å fiske med nett**	[ɔ 'fiskə me 'nɛt]
to cast[throw] the net	**å kaste nettet**	[ɔ 'kastə 'nɛtə]
to haul the net in	**å hale opp nettet**	[ɔ 'halə ɔp 'nɛtə]
to fall into the net	**å bli fanget i nett**	[ɔ 'bli 'faŋət i 'nɛt]
whaler (person)	**hvalfanger** (m)	['val‚faŋər]
whaleboat	**hvalbåt** (m)	['val‚bɔt]
harpoon	**harpun** (m)	[har'pʉn]

159. Games. Billiards

billiards	**biljard** (m)	[bil'ja:d]
billiard room, hall	**biljardsalong** (m)	[bil'ja:d‚sa‚lɔŋ]
ball (snooker, etc.)	**biljardkule** (m/f)	[bil'ja:d‚kʉ:lə]
to pocket a ball	**å støte en kule**	[ɔ 'støtə en 'kʉ:lə]
cue	**kø** (m)	['kø]
pocket	**hull** (n)	['hʉl]

160. Games. Playing cards

diamonds	**ruter** (m pl)	['rʉtər]
spades	**spar** (m pl)	['spar]
hearts	**hjerter** (m)	['jæ:tər]
clubs	**kløver** (m)	['kløvər]
ace	**ess** (n)	['ɛs]
king	**konge** (m)	['kuŋə]
queen	**dame** (m/f)	['damə]
jack, knave	**knekt** (m)	['knɛkt]
playing card	**kort** (n)	['kɔ:t]
cards	**kort** (n pl)	['kɔ:t]
trump	**trumf** (m)	['trʉmf]
deck of cards	**kortstokk** (m)	['kɔ:t‚stɔk]
point	**poeng** (n)	[pɔ'ɛŋ]
to deal (vi, vt)	**å gi, å dele ut**	[ɔ 'ji, ɔ 'delə ʉt]
to shuffle (cards)	**å blande**	[ɔ 'blanə]
lead, turn (n)	**trekk** (n)	['trɛk]
cardsharp	**falskspiller** (m)	['falsk‚spilər]

161. Casino. Roulette

casino	**kasino** (n)	[ka'sinʊ]
roulette (game)	**rulett** (m)	[rʉ'let]

| bet | innsats (m) | ['inˌsɑts] |
| to place bets | å satse | [ɔ 'sɑtsə] |

red	rød (m)	['rø]
black	svart (m)	['svɑːt]
to bet on red	å satse på rød	[ɔ 'sɑtsə pɔ 'rø]
to bet on black	å satse på svart	[ɔ 'sɑtsə pɔ 'svɑːt]

croupier (dealer)	croupier, dealer (m)	[kru'pje], ['dilər]
to spin the wheel	å snurre hjulet	[ɔ 'snʉrə 'jʉle]
rules (of game)	spilleregler (m pl)	['spiləˌrɛglər]
chip	sjetong (m)	[ʂɛ'tɔŋ]

| to win (vi, vt) | å vinne | [ɔ 'vinə] |
| win (winnings) | gevinst (m) | [ge'vinst] |

| to lose (~ 100 dollars) | å tape | [ɔ 'tɑpə] |
| loss (losses) | tap (n) | ['tɑp] |

player	spiller (m)	['spilər]
blackjack (card game)	blackjack (m)	['blekˌsɛk]
craps (dice game)	terningspill (n)	['tæːɲiɲˌspil]
dice (a pair of ~)	terninger (m/f pl)	['tæːɲiɲər]
slot machine	spilleautomat (m)	['spilə aʊtʊ'mɑt]

162. Rest. Games. Miscellaneous

to stroll (vi, vt)	å spasere	[ɔ spɑ'serə]
stroll (leisurely walk)	spasertur (m)	[spɑ'sɛːˌtʉr]
car ride	kjøretur (m)	['çœːrəˌtʉr]
adventure	eventyr (n)	['ɛvənˌtyr]
picnic	piknik (m)	['piknik]

game (chess, etc.)	spill (n)	['spil]
player	spiller (m)	['spilər]
game (one ~ of chess)	parti (n)	[pɑː'ti]

collector (e.g., philatelist)	samler (m)	['sɑmlər]
to collect (stamps, etc.)	å samle	[ɔ 'sɑmlə]
collection	samling (m/f)	['sɑmliŋ]

crossword puzzle	kryssord (n)	['krʏsˌʊːr]
racetrack (horse racing venue)	travbane (m)	['trɑvˌbɑnə]
disco (discotheque)	diskotek (n)	[diskʊ'tek]

sauna	sauna (m)	['saʊnɑ]
lottery	lotteri (n)	[lɔte'ri]
camping trip	campingtur (m)	['kɑmpiɲˌtʉr]
camp	leir (m)	['læjr]

tent (for camping)	telt (n)	['tɛlt]
compass	kompass (m/n)	[kʊm'pas]
camper	camper (m)	['kampər]
to watch (movie, etc.)	å se på	[ɔ 'se pɔ]
viewer	TV-seer (m)	['tɛvɛ ˌse:ər]
TV show (TV program)	TV-show (n)	['tɛvɛ ˌçɔ:w]

163. Photography

camera (photo)	kamera (n)	['kamera]
photo, picture	foto, fotografi (n)	['fɔtɔ], ['fɔtɔgra'fi]
photographer	fotograf (m)	[fɔtɔ'graf]
photo studio	fotostudio (n)	['fɔtɔˌstʉdiɔ]
photo album	fotoalbum (n)	['fɔtɔˌalbʉm]
camera lens	objektiv (n)	[ɔbjɛk'tiv]
telephoto lens	teleobjektiv (n)	['teleɔbjek'tiv]
filter	filter (n)	['filtər]
lens	linse (m/f)	['linsə]
optics (high-quality ~)	optikk (m)	[ɔp'tik]
diaphragm (aperture)	blender (m)	['blenər]
exposure time (shutter speed)	eksponeringstid (m/f)	[ɛkspʊ'neriŋsˌtid]
viewfinder	søker (m)	['søkər]
digital camera	digitalkamera (n)	[digi'tal ˌkamera]
tripod	stativ (m)	[sta'tiv]
flash	blits (m)	['blits]
to photograph (vt)	å fotografere	[ɔ fɔtɔgra'ferə]
to take pictures	å ta bilder	[ɔ 'ta 'bildər]
to have one's picture taken	å bli fotografert	[ɔ 'bli fɔtɔgra'fɛ:t]
focus	fokus (n)	['fɔkʉs]
to focus	å stille skarphet	[ɔ 'stilə 'skarpˌhet]
sharp, in focus (adj)	skarp	['ckarp]
sharpness	skarphet (m)	['skarpˌhet]
contrast	kontrast (m)	[kʊn'trast]
contrast (as adj)	kontrast-	[kʊn'trast-]
picture (photo)	bilde (n)	['bildə]
negative (n)	negativ (m/n)	['negaˌtiv]
film (a roll of ~)	film (m)	['film]
frame (still)	bilde (n)	['bildə]
to print (photos)	å skrive ut	[ɔ skrivə ʉt]

164. Beach. Swimming

beach	badestrand (m/f)	['badə‚stran]
sand	sand (m)	['san]
deserted (beach)	øde	['ødə]
suntan	solbrenthet (m)	['sʊlbrɛnt‚het]
to get a tan	å sole seg	[ɔ 'sʊlə sæj]
tan (adj)	solbrent	['sʊl‚brɛnt]
sunscreen	solkrem (m)	['sʊl‚krɛm]
bikini	bikini (m)	[bi'kini]
bathing suit	badedrakt (m/f)	['badə‚drakt]
swim trunks	badebukser (m/f)	['badə‚bʉksər]
swimming pool	svømmebasseng (n)	['svœmə‚ba'sɛŋ]
to swim (vi)	å svømme	[ɔ 'svœmə]
shower	dusj (m)	['dʉʃ]
to change (one's clothes)	å kle seg om	[ɔ 'kle sæj ‚ɔm]
towel	håndkle (n)	['hɔn‚kle]
boat	båt (m)	['bɔt]
motorboat	motorbåt (m)	['mɔtʊr‚bɔt]
water ski	vannski (m pl)	['van‚ʂi]
paddle boat	pedalbåt (m)	['pe'dal‚bɔt]
surfing	surfing (m/f)	['sørfiŋ]
surfer	surfer (m)	['sørfər]
scuba set	scuba (n)	['skʉba]
flippers (swim fins)	svømmeføtter (m pl)	['svœmə‚fœtər]
mask (diving ~)	maske (m/f)	['maskə]
diver	dykker (m)	['dʏkər]
to dive (vi)	å dykke	[ɔ 'dʏkə]
underwater (adv)	under vannet	['ʉnər 'vanə]
beach umbrella	parasoll (m)	[para'sɔl]
sunbed (lounger)	liggestol (m)	['ligə‚stʉl]
sunglasses	solbriller (m pl)	['sʊl‚brilər]
air mattress	luftmadrass (m)	['lʉftma‚dras]
to play (amuse oneself)	å leke	[ɔ 'lekə]
to go for a swim	å bade	[ɔ 'badə]
beach ball	ball (m)	['bal]
to inflate (vt)	å blåse opp	[ɔ 'blɔːsə ɔp]
inflatable, air (adj)	luft-, oppblåsbar	['lʉft-], [ɔp'blɔːsbar]
wave	bølge (m)	['bølgə]
buoy (line of ~s)	bøye (m)	['bøjə]
to drown (ab. person)	å drukne	[ɔ 'drʉknə]

to save, to rescue	**å redde**	[ɔ 'rɛdə]
life vest	**redningsvest** (m)	['rɛdniŋsˌvɛst]
to observe, to watch	**å observere**	[ɔ ɔbsɛr'verə]
lifeguard	**badevakt** (m/f)	['bɑdəˌvɑkt]

TECHNICAL EQUIPMENT. TRANSPORTATION

Technical equipment

165. Computer

computer	datamaskin (m)	['data ma͵ʃin]
notebook, laptop	bærbar, laptop (m)	['bær͵bar], ['laptɔp]
to turn on	å slå på	[ɔ 'ʂlɔ pɔ]
to turn off	å slå av	[ɔ 'ʂlɔ aː]
keyboard	tastatur (n)	[tasta'tʉr]
key	tast (m)	['tast]
mouse	mus (m/f)	['mʉs]
mouse pad	musematte (m/f)	['mʉsə͵matə]
button	knapp (m)	['knap]
cursor	markør (m)	[mar'kør]
monitor	monitor (m)	['mɔnitɔr]
screen	skjerm (m)	['ʂærm]
hard disk	harddisk (m)	['har͵disk]
hard disk capacity	harddiskkapasitet (m)	['har͵disk kapasi'tet]
memory	minne (n)	['minə]
random access memory	hovedminne (n)	['hɔvəd͵minə]
file	fil (m)	['fil]
folder	mappe (m/f)	['mapə]
to open (vt)	å åpne	[ɔ 'ɔpnə]
to close (vt)	å lukke	[ɔ 'lʉkə]
to save (vt)	å lagre	[ɔ 'lagrə]
to delete (vt)	å slette, å fjerne	[ɔ 'ʂletə], [ɔ 'fjæːɳə]
to copy (vt)	å kopiere	[ɔ kʉ'pjerə]
to sort (vt)	å sortere	[ɔ sɔ:'ʈerə]
to transfer (copy)	å overføre	[ɔ 'ɔvər͵førə]
program	program (n)	[prʉ'gram]
software	programvare (m/f)	[prʉ'gram͵varə]
programmer	programmerer (m)	[prʉgra'merər]
to program (vt)	å programmere	[ɔ prʉgra'merə]
hacker	hacker (m)	['hakər]
password	passord (n)	['pas͵uːr]

virus	virus (m)	['virʉs]
to find, to detect	å oppdage	[ɔ 'ɔp,dɑgə]
byte	byte (m)	['bɑjt]
megabyte	megabyte (m)	['megɑ,bɑjt]
data	data (m pl)	['dɑtɑ]
database	database (m)	['dɑtɑ,bɑsə]
cable (USB, etc.)	kabel (m)	['kɑbəl]
to disconnect (vt)	å koble fra	[ɔ 'kɔblə frɑ]
to connect (sth to sth)	å koble	[ɔ 'kɔblə]

166. Internet. E-mail

Internet	Internett	['intə,nɛt]
browser	nettleser (m)	['nɛt,lesər]
search engine	søkemotor (m)	['søkə,mɔtʉr]
provider	leverandør (m)	[levərɑn'dør]
webmaster	webmaster (m)	['vɛb,mɑstər]
website	webside, hjemmeside (m/f)	['vɛb,sidə], ['jɛmə,sidə]
webpage	nettside (m)	['nɛt,sidə]
address (e-mail ~)	adresse (m)	[ɑ'drɛsə]
address book	adressebok (f)	[ɑ'drɛsə,bʉk]
mailbox	postkasse (m/f)	['pɔst,kɑsə]
mail	post (m)	['pɔst]
full (adj)	full	['fʉl]
message	melding (m/f)	['mɛliŋ]
incoming messages	innkommende meldinger	['in,kɔmenə 'mɛliŋər]
outgoing messages	utgående meldinger	['ʉt,gɔənə 'mɛliŋər]
sender	avsender (m)	['ɑf,sɛnər]
to send (vt)	å sende	[ɔ 'sɛnə]
sending (of mail)	avsending (m)	['ɑf,sɛniŋ]
receiver	mottaker (m)	['mɔt,tɑkər]
to receive (vt)	å motta	[ɔ 'mɔtʉ]
correspondence	korrespondanse (m)	[kʉrespɔn'dɑnsə]
to correspond (vi)	å brevveksle	[ɔ 'brɛv,vɛkslə]
file	fil (m)	['fil]
to download (vt)	å laste ned	[ɔ 'lɑstə 'ne]
to create (vt)	å opprette	[ɔ 'ɔp,rɛtə]
to delete (vt)	å slette, å fjerne	[ɔ 'ʃletə], [ɔ 'fjæːɳə]
deleted (adj)	slettet	['ʃletət]
connection (ADSL, etc.)	forbindelse (m)	[fɔr'binəlsə]

speed	hastighet (m/f)	['hɑstiˌhet]
modem	modem (n)	['mʉ'dɛm]
access	tilgang (m)	['tilˌgɑŋ]
port (e.g., input ~)	port (m)	['pɔ:t]

| connection (make a ~) | tilkobling (m/f) | ['tilˌkɔbliŋ] |
| to connect to … (vi) | å koble | [ɔ 'kɔblə] |

| to select (vt) | å velge | [ɔ 'vɛlgə] |
| to search (for …) | å søke etter … | [ɔ 'søkə ˌɛtər …] |

167. Electricity

electricity	elektrisitet (m)	[ɛlektrisi'tet]
electric, electrical (adj)	elektrisk	[ɛ'lektrisk]
electric power plant	kraftverk (n)	['krɑftˌværk]
energy	energi (m)	[ɛnær'gi]
electric power	elkraft (m/f)	['ɛlˌkrɑft]

light bulb	lyspære (m/f)	['lysˌpærə]
flashlight	lommelykt (m/f)	['lʉməˌlʏkt]
street light	gatelykt (m/f)	['gɑtəˌlʏkt]

light	lys (n)	['lys]
to turn on	å slå på	[ɔ 'ʂlɔ pɔ]
to turn off	å slå av	[ɔ 'ʂlɔ ɑ:]
to turn off the light	å slokke lyset	[ɔ 'ʂløkə 'lysə]

to burn out (vi)	å brenne ut	[ɔ 'brɛnə ʉt]
short circuit	kortslutning (m)	['kʉːʈˌslʉtniŋ]
broken wire	kabelbrudd (n)	['kɑbəlˌbrʉd]
contact (electrical ~)	kontakt (m)	[kʉn'tɑkt]

light switch	strømbryter (m)	['strømˌbrytər]
wall socket	stikkontakt (m)	['stik kʉnˌtɑkt]
plug	støpsel (n)	['støpsəl]
extension cord	skjøteledning (m)	['ʂøtəˌledniŋ]

fuse	sikring (m)	['sikriŋ]
cable, wire	ledning (m)	['ledniŋ]
wiring	ledningsnett (n)	['ledniŋsˌnɛt]

ampere	ampere (m)	[ɑm'pɛr]
amperage	strømstyrke (m)	['strømˌstyrkə]
volt	volt (m)	['vɔlt]
voltage	spenning (m/f)	['spɛniŋ]

electrical device	elektrisk apparat (n)	[ɛ'lektrisk ɑpɑ'rɑt]
indicator	indikator (m)	[indi'kɑtʉr]
electrician	elektriker (m)	[ɛ'lektrikər]

to solder (vt)	**å lodde**	[ɔ 'lɔdə]
soldering iron	**loddebolt** (m)	['lɔdə‚bɔlt]
electric current	**strøm** (m)	['strøm]

168. Tools

tool, instrument	**verktøy** (n)	['værk‚tøj]
tools	**verktøy** (n pl)	['værk‚tøj]
equipment (factory ~)	**utstyr** (n)	['ʉt‚styr]

hammer	**hammer** (m)	['hamər]
screwdriver	**skrutrekker** (m)	['skrʉ‚trɛkər]
ax	**øks** (m/f)	['øks]

saw	**sag** (m/f)	['sɑg]
to saw (vt)	**å sage**	[ɔ 'sɑgə]
plane (tool)	**høvel** (m)	['høvəl]
to plane (vt)	**å høvle**	[ɔ 'høvlə]
soldering iron	**loddebolt** (m)	['lɔdə‚bɔlt]
to solder (vt)	**å lodde**	[ɔ 'lɔdə]

file (tool)	**fil** (m/f)	['fil]
carpenter pincers	**knipetang** (m/f)	['knipə‚taŋ]
lineman's pliers	**flattang** (m/f)	['flat‚taŋ]
chisel	**hoggjern, huggjern** (n)	['hʊg‚jæːn]

drill bit	**bor** (m/n)	['bʊr]
electric drill	**boremaskin** (m)	['bɔre mɑ‚ʂin]
to drill (vi, vt)	**å bore**	[ɔ 'bɔrə]

knife	**kniv** (m)	['kniv]
pocket knife	**lommekniv** (m)	['lʊmə‚kniv]
folding (~ knife)	**folde-**	['fɔlə-]
blade	**blad** (n)	['blɑ]

sharp (blade, etc.)	**skarp**	['skɑrp]
dull, blunt (adj)	**sløv**	['sløv]
to get blunt (dull)	**å bli sløv**	[ɔ 'bli 'sløv]
to sharpen (vt)	**å skjerpe, å slipe**	[ɔ 'ʂɛrpə], [ɔ 'ʂlipə]

bolt	**bolt** (m)	['bɔlt]
nut	**mutter** (m)	['mʉtər]
thread (of a screw)	**gjenge** (n)	['jɛŋə]
wood screw	**skrue** (m)	['skrʉə]

| nail | **spiker** (m) | ['spikər] |
| nailhead | **spikerhode** (n) | ['spikər‚hʊdə] |

| ruler (for measuring) | **linjal** (m) | [li'njal] |
| tape measure | **målebånd** (n) | ['moːlə‚bɔn] |

spirit level	vater, vaterpass (n)	['vatər], ['vatər,pas]
magnifying glass	lupe (m/f)	['lʉpə]
measuring instrument	måleinstrument (n)	['moːlə instrʉ'mɛnt]
to measure (vt)	å måle	[ɔ 'moːlə]
scale	skala (m)	['skala]
(of thermometer, etc.)		
readings	avlesninger (m/f pl)	['av,lesninər]
compressor	kompressor (m)	[kʊm'presʊr]
microscope	mikroskop (n)	[mikrʊ'skʊp]
pump (e.g., water ~)	pumpe (m/f)	['pʉmpə]
robot	robot (m)	['rɔbɔt]
laser	laser (m)	['lasər]
wrench	skrunøkkel (m)	['skrʉ,nøkəl]
adhesive tape	pakketeip (m)	['pakə,tɛjp]
glue	lim (n)	['lim]
sandpaper	sandpapir (n)	['sanpa,pir]
spring	fjær (m/f)	['fjær]
magnet	magnet (m)	[man'net]
gloves	hansker (m pl)	['hanskər]
rope	reip, rep (n)	['ræjp], ['rɛp]
cord	snor (m/f)	['snʊr]
wire (e.g., telephone ~)	ledning (m)	['lednin]
cable	kabel (m)	['kabəl]
sledgehammer	slegge (m/f)	['ʂlegə]
prybar	spett, jernspett (n)	['spɛt], ['jæːn̩,spɛt]
ladder	stige (m)	['stiːə]
stepladder	trappstige (m/f)	['trap,stiːə]
to screw (tighten)	å skru fast	[ɔ 'skrʉ 'fast]
to unscrew (lid, filter, etc.)	å skru løs	[ɔ 'skrʉ ,løs]
to tighten	å klemme	[ɔ 'klemə]
(e.g., with a clamp)		
to glue, to stick	å klistre, å lime	[ɔ 'klistrə], [ɔ 'limə]
to cut (vt)	å skjære	[ɔ 'ʂæːrə]
malfunction (fault)	funksjonsfeil (m)	['fʉnkʂɔns,fæjl]
repair (mending)	reparasjon (m)	[repara'ʂʊn]
to repair, to fix (vt)	å reparere	[ɔ repa'rerə]
to adjust (machine, etc.)	å justere	[ɔ jʉ'sterə]
to check (to examine)	å sjekke	[ɔ 'ʂɛkə]
checking	kontroll (m)	[kʊn'trɔl]
readings	avlesninger (m/f pl)	['av,lesninər]
reliable, solid (machine)	pålitelig	[pɔ'liteli]
complex (adj)	komplisert	[kʊmpli'sɛːt]

to rust (get rusted)	**å ruste**	[ɔ 'rʉstə]
rusty, rusted (adj)	**rusten, rustet**	['rʉstən], ['rʉstət]
rust	**rust** (m/f)	['rʉst]

Transportation

169. Airplane

airplane	**fly** (n)	['fly]
air ticket	**flybillett** (m)	['fly bi'let]
airline	**flyselskap** (n)	['flysəl‚skɑp]
airport	**flyplass** (m)	['fly‚plɑs]
supersonic (adj)	**overlyds-**	['ɔve‚lyds-]
captain	**kaptein** (m)	[kɑp'tæjn]
crew	**besetning** (m/f)	[be'sɛtniŋ]
pilot	**pilot** (m)	[pi'lɔt]
flight attendant (fem.)	**flyvertinne** (m/f)	[flyvɛ:'ţinə]
navigator	**styrmann** (m)	['styr‚mɑn]
wings	**vinger** (m pl)	['viŋər]
tail	**hale** (m)	['hɑlə]
cockpit	**cockpit, førerkabin** (m)	['kɔkpit], ['førərkɑ‚bin]
engine	**motor** (m)	['mɔtʊr]
undercarriage (landing gear)	**landingshjul** (n)	['lɑniŋs‚jʉl]
turbine	**turbin** (m)	[tʉr'bin]
propeller	**propell** (m)	[prʊ'pɛl]
black box	**svart boks** (m)	['svɑ:ţ bɔks]
yoke (control column)	**ratt** (n)	['rɑt]
fuel	**brensel** (n)	['brɛnsəl]
safety card	**sikkerhetsbrosjyre** (m)	['sikərhɛts‚brɔ'şyrə]
oxygen mask	**oksygenmaske** (m/f)	['ɔksygən‚maskə]
uniform	**uniform** (m)	[ʉni'fɔrm]
life vest	**redningsvest** (m)	['rɛdniŋs‚vɛst]
parachute	**fallskjerm** (m)	['fɑl‚şærm]
takeoff	**start** (m)	['stɑ:ţ]
to take off (vi)	**å løfte**	[ɔ 'lœftə]
runway	**startbane** (m)	['stɑ:ţ‚bɑnə]
visibility	**siktbarhet** (m)	['siktbɑr‚het]
flight (act of flying)	**flyging** (m/f)	['flygiŋ]
altitude	**høyde** (m)	['højdə]
air pocket	**lufthull** (n)	['lʉft‚hʉl]
seat	**plass** (m)	['plɑs]
headphones	**hodetelefoner** (n pl)	['hodətelə‚fʉnər]

folding tray (tray table)	klappbord (n)	['klɑp‚bʉr]
airplane window	vindu (n)	['vindʉ]
aisle	midtgang (m)	['mit‚gɑŋ]

170. Train

train	tog (n)	['tɔg]
commuter train	lokaltog (n)	[lɔ'kɑl‚tɔg]
express train	ekspresstog (n)	[ɛks'prɛs‚tɔg]
diesel locomotive	diesellokomotiv (n)	['disəl lʉkɔmɔ'tiv]
steam locomotive	damplokomotiv (n)	['dɑmp lʉkɔmɔ'tiv]

| passenger car | vogn (m) | ['vɔŋn] |
| dining car | restaurantvogn (m/f) | [rɛstʉ'rɑŋ‚vɔŋn] |

rails	skinner (m/f pl)	['ʂinər]
railroad	jernbane (m)	['jæːɳ‚bɑnə]
railway tie	sville (m/f)	['svilə]

platform (railway ~)	perrong, plattform (m/f)	[pɛ'rɔŋ], ['plɑtfɔrm]
track (~ 1, 2, etc.)	spor (n)	['spʉr]
semaphore	semafor (m)	[sema'fʉr]
station	stasjon (m)	[stɑ'ʂʉn]

engineer (train driver)	lokfører (m)	['lʉk‚førər]
porter (of luggage)	bærer (m)	['bærər]
car attendant	betjent (m)	['be'tjɛnt]
passenger	passasjer (m)	[pɑsɑ'ʂɛr]
conductor (ticket inspector)	billett inspektør (m)	[bi'let inspɛk'tør]

| corridor (in train) | korridor (m) | [kʉri'dɔr] |
| emergency brake | nødbrems (m) | ['nød‚brɛms] |

compartment	kupé (m)	[kʉ'pe]
berth	køye (m/f)	['køjə]
upper berth	overkøye (m/f)	['ɔvər‚køjə]
lower berth	underkøye (m/f)	['ʉnər‚køjə]
bed linen, bedding	sengetøy (n)	['sɛŋə‚tøj]

ticket	billett (m)	[bi'let]
schedule	rutetabell (m)	['rʉtə‚tɑ'bɛl]
information display	informasjonstavle (m/f)	[infɔrmɑ'ʂʉns ‚tɑvlə]

to leave, to depart	å avgå	[ɔ 'ɑvgɔ]
departure (of train)	avgang (m)	['ɑv‚gɑŋ]
to arrive (ab. train)	å ankomme	[ɔ 'ɑn‚kɔmə]
arrival	ankomst (m)	['ɑn‚kɔmst]
to arrive by train	å ankomme med toget	[ɔ 'ɑn‚kɔmə me 'tɔgə]
to get on the train	å gå på toget	[ɔ 'gɔ pɔ 'tɔgə]

to get off the train	å gå av toget	[ɔ 'gɔ ɑ: 'tɔge]
train wreck	togulykke (m/n)	['tɔg ʉ'lʏkə]
to derail (vi)	å spore av	[ɔ 'spʉrə ɑ:]
steam locomotive	damplokomotiv (n)	['dɑmp lʉkɔmɔ'tiv]
stoker, fireman	fyrbøter (m)	['fyrˌbøtər]
firebox	fyrrom (n)	['fyrˌrʊm]
coal	kull (n)	['kʉl]

171. Ship

| ship | skip (n) | ['ʂip] |
| vessel | fartøy (n) | ['fɑːˌʈøj] |

steamship	dampskip (n)	['dɑmpˌʂip]
riverboat	elvebåt (m)	['ɛlvəˌbɔt]
cruise ship	cruiseskip (n)	['krʉsˌʂip]
cruiser	krysser (m)	['krʏsər]

yacht	jakt (m/f)	['jakt]
tugboat	bukserbåt (m)	[bʉk'serˌbɔt]
barge	lastepram (m)	['lɑstəˌprɑm]
ferry	ferje, ferge (m/f)	['færjə], ['færgə]

| sailing ship | seilbåt (n) | ['sæjlˌbɔt] |
| brigantine | brigantin (m) | [brigɑn'tin] |

| ice breaker | isbryter (m) | ['isˌbrytər] |
| submarine | ubåt (m) | ['ʉːˌbɔt] |

boat (flat-bottomed ~)	båt (m)	['bɔt]
dinghy	jolle (m/f)	['jɔlə]
lifeboat	livbåt (m)	['livˌbɔt]
motorboat	motorbåt (m)	['mɔtʊrˌbɔt]

captain	kaptein (m)	[kɑp'tæjn]
seaman	matros (m)	[mɑ'trʊs]
sailor	sjømann (m)	['ʂøˌmɑn]
crew	besetning (m/f)	[be'sɛtniŋ]

boatswain	båtsmann (m)	['bɔsˌmɑn]
ship's boy	skipsgutt, jungmann (m)	['ʂipsˌgʉt], ['jʉŋˌmɑn]
cook	kokk (m)	['kʊk]
ship's doctor	skipslege (m)	['ʂipsˌlegə]

deck	dekk (n)	['dɛk]
mast	mast (m/f)	['mɑst]
sail	seil (n)	['sæjl]

| hold | lasterom (n) | ['lɑstəˌrʊm] |
| bow (prow) | baug (m) | ['bæu] |

stern	**akterende** (m)	['aktəˌrɛnə]
oar	**åre** (m)	['oːrə]
screw propeller	**propell** (m)	[prʊ'pɛl]
cabin	**hytte** (m)	['hʏtə]
wardroom	**offisersmesse** (m/f)	[ɔfi'sɛrsˌmɛsə]
engine room	**maskinrom** (n)	[ma'ʂinˌrʊm]
bridge	**kommandobro** (m/f)	[kɔ'mandʊˌbrʊ]
radio room	**radiorom** (m)	['radiʊˌrʊm]
wave (radio)	**bølge** (m)	['bølgə]
logbook	**loggbok** (m/f)	['lɔgˌbʊk]
spyglass	**langkikkert** (m)	['laŋˌkikeːt]
bell	**klokke** (m/f)	['klɔkə]
flag	**flagg** (n)	['flag]
hawser (mooring ~)	**trosse** (m/f)	['trʊsə]
knot (bowline, etc.)	**knute** (m)	['knʉtə]
deckrails	**rekkverk** (n)	['rɛkˌværk]
gangway	**landgang** (m)	['lanˌgaŋ]
anchor	**anker** (n)	['ankər]
to weigh anchor	**å lette anker**	[ɔ 'letə 'ankər]
to drop anchor	**å kaste anker**	[ɔ 'kastə 'ankər]
anchor chain	**ankerkjetting** (m)	['ankərˌçɛtiŋ]
port (harbor)	**havn** (m/f)	['havn]
quay, wharf	**kai** (m/f)	['kaj]
to berth (moor)	**å fortøye**	[ɔ fɔː'tøjə]
to cast off	**å kaste loss**	[ɔ 'kastə lɔs]
trip, voyage	**reise** (m/f)	['ræjsə]
cruise (sea trip)	**cruise** (n)	['krʉs]
course (route)	**kurs** (m)	['kʉʂ]
route (itinerary)	**rute** (m/f)	['rʉtə]
fairway (safe water channel)	**seilrende** (m)	['ʂæjlˌrɛnə]
shallows	**grunne** (m/f)	['grʉnə]
to run aground	**å gå på grunn**	[ɔ 'gɔ pɔ 'grʉn]
storm	**storm** (m)	['stɔrm]
signal	**signal** (n)	[siŋ'nal]
to sink (vi)	**å synke**	[ɔ 'sʏnkə]
Man overboard!	**Mann over bord!**	['man ˌɔvər 'bʊr]
SOS (distress signal)	**SOS** (n)	[ɛsʊ'ɛs]
ring buoy	**livbøye** (m/f)	['livˌbøjə]

172. Airport

airport	**flyplass** (m)	['fly,plɑs]
airplane	**fly** (n)	['fly]
airline	**flyselskap** (n)	['flysəl,skɑp]
air traffic controller	**flygeleder** (m)	['flygə,ledər]
departure	**avgang** (m)	['ɑv,gɑŋ]
arrival	**ankomst** (m)	['ɑn,kɔmst]
to arrive (by plane)	**å ankomme**	[ɔ 'ɑn,kɔmə]
departure time	**avgangstid** (m/f)	['ɑvgɑŋs,tid]
arrival time	**ankomsttid** (m/f)	[ɑn'kɔms,tid]
to be delayed	**å bli forsinket**	[ɔ 'bli fɔ'ṣinkət]
flight delay	**avgangsforsinkelse** (m)	['ɑvgɑŋs fɔ'ṣinkəlsə]
information board	**informasjonstavle** (m/f)	[infɔrmɑ'ṣuns ,tɑvlə]
information	**informasjon** (m)	[infɔrmɑ'ṣun]
to announce (vt)	**å meddele**	[ɔ 'mɛd,delə]
flight (e.g., next ~)	**fly** (n)	['fly]
customs	**toll** (m)	['tɔl]
customs officer	**tollbetjent** (m)	['tɔlbe,tjɛnt]
customs declaration	**tolldeklarasjon** (m)	['tɔldɛklɑrɑ'ṣun]
to fill out (vt)	**å utfylle**	[ɔ 'ʉt,fvlə]
to fill out the declaration	**å utfylle en tolldeklarasjon**	[ɔ 'ʉt,fvlə en 'tɔldɛklɑrɑ,ṣun]
passport control	**passkontroll** (m)	['pɑskʉn,trɔl]
luggage	**bagasje** (m)	[bɑ'gɑṣə]
hand luggage	**håndbagasje** (m)	['hɔn,bɑ'gɑṣə]
luggage cart	**bagasjetralle** (m/f)	[bɑ'gɑṣə,trɑlə]
landing	**landing** (m)	['lɑniŋ]
landing strip	**landingsbane** (m)	['lɑniŋs,bɑnə]
to land (vi)	**å lande**	[ɔ 'lɑnə]
airstairs	**trapp** (m/f)	['trɑp]
check-in	**innsjekking** (m/f)	['in,ṣɛkiŋ]
check-in counter	**innsjekkingsskranke** (m)	['in,ṣɛkiŋs ,skrɑnkə]
to check-in (vi)	**å sjekke inn**	[ɔ 'ṣɛkə in]
boarding pass	**boardingkort** (n)	['bɔːdiŋ,kɔːt]
departure gate	**gate** (m/f)	['gejt]
transit	**transitt** (m)	[trɑn'sit]
to wait (vt)	**å vente**	[ɔ 'vɛntə]
departure lounge	**ventehall** (m)	['vɛntə,hɑl]
to see off	**å ta avskjed**	[ɔ 'tɑ 'ɑf,ṣɛd]
to say goodbye	**å si farvel**	[ɔ 'si fɑr'vɛl]

173. Bicycle. Motorcycle

bicycle	**sykkel** (m)	['sʏkəl]
scooter	**skooter** (m)	['skutər]
motorcycle, bike	**motorsykkel** (m)	['mɔtʊrˌsʏkəl]
to go by bicycle	**å sykle**	[ɔ 'sʏklə]
handlebars	**styre** (n)	['styrə]
pedal	**pedal** (m)	[pe'dɑl]
brakes	**bremser** (m pl)	['brɛmsər]
bicycle seat (saddle)	**sete** (n)	['setə]
pump	**pumpe** (m/f)	['pʉmpə]
luggage rack	**bagasjebrett** (n)	[bɑ'gɑʂəˌbrɛt]
front lamp	**lykt** (m/f)	['lʏkt]
helmet	**hjelm** (m)	['jɛlm]
wheel	**hjul** (n)	['jʉl]
fender	**skjerm** (m)	['ʂærm]
rim	**felg** (m)	['fɛlg]
spoke	**eik** (m/f)	['æjk]

Cars

174. Types of cars

automobile, car	**bil** (m)	['bil]
sports car	**sportsbil** (m)	['spɔ:t̡ʂ‚bil]
limousine	**limousin** (m)	[limʉ'sin]
off-road vehicle	**terrengbil** (m)	[tɛ'rɛŋ‚bil]
convertible (n)	**kabriolet** (m)	[kabriʊ'le]
minibus	**minibuss** (m)	['mini‚bʉs]
ambulance	**ambulanse** (m)	[ambʉ'lansə]
snowplow	**snøplog** (m)	['snø‚plɔg]
truck	**lastebil** (m)	['lastə‚bil]
tanker truck	**tankbil** (m)	['taŋk‚bil]
van (small truck)	**skapbil** (m)	['skap‚bil]
road tractor (trailer truck)	**trekkvogn** (m/f)	['trɛk‚vɔŋn]
trailer	**tilhenger** (m)	['til‚hɛŋər]
comfortable (adj)	**komfortabel**	[kʊmfɔ:'tabəl]
used (adj)	**brukt**	['brʉkt]

175. Cars. Bodywork

hood	**panser** (n)	['pansər]
fender	**skjerm** (m)	['ʂærm]
roof	**tak** (n)	['tak]
windshield	**frontrute** (m/f)	['frɔnt‚rʉtə]
rear-view mirror	**bakspeil** (n)	['bak‚spæjl]
windshield washer	**vindusspyler** (m)	['vindʉs‚spylər]
windshield wipers	**viskerblader** (n pl)	['viskəblaər]
side window	**siderute** (m/f)	['sidə‚rʉtə]
window lift (power window)	**vindusheis** (m)	['vindʉs‚hæjs]
antenna	**antenne** (m)	[an'tɛnə]
sunroof	**takluke** (m/f), **soltak** (n)	['tak‚lʉkə], ['sʊl‚tak]
bumper	**støtfanger** (m)	['støt‚faŋər]
trunk	**bagasjerom** (n)	[ba'gaʂə‚rʊm]
roof luggage rack	**takgrind** (m/f)	['tak‚grin]
door	**dør** (m/f)	['dœr]

door handle	**dørhåndtak** (n)	['dœr,hɔntak]
door lock	**dørlås** (m/n)	['dœr,lɔs]
license plate	**nummerskilt** (n)	['nʉmər,ʂilt]
muffler	**lyddemper** (m)	['lyd,dɛmpər]
gas tank	**bensintank** (m)	[bɛn'sin,tank]
tailpipe	**eksosrør** (n)	['ɛksʉs,rør]
gas, accelerator	**gass** (m)	['gɑs]
pedal	**pedal** (m)	[pe'dɑl]
gas pedal	**gasspedal** (m)	['gɑs pe'dɑl]
brake	**brems** (m)	['brɛms]
brake pedal	**bremsepedal** (m)	['brɛmsə pe'dɑl]
to brake (use the brake)	**å bremse**	[ɔ 'brɛmsə]
parking brake	**håndbrekk** (n)	['hɔn,brɛk]
clutch	**koppling** (m)	['kɔpliŋ]
clutch pedal	**kopplingspedal** (m)	['kɔpliŋs pe'dɑl]
clutch disc	**koplingsskive** (m/f)	['kɔpliŋs,ʂivə]
shock absorber	**støtdemper** (m)	['støt,dɛmpər]
wheel	**hjul** (n)	['jʉl]
spare tire	**reservehjul** (n)	[re'sɛrvə,jʉl]
tire	**dekk** (n)	['dɛk]
hubcap	**hjulkapsel** (m)	['jʉl,kɑpsəl]
driving wheels	**drivhjul** (n pl)	['driv,jʉl]
front-wheel drive (as adj)	**forhjulsdrevet**	['fɔrjʉls,drevət]
rear-wheel drive (as adj)	**bakhjulsdrevet**	['bɑkjʉls,drevət]
all-wheel drive (as adj)	**firehjulsdrevet**	['firəjʉls,drevət]
gearbox	**girkasse** (m/f)	['gir,kɑsə]
automatic (adj)	**automatisk**	[ɑʉtʉ'mɑtisk]
mechanical (adj)	**mekanisk**	[me'kɑnisk]
gear shift	**girspak** (m)	['gi,ʂpɑk]
headlight	**lyskaster** (m)	['lys,kɑstər]
headlights	**lyskastere** (m pl)	['lys,kɑstərə]
low beam	**nærlys** (n)	['nær,lys]
high beam	**fjernlys** (n)	['fjæːn̩,lys]
brake light	**stopplys, bremselys** (n)	['stɔp,lys], ['brɛmsə,lys]
parking lights	**parkeringslys** (n)	[pɑr'keriŋs,lys]
hazard lights	**varselblinklys** (n)	['vɑsəl,blink lys]
fog lights	**tåkelys** (n)	['toːkə,lys]
turn signal	**blinklys** (n)	['blink,lys]
back-up light	**baklys** (n)	['bɑk,lys]

176. Cars. Passenger compartment

car inside (interior)	interiør (n), innredning (m/f)	[inter'jør], ['in‚rɛdniŋ]
leather (as adj)	lær-	['lær-]
velour (as adj)	velur	[ve'lʉr]
upholstery	trekk (n)	['trɛk]
instrument (gage)	instrument (n)	[instrʉ'mɛnt]
dashboard	dashbord (n)	['daʂbɔːd]
speedometer	speedometer (n)	[spidʉ'metər]
needle (pointer)	viser (m)	['visər]
odometer	kilometerteller (m)	[çilu'metər‚tɛlər]
indicator (sensor)	indikator (m)	[indi'katʉr]
level	nivå (n)	[ni'vo]
warning light	varsellampe (m/f)	['vaʂəl‚lampə]
steering wheel	ratt (n)	['rat]
horn	horn (n)	['huːŋ]
button	knapp (m)	['knap]
switch	bryter (m)	['brytər]
seat	sete (n)	['setə]
backrest	seterygg (m)	['setə‚rʏg]
headrest	nakkestøtte (m/f)	['nakə‚stœtə]
seat belt	sikkerhetsbelte (m)	['sikərhɛts‚bɛltə]
to fasten the belt	å spenne fast sikkerhetsbeltet	[ɔ 'spɛnə fast 'sikərhets‚bɛltə]
adjustment (of seats)	justering (m/f)	[jʉ'steriŋ]
airbag	kollisjonspute (m/f)	['kʉliʂʊns‚pʉtə]
air-conditioner	klimaanlegg (n)	['klima'an‚leg]
radio	radio (m)	['radiʊ]
CD player	CD-spiller (m)	['sɛdɛ ‚spilər]
to turn on	å slå på	[ɔ 'ʂlɔ pɔ]
antenna	antenne (m)	[an'tɛnə]
glove box	hanskerom (n)	['hanskə‚rʊm]
ashtray	askebeger (n)	['askə‚begər]

177. Cars. Engine

engine, motor	motor (m)	['mɔtʊr]
diesel (as adj)	diesel-	['disəl-]
gasoline (as adj)	bensin-	[bɛn'sin-]
engine volume	motorvolum (n)	['mɔtʊr vɔ'lʉm]
power	styrke (m)	['styrkə]

horsepower	hestekraft (m/f)	['hɛstəˌkraft]
piston	stempel (n)	['stɛmpəl]
cylinder	sylinder (m)	[sy'lindər]
valve	ventil (m)	[vɛn'til]

injector	injektor (m)	[i'njɛktʊr]
generator (alternator)	generator (m)	[gene'ratʊr]
carburetor	forgasser (m)	[fɔr'gasər]
motor oil	motorolje (m)	['mɔtʊrˌɔljə]

radiator	radiator (m)	[radi'atʊr]
coolant	kjølevæske (m/f)	['çœləˌvæskə]
cooling fan	vifte (m/f)	['viftə]

battery (accumulator)	batteri (n)	[batɛ'ri]
starter	starter (m)	['stɑːtər]
ignition	tenning (m/f)	['tɛniŋ]
spark plug	tennplugg (m)	['tɛnˌplʉg]

terminal (of battery)	klemme (m/f)	['klemə]
positive terminal	plussklemme (m/f)	['plʉsˌklemə]
negative terminal	minusklemme (m/f)	['minʉsˌklemə]
fuse	sikring (m)	['sikriŋ]

air filter	luftfilter (n)	['lʉftˌfiltər]
oil filter	oljefilter (n)	['ɔljəˌfiltər]
fuel filter	brenselsfilter (n)	['brɛnsəlsˌfiltər]

178. Cars. Crash. Repair

car crash	bilulykke (m/f)	['bil ʉ'lʏkə]
traffic accident	trafikkulykke (m/f)	[tra'fik ʉ'lʏkə]
to crash (into the wall, etc.)	å kjøre inn i ...	[ɔ 'çœːrə in i ...]
to get smashed up	å havarere	[ɔ hava'rerə]
damage	skade (m)	['skadə]
intact (unscathed)	uskadd	['ʉˌskad]

breakdown	havari (n)	[hava'ri]
to break down (vi)	å bryte sammen	[ɔ 'brytə 'sɑmən]
towrope	slepetau (n)	['slepəˌtaʊ]

puncture	punktering (m)	[pʉn'teriŋ]
to be flat	å være punktert	[ɔ 'værə pʉnk'tɛːt]
to pump up	å pumpe opp	[ɔ 'pʉmpə ɔp]
pressure	trykk (n)	['trʏk]
to check (to examine)	å sjekke	[ɔ 'ʂɛkə]

| repair | reparasjon (m) | [repara'ʂʊn] |
| auto repair shop | bilverksted (n) | ['bil 'værkˌsted] |

| spare part | reservedel (m) | [re'sɛrvə,del] |
| part | del (m) | ['del] |

bolt (with nut)	bolt (m)	['bɔlt]
screw (fastener)	skrue (m)	['skruə]
nut	mutter (m)	['muter]
washer	skive (m/f)	['ṣivə]
bearing	lager (n)	['lagər]

tube	rør (m)	['rør]
gasket (head ~)	pakning (m/f)	['pakniŋ]
cable, wire	ledning (m)	['ledniŋ]

jack	jekk (m), donkraft (m/f)	['jɛk], ['dɔn,kraft]
wrench	skrunøkkel (m)	['skru,nøkəl]
hammer	hammer (m)	['hamər]
pump	pumpe (m/f)	['pumpə]
screwdriver	skrutrekker (m)	['skru,trɛkər]

| fire extinguisher | brannslukker (n) | ['brɑn,slukər] |
| warning triangle | varseltrekant (m) | ['vaṣəl 'trɛ,kɑnt] |

to stall (vi)	å skjære	[ɔ 'ṣæ:rə]
stall (n)	stans (m), stopp (m/n)	['stɑns], ['stɔp]
to be broken	å være ødelagt	[ɔ 'værə 'ødə,lɑkt]

to overheat (vi)	å bli overopphetet	[ɔ 'bli 'ɔvərɔp,hetət]
to be clogged up	å bli tilstoppet	[ɔ 'bli til'stɔpət]
to freeze up (pipes, etc.)	å fryse	[ɔ 'frysə]
to burst (vi, ab. tube)	å sprekke, å briste	[ɔ 'sprɛkə], [ɔ 'bristə]

pressure	trykk (n)	['trʏk]
level	nivå (n)	[ni'vo]
slack (~ belt)	slakk	['ṣlɑk]

dent	bulk (m)	['bulk]
knocking noise (engine)	bankelyd (m), dunk (m/n)	['bankə,lyd], ['dunk]
crack	sprekk (m)	['sprɛk]
scratch	ripe (m/f)	['ripə]

179. Cars. Road

road	vei (m)	['væj]
highway	hovedvei (m)	['huvəd,væj]
freeway	motorvei (m)	['mɔtur,væj]
direction (way)	retning (m/f)	['rɛtniŋ]
distance	avstand (m)	['af,stɑn]

| bridge | bro (m/f) | ['bru] |
| parking lot | parkeringsplass (m) | [par'keriŋs,plɑs] |

square	**torg** (n)	['tɔr]
interchange	**trafikkmaskin** (m)	[tra'fik mɑˌʂin]
tunnel	**tunnel** (m)	['tʉnəl]
gas station	**bensinstasjon** (m)	[bɛn'sinˌsta'ʂʉn]
parking lot	**parkeringsplass** (m)	[par'keriŋsˌplas]
gas pump (fuel dispenser)	**bensinpumpe** (m/f)	[bɛn'sinˌpʉmpə]
auto repair shop	**bilverksted** (n)	['bil 'værkˌsted]
to get gas (to fill up)	**å tanke opp**	[ɔ 'tankə ɔp]
fuel	**brensel** (n)	['brɛnsəl]
jerrycan	**bensinkanne** (m/f)	[bɛn'sinˌkɑnə]
asphalt	**asfalt** (m)	['asˌfalt]
road markings	**vegoppmerking** (m/f)	['veg 'ɔpˌmærkiŋ]
curb	**fortauskant** (m)	['fɔːtɑʉsˌkant]
guardrail	**autovern, veirekkverk** (n)	['aʉtoˌvæːŋ], ['væjˌrekværk]
ditch	**veigrøft** (m/f)	['væjˌgrœft]
roadside (shoulder)	**veikant** (m)	['væjˌkant]
lamppost	**lyktestolpe** (m)	['lʏktəˌstɔlpə]
to drive (a car)	**å kjøre**	[ɔ 'çœːrə]
to turn (e.g., ~ left)	**å svinge**	[ɔ 'sviŋə]
to make a U-turn	**å ta en U-sving**	[ɔ 'ta en 'ʉːˌsviŋ]
reverse (~ gear)	**revers** (m)	[re'væʂ]
to honk (vi)	**å tute**	[ɔ 'tʉtə]
honk (sound)	**tut** (n)	['tʉt]
to get stuck (in the mud, etc.)	**å kjøre seg fast**	[ɔ 'çœːrə sæj 'fast]
to spin the wheels	**å spinne**	[ɔ 'spinə]
to cut, to turn off (vt)	**å stanse**	[ɔ 'stansə]
speed	**hastighet** (m/f)	['hastiˌhet]
to exceed the speed limit	**å overskride fartsgrensen**	[ɔ 'ɔvəˌskridə 'faːʈsˌgrɛnsən]
to give a ticket	**å gi bot**	[ɔ 'ji 'bʉt]
traffic lights	**trafikklys** (n)	[tra'fikˌlys]
driver's license	**førerkort** (n)	['førərˌkɔːt]
grade crossing	**planovergang** (m)	['plan 'ɔvərˌgaŋ]
intersection	**veikryss** (n)	['væjkrʏs]
crosswalk	**fotgjengerovergang** (m)	['fʉtjɛŋər 'ɔvɔrˌgaŋ]
bend, curve	**kurve** (m)	['kʉrvə]
pedestrian zone	**gågate** (m/f)	['goːˌgatə]

180. Traffic signs

rules of the road	**trafikkregler** (m pl)	[tra'fikˌrɛglər]
road sign (traffic sign)	**trafikkskilt** (n)	[tra'fikˌʂilt]
passing (overtaking)	**forbikjøring** (m/f)	['fɔrbiˌçœriŋ]

curve	Sving	['sviŋ]
U-turn	u-sving, u-vending	['ʉːˌsviŋ], ['ʉːˌvɛniŋ]
traffic circle	rundkjøring	['rʉnˌçœriŋ]

No entry	Innkjøring forbudt	['inˈçœriŋ fɔrˈbʉt]
No vehicles allowed	Trafikkforbud	[traˈfik fɔrˌbʉt]
No passing	Forbikjøring forbudt	['fɔrbiˌçœriŋ fɔrˈbʉt]
No parking	Parkering forbudt	[parˈkeriŋ fɔrˈbʉt]
No stopping	Stans forbudt	['stɑns fɔrˈbʉt]

dangerous bend	Farlig sving	['fɑːʟi ˌsviŋ]
steep descent	Bratt bakke	['brɑt ˌbɑkə]
one-way traffic	Enveiskjøring	['ɛnvæjsˌsøriŋ]
crosswalk	fotgjengerovergang (m)	['fʉtjɛŋər 'ɔverˌgɑn]
slippery road	Glatt kjørebane	['glɑt 'çœːrəˌbɑnə]
YIELD	Vikeplikt	['vikəˌplikt]

PEOPLE. LIFE EVENTS

Life events

181. Holidays. Event

celebration, holiday	**fest** (m)	['fɛst]
national day	**nasjonaldag** (m)	[nɑsʉ'nɑlˌdɑ]
public holiday	**festdag** (m)	['fɛstˌdɑ]
to commemorate (vt)	**å feire**	[ɔ 'fæjrə]
event (happening)	**begivenhet** (m/f)	[be'jivenˌhet]
event (organized activity)	**evenement** (n)	[ɛvenə'mɑŋ]
banquet (party)	**bankett** (m)	[bɑn'kɛt]
reception (formal party)	**resepsjon** (m)	[resɛp'sʉn]
feast	**fest** (n)	['fɛst]
anniversary	**årsdag** (m)	['oːʂˌdɑ]
jubilee	**jubileum** (n)	[jʉbi'leʉm]
to celebrate (vt)	**å feire**	[ɔ 'fæjrə]
New Year	**nytt år** (n)	['nʏt ˌoːr]
Happy New Year!	**Godt nytt år!**	['gɔt nʏt ˌoːr]
Santa Claus	**Julenissen**	['jʉləˌnisən]
Christmas	**Jul** (m/f)	['jʉl]
Merry Christmas!	**Gledelig jul!**	['gledəli 'jʉl]
Christmas tree	**juletre** (n)	['jʉləˌtrɛ]
fireworks (fireworks show)	**fyrverkeri** (n)	[ˌfyrværkə'ri]
wedding	**bryllup** (n)	['brʏlʉp]
groom	**brudgom** (m)	['brʉdˌgɔm]
bride	**brud** (m/f)	['brʉd]
to invite (vt)	**å innby, å invitere**	[ɔ 'inby], [ɔ invi'terə]
invitation card	**innbydelse** (m)	[in'bydəlsə]
guest	**gjest** (m)	['jɛst]
to visit (~ your parents, etc.)	**å besøke**	[ɔ be'søkə]
to meet the guests	**å hilse på gjestene**	[ɔ 'hilsə pɔ 'jɛstenə]
gift, present	**gave** (m/f)	['gɑvə]
to give (sth as present)	**å gi**	[ɔ 'ji]
to receive gifts	**å få gaver**	[ɔ 'fɔ 'gɑvər]

bouquet (of flowers)	bukett (m)	[bʉ'kɛt]
congratulations	lykkønskning (m/f)	['lʏkˌønskniŋ]
to congratulate (vt)	å gratulere	[ɔ gratʉ'lerə]

greeting card	gratulasjonskort (n)	[gratʉla'ʂʊnsˌkɔːt]
to send a postcard	å sende postkort	[ɔ 'sɛnə 'pɔstˌkɔːt]
to get a postcard	å få postkort	[ɔ 'fɔ 'pɔstˌkɔːt]

toast	skål (m/f)	['skɔl]
to offer (a drink, etc.)	å tilby	[ɔ 'tilby]
champagne	champagne (m)	[ʂam'panjə]

to enjoy oneself	å more seg	[ɔ 'mʊrə sæj]
merriment (gaiety)	munterhet (m)	['mʉntərˌhet]
joy (emotion)	glede (m/f)	['gledə]

| dance | dans (m) | ['dans] |
| to dance (vi, vt) | å danse | [ɔ 'dansə] |

| waltz | vals (m) | ['vals] |
| tango | tango (m) | ['taŋgʊ] |

182. Funerals. Burial

cemetery	gravplass, kirkegård (m)	['gravˌplas], ['çirkəˌgɔːr]
grave, tomb	grav (m)	['grav]
cross	kors (n)	['kɔːʂ]
gravestone	gravstein (m)	['grafˌstæjn]
fence	gjerde (n)	['jærə]
chapel	kapell (n)	[ka'pɛl]

death	død (m)	['dø]
to die (vi)	å dø	[ɔ 'dø]
the deceased	den avdøde	[den 'avˌdødə]
mourning	sorg (m/f)	['sɔr]
to bury (vt)	å begrave	[ɔ be'gravə]
funeral home	begravelsesbyrå (n)	[be'gravəlsəs byˌro]
funeral	begravelse (m)	[be'gravəlsə]

wreath	krans (m)	['krans]
casket, coffin	likkiste (m/f)	['likˌçistə]
hearse	likbil (m)	['likˌbil]
shroud	likklede (n)	['likˌkledə]

funeral procession	gravfølge (n)	['gravˌfølgə]
funerary urn	askeurne (m/f)	['askəˌʉːnə]
crematory	krematorium (n)	[krɛma'tʊrium]
obituary	nekrolog (m)	[nekrʊ'lɔg]
to cry (weep)	å gråte	[ɔ 'groːtə]
to sob (vi)	å hulke	[ɔ 'hʉlkə]

183. War. Soldiers

platoon	**tropp** (m)	['trɔp]
company	**kompani** (n)	[kʊmpɑ'ni]
regiment	**regiment** (n)	[rɛgi'mɛnt]
army	**hær** (m)	['hær]
division	**divisjon** (m)	[divi'ʂʊn]
section, squad	**tropp** (m)	['trɔp]
host (army)	**hær** (m)	['hær]
soldier	**soldat** (m)	[sʊl'dɑt]
officer	**offiser** (m)	[ɔfi'sɛr]
private	**menig** (m)	['meni]
sergeant	**sersjant** (m)	[sær'ʂɑnt]
lieutenant	**løytnant** (m)	['løjt,nɑnt]
captain	**kaptein** (m)	[kɑp'tæjn]
major	**major** (m)	[mɑ'jɔr]
colonel	**oberst** (m)	['ʊbɛʂt]
general	**general** (m)	[gene'rɑl]
sailor	**sjømann** (m)	['ʂø,mɑn]
captain	**kaptein** (m)	[kɑp'tæjn]
boatswain	**båtsmann** (m)	['bɔs,mɑn]
artilleryman	**artillerist** (m)	[ˌɑːʈile'rist]
paratrooper	**fallskjermjeger** (m)	['fɑl,ʂærm 'jɛːgər]
pilot	**flyger, flyver** (m)	['flygər], ['flyvər]
navigator	**styrmann** (m)	['styr,mɑn]
mechanic	**mekaniker** (m)	[me'kɑnikər]
pioneer (sapper)	**pioner** (m)	[piʊ'ner]
parachutist	**fallskjermhopper** (m)	['fɑl,ʂærm 'hɔpər]
reconnaissance scout	**oppklaringssoldat** (m)	['ɔp,klɑriŋ sʊl'dɑt]
sniper	**skarpskytte** (m)	['skɑrp,ʂytə]
patrol (group)	**patrulje** (m)	[pɑ'trʉlje]
to patrol (vt)	**å patruljere**	[ɔ patrʉ'ljerə]
sentry, guard	**vakt** (m)	['vɑkt]
warrior	**kriger** (m)	['krigər]
hero	**helt** (m)	['hɛlt]
heroine	**heltinne** (m)	['hɛlt,inə]
patriot	**patriot** (m)	[pɑtri'ɔt]
traitor	**forræder** (m)	[fo'rædər]
to betray (vt)	**å forråde**	[ɔ fo'rɔːdə]
deserter	**desertør** (m)	[desæ:'ʈør]
to desert (vi)	**å desertere**	[ɔ desæ:'ʈerə]
mercenary	**leiesoldat** (m)	['læjəsʊl,dɑt]

| recruit | rekrutt (m) | [re'krʉt] |
| volunteer | frivillig (m) | ['fri,vili] |

dead (n)	drept (m)	['drɛpt]
wounded (n)	såret (m)	['soːrə]
prisoner of war	fange (m)	['faŋə]

184. War. Military actions. Part 1

war	krig (m)	['krig]
to be at war	å være i krig	[ɔ 'værə i ˌkrig]
civil war	borgerkrig (m)	['bɔrgər,krig]

treacherously (adv)	lumsk, forræderisk	['lʉmsk], [fɔ'rædərisk]
declaration of war	krigserklæring (m)	['krigs ær,klæriŋ]
to declare (~ war)	å erklære	[ɔ ær'klærə]
aggression	aggresjon (m)	[agre'sʉn]
to attack (invade)	å angripe	[ɔ 'an,gripə]

to invade (vt)	å invadere	[ɔ inva'derə]
invader	angriper (m)	['an,gripər]
conqueror	erobrer (m)	[ɛ'rʉbrər]

defense	forsvar (n)	['fʉ,svar]
to defend (a country, etc.)	å forsvare	[ɔ fɔ'svarə]
to defend (against ...)	å forsvare seg	[ɔ fɔ'svarə sæj]

enemy	fiende (m)	['fiɛndə]
foe, adversary	motstander (m)	['mʉt,stanər]
enemy (as adj)	fiendtlig	['fjɛntli]

| strategy | strategi (m) | [strate'gi] |
| tactics | taktikk (m) | [tak'tik] |

order	ordre (m)	['ɔrdrə]
command (order)	ordre, kommando (m/f)	['ɔrdrə], ['kʉ'mandʉ]
to order (vt)	å beordre	[ɔ be'ɔrdrə]
mission	oppdrag (m)	['ɔpdrag]
secret (adj)	hemmelig	['hɛməli]

battle	batalje (m)	[ba'taljə]
battle	slag (n)	['ʂlag]
combat	kamp (m)	['kamp]

attack	angrep (n)	['an,grɛp]
charge (assault)	storm (m)	['stɔrm]
to storm (vt)	å storme	[ɔ 'stɔrmə]
siege (to be under ~)	beleiring (m/f)	[be'læjriŋ]
offensive (n)	offensiv (m), angrep (n)	['ɔfen,sif], ['an,grɛp]
to go on the offensive	å angripe	[ɔ 'an,gripə]

| retreat | retrett (m) | [rɛ'trɛt] |
| to retreat (vi) | å retirere | [ɔ reti'rerə] |

| encirclement | omringing (m/f) | ['ɔmˌriŋiŋ] |
| to encircle (vt) | å omringe | [ɔ 'ɔmˌriŋə] |

bombing (by aircraft)	bombing (m/f)	['bʊmbiŋ]
to drop a bomb	å slippe bombe	[ɔ 'ʂlipə 'bʊmbə]
to bomb (vt)	å bombardere	[ɔ bʊmbɑ:'ɖerə]
explosion	eksplosjon (m)	[ɛksplʊ'ʂʊn]

shot	skudd (n)	['skʉd]
to fire (~ a shot)	å skyte av	[ɔ 'ʂytə ɑ:]
firing (burst of ~)	skytning (m/f)	['ʂytniŋ]

to aim (to point a weapon)	å sikte på ...	[ɔ 'siktə pɔ ...]
to point (a gun)	å rette	[ɔ 'rɛtə]
to hit (the target)	å treffe	[ɔ 'trɛfə]

to sink (~ a ship)	å senke	[ɔ 'sɛnkə]
hole (in a ship)	hull (n)	['hʉl]
to founder, to sink (vi)	å synke	[ɔ 'synkə]

front (war ~)	front (m)	['frɔnt]
evacuation	evakuering (m/f)	[ɛvɑkʉ'eriŋ]
to evacuate (vt)	å evakuere	[ɔ ɛvɑkʉ'erə]

trench	skyttergrav (m)	['ʂytəˌgrav]
barbwire	piggtråd (m)	['pigˌtrɔd]
barrier (anti tank ~)	hinder (n), sperring (m/f)	['hinɖər], ['spɛriŋ]
watchtower	vakttårn (n)	['vaktˌtɔ:n]

military hospital	militærsykehus (n)	[mili'tærˌsykə'hʉs]
to wound (vt)	å såre	[ɔ 'so:rə]
wound	sår (n)	['sɔr]
wounded (n)	såret (n)	['so:rə]
to be wounded	å bli såret	[ɔ 'bli 'so:rət]
serious (wound)	alvorlig	[al'vɔ:ɭi]

185. War. Military actions. Part 2

captivity	fangeskap (n)	['faŋəˌskap]
to take captive	å ta til fange	[ɔ 'ta til 'faŋə]
to be held captive	å være i fangeskap	[ɔ 'værə i 'faŋəˌskap]
to be taken captive	å bli tatt til fange	[ɔ 'bli tat til 'faŋə]

concentration camp	konsentrasjonsleir (m)	[kʊnsəntra'ʂʊnsˌlæjr]
prisoner of war	fange (m)	['faŋə]
to escape (vi)	å flykte	[ɔ 'flʏktə]
to betray (vt)	å forråde	[ɔ fɔ'rɔ:də]

betrayer	**forræder** (m)	[fɔ'rædər]
betrayal	**forræderi** (n)	[fɔrædə'ri]
to execute (by firing squad)	**å henrette ved skyting**	[ɔ 'hɛnˌrɛtə ve 'ʂytiŋ]
execution (by firing squad)	**skyting** (m/f)	['ʂytiŋ]
equipment (military gear)	**mundering** (m/f)	[mʉn'dɛriŋ]
shoulder board	**skulderklaff** (m)	['skʉldərˌklaf]
gas mask	**gassmaske** (m/f)	['gasˌmaskə]
field radio	**feltradio** (m)	['fɛltˌradiʊ]
cipher, code	**chiffer** (n)	['ʂifər]
secrecy	**hemmeligholdelse** (m)	['hɛməliˌhɔləlsə]
password	**passord** (n)	['pɑsˌuːr]
land mine	**mine** (m/f)	['minə]
to mine (road, etc.)	**å minelegge**	[ɔ 'minəˌlegə]
minefield	**minefelt** (n)	['minəˌfɛlt]
air-raid warning	**flyalarm** (m)	['fly a'larm]
alarm (alert signal)	**alarm** (m)	[a'larm]
signal	**signal** (n)	[siŋ'nal]
signal flare	**signalrakett** (m)	[siŋ'nal ra'kɛt]
headquarters	**stab** (m)	['stab]
reconnaissance	**oppklaring** (m/f)	['ɔpˌklariŋ]
situation	**situasjon** (m)	[sitʉa'ʂun]
report	**rapport** (m)	[ra'pɔːt]
ambush	**bakhold** (n)	['bakˌhɔl]
reinforcement (of army)	**forsterkning** (m/f)	[fɔ'ʂtærkniŋ]
target	**mål** (n)	['mol]
proving ground	**skytefelt** (n)	['ʂytəˌfɛlt]
military exercise	**manøverer** (m pl)	[ma'nøvər]
panic	**panikk** (m)	[pa'nik]
devastation	**ødeleggelse** (m)	['ødəˌlegəlsə]
destruction, ruins	**ruiner** (m pl)	[rʉ'inər]
to destroy (vt)	**å ødelegge**	[ɔ 'ødəˌlegə]
to survive (vi, vt)	**å overleve**	[ɔ 'ɔvəˌlevə]
to disarm (vt)	**å avvæpne**	[ɔ 'avˌvæpnə]
to handle (~ a gun)	**å handtere**	[ɔ han'terə]
Attention!	**Rett! | Gi-akt!**	['rɛt], ['ji:'ɑkt]
At ease!	**Hvil!**	['vil]
act of courage	**bedrift** (m)	[be'drift]
oath (vow)	**ed** (m)	['ɛd]
to swear (an oath)	**å sverge**	[ɔ 'sværgə]
decoration (medal, etc.)	**belønning** (m/f)	[be'lœniŋ]

to award (give medal to)	å belønne	[ɔ be'lœnə]
medal	medalje (m)	[me'daljə]
order (e.g., ~ of Merit)	orden (m)	['ɔrdən]

victory	seier (m)	['sæjər]
defeat	nederlag (n)	['nedə‚lag]
armistice	våpenhvile (m)	['vɔpən‚vilə]

standard (battle flag)	fane (m)	['fɑnə]
glory (honor, fame)	berømmelse (m)	[be'rœməlsə]
parade	parade (m)	[pɑ'rɑdə]
to march (on parade)	å marsjere	[ɔ mɑ'ʂerə]

186. Weapons

weapons	våpen (n)	['vɔpən]
firearms	skytevåpen (n)	['ʂytə‚vɔpən]
cold weapons (knives, etc.)	blankvåpen (n)	['blɑŋk‚vɔpən]

chemical weapons	kjemisk våpen (n)	['çemisk ‚vɔpən]
nuclear (adj)	kjerne-	['çæːŋə-]
nuclear weapons	kjernevåpen (n)	['çæːŋə‚vɔpən]

| bomb | bombe (m) | ['bʊmbə] |
| atomic bomb | atombombe (m) | [ɑ'tʊm‚bʊmbə] |

pistol (gun)	pistol (m)	[pi'stʊl]
rifle	gevær (n)	[ge'vær]
submachine gun	maskinpistol (m)	[mɑ'ʂin pi‚stʊl]
machine gun	maskingevær (n)	[mɑ'ʂin ge‚vær]

muzzle	munning (m)	['mʉniŋ]
barrel	løp (n)	['løp]
caliber	kaliber (m/n)	[kɑ'libər]

trigger	avtrekker (m)	['ɑv‚trɛkər]
sight (aiming device)	sikte (n)	['siktə]
magazine	magasin (n)	[mɑgɑ'sin]
butt (shoulder stock)	kolbe (m)	['kɔlbə]

| hand grenade | håndgranat (m) | ['hɔn‚grɑ'nɑt] |
| explosive | sprengstoff (n) | ['sprɛŋ‚stɔf] |

bullet	kule (m/f)	['kʉːlə]
cartridge	patron (m)	[pɑ'trʊn]
charge	ladning (m)	['lɑdniŋ]
ammunition	ammunisjon (m)	[ɑmʉni'ʂʊn]
bomber (aircraft)	bombefly (n)	['bʊmbə‚fly]
fighter	jagerfly (n)	['jɑgər‚fly]

helicopter	helikopter (n)	[heli'kɔptər]
anti-aircraft gun	luftvernkanon (m)	['lʉftvɛːn̩ kɑ'nʉn]
tank	stridsvogn (m/f)	['strids‚vɔŋn]
tank gun	kanon (m)	[kɑ'nʉn]

artillery	artilleri (n)	[‚ɑːṭile'ri]
gun (cannon, howitzer)	kanon (m)	[kɑ'nʉn]
to lay (a gun)	å rette	[ɔ 'rɛtə]

shell (projectile)	projektil (m)	[prʉek'til]
mortar bomb	granat (m/f)	[grɑ'nɑt]
mortar	granatkaster (m)	[grɑ'nɑt‚kɑstər]
splinter (shell fragment)	splint (m)	['splint]

submarine	ubåt (m)	['ʉːˌbɔt]
torpedo	torpedo (m)	[tʉr'pedʉ]
missile	rakett (m)	[rɑ'kɛt]

to load (gun)	å lade	[ɔ 'lɑdə]
to shoot (vi)	å skyte	[ɔ 'ṣytə]
to point at (the cannon)	å sikte på ...	[ɔ 'siktə pɔ ...]
bayonet	bajonett (m)	[bɑjo'nɛt]

rapier	kårde (m)	['koːrdə]
saber (e.g., cavalry ~)	sabel (m)	['sɑbəl]
spear (weapon)	spyd (n)	['spyd]
bow	bue (m)	['bʉːə]
arrow	pil (m/f)	['pil]
musket	muskett (m)	[mʉ'skɛt]
crossbow	armbrøst (m)	['ɑrm‚brøst]

187. Ancient people

primitive (prehistoric)	ur-	['ʉr-]
prehistoric (adj)	forhistorisk	['fɔrhi‚stʉrisk]
ancient (~ civilization)	oldtidens, antikkens	['ɔl‚tidəns], [ɑn'tikəns]

Stone Age	Steinalderen	['stæjn‚ɑlderən]
Bronze Age	bronsealder (m)	['brɔnsə‚ɑldər]
Ice Age	istid (m/f)	['is‚tid]

tribe	stamme (m)	['stɑmə]
cannibal	kannibal (m)	[kɑni'bɑl]
hunter	jeger (m)	['jɛːgər]
to hunt (vi, vt)	å jage	[ɔ 'jɑgə]
mammoth	mammut (m)	['mɑmʉt]

cave	grotte (m/f)	['grɔtə]
fire	ild (m)	['il]
campfire	bål (n)	['bɔl]

cave painting	**helleristning** (m/f)	['hɛlə,ristniŋ]
tool (e.g., stone ax)	**redskap** (m/n)	['rɛd,skɑp]
spear	**spyd** (n)	['spyd]
stone ax	**steinøks** (m/f)	['stæjn,øks]
to be at war	**å være i krig**	[ɔ 'værə i ,krig]
to domesticate (vt)	**å temme**	[ɔ 'tɛmə]
idol	**idol** (n)	[i'dʊl]
to worship (vt)	**å dyrke**	[ɔ 'dyrkə]
superstition	**overtro** (m)	['ɔvə,trʊ]
rite	**ritual** (n)	[ritʉ'ɑl]
evolution	**evolusjon** (m)	[ɛvɔlʉ'ʂʊn]
development	**utvikling** (m/f)	['ʉt,vikliŋ]
disappearance (extinction)	**forsvinning** (m/f)	[fɔ'ʂviniŋ]
to adapt oneself	**å tilpasse seg**	[ɔ 'til,pɑsə sæj]
archeology	**arkeologi** (m)	[,ɑrkeʊlʊ'gi]
archeologist	**arkeolog** (m)	[,ɑrkeʊ'lɔg]
archeological (adj)	**arkeologisk**	[,ɑrkeʊ'lɔgisk]
excavation site	**utgravingssted** (n)	['ʉt,gravins ,sted]
excavations	**utgravinger** (m/f pl)	['ʉt,gravinər]
find (object)	**funn** (n)	['fʉn]
fragment	**fragment** (n)	[frɑg'mɛnt]

188. Middle Ages

people (ethnic group)	**folk** (n)	['fɔlk]
peoples	**folk** (n pl)	['fɔlk]
tribe	**stamme** (m)	['stɑmə]
tribes	**stammer** (m pl)	['stɑmər]
barbarians	**barbarer** (m pl)	[bɑr'bɑrər]
Gauls	**gallere** (m pl)	['gɑlere]
Goths	**gotere** (m pl)	['gɔterə]
Slavs	**slavere** (m pl)	['slɑvɛrə]
Vikings	**vikinger** (m pl)	['vikiŋər]
Romans	**romere** (m pl)	['rʊmerə]
Roman (adj)	**romersk**	['rʊmæʂk]
Byzantines	**bysantiner** (m pl)	[bysɑn'tinər]
Byzantium	**Bysants**	[by'sɑnts]
Byzantine (adj)	**bysantinsk**	[bysɑn'tinsk]
emperor	**keiser** (m)	['kæjsər]
leader, chief (tribal ~)	**høvding** (m)	['høvdiŋ]
powerful (~ king)	**mektig**	['mɛkti]
king	**konge** (m)	['kʊŋə]

ruler (sovereign)	**hersker** (m)	['hæʂkər]
knight	**ridder** (m)	['ridər]
feudal lord	**føydalherre** (m)	['føjdɑlˌhɛrə]
feudal (adj)	**føydal**	['føjdɑl]
vassal	**vasall** (m)	[vɑ'sɑl]
duke	**hertug** (m)	['hæːʈʉg]
earl	**greve** (m)	['grevə]
baron	**baron** (m)	[bɑ'rʊn]
bishop	**biskop** (m)	['biskɔp]
armor	**rustning** (m/f)	['rʉstniŋ]
shield	**skjold** (n)	['ʂɔl]
sword	**sverd** (n)	['sværd]
visor	**visir** (n)	[vi'sir]
chainmail	**ringbrynje** (m/f)	['riŋˌbrynjə]
Crusade	**korstog** (n)	['kɔːʂˌtog]
crusader	**korsfarer** (m)	['kɔːʂˌfɑrər]
territory	**territorium** (n)	[tɛri'tʊrium]
to attack (invade)	**å angripe**	[ɔ 'ɑnˌgripə]
to conquer (vt)	**å erobre**	[ɔ ɛ'rʊbrə]
to occupy (invade)	**å okkupere**	[ɔ ɔkʉ'perə]
siege (to be under ~)	**beleiring** (m/f)	[be'læjriŋ]
besieged (adj)	**beleiret**	[be'læjrət]
to besiege (vt)	**å beleire**	[ɔ be'læjre]
inquisition	**inkvisisjon** (m)	[inkvisi'ʂʊn]
inquisitor	**inkvisitor** (m)	[inkvi'sitʊr]
torture	**tortur** (m)	[tɔː'ʈʉr]
cruel (adj)	**brutal**	[brʉ'tɑl]
heretic	**kjetter** (m)	['çɛtər]
heresy	**kjetteri** (n)	[çɛtə'ri]
seafaring	**sjøfart** (m)	['ʂøˌfɑːʈ]
pirate	**pirat, sjørøver** (m)	['pi'rɑt], ['ʂøˌrøvər]
piracy	**sjørøveri** (n)	['ʂø røvɛ'ri]
boarding (attack)	**entring** (m/f)	['ɛntriŋ]
loot, booty	**bytte** (n)	['bytə]
treasures	**skatter** (m pl)	['skɑtər]
discovery	**oppdagelse** (m)	['ɔpˌdɑgəlsə]
to discover (new land, etc.)	**å oppdage**	[ɔ 'ɔpˌdɑgə]
expedition	**ekspedisjon** (m)	[ɛkspedi'ʂʊn]
musketeer	**musketer** (m)	[mʉskə'ter]
cardinal	**kardinal** (m)	[kɑːɖi'nɑl]
heraldry	**heraldikk** (m)	[herɑl'dik]
heraldic (adj)	**heraldisk**	[he'rɑldisk]

189. Leader. Chief. Authorities

king	**konge** (m)	['kʊŋə]
queen	**dronning** (m/f)	['drɔniŋ]
royal (adj)	**kongelig**	['kʊŋəli]
kingdom	**kongerike** (n)	['kʊŋəˌrikə]
prince	**prins** (m)	['prins]
princess	**prinsesse** (m/f)	[prin'sɛsə]
president	**president** (m)	[prɛsi'dɛnt]
vice-president	**visepresident** (m)	['visə prɛsi'dɛnt]
senator	**senator** (m)	[se'natʊr]
monarch	**monark** (m)	[mʊ'nɑrk]
ruler (sovereign)	**hersker** (m)	['hæʂkər]
dictator	**diktator** (m)	[dik'tatʊr]
tyrant	**tyrann** (m)	[ty'rɑn]
magnate	**magnat** (m)	[mɑŋ'nɑt]
director	**direktør** (m)	[dirɛk'tør]
chief	**sjef** (m)	['ʂɛf]
manager (director)	**forstander** (m)	[fo'ʂtɑndər]
boss	**boss** (m)	['bɔs]
owner	**eier** (m)	['æjər]
leader	**leder** (m)	['ledər]
head (~ of delegation)	**leder** (m)	['ledər]
authorities	**myndigheter** (m pl)	['mʏndiˌhetər]
superiors	**overordnede** (pl)	['ɔverˌɔrdnedə]
governor	**guvernør** (m)	[gʉver'nør]
consul	**konsul** (m)	['kʊnˌsʉl]
diplomat	**diplomat** (m)	[diplʊ'mɑt]
mayor	**borgermester** (m)	[bɔrgər'mɛstər]
sheriff	**sheriff** (m)	[ʂɛ'rif]
emperor	**keiser** (m)	['kæjsər]
tsar, czar	**tsar** (m)	['tsɑr]
pharaoh	**farao** (m)	['fɑrɑu]
khan	**khan** (m)	['kʉn]

190. Road. Way. Directions

road	**vei** (m)	['væj]
way (direction)	**vei** (m)	['væj]
freeway	**motorvei** (m)	['mɔtʊrˌvæj]
highway	**hovedvei** (m)	['hʊvədˌvæj]

interstate	riksvei (m)	['riks‚væj]
main road	hovedvei (m)	['hʊvəd‚væj]
dirt road	bygdevei (m)	['bʏgdə‚væj]

| pathway | sti (m) | ['sti] |
| footpath (troddenpath) | sti (m) | ['sti] |

Where?	Hvor?	['vʊr]
Where (to)?	Hvorhen?	['vʊrhen]
From where?	Hvorfra?	['vʊrfrɑ]

| direction (way) | retning (m/f) | ['rɛtniŋ] |
| to point (~ the way) | å peke | [ɔ 'pekə] |

to the left	til venstre	[til 'vɛnstrə]
to the right	til høyre	[til 'højrə]
straight ahead (adv)	rett frem	['rɛt frem]
back (e.g., to turn ~)	tilbake	[til'bɑkə]
bend, curve	kurve (m)	['kʉrvə]
to turn (e.g., ~ left)	å svinge	[ɔ 'sviŋə]
to make a U-turn	å ta en U-sving	[ɔ 'tɑ en 'ʉːˌsviŋ]

| to be visible (mountains, castle, etc.) | å være synlig | [ɔ 'værə 'sʏnli] |
| to appear (come into view) | å vise seg | [ɔ 'visə sæj] |

stop, halt (e.g., during a trip)	stopp (m), hvile (m/f)	['stɔp], ['vilə]
to rest, to pause (vi)	å hvile	[ɔ 'vilə]
rest (pause)	hvile (m/f)	['vilə]

to lose one's way	å gå seg vill	[ɔ 'gɔ sæj 'vil]
to lead to ... (ab. road)	å føre til ...	[ɔ 'førə til ...]
to come out (e.g., on the highway)	å komme ut ...	[ɔ 'kɔmə ʉt ...]
stretch (of road)	strekning (m)	['strɛkniŋ]

asphalt	asfalt (m)	['ɑsˌfɑlt]
curb	fortauskant (m)	['fɔːˌtaʊsˌkɑnt]
ditch	veigrøft (m/f)	['væjˌgrœft]
manhole	kum (m), kumlokk (n)	['kʉm], ['kʉmˌlɔk]
roadside (shoulder)	veikant (m)	['væjˌkɑnt]
pit, pothole	grop (m/f)	['grʊp]

| to go (on foot) | å gå | [ɔ 'gɔ] |
| to pass (overtake) | å passere | [ɔ pɑ'serə] |

step (footstep)	skritt (n)	['skrit]
on foot (adv)	til fots	[til 'fʊts]
to block (road)	å sperre	[ɔ 'spɛrə]
boom gate	bom (m)	['bʊm]
dead end	blindgate (m/f)	['blinˌgɑtə]

191. Breaking the law. Criminals. Part 1

bandit	**banditt** (m)	[ban'dit]
crime	**forbrytelse** (m)	[fɔr'brytəlsə]
criminal (person)	**forbryter** (m)	[fɔr'brytər]
thief	**tyv** (m)	['tyv]
to steal (vi, vt)	**å stjele**	[ɔ 'stjelə]
to kidnap (vt)	**å kidnappe**	[ɔ 'kidˌnɛpə]
kidnapping	**kidnapping** (m)	['kidˌnɛpiŋ]
kidnapper	**kidnapper** (m)	['kidˌnɛpər]
ransom	**løsepenger** (m pl)	['løsəˌpɛŋər]
to demand ransom	**å kreve løsepenger**	[ɔ 'krevə 'løsəˌpɛŋər]
to rob (vt)	**å rane**	[ɔ 'ranə]
robbery	**ran** (n)	['ran]
robber	**raner** (m)	['ranər]
to extort (vt)	**å presse ut**	[ɔ 'prɛsə ʉt]
extortionist	**utpresser** (m)	['ʉtˌprɛsər]
extortion	**utpressing** (m/f)	['ʉtˌprɛsiŋ]
to murder, to kill	**å myrde**	[ɔ 'myːɖə]
murder	**mord** (n)	['mʊr]
murderer	**morder** (m)	['mʊrdər]
gunshot	**skudd** (n)	['skʉd]
to fire (~ a shot)	**å skyte av**	[ɔ 'ʂytə aː]
to shoot to death	**å skyte ned**	[ɔ 'ʂytə ne]
to shoot (vi)	**å skyte**	[ɔ 'ʂytə]
shooting	**skyting, skytning** (m/f)	['ʂytiŋ], ['ʂytniŋ]
incident (fight, etc.)	**hendelse** (m)	['hɛndəlsə]
fight, brawl	**slagsmål** (n)	['ʂlaksˌmol]
Help!	**Hjelp!**	['jɛlp]
victim	**offer** (n)	['ɔfər]
to damage (vt)	**å skade**	[ɔ 'skadə]
damage	**skade** (m)	['skadə]
dead body, corpse	**lik** (n)	['lik]
grave (~ crime)	**alvorlig**	[al'voːli]
to attack (vt)	**å anfalle**	[ɔ 'anˌfalə]
to beat (to hit)	**å slå**	[ɔ 'ʂlɔ]
to beat up	**å klå opp**	[ɔ 'klɔ ɔp]
to take (rob of sth)	**å berøve**	[ɔ be'røvə]
to stab to death	**å stikke i hjel**	[ɔ 'stikə i 'jel]
to maim (vt)	**å lemleste**	[ɔ 'lemˌlestə]
to wound (vt)	**å såre**	[ɔ 'soːrə]

blackmail	utpressing (m/f)	['ʉt,prɛsiŋ]
to blackmail (vt)	å utpresse	[ɔ 'ʉt,prɛsə]
blackmailer	utpresser (m)	['ʉt,prɛsər]

protection racket	utpressing (m/f)	['ʉt,prɛsiŋ]
racketeer	utpresser (m)	['ʉt,prɛsər]
gangster	gangster (m)	['gɛŋstər]
mafia, Mob	mafia (m)	['mafia]

pickpocket	lommetyv (m)	['lʊmə,tyv]
burglar	innbruddstyv (m)	['inbrʉds,tyv]
smuggling	smugling (m/f)	['smʉgliŋ]
smuggler	smugler (m)	['smʉglər]

forgery	forfalskning (m/f)	[fɔr'falskniŋ]
to forge (counterfeit)	å forfalske	[ɔ fɔr'falskə]
fake (forged)	falsk	['falsk]

192. Breaking the law. Criminals. Part 2

rape	voldtekt (m)	['vɔl,tɛkt]
to rape (vt)	å voldta	[ɔ 'vɔl,ta]
rapist	voldtektsmann (m)	['vɔl,tɛkts man]
maniac	maniker (m)	['manikər]

prostitute (fem.)	prostituert (m)	[prʊstitʉ'e:t]
prostitution	prostitusjon (m)	[prʊstitʉ'ʂʊn]
pimp	hallik (m)	['halik]

| drug addict | narkoman (m) | [narkʊ'man] |
| drug dealer | narkolanger (m) | ['narkɔ,laŋər] |

to blow up (bomb)	å sprenge	[ɔ 'sprɛŋə]
explosion	eksplosjon (m)	[ɛksplʊ'ʂʊn]
to set fire	å sette fyr	[ɔ 'sɛtə ,fyr]
arsonist	brannstifter (m)	['bran,stiftər]

terrorism	terrorisme (m)	[tɛrʊ'rismə]
terrorist	terrorist (m)	[tɛrʊ'rist]
hostage	gissel (m)	['jisəl]

to swindle (deceive)	å bedra	[ɔ be'dra]
swindle, deception	bedrag (n)	[be'drag]
swindler	bedrager, svindler (m)	[be'dragər], ['svindlər]

to bribe (vt)	å bestikke	[ɔ be'stikə]
bribery	bestikkelse (m)	[be'stikəlsə]
bribe	bestikkelse (m)	[be'stikəlsə]
poison	gift (m/f)	['jift]
to poison (vt)	å forgifte	[ɔ fɔr'jiftə]

to poison oneself	å forgifte seg selv	[ɔ for'jiftə sæj sɛl]
suicide (act)	selvmord (n)	['sɛl̩mʊr]
suicide (person)	selvmorder (m)	['sɛl̩mʊrdər]

to threaten (vt)	å true	[ɔ 'trʉə]
threat	trussel (m)	['trʉsəl]
to make an attempt	å begå mordforsøk	[ɔ be'gɔ 'mʊrdfɔ̩søk]
attempt (attack)	mordforsøk (n)	['mʊrdfɔ̩søk]

| to steal (a car) | å stjele | [ɔ 'stjelə] |
| to hijack (a plane) | å kapre | [ɔ 'kaprə] |

| revenge | hevn (m) | ['hɛvn] |
| to avenge (get revenge) | å hevne | [ɔ 'hɛvnə] |

to torture (vt)	å torturere	[ɔ tɔ:tʉ'rerə]
torture	tortur (m)	[tɔ:'tʉr]
to torment (vt)	å plage	[ɔ 'plagə]

pirate	pirat, sjørøver (m)	['pi'rat], ['ʂø̩røvər]
hooligan	bølle (m)	['bølə]
armed (adj)	bevæpnet	[be'væpnət]
violence	vold (m)	['vɔl]
illegal (unlawful)	illegal	['ile̩gal]

| spying (espionage) | spionasje (m) | [spiʊ'naʂə] |
| to spy (vi) | å spionere | [ɔ spiʊ'nerə] |

193. Police. Law. Part 1

| justice | justis (m), rettspleie (m/f) | ['jʉ'stis], ['rɛts̩plæje] |
| court (see you in ~) | rettssal (m) | ['rɛts̩sal] |

judge	dommer (m)	['dɔmər]
jurors	lagrettemedlemmer (n pl)	['lag̩rɛtə medle'mer]
jury trial	lagrette, juryordning (m)	['lag̩rɛtə], ['jʉri̩ordniŋ]
to judge (vt)	å dømme	[ɔ 'dœmə]

lawyer, attorney	advokat (m)	[advʊ'kat]
defendant	anklaget (ui)	['an̩klagət]
dock	anklagebenk (m)	[an'klagə̩bɛnk]

| charge | anklage (m) | ['an̩klagə] |
| accused | anklagede (m) | ['an̩klagədə] |

| sentence | dom (m) | ['dɔm] |
| to sentence (vt) | å dømme | [ɔ 'dœmə] |

| guilty (culprit) | skyldige (m) | ['ʂyldiə] |
| to punish (vt) | å straffe | [ɔ 'strafə] |

punishment	straff, avstraffelse (m)	['strɑf], ['ɑfˌstrɑfəlsə]
fine (penalty)	bot (m/f)	['bʊt]
life imprisonment	livsvarig fengsel (n)	['lifsˌvɑri 'fɛŋsəl]
death penalty	dødsstraff (m/f)	['dødˌstrɑf]
electric chair	elektrisk stol (m)	[ɛ'lektrisk ˌstʊl]
gallows	galge (m)	['gɑlgə]

| to execute (vt) | å henrette | [ɔ 'hɛnˌrɛtə] |
| execution | henrettelse (m) | ['hɛnˌrɛtəlsə] |

| prison, jail | fengsel (n) | ['fɛŋsəl] |
| cell | celle (m) | ['sɛlə] |

escort	eskorte (m)	[ɛs'kɔːtə]
prison guard	fangevokter (m)	['fɑŋəˌvɔktər]
prisoner	fange (m)	['fɑŋə]

| handcuffs | håndjern (n pl) | ['hɔnˌjæːn] |
| to handcuff (vt) | å sette håndjern | [ɔ 'sɛtə 'hɔnˌjæːn] |

prison break	flykt (m/f)	['flʏkt]
to break out (vi)	å flykte, å rømme	[ɔ 'flʏktə], [ɔ 'rœmə]
to disappear (vi)	å forsvinne	[ɔ fɔ'ʂvinə]
to release (from prison)	å løslate	[ɔ 'løsˌlatə]
amnesty	amnesti (m)	[ɑmnɛ'sti]

police	politi (n)	[pʊli'ti]
police officer	politi (m)	[pʊli'ti]
police station	politistasjon (m)	[pʊli'tiˌsta'ʂʊn]
billy club	gummikølle (m/f)	['gʉmiˌkølə]
bullhorn	megafon (m)	[mega'fʉn]

patrol car	patruljebil (m)	[pa'trʉljəˌbil]
siren	sirene (m/f)	[si'renə]
to turn on the siren	å slå på sirenen	[ɔ 'ʂlɔ pɔ si'renən]
siren call	sirene hyl (n)	[si'renə ˌhyl]

crime scene	åsted (n)	['ɔsted]
witness	vitne (n)	['vitnə]
freedom	frihet (m)	['friˌhet]
accomplice	medskyldig (m)	['mɛˌʂyldi]
to flee (vi)	å flykte	[ɔ 'flʏktə]
trace (to leave a ~)	spor (n)	['spʊr]

194. Police. Law. Part 2

search (investigation)	ettersøking (m/f)	['ɛtəˌsøkiŋ]
to look for ...	å søke etter ...	[ɔ 'søkə ˌɛtər ...]
suspicion	mistanke (m)	['misˌtɑŋkə]
suspicious (e.g., ~ vehicle)	mistenkelig	[mis'tɛnkəli]

to stop (cause to halt)	**å stoppe**	[ɔ 'stɔpə]
to detain (keep in custody)	**å anholde**	[ɔ 'anˌhɔlə]
case (lawsuit)	**sak** (m/f)	['sɑk]
investigation	**etterforskning** (m/f)	['ɛtərˌfɔʂkniŋ]
detective	**detektiv** (m)	[detɛk'tiv]
investigator	**etterforsker** (m)	['ɛtərˌfɔʂkər]
hypothesis	**versjon** (m)	[væ'ʂʊn]
motive	**motiv** (n)	[mʊ'tiv]
interrogation	**forhør** (n)	[fɔr'hør]
to interrogate (vt)	**å forhøre**	[ɔ fɔr'hørə]
to question (~ neighbors, etc.)	**å avhøre**	[ɔ 'avˌhørə]
check (identity ~)	**sjekking** (m/f)	['ʂɛkiŋ]
round-up	**rassia, razzia** (m)	['rɑsiɑ]
search (~ warrant)	**ransakelse** (m)	['ranˌsɑkəlsə]
chase (pursuit)	**jakt** (m/f)	['jɑkt]
to pursue, to chase	**å forfølge**	[ɔ fɔr'følə]
to track (a criminal)	**å spore**	[ɔ 'spʊrə]
arrest	**arrest** (m)	[ɑ'rɛst]
to arrest (sb)	**å arrestere**	[ɔ ɑrɛ'sterə]
to catch (thief, etc.)	**å fange**	[ɔ 'fɑŋə]
capture	**pågripelse** (m)	['pɔˌgripəlsə]
document	**dokument** (n)	[dɔkʉ'mɛnt]
proof (evidence)	**bevis** (n)	[be'vis]
to prove (vt)	**å bevise**	[ɔ be'visə]
footprint	**fotspor** (n)	['fʊtˌspʊr]
fingerprints	**fingeravtrykk** (n pl)	['fiŋərˌɑvtrʏk]
piece of evidence	**bevis** (n)	[be'vis]
alibi	**alibi** (n)	['ɑlibi]
innocent (not guilty)	**uskyldig**	[ʉ'ʂʏldi]
injustice	**urettferdighet** (m)	['ʉrɛtfærdiˌhet]
unjust, unfair (adj)	**urettferdig**	['ʉrɛtˌfærdi]
criminal (adj)	**kriminell**	[krimi'nɛl]
to confiscate (vt)	**å konfiskere**	[ɔ kʉnfi'skerə]
drug (illegal substance)	**narkotika** (m)	[nar'kɔtikɑ]
weapon, gun	**våpen** (n)	['vɔpən]
to disarm (vt)	**å avvæpne**	[ɔ 'avˌvæpnə]
to order (command)	**å befale**	[ɔ be'fɑlə]
to disappear (vi)	**å forsvinne**	[ɔ fɔ'ʂvinə]
law	**lov** (m)	['lɔv]
legal, lawful (adj)	**lovlig**	['lɔvli]
illegal, illicit (adj)	**ulovlig**	[ʉ'lɔvli]
responsibility (blame)	**ansvar** (n)	['anˌsvɑr]
responsible (adj)	**ansvarlig**	[ɑns'vɑːli]

NATURE

The Earth. Part 1

195. Outer space

space	**rommet, kosmos** (n)	['rʊmə], ['kɔsmɔs]
space (as adj)	**rom-**	['rʊm-]
outer space	**ytre rom** (n)	['ytrə ˌrʊm]
world	**verden** (m)	['værdən]
universe	**univers** (n)	[ʉni'væʂ]
galaxy	**galakse** (m)	[ga'laksə]
star	**stjerne** (m/f)	['stjæ:ŋə]
constellation	**stjernebilde** (n)	['stjæ:ŋəˌbildə]
planet	**planet** (m)	[pla'net]
satellite	**satellitt** (m)	[satɛ'lit]
meteorite	**meteoritt** (m)	[meteʊ'rit]
comet	**komet** (m)	[kʊ'met]
asteroid	**asteroide** (n)	[asterʊ'idə]
orbit	**bane** (m)	['banə]
to revolve (~ around the Earth)	**å rotere**	[ɔ rɔ'terə]
atmosphere	**atmosfære** (m)	[atmʊ'sfærə]
the Sun	**Solen**	['sʊlən]
solar system	**solsystem** (n)	['sʊl sy'stem]
solar eclipse	**solformørkelse** (m)	['sʊl fɔr'mœrkəlsə]
the Earth	**Jorden**	['ju:rən]
the Moon	**Månen**	['mo:nən]
Mars	**Mars**	['maʂ]
Venus	**Venus**	['venʉs]
Jupiter	**Jupiter**	['jʉpitər]
Saturn	**Saturn**	['saˌtʉ:ŋ]
Mercury	**Merkur**	[mær'kʉr]
Uranus	**Uranus**	[ʉ'ranʉs]
Neptune	**Neptun**	[nɛp'tʉn]
Pluto	**Pluto**	['plʉtʊ]
Milky Way	**Melkeveien**	['mɛlkəˌvæjən]
Great Bear (Ursa Major)	**den Store Bjørn**	['dən 'stʊrə ˌbjœ:ŋ]

North Star	Nordstjernen, Polaris	['nuːrˌstjæːnən], [poˈlaris]
Martian	marsbeboer (m)	['masˌbebʊər]
extraterrestrial (n)	utenomjordisk vesen (n)	['ʉtənɔmjuːrdisk 'vesən]
alien	romvesen (n)	['rʊmˌvesən]
flying saucer	flygende tallerken (m)	['flygənə taˈlærkən]
spaceship	romskip (n)	['rʊmˌʂip]
space station	romstasjon (m)	['rʊmˌstaˈʂʊn]
blast-off	start (m), oppskyting (m/f)	['staːt], ['ɔpˌʂytiŋ]
engine	motor (m)	['mɔtʊr]
nozzle	dyse (m)	['dysə]
fuel	brensel (n), drivstoff (n)	['brɛnsəl], ['drifˌstɔf]
cockpit, flight deck	cockpit (m), flydekk (n)	['kɔkpit], ['flyˌdɛk]
antenna	antenne (m)	[ɑnˈtɛnə]
porthole	koøye (n)	['kʊˌøjə]
solar panel	solbatteri (n)	['sʊl batɛˈri]
spacesuit	romdrakt (m/f)	['rʊmˌdrɑkt]
weightlessness	vektløshet (m/f)	['vɛktløsˌhet]
oxygen	oksygen (n)	['ɔksyˈgen]
docking (in space)	dokking (m/f)	['dɔkiŋ]
to dock (vi, vt)	å dokke	[ɔ 'dɔkə]
observatory	observatorium (n)	[ɔbsərvaˈtʊrium]
telescope	teleskop (n)	[teleˈskʊp]
to observe (vt)	å observere	[ɔ ɔbsɛrˈverə]
to explore (vt)	å utforske	[ɔ 'ʉtˌfɔʂkə]

196. The Earth

the Earth	Jorden	['juːrən]
the globe (the Earth)	jordklode (m)	['juːrˌklɔdə]
planet	planet (m)	[plɑˈnet]
atmosphere	atmosfære (m)	[ɑtmʊˈsfærə]
geography	geografi (m)	[geʊgrɑˈfi]
nature	natur (m)	[nɑˈtʉr]
globe (table ~)	globus (m)	['glɔbʉs]
map	kart (n)	['kɑːt]
atlas	atlas (n)	['ɑtlɑs]
Europe	Europa	[ɛʉˈrʊpɑ]
Asia	Asia	['ɑsiɑ]
Africa	Afrika	['ɑfrikɑ]
Australia	Australia	[aʉˈstrɑliɑ]
America	Amerika	[ɑˈmerikɑ]

North America	**Nord-Amerika**	['nuːr ɑ'merikɑ]
South America	**Sør-Amerika**	['sør ɑ'merikɑ]
Antarctica	**Antarktis**	[ɑn'tɑrktis]
the Arctic	**Arktis**	['ɑrktis]

197. Cardinal directions

north	**nord** (n)	['nuːr]
to the north	**mot nord**	[mʊt 'nuːr]
in the north	**i nord**	[i 'nuːr]
northern (adj)	**nordlig**	['nuːrli]
south	**syd, sør**	['syd], ['sør]
to the south	**mot sør**	[mʊt 'sør]
in the south	**i sør**	[i 'sør]
southern (adj)	**sydlig, sørlig**	['sydli], ['søː[i]
west	**vest** (m)	['vɛst]
to the west	**mot vest**	[mʊt 'vɛst]
in the west	**i vest**	[i 'vɛst]
western (adj)	**vestlig, vest-**	['vɛstli]
east	**øst** (m)	['øst]
to the east	**mot øst**	[mʊt 'øst]
in the east	**i øst**	[i 'øst]
eastern (adj)	**østlig**	['østli]

198. Sea. Ocean

sea	**hav** (n)	['hɑv]
ocean	**verdenshav** (n)	[værdəns'hɑv]
gulf (bay)	**bukt** (m/f)	['bʉkt]
straits	**sund** (n)	['sʉn]
land (solid ground)	**fastland** (n)	['fɑst̩lɑn]
continent (mainland)	**fastland, kontinent** (n)	['fɑst̩lɑn], [kʊnti'nɛnt]
island	**øy** (m/f)	['øj]
peninsula	**halvøy** (m/f)	['hɑl̩øːj]
archipelago	**skjærgård** (m), **arkipel** (n)	['sær̩gɔr], [ɑrkipe'lɑg]
bay, cove	**bukt** (m/f)	['bʉkt]
harbor	**havn** (m/f)	['hɑvn]
lagoon	**lagune** (m)	[lɑ'gʉnə]
cape	**nes** (n), **kapp** (n)	['nes], ['kɑp]
atoll	**atoll** (m)	[ɑ'tɔl]
reef	**rev** (n)	['rev]

| coral | korall (m) | [kʊˈrɑl] |
| coral reef | korallrev (n) | [kʊˈrɑlˌrɛv] |

deep (adj)	dyp	[ˈdyp]
depth (deep water)	dybde (m)	[ˈdʏbdə]
abyss	avgrunn (m)	[ˈɑvˌɡrʉn]
trench (e.g., Mariana ~)	dyphavsgrop (m/f)	[ˈdyphɑfsˌɡrɔp]

| current (Ocean ~) | strøm (m) | [ˈstrøm] |
| to surround (bathe) | å omgi | [ɔ ˈɔmˌji] |

| shore | kyst (m) | [ˈçyst] |
| coast | kyst (m) | [ˈçyst] |

flow (flood tide)	flo (m/f)	[ˈflʊ]
ebb (ebb tide)	ebbe (m), fjære (m/f)	[ˈɛbə], [ˈfjærə]
shoal	sandbanke (m)	[ˈsɑnˌbɑnkə]
bottom (~ of the sea)	bunn (m)	[ˈbʉn]

wave	bølge (m)	[ˈbølɡə]
crest (~ of a wave)	bølgekam (m)	[ˈbølɡəˌkɑm]
spume (sea foam)	skum (n)	[ˈskʉm]

storm (sea storm)	storm (m)	[ˈstɔrm]
hurricane	orkan (m)	[ɔrˈkɑn]
tsunami	tsunami (m)	[tsʉˈnɑmi]
calm (dead ~)	stille (m/f)	[ˈstilə]
quiet, calm (adj)	stille	[ˈstilə]

| pole | pol (m) | [ˈpʊl] |
| polar (adj) | pol-, polar | [ˈpʊl-], [pʊˈlɑr] |

latitude	bredde, latitude (m)	[ˈbrɛdə], [ˈlɑtiˌtʉdə]
longitude	lengde (m/f)	[ˈlɛŋdə]
parallel	breddegrad (m)	[ˈbrɛdəˌɡrɑd]
equator	ekvator (m)	[ɛˈkvɑtʊr]

sky	himmel (m)	[ˈhiməl]
horizon	horisont (m)	[hʊriˈsɔnt]
air	luft (f)	[ˈlʉft]

lighthouse	fyr (n)	[ˈfyɪ]
to dive (vi)	å dykke	[ɔ ˈdʏkə]
to sink (ab. boat)	å synke	[ɔ ˈsʏnkə]
treasures	skatter (m pl)	[ˈskɑtər]

199. Seas' and Oceans' names

| Atlantic Ocean | Atlanterhavet | [ɑtˈlɑntərˌhɑve] |
| Indian Ocean | Indiahavet | [ˈindiɑˌhɑve] |

| Pacific Ocean | **Stillehavet** | ['stilə,have] |
| Arctic Ocean | **Polhavet** | ['pɔl,have] |

Black Sea	**Svartehavet**	['svɑ:ʈə,have]
Red Sea	**Rødehavet**	['rødə,have]
Yellow Sea	**Gulehavet**	['gʉlə,have]
White Sea	**Kvitsjøen, Hvitehavet**	['kvit,ʂø:n], ['vit,have]

Caspian Sea	**Kaspihavet**	['kɑspi,have]
Dead Sea	**Dødehavet**	['dødə'have]
Mediterranean Sea	**Middelhavet**	['midəl,have]

| Aegean Sea | **Egeerhavet** | [ɛ'ge:ər,have] |
| Adriatic Sea | **Adriahavet** | ['adria,have] |

Arabian Sea	**Arabiahavet**	[a'rabia,have]
Sea of Japan	**Japanhavet**	['japan,have]
Bering Sea	**Beringhavet**	['beriŋ,have]
South China Sea	**Sør-Kina-havet**	['sør,çina 'have]

Coral Sea	**Korallhavet**	[kʊ'ral,have]
Tasman Sea	**Tasmanhavet**	[tas'man,have]
Caribbean Sea	**Karibhavet**	[ka'rib,have]

| Barents Sea | **Barentshavet** | ['barɛns,have] |
| Kara Sea | **Karahavet** | ['kara,have] |

North Sea	**Nordsjøen**	['nʊ:r,ʂø:n]
Baltic Sea	**Østersjøen**	['østə,ʂø:n]
Norwegian Sea	**Norskehavet**	['nɔʂkə,have]

200. Mountains

mountain	**fjell** (n)	['fjɛl]
mountain range	**fjellkjede** (m)	['fjɛl,çɛ:də]
mountain ridge	**fjellrygg** (m)	['fjɛl,rʏg]

summit, top	**topp** (m)	['tɔp]
peak	**tind** (m)	['tin]
foot (~ of the mountain)	**fot** (m)	['fʊt]
slope (mountainside)	**skråning** (m)	['skrɔniŋ]

volcano	**vulkan** (m)	[vʉl'kan]
active volcano	**virksom vulkan** (m)	['virksɔm vʉl'kan]
dormant volcano	**utslukt vulkan** (m)	['ʉt,slʉkt vʉl'kan]

eruption	**utbrudd** (n)	['ʉt,brʉd]
crater	**krater** (n)	['kratər]
magma	**magma** (m/n)	['magma]
lava	**lava** (m)	['lava]

molten (~ lava)	**glødende**	['gløðenə]
canyon	**canyon** (m)	['kanjən]
gorge	**gjel** (n), **kløft** (m)	['jel], ['klœft]
crevice	**renne** (m/f)	['rɛnə]
abyss (chasm)	**avgrunn** (m)	['ɑv‚grʉn]
pass, col	**pass** (n)	['pɑs]
plateau	**platå** (n)	[plɑ'to]
cliff	**klippe** (m)	['klipə]
hill	**ås** (m)	['ɔs]
glacier	**bre, jøkel** (m)	['bre], ['jøkəl]
waterfall	**foss** (m)	['fɔs]
geyser	**geysir** (m)	['gɛjsir]
lake	**innsjø** (m)	['in‚ʂø]
plain	**slette** (m/f)	['ʂletə]
landscape	**landskap** (n)	['lɑn‚skɑp]
echo	**ekko** (n)	['ɛkʊ]
alpinist	**alpinist** (m)	[ɑlpi'nist]
rock climber	**fjellklatrer** (m)	['fjɛl‚klɑtrər]
to conquer (in climbing)	**å erobre**	[ɔ ɛ'rʊbrə]
climb (an easy ~)	**bestigning** (m/f)	[be'stigniŋ]

201. Mountains names

The Alps	**Alpene**	['ɑlpenə]
Mont Blanc	**Mont Blanc**	[‚mɔn'blɑn]
The Pyrenees	**Pyreneene**	[pyre'neːənə]
The Carpathians	**Karpatene**	[kɑr'pɑtenə]
The Ural Mountains	**Uralfjellene**	[ʉ'rɑl‚fjɛlenə]
The Caucasus Mountains	**Kaukasus**	['kɑʊkɑsʉs]
Mount Elbrus	**Elbrus**	[ɛl'brʉs]
The Altai Mountains	**Altaj**	[ɑl'tɑj]
The Tian Shan	**Tien Shan**	[ti'en‚ʂɑn]
The Pamir Mountains	**Pamir**	[pɑ'mir]
The Himalayas	**Himalaya**	[himɑ'lɑjɑ]
Mount Everest	**Everest**	['ɛve'rɛst]
The Andes	**Andes**	['ɑndəs]
Mount Kilimanjaro	**Kilimanjaro**	[kilimɑn'dʂɑrʊ]

202. Rivers

| river | **elv** (m/f) | ['ɛlv] |
| spring (natural source) | **kilde** (m) | ['çildə] |

riverbed (river channel)	**elveleie** (n)	['ɛlvəˌlæjə]
basin (river valley)	**flodbasseng** (n)	['flʊd baˌseŋ]
to flow into …	**å munne ut …**	[ɔ 'mʉnə ʉt …]
tributary	**bielv** (m/f)	['biˌelv]
bank (of river)	**bredd** (m)	['brɛd]
current (stream)	**strøm** (m)	['strøm]
downstream (adv)	**medstrøms**	['meˌstrøms]
upstream (adv)	**motstrøms**	['mʊtˌstrøms]
inundation	**oversvømmelse** (m)	['ɔvəˌsvœməlsə]
flooding	**flom** (m)	['flɔm]
to overflow (vi)	**å overflø**	[ɔ 'ɔvərˌflø]
to flood (vt)	**å oversvømme**	[ɔ 'ɔvəˌsvœmə]
shallow (shoal)	**grunne** (m/f)	['grʉnə]
rapids	**stryk** (m/n)	['stryk]
dam	**demning** (m)	['dɛmniŋ]
canal	**kanal** (m)	[kɑ'nɑl]
reservoir (artificial lake)	**reservoar** (n)	[resɛrvʊ'ɑr]
sluice, lock	**sluse** (m)	['ʂlʉsə]
water body (pond, etc.)	**vannmasse** (m)	['vɑnˌmɑsə]
swamp (marshland)	**myr, sump** (m)	['myr], ['sʉmp]
bog, marsh	**hengemyr** (m)	['hɛŋəˌmyr]
whirlpool	**virvel** (m)	['virvəl]
stream (brook)	**bekk** (m)	['bɛk]
drinking (ab. water)	**drikke-**	['drikə-]
fresh (~ water)	**fersk-**	['fæʂk-]
ice	**is** (m)	['is]
to freeze over (ab. river, etc.)	**å fryse til**	[ɔ 'frysə til]

203. Rivers' names

Seine	**Seine**	['sɛːn]
Loire	**Loire**	[lu'ɑːr]
Thames	**Themsen**	['tɛmsən]
Rhine	**Rhinen**	['riːnən]
Danube	**Donau**	['dɔnaʊ]
Volga	**Volga**	['vɔlgɑ]
Don	**Don**	['dɔn]
Lena	**Lena**	['lenɑ]
Yellow River	**Huang He**	[ˌhwɑn'hɛ]

Yangtze	**Yangtze**	[ˈjɑŋtse]
Mekong	**Mekong**	[meˈkɔŋ]
Ganges	**Ganges**	[ˈgɑŋes]

Nile River	**Nilen**	[ˈnilən]
Congo River	**Kongo**	[ˈkɔngʊ]
Okavango River	**Okavango**	[ʊkɑˈvɑngʊ]
Zambezi River	**Zambezi**	[sɑmˈbesi]
Limpopo River	**Limpopo**	[limpɔˈpɔ]
Mississippi River	**Mississippi**	[ˈmisiˈsipi]

204. Forest

| forest, wood | **skog** (m) | [ˈskʊg] |
| forest (as adj) | **skog-** | [ˈskʊg-] |

thick forest	**tett skog** (n)	[ˈtɛt ˌskʊg]
grove	**lund** (m)	[ˈlʉn]
forest clearing	**glenne** (m/f)	[ˈglenə]

| thicket | **krattskog** (m) | [ˈkrɑtˌskʊg] |
| scrubland | **kratt** (n) | [ˈkrɑt] |

| footpath (troddenpath) | **sti** (m) | [ˈsti] |
| gully | **ravine** (m) | [rɑˈvinə] |

tree	**tre** (n)	[ˈtrɛ]
leaf	**blad** (n)	[ˈblɑ]
leaves (foliage)	**løv** (n)	[ˈløv]

fall of leaves	**løvfall** (n)	[ˈløvˌfɑl]
to fall (ab. leaves)	**å falle**	[ɔ ˈfɑlə]
top (of the tree)	**tretopp** (m)	[ˈtrɛˌtɔp]

branch	**kvist, gren** (m)	[ˈkvist], [ˈgren]
bough	**gren, grein** (m/f)	[ˈgren], [ˈgræjn]
bud (on shrub, tree)	**knopp** (m)	[ˈknɔp]
needle (of pine tree)	**nål** (m/f)	[ˈnɔl]
pine cone	**kongle** (m/f)	[ˈkʊŋlə]

hollow (in a tree)	**trehull** (n)	[ˈtrɛˌhʉl]
nest	**reir** (n)	[ˈræjr]
burrow (animal hole)	**hule** (m/f)	[ˈhʉlə]

trunk	**stamme** (m)	[ˈstɑmə]
root	**rot** (m/f)	[ˈrʊt]
bark	**bark** (m)	[ˈbɑrk]
moss	**mose** (m)	[ˈmʊsə]
to uproot (remove trees or tree stumps)	**å rykke opp med roten**	[ɔ ˈrʏkə ɔp me ˈrutən]

to chop down	å felle	[ɔ 'fɛlə]
to deforest (vt)	å hogge ned	[ɔ 'hɔgə 'ne]
tree stump	stubbe (m)	['stʉbə]

campfire	bål (n)	['bɔl]
forest fire	skogbrann (m)	['skʊg̩brɑn]
to extinguish (vt)	å slokke	[ɔ 'ʂløkə]

forest ranger	skogvokter (m)	['skʊg̩vɔktər]
protection	vern (n), beskyttelse (m)	['væːn̩], ['be'ʂytəlsə]
to protect (~ nature)	å beskytte	[ɔ be'ʂytə]
poacher	tyvskytter (m)	['tyf̩sytər]
steel trap	saks (m/f)	['sɑks]

| to gather, to pick (vt) | å plukke | [ɔ 'plʉkə] |
| to lose one's way | å gå seg vill | [ɔ 'gɔ sæj 'vil] |

205. Natural resources

natural resources	naturressurser (m pl)	[nɑ'tʉr rɛ'sʉʂər]
minerals	mineraler (n pl)	[minə'rɑlər]
deposits	forekomster (m pl)	['fɔrə̩kɔmstər]
field (e.g., oilfield)	felt (m)	['fɛlt]

to mine (extract)	å utvinne	[ɔ 'ʉt̩vinə]
mining (extraction)	utvinning (m/f)	['ʉt̩viniŋ]
ore	malm (m)	['mɑlm]
mine (e.g., for coal)	gruve (m/f)	['grʉvə]
shaft (mine ~)	gruvesjakt (m/f)	['grʉvə̩sɑkt]
miner	gruvearbeider (m)	['grʉvə'ɑr̩bæjdər]

| gas (natural ~) | gass (m) | ['gɑs] |
| gas pipeline | gassledning (m) | ['gɑs̩ledniŋ] |

oil (petroleum)	olje (m)	['ɔljə]
oil pipeline	oljeledning (m)	['ɔljə̩ledniŋ]
oil well	oljebrønn (m)	['ɔljə̩brœn]
derrick (tower)	boretårn (n)	['boːrə̩tɔːn̩]
tanker	tankskip (n)	['tɑnk̩ʂip]

sand	sand (m)	['sɑn]
limestone	kalkstein (m)	['kɑlk̩stæjn]
gravel	grus (m)	['grʉs]
peat	torv (m/f)	['tɔrv]
clay	leir (n)	['læjr]
coal	kull (n)	['kʉl]

iron (ore)	jern (n)	['jæːn̩]
gold	gull (n)	['gʉl]
silver	sølv (n)	['søl]

nickel	**nikkel** (m)	['nikəl]
copper	**kobber** (n)	['kɔbər]
zinc	**sink** (m/n)	['sink]
manganese	**mangan** (m/n)	[ma'ŋan]
mercury	**kvikksølv** (n)	['kvik‚søl]
lead	**bly** (n)	['bly]
mineral	**mineral** (n)	[minə'ral]
crystal	**krystall** (m/n)	[kry'stal]
marble	**marmor** (m/n)	['marmʊr]
uranium	**uran** (m/n)	[ʉ'ran]

The Earth. Part 2

206. Weather

weather	vær (n)	['vær]
weather forecast	værvarsel (n)	['vær͵vɑʂəl]
temperature	temperatur (m)	[tɛmpərɑ'tʉr]
thermometer	termometer (n)	[tɛrmʊ'metər]
barometer	barometer (n)	[bɑrʊ'metər]
humid (adj)	fuktig	['fʉkti]
humidity	fuktighet (m)	['fʉkti͵het]
heat (extreme ~)	hete (m)	['he:tə]
hot (torrid)	het	['het]
it's hot	det er hett	[de ær 'het]
it's warm	det er varmt	[de ær 'vɑrmt]
warm (moderately hot)	varm	['vɑrm]
it's cold	det er kaldt	[de ær 'kɑlt]
cold (adj)	kald	['kɑl]
sun	sol (m/f)	['sʊl]
to shine (vi)	å skinne	[ɔ 'ʂinə]
sunny (day)	solrik	['sʊl͵rik]
to come up (vi)	å gå opp	[ɔ 'gɔ ɔp]
to set (vi)	å gå ned	[ɔ 'gɔ ne]
cloud	sky (m)	['ʂy]
cloudy (adj)	skyet	['ʂy:ət]
rain cloud	regnsky (m/f)	['ræjn͵ʂy]
somber (gloomy)	mørk	['mœrk]
rain	regn (n)	['ræjn]
it's raining	det regner	[de 'ræjnər]
rainy (~ day, weather)	regnværs-	['ræjn͵væʂ-]
to drizzle (vi)	å småregne	[ɔ 'smɔ:ræjnə]
pouring rain	piskende regn (n)	['piskenə ͵ræjn]
downpour	styrtregn (n)	['sty:ʈ͵ræjn]
heavy (e.g., ~ rain)	kraftig, sterk	['krɑfti], ['stærk]
puddle	vannpytt (m)	['vɑn͵pʏt]
to get wet (in rain)	å bli våt	[ɔ 'bli 'vɔt]
fog (mist)	tåke (m/f)	['to:kə]
foggy	tåke	['to:kə]

| snow | snø (m) | ['snø] |
| it's snowing | det snør | [de 'snør] |

207. Severe weather. Natural disasters

thunderstorm	tordenvær (n)	['turdən̩vær]
lightning (~ strike)	lyn (n)	['lyn]
to flash (vi)	å glimte	[ɔ 'glimtə]

thunder	torden (m)	['turdən]
to thunder (vi)	å tordne	[ɔ 'turdnə]
it's thundering	det tordner	[de 'turdnər]

| hail | hagle (m/f) | ['haglə] |
| it's hailing | det hagler | [de 'haglər] |

| to flood (vt) | å oversvømme | [ɔ 'ɔvə̩svœmə] |
| flood, inundation | oversvømmelse (m) | ['ɔvə̩svœməlsə] |

earthquake	jordskjelv (n)	['ju:r̩sɛlv]
tremor, quake	skjelv (n)	['sɛlv]
epicenter	episenter (n)	[ɛpi'sɛntər]
eruption	utbrudd (n)	['ʉt̩brʉd]
lava	lava (m)	['lava]

twister	skypumpe (m/f)	['sy̩pʉmpə]
tornado	tornado (m)	[tʊ'nɑdʊ]
typhoon	tyfon (m)	[ty'fʊn]

hurricane	orkan (m)	[ɔr'kan]
storm	storm (m)	['stɔrm]
tsunami	tsunami (m)	[tsʉ'nami]

cyclone	syklon (m)	[sy'klun]
bad weather	uvær (n)	['ʉːˌvær]
fire (accident)	brann (m)	['bran]
disaster	katastrofe (m)	[kata'strofə]
meteorite	meteoritt (m)	[meteʉ'rit]

avalanche	lavine (m)	[la'vino]
snowslide	snøskred, snøras (n)	['snø̩skred], ['snøras]
blizzard	snøstorm (m)	['snø̩stɔrm]
snowstorm	snøstorm (m)	['snø̩stɔrm]

208. Noises. Sounds

| silence (quiet) | stillhet (m/f) | ['stil̩het] |
| sound | lyd (m) | ['lyd] |

noise	**støy** (m)	['støj]
to make noise	**å støye**	[ɔ 'støjə]
noisy (adj)	**støyende**	['støjənə]

loudly (to speak, etc.)	**høylytt**	['højlʏt]
loud (voice, etc.)	**høy**	['høj]
constant (e.g., ~ noise)	**konstant**	[kʊn'stɑnt]

cry, shout (n)	**skrik** (n)	['skrik]
to cry, to shout (vi)	**å skrike**	[ɔ 'skrikə]
whisper	**hvisking** (m/f)	['viskiŋ]
to whisper (vi, vt)	**å hviske**	[ɔ 'viskə]

| barking (dog's ~) | **gjøing** (m/f) | ['jøːiŋ] |
| to bark (vi) | **å gjø** | [ɔ 'jø] |

groan (of pain, etc.)	**stønn** (n)	['stœn]
to groan (vi)	**å stønne**	[ɔ 'stœnə]
cough	**hoste** (m)	['hʊstə]
to cough (vi)	**å hoste**	[ɔ 'hʊstə]

whistle	**plystring** (m/f)	['plʏstriŋ]
to whistle (vi)	**å plystre**	[ɔ 'plʏstrə]
knock (at the door)	**knakk** (m/n)	['knɑk]
to knock (at the door)	**å knakke**	[ɔ 'knɑkə]

| to crack (vi) | **å knake** | [ɔ 'knɑkə] |
| crack (cracking sound) | **knak** (n) | ['knɑk] |

siren	**sirene** (m/f)	[si'renə]
whistle (factory ~, etc.)	**fløyte** (m/f)	['fløjtə]
to whistle (ab. train)	**å tute**	[ɔ 'tʉtə]
honk (car horn sound)	**tut** (n)	['tʉt]
to honk (vi)	**å tute**	[ɔ 'tʉtə]

209. Winter

winter (n)	**vinter** (m)	['vintər]
winter (as adj)	**vinter-**	['vintər-]
in winter	**om vinteren**	[ɔm 'vintərən]

snow	**snø** (m)	['snø]
it's snowing	**det snør**	[de 'snør]
snowfall	**snøfall** (n)	['snøˌfɑl]
snowdrift	**snødrive** (m/f)	['snøˌdrivə]

snowflake	**snøfnugg** (n)	['snøˌfnʉg]
snowball	**snøball** (m)	['snøˌbɑl]
snowman	**snømann** (m)	['snøˌmɑn]
icicle	**istapp** (m)	['isˌtɑp]

December	desember (m)	[de'sɛmbər]
January	januar (m)	['janʉˌɑr]
February	februar (m)	['febrʉˌɑr]
frost (severe ~, freezing cold)	frost (m/f)	['frɔst]
frosty (weather, air)	frost	['frɔst]
below zero (adv)	under null	['ʉnər nʉl]
first frost	lett frost (m)	['let 'frɔst]
hoarfrost	rimfrost (m)	['rimˌfrɔst]
cold (cold weather)	kulde (m/f)	['kʉlə]
it's cold	det er kaldt	[de ær 'kalt]
fur coat	pels (m), pelskåpe (m/f)	['pɛls], ['pɛlsˌkoːpə]
mittens	votter (m pl)	['vɔtər]
to get sick	å bli syk	[ɔ 'bli 'syk]
cold (illness)	forkjølelse (m)	[fɔr'çœləlsə]
to catch a cold	å forkjøle seg	[ɔ fɔr'çœlə sæj]
ice	is (m)	['is]
black ice	islag (n)	['isˌlɑg]
to freeze over (ab. river, etc.)	å fryse til	[ɔ 'frysə til]
ice floe	isflak (n)	['isˌflɑk]
skis	ski (m/f pl)	['ʂi]
skier	skigåer (m)	['ʂiˌgoər]
to ski (vi)	å gå på ski	[ɔ 'gɔ pɔ 'ʂi]
to skate (vi)	å gå på skøyter	[ɔ 'gɔ pɔ 'ʂøjtər]

Fauna

210. Mammals. Predators

predator	rovdyr (n)	['rɔvˌdyr]
tiger	tiger (m)	['tigər]
lion	løve (m/f)	['løve]
wolf	ulv (m)	['ʉlv]
fox	rev (m)	['rev]
jaguar	jaguar (m)	[jagʉ'ɑr]
leopard	leopard (m)	[leʉ'pɑrd]
cheetah	gepard (m)	[ge'pɑrd]
black panther	panter (m)	['pɑntər]
puma	puma (m)	['pʉmɑ]
snow leopard	snøleopard (m)	['snø leʉ'pɑrd]
lynx	gaupe (m/f)	['gɑʉpə]
coyote	coyote, prærieulv (m)	[kɔ'jotə], ['præriˌʉlv]
jackal	sjakal (m)	[ʂa'kɑl]
hyena	hyene (m)	[hy'enə]

211. Wild animals

animal	dyr (n)	['dyr]
beast (animal)	best, udyr (n)	['bɛst], ['ʉˌdyr]
squirrel	ekorn (n)	['ɛkuːn]
hedgehog	pinnsvin (n)	['pinˌsvin]
hare	hare (m)	['hɑrə]
rabbit	kanin (m)	[kɑ'nin]
badger	grevling (m)	['grɛvliŋ]
raccoon	vaskebjørn (m)	['vaskəˌbjœːn]
hamster	hamster (m)	['hɑmstər]
marmot	murmeldyr (n)	['mʉrmələˌdyr]
mole	muldvarp (m)	['mʉlˌvɑrp]
mouse	mus (m/f)	['mʉs]
rat	rotte (m/f)	['rɔtə]
bat	flaggermus (m/f)	['flagərˌmʉs]
ermine	røyskatt (m)	['røjskat]
sable	sobel (m)	['sʉbəl]

marten	mår (m)	['mɔr]
weasel	snømus (m/f)	['snø,mʉs]
mink	mink (m)	['mink]
beaver	bever (m)	['bevər]
otter	oter (m)	['ʊtər]
horse	hest (m)	['hɛst]
moose	elg (m)	['ɛlg]
deer	hjort (m)	['jɔːt]
camel	kamel (m)	[ka'mel]
bison	bison (m)	['bisɔn]
aurochs	urokse (m)	['ʉr,ʊksə]
buffalo	bøffel (m)	['bøfəl]
zebra	sebra (m)	['sebra]
antelope	antilope (m)	[anti'lʊpə]
roe deer	rådyr (n)	['rɔ,dyr]
fallow deer	dåhjort, dådyr (n)	['dɔ,jɔːt], ['dɔ,dyr]
chamois	gemse (m)	['gɛmsə]
wild boar	villsvin (n)	['vil,svin]
whale	hval (m)	['val]
seal	sel (m)	['sel]
walrus	hvalross (m)	['val,rɔs]
fur seal	pelssel (m)	['pɛls,sel]
dolphin	delfin (m)	[dɛl'fin]
bear	bjørn (m)	['bjœːɳ]
polar bear	isbjørn (m)	['is,bjœːɳ]
panda	panda (m)	['panda]
monkey	ape (m/f)	['apə]
chimpanzee	sjimpanse (m)	[ʂim'pansə]
orangutan	orangutang (m)	[ʊ'rangʉ,taŋ]
gorilla	gorilla (m)	[gɔ'rila]
macaque	makak (m)	[ma'kak]
gibbon	gibbon (m)	['gibʊn]
elephant	elefant (m)	[ɛle'fant]
rhinoceros	neshorn (n)	['nɛs,hʉːɳ]
giraffe	sjiraff (m)	[ʂi'raf]
hippopotamus	flodhest (m)	['flʊd,hɛst]
kangaroo	kenguru (m)	['kɛŋgʉrʉ]
koala (bear)	koala (m)	[kʊ'ala]
mongoose	mangust, mungo (m)	[maŋ'gʉst], ['mʉŋgu]
chinchilla	chinchilla (m)	[ʂin'ʂila]
skunk	skunk (m)	['skunk]
porcupine	hulepinnsvin (n)	['hʉlə,pinsvin]

212. Domestic animals

cat	katt (m)	['kat]
tomcat	hannkatt (m)	['hanˌkat]
dog	hund (m)	['hʉɳ]

horse	hest (m)	['hɛst]
stallion (male horse)	hingst (m)	['hiŋst]
mare	hoppe, merr (m/f)	['hɔpə], ['mɛr]

cow	ku (f)	['kʉ]
bull	tyr (m)	['tyr]
ox	okse (m)	['ɔksə]

sheep (ewe)	sau (m)	['saʉ]
ram	vær, saubukk (m)	['vær], ['saʉˌbʉk]
goat	geit (m/f)	['jæjt]
billy goat, he-goat	geitebukk (m)	['jæjtəˌbʉk]

| donkey | esel (n) | ['ɛsəl] |
| mule | muldyr (n) | ['mʉlˌdyr] |

pig, hog	svin (n)	['svin]
piglet	gris (m)	['gris]
rabbit	kanin (m)	[ka'nin]

| hen (chicken) | høne (m/f) | ['hønə] |
| rooster | hane (m) | ['hanə] |

duck	and (m/f)	['an]
drake	andrik (m)	['andrik]
goose	gås (m/f)	['gɔs]

| tom turkey, gobbler | kalkunhane (m) | [kal'kʉnˌhanə] |
| turkey (hen) | kalkunhøne (m/f) | [kal'kʉnˌhønə] |

domestic animals	husdyr (n pl)	['hʉsˌdyr]
tame (e.g., ~ hamster)	tam	['tam]
to tame (vt)	å temme	[ɔ 'tɛmə]
to breed (vt)	å avle, å oppdrette	[ɔ 'avlə], [ɔ 'ɔpˌdrɛtə]

farm	farm, gård (m)	['farm], ['gɔːr]
poultry	fjærfe (n)	['fjærˌfɛ]
cattle	kveg (n)	['kvɛg]
herd (cattle)	flokk, bøling (m)	['flɔk], ['bøliŋ]

stable	stall (m)	['stal]
pigpen	grisehus (n)	['grisəˌhʉs]
cowshed	kufjøs (m/n)	['kuˌfjøs]
rabbit hutch	kaninbur (n)	[ka'ninˌbʉr]
hen house	hønsehus (n)	['hønsəˌhʉs]

213. Dogs. Dog breeds

dog	hund (m)	['hʉŋ]
sheepdog	fårehund (m)	['foːrə‚hʉn]
German shepherd	schäferhund (m)	['ʂɛfær‚hʉn]
poodle	puddel (m)	['pʉdəl]
dachshund	dachshund (m)	['daʂ‚hʉn]
bulldog	bulldogg (m)	['bʉl‚dog]
boxer	bokser (m)	['boksər]
mastiff	mastiff (m)	[mɑsˈtif]
Rottweiler	rottweiler (m)	['rɔt‚væjlər]
Doberman	dobermann (m)	['dobermɑn]
basset	basset (m)	['basɛt]
bobtail	bobtail (m)	['bobtɛjl]
Dalmatian	dalmatiner (m)	[dɑlmaˈtinər]
cocker spaniel	cocker spaniel (m)	['koker ‚spaniəl]
Newfoundland	newfoundlandshund (m)	[njʉ'fawnd‚lənds 'hʉn]
Saint Bernard	sankt bernhardshund (m)	[‚sankt 'bɛːnɑds‚hʉn]
husky	husky (m)	['hɑski]
Chow Chow	chihuahua (m)	[tʂiˈvava]
spitz	spisshund (m)	['spis‚hʉn]
pug	mops (m)	['mɔps]

214. Sounds made by animals

barking (n)	gjøing (m/f)	['jøːiŋ]
to bark (vi)	å gjø	[ɔ 'jø]
to meow (vi)	å mjaue	[ɔ 'mjaʊe]
to purr (vi)	å spinne	[ɔ 'spinə]
to moo (vi)	å raute	[ɔ 'raʊte]
to bellow (bull)	å belje, å brøle	[ɔ 'belje], [ɔ 'brøle]
to growl (vi)	å knurre	[ɔ 'knʉrə]
howl (n)	hyl (n)	['hyl]
to howl (vi)	å hyle	[ɔ 'hylə]
to whine (vi)	å klynke	[ɔ 'klʏnkə]
to bleat (sheep)	å breke	[ɔ 'brekə]
to oink, to grunt (pig)	å grynte	[ɔ 'grʏntə]
to squeal (vi)	å hvine	[ɔ 'vinə]
to croak (vi)	å kvekke	[ɔ 'kvɛkə]
to buzz (insect)	å surre	[ɔ 'sʉrə]
to chirp (crickets, grasshopper)	å gnisse	[ɔ 'gnisə]

215. Young animals

cub	unge (m)	['ʉŋə]
kitten	kattunge (m)	['kat̩ʉŋə]
baby mouse	museunge (m)	['mʉsə̩ʉŋə]
puppy	valp (m)	['valp]
leveret	hareunge (m)	['harə̩ʉŋə]
baby rabbit	kaninunge (m)	[ka'nin̩ʉŋə]
wolf cub	ulvunge (m)	['ʉlv̩ʉŋə]
fox cub	revevalp (m)	['revə̩valp]
bear cub	bjørnunge (m)	['bjœ:n̩ʉŋə]
lion cub	løveunge (m)	['løvə̩ʉŋə]
tiger cub	tigerunge (m)	['tigər̩ʉŋə]
elephant calf	elefantunge (m)	[ɛle'fant̩ʉŋə]
piglet	gris (m)	['gris]
calf (young cow, bull)	kalv (m)	['kalv]
kid (young goat)	kje (n), geitekilling (m)	['çe], ['jæjtə̩çiliŋ]
lamb	lam (n)	['lam]
fawn (young deer)	hjortekalv (m)	['jɔ:ʈə̩kalv]
young camel	kamelunge (m)	[ka'mel̩ʉŋə]
snakelet (baby snake)	slangeyngel (m)	['ʂlaŋə̩yŋəl]
froglet (baby frog)	froskeunge (m)	['frɔskə̩ʉŋə]
baby bird	fugleunge (m)	['fʉlə̩ʉŋə]
chick (of chicken)	kylling (m)	['çyliŋ]
duckling	andunge (m)	['an̩ʉŋə]

216. Birds

bird	fugl (m)	['fʉl]
pigeon	due (m/f)	['dʉə]
sparrow	spurv (m)	['spʉrv]
tit (great tit)	kjøttmeis (m/f)	['çœt̩mæjs]
magpie	skjære (m/f)	['særə]
raven	ravn (m)	['ravn]
crow	kråke (m)	['kro:kə]
jackdaw	kaie (m/f)	['kajə]
rook	kornkråke (m/f)	['kʉ:n̩kro:kə]
duck	and (m/f)	['an]
goose	gås (m/f)	['gɔs]
pheasant	fasan (m)	[fa'san]
eagle	ørn (m/f)	['œ:n̩]
hawk	hauk (m)	['haʉk]

falcon	**falk** (m)	['falk]
vulture	**gribb** (m)	['grib]
condor (Andean ~)	**kondor** (m)	[kʊn'dʊr]
swan	**svane** (m/f)	['svanə]
crane	**trane** (m/f)	['tranə]
stork	**stork** (m)	['stɔrk]
parrot	**papegøye** (m)	[pape'gøjə]
hummingbird	**kolibri** (m)	[kʊ'libri]
peacock	**påfugl** (m)	['pɔˌfʉl]
ostrich	**struts** (m)	['strʉts]
heron	**hegre** (m)	['hæjrə]
flamingo	**flamingo** (m)	[fla'mingʊ]
pelican	**pelikan** (m)	[peli'kan]
nightingale	**nattergal** (m)	['natərˌgal]
swallow	**svale** (m/f)	['svalə]
thrush	**trost** (m)	['trʊst]
song thrush	**måltrost** (m)	['moːlˌtrʊst]
blackbird	**svarttrost** (m)	['svaːˌtrʊst]
swift	**tårnseiler** (m),	['tɔːˌnˌsæjlə],
	tårnsvale (m/f)	['tɔːˌnˌsvalə]
lark	**lerke** (m/f)	['lærkə]
quail	**vaktel** (m)	['vaktəl]
woodpecker	**hakkespett** (m)	['hakəˌspɛt]
cuckoo	**gjøk, gauk** (m)	['jøk], ['gaʊk]
owl	**ugle** (m/f)	['ʉglə]
eagle owl	**hubro** (m)	['hʉbrʊ]
wood grouse	**storfugl** (m)	['stʊrˌfʉl]
black grouse	**orrfugl** (m)	['ɔrˌfʉl]
partridge	**rapphøne** (m/f)	['rapˌhønə]
starling	**stær** (m)	['stær]
canary	**kanarifugl** (m)	[ka'nariˌfʉl]
hazel grouse	**jerpe** (m/f)	['jærpə]
chaffinch	**bokfink** (m)	['bʊkˌfink]
bullfinch	**dompap** (m)	['dʊmpap]
seagull	**måke** (m/f)	['moːkə]
albatross	**albatross** (m)	['albaˌtrɔs]
penguin	**pingvin** (m)	[piŋ'vin]

217. Birds. Singing and sounds

| to sing (vi) | **å synge** | [ɔ 'sʏŋə] |
| to call (animal, bird) | **å skrike** | [ɔ 'skrikə] |

| to crow (rooster) | å gale | [ɔ 'gɑlə] |
| cock-a-doodle-doo | kykeliky | [kykəli'ky:] |

to cluck (hen)	å kakle	[ɔ 'kɑklə]
to caw (vi)	å krae	[ɔ 'krɑe]
to quack (duck)	å snadre, å rappe	[ɔ 'snɑdrə], [ɔ 'rɑpə]
to cheep (vi)	å pipe	[ɔ 'pipə]
to chirp, to twitter	å kvitre	[ɔ 'kvitrə]

218. Fish. Marine animals

bream	brasme (m/f)	['brɑsmə]
carp	karpe (m)	['kɑrpə]
perch	åbor (m)	['obɔr]
catfish	malle (m)	['mɑlə]
pike	gjedde (m/f)	['jɛdə]

| salmon | laks (m) | ['lɑks] |
| sturgeon | stør (m) | ['stør] |

herring	sild (m/f)	['sil]
Atlantic salmon	atlanterhavslaks (m)	[ɑt'lɑntərhɑfs‚lɑks]
mackerel	makrell (m)	[mɑ'krɛl]
flatfish	rødspette (m/f)	['rø‚spɛtə]

zander, pike perch	gjørs (m)	['jø:ṣ]
cod	torsk (m)	['tɔṣk]
tuna	tunfisk (m)	['tʉn‚fisk]
trout	ørret (m)	['øret]
eel	ål (m)	['ɔl]
electric ray	elektrisk rokke (m/f)	[ɛ'lektrisk ‚rɔkə]
moray eel	murene (m)	[mʉ'rɛnə]
piranha	piraja (m)	[pi'rɑja]

shark	hai (m)	['hɑj]
dolphin	delfin (m)	[dɛl'fin]
whale	hval (m)	['vɑl]

crab	krabbe (m)	['krɑbə]
jellyfish	manet (m/f), meduse (m)	['mɑnet], [me'dʉsə]
octopus	blekksprut (m)	['blek‚sprʉt]

starfish	sjøstjerne (m/f)	['ṣø‚stjæ:ŋə]
sea urchin	sjøpinnsvin (n)	['ṣø:'pin‚svin]
seahorse	sjøhest (m)	['ṣø‚hɛst]

oyster	østers (m)	['østəṣ]
shrimp	reke (m/f)	['rekə]
lobster	hummer (m)	['hʉmər]
spiny lobster	langust (m)	[lɑŋ'gʉst]

219. Amphibians. Reptiles

snake	**slange** (m)	['ʂlaŋə]
venomous (snake)	**giftig**	['jifti]
viper	**hoggorm, huggorm** (m)	['hʊgˌɔrm], ['hʉgˌɔrm]
cobra	**kobra** (m)	['kʊbra]
python	**pyton** (m)	['pytɔn]
boa	**boaslange** (m)	['bɔaˌslaŋə]
grass snake	**snok** (m)	['snʊk]
rattle snake	**klapperslange** (m)	['klapəˌslaŋə]
anaconda	**anakonda** (m)	[anaˈkɔnda]
lizard	**øgle** (m/f)	['øglə]
iguana	**iguan** (m)	[igʉˈan]
monitor lizard	**varan** (n)	[vaˈran]
salamander	**salamander** (m)	[salaˈmandər]
chameleon	**kameleon** (m)	[kaməleˈʊn]
scorpion	**skorpion** (m)	[skɔrpiˈʊn]
turtle	**skilpadde** (m/f)	['ʂilˌpadə]
frog	**frosk** (m)	['frɔsk]
toad	**padde** (m/f)	['padə]
crocodile	**krokodille** (m)	[krʊkəˈdilə]

220. Insects

insect, bug	**insekt** (n)	['insɛkt]
butterfly	**sommerfugl** (m)	['sɔmərˌfʉl]
ant	**maur** (m)	['maʊr]
fly	**flue** (m/f)	['flʉə]
mosquito	**mygg** (m)	['myg]
beetle	**bille** (m)	['bilə]
wasp	**veps** (m)	['vɛps]
bee	**bie** (m/f)	['biə]
bumblebee	**humle** (m/f)	['hʉmlə]
gadfly (botfly)	**brems** (m)	['brɛmɔ]
spider	**edderkopp** (m)	['ɛdərˌkɔp]
spiderweb	**edderkoppnett** (n)	['ɛdərkɔpˌnɛt]
dragonfly	**øyenstikker** (m)	['øjənˌstikər]
grasshopper	**gresshoppe** (m/f)	['grɛsˌhɔpə]
moth (night butterfly)	**nattsvermer** (m)	['natˌsværmər]
cockroach	**kakerlakk** (m)	[kakəˈlak]
tick	**flått, midd** (m)	['flɔt], ['mid]

| flea | **loppe** (f) | ['lɔpə] |
| midge | **knott** (m) | ['knɔt] |

locust	**vandgresshoppe** (m/f)	['vɑn 'grɛsˌhɔpə]
snail	**snegl** (m)	['snæjl]
cricket	**siriss** (m)	['siˌris]

lightning bug	**ildflue** (m/f), **lysbille** (m)	['ilˌflʉe], ['lysˌbilə]
ladybug	**marihøne** (m/f)	['mɑriˌhønə]
cockchafer	**oldenborre** (f)	['ɔldənˌbɔrə]

leech	**igle** (m/f)	['iglə]
caterpillar	**sommerfugllarve** (m/f)	['sɔmərfʉlˌlɑrvə]
earthworm	**meitemark** (m)	['mæjtəˌmɑrk]
larva	**larve** (m/f)	['lɑrvə]

221. Animals. Body parts

beak	**nebb** (n)	['nɛb]
wings	**vinger** (m pl)	['viŋər]
foot (of bird)	**fot** (m)	['fʊt]
feathers (plumage)	**fjærdrakt** (m/f)	['fjærˌdrɑkt]

| feather | **fjær** (m/f) | ['fjær] |
| crest | **fjærtopp** (m) | ['fjæːˌtɔp] |

gills	**gjeller** (m/f pl)	['jɛlər]
spawn	**rogn** (m/f)	['rɔŋn]
larva	**larve** (m/f)	['lɑrvə]

| fin | **finne** (m) | ['finə] |
| scales (of fish, reptile) | **skjell** (n) | ['ʂɛl] |

fang (canine)	**hoggtann** (m/f)	['hɔgˌtɑn]
paw (e.g., cat's ~)	**pote** (m)	['poːtə]
muzzle (snout)	**snute** (m/f)	['snʉtə]
mouth (of cat, dog)	**kjeft** (m)	['çɛft]

| tail | **hale** (m) | ['hɑlə] |
| whiskers | **værhår** (n) | ['værˌhɔr] |

| hoof | **klov, hov** (m) | ['klɔv], ['hɔv] |
| horn | **horn** (n) | ['hʊːɳ] |

carapace	**ryggskjold** (n)	['rygˌʂɔl]
shell (of mollusk)	**skall** (n)	['skɑl]
eggshell	**eggeskall** (n)	['ɛgəˌskɑl]

| animal's hair (pelage) | **pels** (m) | ['pɛls] |
| pelt (hide) | **skinn** (n) | ['ʂin] |

222. Actions of animals

to fly (vi)	**å fly**	[ɔ 'fly]
to fly in circles	**å kretse**	[ɔ 'krɛtsə]
to fly away	**å fly bort**	[ɔ 'fly ˌbʊːt]
to flap (~ the wings)	**å flakse**	[ɔ 'flɑksə]
to peck (vi)	**å pikke**	[ɔ 'pikə]
to sit on eggs	**å ruge på eggene**	[ɔ 'rʉgə pɔ 'ɛgenə]
to hatch out (vi)	**å klekkes**	[ɔ 'klekəs]
to build a nest	**å bygge reir**	[ɔ 'bʏgə 'ræir]
to slither, to crawl	**å krype**	[ɔ 'krypə]
to sting, to bite (insect)	**å stikke**	[ɔ 'stikə]
to bite (ab. animal)	**å bite**	[ɔ 'bitə]
to sniff (vt)	**å snuse**	[ɔ 'snʉsə]
to bark (vi)	**å gjø**	[ɔ 'jø]
to hiss (snake)	**å hvese**	[ɔ 'vesə]
to scare (vt)	**å skremme**	[ɔ 'skrɛmə]
to attack (vt)	**å overfalle**	[ɔ 'ɔvərˌfɑlə]
to gnaw (bone, etc.)	**å gnage**	[ɔ 'gnɑgə]
to scratch (with claws)	**å klore**	[ɔ 'klɔrə]
to hide (vi)	**å gjemme seg**	[ɔ 'jɛmə sæj]
to play (kittens, etc.)	**å leke**	[ɔ 'lekə]
to hunt (vi, vt)	**å jage**	[ɔ 'jagə]
to hibernate (vi)	**å ligge i dvale**	[ɔ 'ligə i 'dvalə]
to go extinct	**å dø ut**	[ɔ 'dø ʉt]

223. Animals. Habitats

habitat	**habitat** (n)	[hɑbi'tɑt]
migration	**migrasjon** (m)	[migrɑ'ʂʊn]
mountain	**fjell** (n)	['fjɛl]
reef	**rev** (n)	['rev]
cliff	**klippe** (m)	['klipə]
forest	**skog** (m)	['skʊg]
jungle	**jungel** (m)	['jʉŋəl]
savanna	**savanne** (m)	[sɑ'vanə]
tundra	**tundra** (m)	['tʉndrɑ]
steppe	**steppe** (m)	['stɛpə]
desert	**ørken** (m)	['œrkən]
oasis	**oase** (m)	[ʊ'ɑsə]
sea	**hav** (n)	['hɑv]

lake	innsjø (m)	['in'ʂø]
ocean	verdenshav (n)	[værdəns'hav]
swamp (marshland)	myr (m/f)	['myr]
freshwater (adj)	ferskvanns-	['fæʂkˌvɑns-]
pond	dam (m)	['dɑm]
river	elv (m/f)	['ɛlv]
den (bear's ~)	hi (n)	['hi]
nest	reir (n)	['ræjr]
hollow (in a tree)	trehull (n)	['trɛˌhʉl]
burrow (animal hole)	hule (m/f)	['hʉlə]
anthill	maurtue (m/f)	['mɑʉːˌtʉə]

224. Animal care

zoo	zoo, dyrepark (m)	['sʉː], [dyrə'pɑrk]
nature preserve	naturreservat (n)	[nɑ'tʉr resɛr'vɑt]
breeder (cattery, kennel, etc.)	oppdretter (m)	['ɔpˌdrɛtər]
open-air cage	voliere (m)	[vɔ'ljer]
cage	bur (n)	['bʉr]
doghouse (kennel)	kennel (m)	['kɛnəl]
dovecot	duehus (n)	['dʉəˌhʉs]
aquarium (fish tank)	akvarium (n)	[ɑ'kvɑrium]
dolphinarium	delfinarium (n)	[dɛlfi'nɑrium]
to breed (animals)	å avle, å oppdrette	[ɔ 'ɑvlə], [ɔ 'ɔpˌdrɛtə]
brood, litter	avkom (n)	['ɑvˌkɔm]
to tame (vt)	å temme	[ɔ 'tɛmə]
feed (fodder, etc.)	fôr (n)	['fʉr]
to feed (vt)	å utfore	[ɔ 'ʉtˌforə]
to train (animals)	å dressere	[ɔ drɛ'serə]
pet store	dyrebutikk (m)	['dyrəbʉ'tik]
muzzle (for dog)	munnkurv (m)	['mʉnˌkʉrv]
collar (e.g., dog ~)	halsbånd (n)	['hɑlsˌbɔn]
name (of animal)	navn (n)	['nɑvn]
pedigree (of dog)	stamtavle (m/f)	['stɑmˌtɑvlə]

225. Animals. Miscellaneous

pack (wolves)	flokk (m)	['flɔk]
flock (birds)	flokk (m)	['flɔk]
shoal, school (fish)	stim (m/n)	['stim]
herd (horses)	flokk (m)	['flɔk]

| male (n) | hann (m) | ['han] |
| female (n) | hunn (m) | ['hʉn] |

hungry (adj)	**sulten**	['sʉltən]
wild (adj)	**vill**	['vil]
dangerous (adj)	**farlig**	['fɑːli̯]

226. Horses

| horse | hest (m) | ['hɛst] |
| breed (race) | rase (m) | ['rɑsə] |

| foal | føll (n) | ['føl] |
| mare | hoppe, merr (m/f) | ['hɔpə], ['mɛr] |

mustang	mustang (m)	['mʉstaŋ]
pony	ponni (m)	['pɔni]
draft horse	kaldblodshest (m)	['kɑlblʉds,hɛst]

| mane | man (m/f) | ['man] |
| tail | hale (m) | ['hɑlə] |

hoof	hov (m)	['hɔv]
horseshoe	hestesko (m)	['hɛstə,skʉ]
to shoe (vt)	å sko	[ɔ 'skʉː]
blacksmith	smed, hovslager (m)	['sme], ['hɔfs,lɑgər]

saddle	sal (m)	['sɑl]
stirrup	stigbøyle (m)	['stig,bøjlə]
bridle	bissel (n)	['bisəl]
reins	tømmer (m pl)	['tœmər]
whip (for riding)	pisk (m)	['pisk]

rider	rytter (m)	['rʏtər]
to saddle up (vt)	å sale	[ɔ 'sɑlə]
to mount a horse	å stige opp på hesten	[ɔ 'stiːə ɔp pɔ 'hɛstən]

gallop	galopp (m)	[gɑ'lɔp]
to gallop (vi)	å galoppere	[ɔ gɑlɔ'perə]
trot (n)	trav (n)	['tɾɑv]
at a trot (adv)	i trav	[i 'trɑv]
to go at a trot	å trave	[ɔ 'trɑvə]

| racehorse | veddeløpshest (m) | ['vɛdə,løps hɛst] |
| horse racing | hesteveddeløp (n) | ['hɛstə 'vedə,løp] |

stable	stall (m)	['stɑl]
to feed (vt)	å utfore	[ɔ 'ʉt,forə]
hay	høy (n)	['høj]
to water (animals)	å vanne	[ɔ 'vanə]

225

to wash (horse)	**å børste**	[ɔ 'bøʂtə]
horse-drawn cart	**hestevogn** (m/f)	['hɛstəˌvɔŋn]
to graze (vi)	**å beite**	[ɔ 'bæjtə]
to neigh (vi)	**å vrinske, å knegge**	[ɔ 'vrinskə], [ɔ 'knɛgə]
to kick (about horse)	**å sparke bakut**	[ɔ 'spɑrkə 'bɑkˌʉt]

Flora

227. Trees

tree	**tre** (n)	['trɛ]
deciduous (adj)	**løv-**	['løv-]
coniferous (adj)	**bar-**	['bɑr-]
evergreen (adj)	**eviggrønt**	['ɛviˌgrœnt]
apple tree	**epletre** (n)	['ɛpləˌtrɛ]
pear tree	**pæretre** (n)	['pærəˌtrɛ]
sweet cherry tree	**morelltre** (n)	[mʊ'rɛlˌtrɛ]
sour cherry tree	**kirsebærtre** (n)	['çisəbærˌtrɛ]
plum tree	**plommetre** (n)	['plʊməˌtrɛ]
birch	**bjørk** (f)	['bjœrk]
oak	**eik** (f)	['æjk]
linden tree	**lind** (m/f)	['lin]
aspen	**osp** (m/f)	['ɔsp]
maple	**lønn** (m/f)	['lœn]
spruce	**gran** (m/f)	['grɑn]
pine	**furu** (m/f)	['fʉrʉ]
larch	**lerk** (m)	['lærk]
fir tree	**edelgran** (m/f)	['ɛdəlˌgrɑn]
cedar	**seder** (m)	['sedər]
poplar	**poppel** (m)	['pɔpəl]
rowan	**rogn** (m/f)	['rɔŋn]
willow	**pil** (m/f)	['pil]
alder	**or, older** (m/f)	['ʊr], ['ɔldər]
beech	**bøk** (m)	['bøk]
elm	**alm** (m)	['ɑlm]
ash (tree)	**ask** (m/f)	['ɑsk]
chestnut	**kastanjetre** (n)	[kɑ'stɑnjeˌtrɛ]
magnolia	**magnolia** (m)	[mɑŋ'nʉlia]
palm tree	**palme** (m)	['pɑlmə]
cypress	**sypress** (m)	[sʏ'prɛs]
mangrove	**mangrove** (m)	[mɑŋ'grʊvə]
baobab	**apebrødtre** (n)	['ɑpebrøˌtrɛ]
eucalyptus	**eukalyptus** (m)	[ɛvkɑ'lyptʉs]
sequoia	**sequoia** (m)	['sekˌvɔja]

228. Shrubs

bush	**busk** (m)	['bʉsk]
shrub	**busk** (m)	['bʉsk]
grapevine	**vinranke** (m)	['vin,rɑnkə]
vineyard	**vinmark** (m/f)	['vin,mɑrk]
raspberry bush	**bringebærbusk** (m)	['briŋə,bær bʉsk]
blackcurrant bush	**solbærbusk** (m)	['sʉlbær,bʉsk]
redcurrant bush	**ripsbusk** (m)	['rips,bʉsk]
gooseberry bush	**stikkelsbærbusk** (m)	['stikəlsbær,bʉsk]
acacia	**akasie** (m)	[ɑ'kɑsiə]
barberry	**berberis** (m)	['bærberis]
jasmine	**sjasmin** (m)	[ʂɑs'min]
juniper	**einer** (m)	['æjnər]
rosebush	**rosenbusk** (m)	['rʉsən,bʉsk]
dog rose	**steinnype** (m/f)	['stæjn,nypə]

229. Mushrooms

mushroom	**sopp** (m)	['sɔp]
edible mushroom	**spiselig sopp** (m)	['spisəli ,sɔp]
poisonous mushroom	**giftig sopp** (m)	['jifti ,sɔp]
cap (of mushroom)	**hatt** (m)	['hɑt]
stipe (of mushroom)	**stilk** (m)	['stilk]
cep (Boletus edulis)	**steinsopp** (m)	['stæjn,sɔp]
orange-cap boletus	**rødskrubb** (m/n)	['rø,skrʉb]
birch bolete	**brunskrubb** (m/n)	['brʉn,skrʉb]
chanterelle	**kantarell** (m)	[kɑntɑ'rel]
russula	**kremle** (m/f)	['krɛmlə]
morel	**morkel** (m)	['mɔrkəl]
fly agaric	**fluesopp** (m)	['flʉə,sɔp]
death cap	**grønn fluesopp** (m)	['grœn 'flʉə,sɔp]

230. Fruits. Berries

fruit	**frukt** (m/f)	['frʉkt]
fruits	**frukter** (m/f pl)	['frʉktər]
apple	**eple** (n)	['ɛplə]
pear	**pære** (m/f)	['pærə]
plum	**plomme** (m/f)	['plʉmə]
strawberry (garden ~)	**jordbær** (n)	['juːr,bær]

sour cherry	**kirsebær** (n)	['çiʂə‚bær]
sweet cherry	**morell** (m)	[mʊ'rɛl]
grape	**drue** (m)	['drʉə]
raspberry	**bringebær** (n)	['briŋə‚bær]
blackcurrant	**solbær** (n)	['sʊl‚bær]
redcurrant	**rips** (m)	['rips]
gooseberry	**stikkelsbær** (n)	['stikəls‚bær]
cranberry	**tranebær** (n)	['trɑnə‚bær]
orange	**appelsin** (m)	[ɑpel'sin]
mandarin	**mandarin** (m)	[mɑndɑ'rin]
pineapple	**ananas** (m)	['ɑnɑnɑs]
banana	**banan** (m)	[bɑ'nɑn]
date	**daddel** (m)	['dɑdəl]
lemon	**sitron** (m)	[si'trʊn]
apricot	**aprikos** (m)	[ɑpri'kʊs]
peach	**fersken** (m)	['fæʂkən]
kiwi	**kiwi** (m)	['kivi]
grapefruit	**grapefrukt** (m/f)	['grɛjp‚frʉkt]
berry	**bær** (n)	['bær]
berries	**bær** (n pl)	['bær]
cowberry	**tyttebær** (n)	['tʏtə‚bær]
wild strawberry	**markjordbær** (n)	['mɑrk juːr‚bær]
bilberry	**blåbær** (n)	['blɔ‚bær]

231. Flowers. Plants

flower	**blomst** (m)	['blɔmst]
bouquet (of flowers)	**bukett** (m)	[bʉ'kɛt]
rose (flower)	**rose** (m/f)	['rʊsə]
tulip	**tulipan** (m)	[tʉli'pɑn]
carnation	**nellik** (m)	['nɛlik]
gladiolus	**gladiolus** (m)	[glɑdi'ɔlʉs]
cornflower	**kornblomst** (m)	['kʊːn‚blɔmst]
harebell	**blåklokke** (m/f)	['blɔ‚klɔkə]
dandelion	**løvetann** (m/f)	['løvə‚tɑn]
camomile	**kamille** (m)	[kɑ'milə]
aloe	**aloe** (m)	['ɑlʊe]
cactus	**kaktus** (m)	['kɑktʉs]
rubber plant, ficus	**gummiplante** (m/f)	['gʉmi‚plɑntə]
lily	**lilje** (m)	['liljə]
geranium	**geranium** (m)	[ge'rɑnium]
hyacinth	**hyasint** (m)	[hiɑ'sint]

mimosa	mimose (m/f)	[mi'mɔsə]
narcissus	narsiss (m)	[na'şis]
nasturtium	blomkarse (m)	['blɔm͵kaşə]
orchid	orkidé (m)	[ɔrki'de]
peony	peon, pion (m)	[pe'ʊn], [pi'ʊn]
violet	fiol (m)	[fi'ʊl]
pansy	stemorsblomst (m)	['stemʊş͵blɔmst]
forget-me-not	forglemmegei (m)	[fɔr'glemə jæj]
daisy	tusenfryd (m)	['tʉsən͵fryd]
poppy	valmue (m)	['valmʉə]
hemp	hamp (m)	['hamp]
mint	mynte (m/f)	['myntə]
lily of the valley	liljekonvall (m)	['liljə kɔn'val]
snowdrop	snøklokke (m/f)	['snø͵klɔkə]
nettle	nesle (m/f)	['nɛslə]
sorrel	syre (m/f)	['syrə]
water lily	nøkkerose (m/f)	['nøkə͵rʊse]
fern	bregne (m/f)	['brɛjnə]
lichen	lav (m/n)	['lav]
greenhouse (tropical ~)	drivhus (n)	['driv͵hʉs]
lawn	gressplen (m)	['grɛs͵plen]
flowerbed	blomsterbed (n)	['blɔmstər͵bed]
plant	plante (m/f), vekst (m)	['plantə], ['vɛkst]
grass	gras (n)	['gras]
blade of grass	grasstrå (n)	['gras͵strɔ]
leaf	blad (n)	['blɑ]
petal	kronblad (n)	['krɔn͵blɑ]
stem	stilk (m)	['stilk]
tuber	rotknoll (m)	['rʊt͵knɔl]
young plant (shoot)	spire (m/f)	['spirə]
thorn	torn (m)	['tʊːɳ]
to blossom (vi)	å blomstre	[ɔ 'blɔmstrə]
to fade, to wither	å visne	[ɔ 'visnə]
smell (odor)	lukt (m/f)	['lʉkt]
to cut (flowers)	å skjære av	[ɔ 'şæːrə ɑː]
to pick (a flower)	å plukke	[ɔ 'plʉkə]

232. Cereals, grains

grain	korn (n)	['kʊːɳ]
cereal crops	cerealer (n pl)	[sere'alər]

ear (of barley, etc.)	**aks** (n)	['ɑks]
wheat	**hvete** (m)	['vetə]
rye	**rug** (m)	['rʉg]
oats	**havre** (m)	['hɑvrə]
millet	**hirse** (m)	['hiṣə]
barley	**bygg** (m/n)	['bɤg]
corn	**mais** (m)	['mɑis]
rice	**ris** (m)	['ris]
buckwheat	**bokhvete** (m)	['bʉk͵vetə]
pea plant	**ert** (m/f)	['æːʈ]
kidney bean	**bønne** (m/f)	['bœnə]
soy	**soya** (m)	['sɔja]
lentil	**linse** (m/f)	['linsə]
beans (pulse crops)	**bønner** (m/f pl)	['bœnər]

233. Vegetables. Greens

vegetables	**grønnsaker** (m pl)	['grœn͵sɑkər]
greens	**grønnsaker** (m pl)	['grœn͵sɑkər]
tomato	**tomat** (m)	[tʊ'mɑt]
cucumber	**agurk** (m)	[ɑ'gʉrk]
carrot	**gulrot** (m/f)	['gʉl͵rʊt]
potato	**potet** (m/f)	[pʊ'tet]
onion	**løk** (m)	['løk]
garlic	**hvitløk** (m)	['vit͵løk]
cabbage	**kål** (m)	['kɔl]
cauliflower	**blomkål** (m)	['blɔm͵kɔl]
Brussels sprouts	**rosenkål** (m)	['rʊsən͵kɔl]
broccoli	**brokkoli** (m)	['brɔkɔli]
beetroot	**rødbete** (m/f)	['røː͵betə]
eggplant	**aubergine** (m)	[ɔbɛr'ṣin]
zucchini	**squash** (m)	['skvɔṣ]
pumpkin	**gresskar** (n)	['grɛskɑr]
turnip	**nepe** (m/f)	['nepə]
parsley	**persille** (m/f)	[pæ'ṣilə]
dill	**dill** (m)	['dil]
lettuce	**salat** (m)	[sɑ'lɑt]
celery	**selleri** (m/n)	[sɛle͵ri]
asparagus	**asparges** (m)	[ɑ'spɑrṣəs]
spinach	**spinat** (m)	[spi'nɑt]
pea	**erter** (m pl)	['æːʈər]
beans	**bønner** (m/f pl)	['bœnər]
corn (maize)	**mais** (m)	['mɑis]

kidney bean	**bønne** (m/f)	['bœnə]
pepper	**pepper** (m)	['pɛpər]
radish	**reddik** (m)	['rɛdik]
artichoke	**artisjokk** (m)	[ˌɑːtʃiˈsɔk]

REGIONAL GEOGRAPHY

Countries. Nationalities

234. Western Europe

Europe	**Europa**	[ɛʉ'rʊpa]
European Union	**Den Europeiske Union**	[den ɛʉrʊ'pɛiskə ʉni'ɔn]
European (n)	**europeer** (m)	[ɛʉrʊ'peər]
European (adj)	**europeisk**	[ɛʉrʊ'pɛisk]
Austria	**Østerrike**	['østə,rikə]
Austrian (masc.)	**østerriker** (m)	['østə,rikər]
Austrian (fem.)	**østerriksk kvinne** (m/f)	['østə,riksk ,kvinə]
Austrian (adj)	**østerriksk**	['østə,riksk]
Great Britain	**Storbritannia**	['stʊr bri,tania]
England	**England**	['ɛŋlan]
British (masc.)	**brite** (m)	['britə]
British (fem.)	**brite** (m)	['britə]
English, British (adj)	**engelsk, britisk**	['ɛŋelsk], ['britisk]
Belgium	**Belgia**	['bɛlgia]
Belgian (masc.)	**belgier** (m)	['bɛlgiər]
Belgian (fem.)	**belgisk kvinne** (m/f)	['bɛlgisk ,kvinə]
Belgian (adj)	**belgisk**	['bɛlgisk]
Germany	**Tyskland**	['tʏsklan]
German (masc.)	**tysker** (m)	['tʏskər]
German (fem.)	**tysk kvinne** (m/f)	['tʏsk ,kvinə]
German (adj)	**tysk**	['tʏsk]
Netherlands	**Nederland**	['nedə,lan]
Holland	**Holland**	['hɔlan]
Dutch (masc.)	**hollender** (m)	['hɔ,lendər]
Dutch (fem.)	**hollandsk kvinne** (m/f)	['hɔ,lansk ,kvinə]
Dutch (adj)	**hollandsk**	['hɔ,lansk]
Greece	**Hellas**	['hɛlas]
Greek (masc.)	**greker** (m)	['grekər]
Greek (fem.)	**gresk kvinne** (m/f)	['grɛsk ,kvinə]
Greek (adj)	**gresk**	['grɛsk]
Denmark	**Danmark**	['danmark]
Dane (masc.)	**danske** (m)	['danskə]

Dane (fem.)	**dansk kvinne** (m/f)	['dɑnsk ˌkvinə]
Danish (adj)	**dansk**	['dɑnsk]
Ireland	**Irland**	['irlɑn]
Irish (masc.)	**irlender, irlending** (m)	['irˌlenər], ['irˌleniŋ]
Irish (fem.)	**irsk kvinne** (m/f)	['iːʂk ˌkvinə]
Irish (adj)	**irsk**	['iːʂk]
Iceland	**Island**	['islɑn]
Icelander (masc.)	**islending** (m)	['isˌleniŋ]
Icelander (fem.)	**islandsk kvinne** (m/f)	['isˌlɑnsk ˌkvinə]
Icelandic (adj)	**islandsk**	['isˌlɑnsk]
Spain	**Spania**	['spɑniɑ]
Spaniard (masc.)	**spanier** (m)	['spɑniər]
Spaniard (fem.)	**spansk kvinne** (m/f)	['spɑnsk ˌkvinə]
Spanish (adj)	**spansk**	['spɑnsk]
Italy	**Italia**	[i'tɑliɑ]
Italian (masc.)	**italiener** (m)	[itɑ'ljɛnər]
Italian (fem.)	**italiensk kvinne** (m/f)	[itɑ'ljɛnsk ˌkvinə]
Italian (adj)	**italiensk**	[itɑ'ljɛnsk]
Cyprus	**Kypros**	['kyprʊs]
Cypriot (masc.)	**kypriot** (m)	[kypri'ʊt]
Cypriot (fem.)	**kypriotisk kvinne** (m/f)	[kypri'ʊtisk ˌkvinə]
Cypriot (adj)	**kypriotisk**	[kypri'ʊtisk]
Malta	**Malta**	['mɑltɑ]
Maltese (masc.)	**malteser** (m)	[mɑl'tesər]
Maltese (fem.)	**maltesisk kvinne** (m/f)	[mɑl'tesisk ˌkvinə]
Maltese (adj)	**maltesisk**	[mɑl'tesisk]
Norway	**Norge**	['nɔrgə]
Norwegian (masc.)	**nordmann** (m)	['nuːrmɑn]
Norwegian (fem.)	**norsk kvinne** (m/f)	['nɔʂk ˌkvinə]
Norwegian (adj)	**norsk**	['nɔʂk]
Portugal	**Portugal**	[pɔːʈʉ'gɑl]
Portuguese (masc.)	**portugiser** (m)	[pɔːʈʉ'gisər]
Portuguese (fem.)	**portugisisk kvinne** (m/f)	[pɔːʈʉ'gisisk ˌkvinə]
Portuguese (adj)	**portugisisk**	[pɔːʈʉ'gisisk]
Finland	**Finland**	['finlɑn]
Finn (masc.)	**finne** (m)	['finə]
Finn (fem.)	**finsk kvinne** (m/f)	['finsk ˌkvinə]
Finnish (adj)	**finsk**	['finsk]
France	**Frankrike**	['frɑnkrikə]
French (masc.)	**franskmann** (m)	['frɑnskˌmɑn]
French (fem.)	**fransk kvinne** (m/f)	['frɑnsk ˌkvinə]
French (adj)	**fransk**	['frɑnsk]

Sweden	**Sverige**	['sværiə]
Swede (masc.)	**svenske** (m)	['svɛnskə]
Swede (fem.)	**svensk kvinne** (m/f)	['svɛnsk ˌkvinə]
Swedish (adj)	**svensk**	['svɛnsk]

Switzerland	**Sveits**	['svæjts]
Swiss (masc.)	**sveitser** (m)	['svæjtsər]
Swiss (fem.)	**sveitsisk kvinne** (m/f)	['svæjtsisk ˌkvinə]
Swiss (adj)	**sveitsisk**	['svæjtsisk]

Scotland	**Skottland**	['skɔtlɑn]
Scottish (masc.)	**skotte** (m)	['skɔtə]
Scottish (fem.)	**skotsk kvinne** (m/f)	['skɔtsk ˌkvinə]
Scottish (adj)	**skotsk**	['skɔtsk]

Vatican	**Vatikanet**	['vɑtiˌkɑne]
Liechtenstein	**Liechtenstein**	['lihtɛnˌstæjn]
Luxembourg	**Luxembourg**	['lʉksɛmˌbʉrg]
Monaco	**Monaco**	[mʊ'nɑkʊ]

235. Central and Eastern Europe

Albania	**Albania**	[al'bɑniɑ]
Albanian (masc.)	**albaner** (m)	[al'bɑnər]
Albanian (fem.)	**albansk kvinne** (m)	[al'bɑnsk ˌkvinə]
Albanian (adj)	**albansk**	[al'bɑnsk]

Bulgaria	**Bulgaria**	[bʉl'gɑriɑ]
Bulgarian (masc.)	**bulgarer** (m)	[bʉl'gɑrər]
Bulgarian (fem.)	**bulgarsk kvinne** (m/f)	[bʉl'gɑs̺k ˌkvinə]
Bulgarian (adj)	**bulgarsk**	[bʉl'gɑs̺k]

Hungary	**Ungarn**	['ʉŋɑːɳ]
Hungarian (masc.)	**ungarer** (m)	['ʉŋɑrər]
Hungarian (fem.)	**ungarsk kvinne** (m/f)	['ʉŋɑs̺k ˌkvinə]
Hungarian (adj)	**ungarsk**	['ʉŋɑs̺k]

Latvia	**Latvia**	['lɑtviɑ]
Latvian (masc.)	**latvier** (m)	['lɑtviər]
Latvian (fem.)	**latvisk kvinne** (m/f)	['lʉlvisk ˌkvinə]
Latvian (adj)	**latvisk**	['lɑtvisk]

Lithuania	**Litauen**	['liˌtaʋən]
Lithuanian (masc.)	**litauer** (m)	['liˌtaʋər]
Lithuanian (fem.)	**litauisk kvinne** (m/f)	['liˌtaʋisk ˌkvinə]
Lithuanian (adj)	**litauisk**	['liˌtaʋisk]

Poland	**Polen**	['pʊlen]
Pole (masc.)	**polakk** (m)	[pʊ'lɑk]
Pole (fem.)	**polsk kvinne** (m/f)	['pʊlsk ˌkvinə]

235

Polish (adj)	polsk	['pulsk]
Romania	Romania	[ru'mania]
Romanian (masc.)	rumener (m)	[ru'menər]
Romanian (fem.)	rumensk kvinne (m/f)	[ru'mɛnsk ˌkvinə]
Romanian (adj)	rumensk	[ru'mɛnsk]

Serbia	Serbia	['særbia]
Serbian (masc.)	serber (m)	['særbər]
Serbian (fem.)	serbisk kvinne (m/f)	['særbisk ˌkvinə]
Serbian (adj)	serbisk	['særbisk]

Slovakia	Slovakia	[ṣlu'vakia]
Slovak (masc.)	slovak (m)	[ṣlu'vak]
Slovak (fem.)	slovakisk kvinne (m/f)	[ṣlu'vakisk ˌkvinə]
Slovak (adj)	slovakisk	[ṣlu'vakisk]

Croatia	Kroatia	[kru'atia]
Croatian (masc.)	kroat (m)	[kru'at]
Croatian (fem.)	kroatisk kvinne (m/f)	[kru'atisk ˌkvinə]
Croatian (adj)	kroatisk	[kru'atisk]

Czech Republic	Tsjekkia	['tʂɛkija]
Czech (masc.)	tsjekker (m)	['tʂɛkər]
Czech (fem.)	tsjekkisk kvinne (m/f)	['tʂɛkisk ˌkvinə]
Czech (adj)	tsjekkisk	['tʂɛkisk]

Estonia	Estland	['ɛstlan]
Estonian (masc.)	estlender (m)	['ɛstˌlendər]
Estonian (fem.)	estisk kvinne (m/f)	['ɛstisk ˌkvinə]
Estonian (adj)	estisk	['ɛstisk]

Bosnia and Herzegovina	Bosnia-Hercegovina	['bosnia hersegoˌvina]
Macedonia (Republic of ~)	Makedonia	[make'donia]
Slovenia	Slovenia	[ṣlu'venia]
Montenegro	Montenegro	['montəˌnɛgru]

236. Former USSR countries

Azerbaijan	Aserbajdsjan	[aserbajd'ʂan]
Azerbaijani (masc.)	aserbajdsjaner (m)	[aserbajd'ʂanər]
Azerbaijani (fem.)	aserbajdsjansk kvinne (m)	[aserbajd'ʂansk ˌkvinə]
Azerbaijani, Azeri (adj)	aserbajdsjansk	[aserbajd'ʂansk]

Armenia	Armenia	[ar'menia]
Armenian (masc.)	armener (m)	[ar'menər]
Armenian (fem.)	armensk kvinne (m)	[ar'mensk ˌkvinə]
Armenian (adj)	armensk	[ar'mensk]
Belarus	Hviterussland	['vitəˌruslan]
Belarusian (masc.)	hviterusser (m)	['vitəˌrusər]

| Belarusian (fem.) | hviterussisk kvinne (m/f) | ['vitə,rʉsisk ,kvinə] |
| Belarusian (adj) | hviterussisk | ['vitə,rʉsisk] |

Georgia	Georgia	[ge'ɔrgia]
Georgian (masc.)	georgier (m)	[ge'ɔrgiər]
Georgian (fem.)	georgisk kvinne (m/f)	[ge'ɔrgisk ,kvinə]
Georgian (adj)	georgisk	[ge'ɔrgisk]

Kazakhstan	Kasakhstan	[ka'sak,stan]
Kazakh (masc.)	kasakh (m)	[ka'sak]
Kazakh (fem.)	kasakhisk kvinne (m/f)	[ka'sakisk ,kvinə]
Kazakh (adj)	kasakhisk	[ka'sakisk]
Kirghizia	Kirgisistan	[kir'gisi,stan]
Kirghiz (masc.)	kirgiser (m)	[kir'gisər]
Kirghiz (fem.)	kirgisisk kvinne (m/f)	[kir'gisisk ,kvinə]
Kirghiz (adj)	kirgisisk	[kir'gisisk]

Moldova, Moldavia	Moldova	[mɔl'dɔva]
Moldavian (masc.)	moldover (m)	[mɔl'dɔvər]
Moldavian (fem.)	moldovsk kvinne (m/f)	[mɔl'dɔvsk ,kvinə]
Moldavian (adj)	moldovsk	[mɔl'dɔvsk]

Russia	Russland	['rʉslan]
Russian (masc.)	russer (m)	['rʉsər]
Russian (fem.)	russisk kvinne (m/f)	['rʉsisk ,kvinə]
Russian (adj)	russisk	['rʉsisk]
Tajikistan	Tadsjikistan	[ta'dʂiki,stan]
Tajik (masc.)	tadsjik, tadsjiker (m)	[ta'dʂik], [ta'dʂikər]
Tajik (fem.)	tadsjikisk kvinne (m/f)	[ta'dʂikisk ,kvinə]
Tajik (adj)	tadsjikisk	[ta'dʂikisk]

Turkmenistan	Turkmenistan	[tʉrk'meni,stan]
Turkmen (masc.)	turkmen (m)	[tʉrk'men]
Turkmen (fem.)	turkmensk kvinne (m/f)	[tʉrk'mensk ,kvinə]
Turkmenian (adj)	turkmensk	[tʉrk'mensk]

Uzbekistan	Usbekistan	[ʉs'beki,stan]
Uzbek (masc.)	usbek, usbeker (m)	[ʉs'bek], [ʉs'bekər]
Uzbek (fem.)	usbekisk kvinne (m/f)	[ʉs'bekisk ,kvinə]
Uzbek (adj)	usbekisk	[ʉs'bekisk]

Ukraine	Ukraina	[ʉkra'inu]
Ukrainian (masc.)	ukrainer (m)	[ʉkra'inər]
Ukrainian (fem.)	ukrainsk kvinne (m/f)	[ʉkra'insk ,kvinə]
Ukrainian (adj)	ukrainsk	[ʉkra'insk]

237. Asia

| Asia | Asia | ['asia] |
| Asian (adj) | asiatisk | [asi'atisk] |

Vietnam	**Vietnam**	['vjɛtnam]
Vietnamese (masc.)	**vietnameser** (m)	[vjɛtna'mesər]
Vietnamese (fem.)	**vietnamesisk kvinne** (m/f)	[vjɛtna'mesisk ˌkvinə]
Vietnamese (adj)	**vietnamesisk**	[vjɛtna'mesisk]
India	**India**	['india]
Indian (masc.)	**inder** (m)	['indər]
Indian (fem.)	**indisk kvinne** (m/f)	['indisk ˌkvinə]
Indian (adj)	**indisk**	['indisk]
Israel	**Israel**	['israəl]
Israeli (masc.)	**israeler** (m)	[isra'elər]
Israeli (fem.)	**israelsk kvinne** (m/f)	[isra'elsk ˌkvinə]
Israeli (adj)	**israelsk**	[isra'elsk]
Jew (n)	**jøde** (m)	['jødə]
Jewess (n)	**jødisk kvinne** (m/f)	['jødisk ˌkvinə]
Jewish (adj)	**jødisk**	['jødisk]
China	**Kina**	['çina]
Chinese (masc.)	**kineser** (m)	[çi'nesər]
Chinese (fem.)	**kinesisk kvinne** (m/f)	[çi'nesisk ˌkvinə]
Chinese (adj)	**kinesisk**	[çi'nesisk]
Korean (masc.)	**koreaner** (m)	[kʊre'anər]
Korean (fem.)	**koreansk kvinne** (m/f)	[kʊre'ansk ˌkvinə]
Korean (adj)	**koreansk**	[kʊre'ansk]
Lebanon	**Libanon**	['libanɔn]
Lebanese (masc.)	**libaneser** (m)	[liba'nesər]
Lebanese (fem.)	**libanesisk kvinne** (m/f)	[liba'nesisk ˌkvinə]
Lebanese (adj)	**libanesisk**	[liba'nesisk]
Mongolia	**Mongolia**	[mʊŋ'gulia]
Mongolian (masc.)	**mongol** (m)	[mʊŋ'gul]
Mongolian (fem.)	**mongolsk kvinne** (m/f)	[mʊn'gɔlsk ˌkvinə]
Mongolian (adj)	**mongolsk**	[mʊn'gɔlsk]
Malaysia	**Malaysia**	[ma'lajsia]
Malaysian (masc.)	**malayer** (m)	[ma'lajər]
Malaysian (fem.)	**malayisk kvinne** (m/f)	[ma'lajisk ˌkvinə]
Malaysian (adj)	**malayisk**	[ma'lajisk]
Pakistan	**Pakistan**	['pakiˌstan]
Pakistani (masc.)	**pakistaner** (m)	[paki'stanər]
Pakistani (fem.)	**pakistansk kvinne** (m/f)	[paki'stansk ˌkvinə]
Pakistani (adj)	**pakistansk**	[paki'stansk]
Saudi Arabia	**Saudi-Arabia**	['saʊdi a'rabia]
Arab (masc.)	**araber** (m)	[a'rabər]
Arab (fem.)	**arabisk kvinne** (m)	[a'rabisk ˌkvinə]
Arab, Arabic (adj)	**arabisk**	[a'rabisk]

Thailand	**Thailand**	['tajlan]
Thai (masc.)	**thailender** (m)	['tajlendər]
Thai (fem.)	**thailandsk kvinne** (m/f)	['tajlansk ˌkvinə]
Thai (adj)	**thailandsk**	['tajlansk]

Taiwan	**Taiwan**	['taj ˌvan]
Taiwanese (masc.)	**taiwaner** (m)	[taj'vanər]
Taiwanese (fem.)	**taiwansk kvinne** (m/f)	[taj'vansk ˌkvinə]
Taiwanese (adj)	**taiwansk**	[taj'vansk]

Turkey	**Tyrkia**	[tyrkia]
Turk (masc.)	**tyrker** (m)	['tyrkər]
Turk (fem.)	**tyrkisk kvinne** (m/f)	['tyrkisk ˌkvinə]
Turkish (adj)	**tyrkisk**	['tyrkisk]

Japan	**Japan**	['japan]
Japanese (masc.)	**japaner** (m)	[ja'panər]
Japanese (fem.)	**japansk kvinne** (m/f)	['japansk ˌkvinə]
Japanese (adj)	**japansk**	['japansk]

Afghanistan	**Afghanistan**	[af'gani ˌstan]
Bangladesh	**Bangladesh**	[bangla'dɛʂ]
Indonesia	**Indonesia**	[indʊ'nesia]
Jordan	**Jordan**	['jɔrdan]

Iraq	**Irak**	['irak]
Iran	**Iran**	['iran]
Cambodia	**Kambodsja**	[kam'bɔdʂa]
Kuwait	**Kuwait**	['kʊvajt]

Laos	**Laos**	['laɔs]
Myanmar	**Myanmar**	['mjænma]
Nepal	**Nepal**	['nepal]
United Arab Emirates	**Forente Arabiske Emiratene**	[fo'rentə a'rabiskə ɛmi'ratenə]

Syria	**Syria**	['syria]
Palestine	**Palestina**	[pale'stina]
South Korea	**Sør-Korea**	['sør kʊˌrea]
North Korea	**Nord-Korea**	['nʊːr kʊ'rɛa]

238. North America

United States of America	**Amerikas Forente Stater**	[ɑ'merikas fɔ'rɛntə 'statər]
American (masc.)	**amerikaner** (m)	[ameri'kanər]
American (fem.)	**amerikansk kvinne** (m)	[ameri'kansk ˌkvinə]
American (adj)	**amerikansk**	[ameri'kansk]

| Canada | **Canada** | ['kanada] |
| Canadian (masc.) | **kanadier** (m) | [ka'nadiər] |

Canadian (fem.)	kanadisk kvinne (m/f)	[ka'nadisk ˌkvinə]
Canadian (adj)	kanadisk	[ka'nadisk]

Mexico	Mexico	['mɛksikʊ]
Mexican (masc.)	meksikaner (m)	[mɛksi'kanər]
Mexican (fem.)	meksikansk kvinne (m/f)	[mɛksi'kansk ˌkvinə]
Mexican (adj)	meksikansk	[mɛksi'kansk]

239. Central and South America

Argentina	Argentina	[argɛn'tina]
Argentinian (masc.)	argentiner (m)	[argɛn'tinər]
Argentinian (fem.)	argentinsk kvinne (m)	[argɛn'tinsk ˌkvinə]
Argentinian (adj)	argentinsk	[argɛn'tinsk]

Brazil	Brasilia	[bra'silia]
Brazilian (masc.)	brasilianer (m)	[brasili'anər]
Brazilian (fem.)	brasiliansk kvinne (m/f)	[brasili'ansk ˌkvinə]
Brazilian (adj)	brasiliansk	[brasili'ansk]

Colombia	Colombia	[kɔ'lʊmbia]
Colombian (masc.)	colombianer (m)	[kɔlʊmbi'anər]
Colombian (fem.)	colombiansk kvinne (m/f)	[kɔlʊmbi'ansk ˌkvinə]
Colombian (adj)	colombiansk	[kɔlʊmbi'ansk]

Cuba	Cuba	['kʉba]
Cuban (masc.)	kubaner (m)	[kʉ'banər]
Cuban (fem.)	kubansk kvinne (m/f)	[kʉ'bansk ˌkvinə]
Cuban (adj)	kubansk	[kʉ'bansk]

Chile	Chile	['tʂilə]
Chilean (masc.)	chilener (m)	[tʂi'lenər]
Chilean (fem.)	chilensk kvinne (m/f)	[tʂi'lensk ˌkvinə]
Chilean (adj)	chilensk	[tʂi'lensk]

Bolivia	Bolivia	[bɔ'livia]
Venezuela	Venezuela	[venesʉ'ɛla]
Paraguay	Paraguay	[parag'waj]
Peru	Peru	[pe'ruː]

Suriname	Surinam	['sʉriˌnam]
Uruguay	Uruguay	[ʉrygʊ'aj]
Ecuador	Ecuador	[ɛkʊa'dɔr]

The Bahamas	Bahamas	[ba'hamas]
Haiti	Haiti	[ha'iti]
Dominican Republic	Dominikanske Republikken	[dʉmini'kanskə repʉ'blikən]

Panama	Panama	['panama]
Jamaica	Jamaica	[ʂa'majka]

240. Africa

Egypt	**Egypt**	[ɛ'gypt]
Egyptian (masc.)	**egypter** (m)	[ɛ'gyptər]
Egyptian (fem.)	**egyptisk kvinne** (m/f)	[ɛ'gyptisk ˌkvinə]
Egyptian (adj)	**egyptisk**	[ɛ'gyptisk]
Morocco	**Marokko**	[ma'rɔkʊ]
Moroccan (masc.)	**marokkaner** (m)	[marɔ'kanər]
Moroccan (fem.)	**marokkansk kvinne** (m/f)	[marɔ'kansk ˌkvinə]
Moroccan (adj)	**marokkansk**	[marɔ'kansk]
Tunisia	**Tunisia**	['tʉ'nisia]
Tunisian (masc.)	**tuneser** (m)	[tʉ'nesər]
Tunisian (fem.)	**tunesisk kvinne** (m/f)	[tʉ'nesisk ˌkvinə]
Tunisian (adj)	**tunesisk**	[tʉ'nesisk]
Ghana	**Ghana**	['gana]
Zanzibar	**Zanzibar**	['sansibar]
Kenya	**Kenya**	['kenya]
Libya	**Libya**	['libia]
Madagascar	**Madagaskar**	[mada'gaskar]
Namibia	**Namibia**	[na'mibia]
Senegal	**Senegal**	[sene'gal]
Tanzania	**Tanzania**	['tansaˌnia]
South Africa	**Republikken Sør-Afrika**	[repʉ'bliken 'sørˌafrika]
African (masc.)	**afrikaner** (m)	[afri'kanər]
African (fem.)	**afrikansk kvinne** (m)	[afri'kansk ˌkvinə]
African (adj)	**afrikansk**	[afri'kansk]

241. Australia. Oceania

Australia	**Australia**	[aʊ'stralia]
Australian (masc.)	**australier** (m)	[aʊ'straliər]
Australian (fem.)	**australsk kvinne** (m/f)	[aʊ'strʉlsk ˌkvinə]
Australian (adj)	**australsk**	[aʊ'stralsk]
New Zealand	**New Zealand**	[njʉ'selan]
New Zealander (masc.)	**newzealender** (m)	[njʉ'selendər]
New Zealander (fem.)	**newzealandsk kvinne** (m/f)	[njʉ'selansk ˌkvinə]
New Zealand (as adj)	**newzealandsk**	[njʉ'selansk]
Tasmania	**Tasmania**	[tas'mania]
French Polynesia	**Fransk Polynesia**	['fransk poly'nesia]

242. Cities

Amsterdam	**Amsterdam**	['amstɛrˌdam]
Ankara	**Ankara**	['ankara]
Athens	**Athen, Aten**	[a'ten]
Baghdad	**Bagdad**	['bagdad]
Bangkok	**Bangkok**	['bankɔk]
Barcelona	**Barcelona**	[barsə'luna]
Beijing	**Peking, Beijing**	['pekiŋ], ['bɛjʒin]
Beirut	**Beirut**	['bæejˌrʉt]
Berlin	**Berlin**	[bɛr'lin]
Mumbai (Bombay)	**Bombay**	['bɔmbɛj]
Bonn	**Bonn**	['bɔn]
Bordeaux	**Bordeaux**	[bɔr'dɔː]
Bratislava	**Bratislava**	[brati'slava]
Brussels	**Brussel**	['brʉsɛl]
Bucharest	**Bukarest**	['bʉka'rɛst]
Budapest	**Budapest**	['bʉdapɛst]
Cairo	**Kairo**	['kajrʊ]
Kolkata (Calcutta)	**Calcutta**	[kal'kʉta]
Chicago	**Chicago**	[ʂi'kagʊ]
Copenhagen	**København**	['çøbənˌhavn]
Dar-es-Salaam	**Dar-es-Salaam**	['daresaˌlam]
Delhi	**Delhi**	['dɛli]
Dubai	**Dubai**	['dʉbaj]
Dublin	**Dublin**	['døblin]
Düsseldorf	**Düsseldorf**	['dʉsəlˌdɔrf]
Florence	**Firenze**	[fi'rɛnsə]
Frankfurt	**Frankfurt**	['frankfʉːt]
Geneva	**Genève**	[ʂe'nɛv]
The Hague	**Haag**	['hag]
Hamburg	**Hamburg**	['hambʉrg]
Hanoi	**Hanoi**	['hanɔj]
Havana	**Havana**	[ha'vana]
Helsinki	**Helsinki**	['hɛlsinki]
Hiroshima	**Hiroshima**	[hirʊ'ʂima]
Hong Kong	**Hongkong**	['hɔnˌkɔn]
Istanbul	**Istanbul**	['istanbʉl]
Jerusalem	**Jerusalem**	[je'rʉsalem]
Kyiv	**Kiev**	['kiːef]
Kuala Lumpur	**Kuala Lumpur**	[kʉ'ala 'lʉmpʉr]
Lisbon	**Lisboa**	['lisbʊa]
London	**London**	['lɔndɔn]
Los Angeles	**Los Angeles**	[ˌlɔs'ændʒələs]

Lyons	Lyon	[li'ɔn]
Madrid	Madrid	[mɑ'drid]
Marseille	Marseille	[mɑr'sɛj]
Mexico City	Mexico City	['mɛksikʊ 'siti]

Miami	Miami	[mɑ'jami]
Montreal	Montreal	[mɔntri'ɔl]
Moscow	Moskva	[mɔ'skvɑ]
Munich	München	['mʉnhən]

Nairobi	Nairobi	[nɑj'rʊbi]
Naples	Napoli	['nɑpʊli]
New York	New York	[njʉ 'jork]
Nice	Nice	['nis]
Oslo	Oslo	['ɔʂlʊ]
Ottawa	Ottawa	['ɔtɑvɑ]

Paris	Paris	[pɑ'ris]
Prague	Praha	['prɑhɑ]
Rio de Janeiro	Rio de Janeiro	['riu de ʂɑ'næjrʊ]
Rome	Roma	['rʊmɑ]

Saint Petersburg	Sankt Petersburg	[ˌsɑnkt 'petɛʂˌbʉrg]
Seoul	Seoul	[se'u:l]
Shanghai	Shanghai	['ʂɑŋhɑj]
Singapore	Singapore	['siŋɑ'pɔr]
Stockholm	Stockholm	['stɔkhɔlm]
Sydney	Sydney	['sidni]

Taipei	Taipei	['tɑjpæj]
Tokyo	Tokyo	['tɔkiʊ]
Toronto	Toronto	[to'rɔntʊ]

Venice	Venezia	[ve'netsiɑ]
Vienna	Wien	['vin]
Warsaw	Warszawa	[vɑ'ʂɑvɑ]
Washington	Washington	['vɔʂiŋtən]

243. Politics. Government. Part 1

politics	politikk (m)	[pʊli'tik]
political (adj)	politisk	[pʊ'litisk]
politician	politiker (m)	[pʊ'litikər]

state (country)	stat (m)	['stɑt]
citizen	statsborger (m)	['stɑtsˌbɔrgər]
citizenship	statsborgerskap (n)	['stɑtsbɔrgəˌskɑp]

| national emblem | riksvåpen (n) | ['riksˌvɔpən] |
| national anthem | nasjonalsang (m) | [nɑʂʊ'nɑlˌsɑn] |

government	regjering (m/f)	[rɛ'jeriŋ]
head of state	landets leder (m)	['lanɛts ˌledər]
parliament	parlament (n)	[pɑːⁱa'mɛnt]
party	parti (n)	[pɑː'ti]

| capitalism | kapitalisme (n) | [kapita'lismə] |
| capitalist (adj) | kapitalistisk | [kapita'listisk] |

| socialism | sosialisme (m) | [sʊsia'lismə] |
| socialist (adj) | sosialistisk | [sʊsia'listisk] |

communism	kommunisme (m)	[kʊmʉ'nismə]
communist (adj)	kommunistisk	[kʊmʉ'nistisk]
communist (n)	kommunist (m)	[kʊmʉ'nist]

democracy	demokrati (n)	[demʊkra'ti]
democrat	demokrat (m)	[demʊ'krat]
democratic (adj)	demokratisk	[demʊ'kratisk]
Democratic party	demokratisk parti (n)	[demʊ'kratisk pɑː'ti]

| liberal (n) | liberaler (m) | [libə'ralər] |
| liberal (adj) | liberal | [libə'ral] |

| conservative (n) | konservativ (m) | [kʊn'sɛrvaˌtiv] |
| conservative (adj) | konservativ | [kʊn'sɛrvaˌtiv] |

republic (n)	republikk (m)	[repʉ'blik]
republican (n)	republikaner (m)	[repʉbli'kanər]
Republican party	republikanske parti (n)	[repʉbli'kanskə pɑː'ti]

elections	valg (n)	['valg]
to elect (vt)	å velge	[ɔ 'vɛlgə]
elector, voter	velger (m)	['vɛlgər]
election campaign	valgkampanje (m)	['valg kam'panjə]

voting (n)	avstemning, votering (m)	['afˌstɛmniŋ], ['votəriŋ]
to vote (vi)	å stemme	[ɔ 'stɛmə]
suffrage, right to vote	stemmerett (m)	['stɛməˌrɛt]

candidate	kandidat (m)	[kandi'dat]
to be a candidate	å kandidere	[ɔ kandi'derə]
campaign	kampanje (m)	[kam'panjə]

| opposition (as adj) | opposisjons- | [ɔpʊsi'ʂʊns-] |
| opposition (n) | opposisjon (m) | [ɔpʊsi'ʂʊn] |

visit	besøk (n)	[be'søk]
official visit	offisielt besøk (n)	[ɔfi'sjɛlt be'søk]
international (adj)	internasjonal	['intɛːnɑʂʊˌnal]

| negotiations | forhandlinger (m pl) | [fɔr'handliŋər] |
| to negotiate (vi) | å forhandle | [ɔ fɔr'handlə] |

244. Politics. Government. Part 2

society	**samfunn** (n)	['sɑmˌfʉn]
constitution	**grunnlov** (m)	['grʉnˌlɔv]
power (political control)	**makt** (m)	['mɑkt]
corruption	**korrupsjon** (m)	[kʉrʉp'ʂʊn]
law (justice)	**lov** (m)	['lɔv]
legal (legitimate)	**lovlig**	['lɔvli]
justice (fairness)	**rettferdighet** (m)	[rɛt'færdiˌhet]
just (fair)	**rettferdig**	[rɛt'færdi]
committee	**komité** (m)	[kʊmi'te]
bill (draft law)	**lovforslag** (n)	['lɔvˌfɔʂlɑg]
budget	**budsjett** (n)	[bʉd'ʂɛt]
policy	**politikk** (m)	[pʊli'tik]
reform	**reform** (m/f)	[rɛ'fɔrm]
radical (adj)	**radikal**	[rɑdi'kɑl]
power (strength, force)	**kraft** (m/f)	['krɑft]
powerful (adj)	**mektig**	['mɛkti]
supporter	**tilhenger** (m)	['tilˌhɛŋər]
influence	**innflytelse** (m)	['inˌflytəlsə]
regime (e.g., military ~)	**regime** (n)	[rɛ'ʂimə]
conflict	**konflikt** (m)	[kʊn'flikt]
conspiracy (plot)	**sammensvergelse** (m)	['sɑmənˌsværgəlsə]
provocation	**provokasjon** (m)	[prʊvʊkɑ'ʂʊn]
to overthrow (regime, etc.)	**å styrte**	[ɔ 'sty:tə]
overthrow (of government)	**styrting** (m/f)	['sty:tiŋ]
revolution	**revolusjon** (m)	[revʊlʉ'ʂʊn]
coup d'état	**statskupp** (n)	['stɑtsˌkʉp]
military coup	**militærkupp** (n)	[mili'tærˌkʉp]
crisis	**krise** (m/f)	['krisə]
economic recession	**økonomisk nedgang** (m)	[økʊ'nʊmisk 'nedˌgɑŋ]
demonstrator (protestor)	**demonstrant** (m)	[demʊn'strɑnt]
demonstration	**demonstrasjon** (m)	[demɔnstrʉ'ʂʊn]
martial law	**krigstilstand** (m)	['krigstilˌstɑn]
military base	**militærbase** (m)	[mili'tærˌbɑsə]
stability	**stabilitet** (m)	[stɑbili'tet]
stable (adj)	**stabil**	[stɑ'bil]
exploitation	**utbytting** (m/f)	['ʉtˌbytiŋ]
to exploit (workers)	**å utbytte**	[ɔ 'ʉtˌbytə]
racism	**rasisme** (m)	[rɑ'sismə]
racist	**rasist** (m)	[rɑ'sist]

| fascism | fascisme (m) | [fɑ'ʂismə] |
| fascist | fascist (m) | [fɑ'ʂist] |

245. Countries. Miscellaneous

foreigner	utlending (m)	['ʉtˌleniŋ]
foreign (adj)	utenlandsk	['ʉtənˌlɑnsk]
abroad	i utlandet	[i 'ʉtˌlɑnə]
(in a foreign country)		

emigrant	emigrant (m)	[ɛmi'grɑnt]
emigration	emigrasjon (m)	[ɛmigrɑ'ʂʉn]
to emigrate (vi)	å emigrere	[ɔ ɛmi'grɛrə]

the West	Vesten	['vɛstən]
the East	Østen	['østən]
the Far East	Det fjerne østen	['de 'fjæːŋə ˌøstɛn]

civilization	sivilisasjon (m)	[sivilisɑ'ʂʉn]
humanity (mankind)	menneskehet (m)	['mɛnəskeˌhet]
the world (earth)	verden (m)	['værdən]
peace	fred (m)	['frɛd]
worldwide (adj)	verdens-	['værdəns-]

homeland	fedreland (n)	['fædrəˌlɑn]
people (population)	folk (n)	['folk]
population	befolkning (m)	[be'folkniŋ]

people (a lot of ~)	folk (n)	['folk]
nation (people)	nasjon (m)	[nɑ'ʂʉn]
generation	generasjon (m)	[generɑ'ʂʉn]

territory (area)	territorium (n)	[tɛri'tʉrium]
region	region (m)	[rɛgi'ʉn]
state (part of a country)	delstat (m)	['delˌstɑt]

tradition	tradisjon (m)	[trɑdi'ʂʉn]
custom (tradition)	skikk, sedvane (m)	['ʂik], ['sɛdˌvɑnə]
ecology	økologi (m)	[økʉlʉ'gi]

Indian (Native American)	indianer (m)	[indi'ɑnər]
Gypsy (masc.)	sigøyner (m)	[si'gøjnər]
Gypsy (fem.)	sigøynerske (m/f)	[si'gøjnəʂkə]
Gypsy (adj)	sigøynersk	[si'gøjnəʂk]

empire	imperium, keiserrike (n)	['im'perium], ['kæjsəˌrike]
colony	koloni (m)	[kʉlu'ni]
slavery	slaveri (n)	[slɑvɛ'ri]
invasion	invasjon (m)	[invɑ'ʂʉn]
famine	hungersnød (m/f)	['hʉŋɛʂˌnød]

246. Major religious groups. Confessions

religion	religion (m)	[religi'ʊn]
religious (adj)	religiøs	[reli'gjøs]
faith, belief	tro (m)	['trʊ]
to believe (in God)	å tro	[ɔ 'trʊ]
believer	troende (m)	['trʊenə]
atheism	ateisme (m)	[ate'ismə]
atheist	ateist (m)	[ate'ist]
Christianity	kristendom (m)	['kristən‚dɔm]
Christian (n)	kristen (m)	['kristən]
Christian (adj)	kristelig	['kristəli]
Catholicism	katolisisme (m)	[katʊli'sismə]
Catholic (n)	katolikk (m)	[katʊ'lik]
Catholic (adj)	katolsk	[ka'tʊlsk]
Protestantism	protestantisme (m)	[prʊtɛstan'tismə]
Protestant Church	den protestantiske kirke	[den prʊtɛ'stantiskə ‚çirkə]
Protestant (n)	protestant (m)	[prʊtɛ'stant]
Orthodoxy	ortodoksi (m)	[ɔ:ʈʊdʊk'si]
Orthodox Church	den ortodokse kirke	[den ɔ:ʈʊ'dɔksə ‚çirkə]
Orthodox (n)	ortodoks (n)	[ɔ:ʈʊ'dɔks]
Presbyterianism	presbyterianisme (m)	[prɛsbytæria'nismə]
Presbyterian Church	den presbyterianske kirke	[den prɛsbyteri'anskə ‚çirkə]
Presbyterian (n)	presbyterianer (m)	[prɛsbytæri'anər]
Lutheranism	lutherdom (m)	[lʉtər'dɔm]
Lutheran (n)	lutheraner (m)	[lʉtə'ranər]
Baptist Church	baptisme (m)	[bap'tismə]
Baptist (n)	baptist (m)	[bap'tist]
Anglican Church	den anglikanske kirke	[den aŋli'kanskə ‚çirkə]
Anglican (n)	anglikaner (m)	[aŋli'kanər]
Mormonism	mormonisme (m)	[mɔrmʊ'nismə]
Mormon (n)	mormon (m)	[mʊr'mʊn]
Judaism	judaisme (m)	['jʉda‚ismə]
Jew (n)	judeer (m)	['jʉ'deər]
Buddhism	buddhisme (m)	[bʉ'dismə]
Buddhist (n)	buddhist (m)	[bʉ'dist]
Hinduism	hinduisme (m)	[hindʉ'ismə]
Hindu (n)	hindu (m)	['hindʉ]

Islam	islam	['islɑm]
Muslim (n)	muslim (m)	[mʉ'slim]
Muslim (adj)	muslimsk	[mʉ'slimsk]
Shiah Islam	sjiisme (m)	[ʂi'ismə]
Shiite (n)	sjiitt (m)	[ʂi'it]
Sunni Islam	sunnisme (m)	[sʉ'nismə]
Sunnite (n)	sunnimuslim (m)	['sʉni mʉs,lim]

247. Religions. Priests

priest	prest (m)	['prɛst]
the Pope	Paven	['pɑvən]
monk, friar	munk (m)	['mʉnk]
nun	nonne (m/f)	['nɔnə]
pastor	pastor (m)	['pɑstʊr]
abbot	abbed (m)	['ɑbed]
vicar (parish priest)	sogneprest (m)	['sɔŋnə,prɛst]
bishop	biskop (m)	['biskɔp]
cardinal	kardinal (m)	[kɑːɖi'nɑl]
preacher	predikant (m)	[prɛdi'kɑnt]
preaching	preken (m)	['prɛkən]
parishioners	menighet (m/f)	['meni,het]
believer	troende (m)	['trʊenə]
atheist	ateist (m)	[ate'ist]

248. Faith. Christianity. Islam

Adam	Adam	['ɑdɑm]
Eve	Eva	['ɛvɑ]
God	Gud (m)	['gʉd]
the Lord	Herren	['hærən]
the Almighty	Den Allmektige	[den ɑl'mɛktiə]
sin	synd (m/f)	['sʏn]
to sin (vi)	å synde	[ɔ 'sʏnə]
sinner (masc.)	synder (m)	['sʏnər]
sinner (fem.)	synderinne (m)	['sʏnə,rinə]
hell	helvete (n)	['hɛlvetə]
paradise	paradis (n)	['pɑrɑ,dis]
Jesus	Jesus	['jesʉs]
Jesus Christ	Jesus Kristus	['jesʉs ,kristʉs]

the Holy Spirit	**Den Hellige Ånd**	[dən 'hɛliə ˌɔn]
the Savior	**Frelseren**	['frɛlserən]
the Virgin Mary	**Jomfru Maria**	['jɔmfrʉ maˌria]

the Devil	**Djevel** (m)	['djevəl]
devil's (adj)	**djevelsk**	['djevəlsk]
Satan	**Satan**	['satan]
satanic (adj)	**satanisk**	[sɑ'tanisk]

angel	**engel** (m)	['ɛŋəl]
guardian angel	**skytsengel** (m)	['syts'ɛŋəl]
angelic (adj)	**engle-**	['ɛŋlə-]

apostle	**apostel** (m)	[ɑ'pɔstəl]
archangel	**erkeengel** (m)	['ærkəˌæŋəl]
the Antichrist	**Antikrist**	['anti'krist]

Church	**kirken** (m)	['çirkən]
Bible	**bibel** (m)	['bibəl]
biblical (adj)	**bibelsk**	['bibəlsk]

Old Testament	**Det Gamle Testamente**	[de 'gamlə tɛstɑ'mentə]
New Testament	**Det Nye Testamente**	[de 'nye tɛstɑ'mentə]
Gospel	**evangelium** (n)	[ɛvɑn'gelium]
Holy Scripture	**Den Hellige Skrift**	[dən 'hɛliə ˌskrift]
Heaven	**Himmerike** (n)	['himəˌrikə]

Commandment	**bud** (n)	['bʉd]
prophet	**profet** (m)	[prʉ'fet]
prophecy	**profeti** (m)	[prʉfe'ti]

Allah	**Allah**	['ala]
Mohammed	**Muhammed**	[mʉ'hamed]
the Koran	**Koranen**	[kʉ'ranən]

mosque	**moské** (m)	[mʉ'ske]
mullah	**mulla** (m)	['mʉla]
prayer	**bønn** (m)	['bœn]
to pray (vi, vt)	**å be**	[ɔ 'be]

pilgrimage	**pilegrimsreise** (m/f)	['piləgrimsˌræjsə]
pilgrim	**pilegrim** (m)	['piləgrim]
Mecca	**Mekka**	['mɛka]

church	**kirke** (m/f)	['çirkə]
temple	**tempel** (n)	['tɛmpəl]
cathedral	**katedral** (m)	[kate'dral]
Gothic (adj)	**gotisk**	['gɔtisk]
synagogue	**synagoge** (m)	[synɑ'gʉgə]
mosque	**moské** (m)	[mʉ'ske]
chapel	**kapell** (n)	[kɑ'pɛl]
abbey	**abbedi** (n)	['abedi]

convent	kloster (n)	['klɔstər]
monastery	kloster (n)	['klɔstər]
bell (church ~s)	klokke (m/f)	['klɔkə]
bell tower	klokketårn (n)	['klɔkəˌtoːn]
to ring (ab. bells)	å ringe	[ɔ 'riŋə]
cross	kors (n)	['kɔːʂ]
cupola (roof)	kuppel (m)	['kʉpəl]
icon	ikon (m/n)	[i'kʊn]
soul	sjel (m)	['ʂɛl]
fate (destiny)	skjebne (m)	['ʂɛbnə]
evil (n)	ondskap (n)	['ʊnˌskɑp]
good (n)	godhet (m)	['gʊˌhet]
vampire	vampyr (m)	[vɑm'pyr]
witch (evil ~)	heks (m)	['hɛks]
demon	demon (m)	[de'mʊn]
spirit	ånd (m)	['ɔn]
redemption (giving us ~)	forløsning (m/f)	[fɔː'løsniŋ]
to redeem (vt)	å sone	[ɔ 'sʊnə]
church service, mass	gudstjeneste (m)	['gʉtsˌtjenɛstə]
to say mass	å holde gudstjeneste	[ɔ 'hɔldə 'gʉtsˌtjenɛstə]
confession	skriftemål (n)	['skriftəˌmol]
to confess (vi)	å skrifte	[ɔ 'skriftə]
saint (n)	helgen (m)	['hɛlgən]
sacred (holy)	hellig	['hɛli]
holy water	vievann (n)	['viəˌvɑn]
ritual (n)	ritual (n)	[ritʉ'ɑl]
ritual (adj)	rituell	[ritʉ'ɛl]
sacrifice	ofring (m/f)	['ɔfriŋ]
superstition	overtro (m)	['ɔvəˌtrʊ]
superstitious (adj)	overtroisk	['ɔvəˌtrʊisk]
afterlife	livet etter dette	['livə ˌɛtər 'dɛtə]
eternal life	det evige liv	[de ˌeviə 'liv]

MISCELLANEOUS

249. Various useful words

background (green ~)	**bakgrunn** (m)	['bɑkˌgrʉn]
balance (of situation)	**balanse** (m)	[bɑ'lɑnsə]
barrier (obstacle)	**hinder** (n)	['hindər]
base (basis)	**basis** (n)	['bɑsis]
beginning	**begynnelse** (m)	[be'jinəlsə]
category	**kategori** (m)	[kɑtegʉ'ri]
cause (reason)	**årsak** (m/f)	['oːˌsɑk]
choice	**valg** (n)	['vɑlg]
coincidence	**sammenfall** (n)	['sɑmənˌfɑl]
comfortable (~ chair)	**bekvem**	[be'kvem]
comparison	**sammenlikning** (m)	['sɑmənˌlikniŋ]
compensation	**kompensasjon** (m)	[kʉmpɛnsɑ'ʂʉn]
degree (extent, amount)	**grad** (m)	['grɑd]
development	**utvikling** (m/f)	['ʉtˌvikliŋ]
difference	**skilnad, forskjell** (m)	['ʂilnɑd], ['fɔːʂɛl]
effect (e.g., of drugs)	**effekt** (m)	[ɛ'fɛkt]
effort (exertion)	**anstrengelse** (m)	['ɑnˌstrɛŋəlsə]
element	**element** (n)	[ɛle'mɛnt]
end (finish)	**slutt** (m)	['ʂlʉt]
example (illustration)	**eksempel** (n)	[ɛk'sɛmpəl]
fact	**faktum** (n)	['fɑktum]
frequent (adj)	**hyppig**	['hʏpi]
growth (development)	**vekst** (m)	['vɛkst]
help	**hjelp** (m)	['jɛlp]
ideal	**ideal** (n)	[ide'ɑl]
kind (sort, type)	**slags** (n)	['ʂlɑks]
labyrinth	**labyrint** (m)	[lɑby'rlnt]
mistake, error	**feil** (m)	['fæjl]
moment	**moment** (n)	[mɔ'mɛnt]
object (thing)	**objekt** (n)	[ɔb'jɛkt]
obstacle	**hindring** (m/f)	['hindriŋ]
original (original copy)	**original** (m)	[ɔrigi'nɑl]
part (~ of sth)	**del** (m)	['del]
particle, small part	**partikkel** (m)	[pɑːˈʈikəl]
pause (break)	**pause** (m)	['paʉsə]

position	posisjon (m)	[pɔsi'ʂʊn]
principle	prinsipp (n)	[prin'sip]
problem	problem (n)	[prʊ'blem]

process	prosess (m)	[prʊ'sɛs]
progress	fremskritt (n)	['frɛmˌskrit]
property (quality)	egenskap (m)	['ɛgənˌskɑp]
reaction	reaksjon (m)	[rɛak'ʂʊn]
risk	risiko (m)	['risikʊ]

secret	hemmelighet (m/f)	['hɛmǝliˌhet]
series	serie (m)	['seriǝ]
shape (outer form)	form (m/f)	['fɔrm]
situation	situasjon (m)	[sitɥɑ'ʂʊn]
solution	løsning (m)	['løsniŋ]

standard (adj)	standard-	['stɑnˌdɑr-]
standard (level of quality)	standard (m)	['stɑnˌdɑr]
stop (pause)	stopp (m), hvile (m/f)	['stɔp], ['vilǝ]
style	stil (m)	['stil]

system	system (n)	[sʏ'stem]
table (chart)	tabell (m)	[tɑ'bɛl]
tempo, rate	tempo (n)	['tɛmpʊ]
term (word, expression)	term (m)	['tɛrm]

thing (object, item)	ting (m)	['tiŋ]
truth (e.g., moment of ~)	sannhet (m)	['sɑnˌhet]
turn (please wait your ~)	tur (m)	['tɵr]
type (sort, kind)	type (m)	['typǝ]
urgent (adj)	omgående	['ɔmˌgɔːnǝ]

urgently (adv)	omgående	['ɔmˌgɔːnǝ]
utility (usefulness)	nytte (m/f)	['nʏtǝ]
variant (alternative)	variant (m)	[vɑri'ɑnt]
way (means, method)	måte (m)	['moːtǝ]
zone	sone (m/f)	['sʊnǝ]

250. Modifiers. Adjectives. Part 1

additional (adj)	ytterligere	['ytǝˌliǝrǝ]
ancient (~ civilization)	oldtidens, antikkens	['ɔlˌtidǝns], [ɑn'tikǝns]
artificial (adj)	kunstig	['kɵnsti]
back, rear (adj)	bak-	['bɑk-]
bad (adj)	dårlig	['doːli]

beautiful (~ palace)	vakker	['vɑkǝr]
beautiful (person)	vakker	['vɑkǝr]
big (in size)	stor	['stʊr]

bitter (taste)	**bitter**	['bitər]
blind (sightless)	**blind**	['blin]
calm, quiet (adj)	**rolig**	['rʊli]
careless (negligent)	**slurvet**	['slʉrvət]
caring (~ father)	**omsorgsfull**	['ɔm,sɔrgsfʉl]
central (adj)	**sentral**	[sɛn'tral]
cheap (low-priced)	**billig**	['bili]
cheerful (adj)	**glad, munter**	['gla], ['mʉntər]
children's (adj)	**barne-**	['bɑːŋə-]
civil (~ law)	**sivil**	[si'vil]
clandestine (secret)	**hemmelig**	['hɛməli]
clean (free from dirt)	**ren**	['ren]
clear (explanation, etc.)	**klar**	['klɑr]
clever (smart)	**klok**	['klʊk]
close (near in space)	**nær**	['nær]
closed (adj)	**stengt**	['stɛŋt]
cloudless (sky)	**skyfri**	['ʂy,fri]
cold (drink, weather)	**kald**	['kal]
compatible (adj)	**forenelig**	[fo'renli]
contented (satisfied)	**nøgd, tilfreds**	['nøgd], [til'frɛds]
continuous (uninterrupted)	**uavbrutt**	[ʉːʼav,brʉt]
cool (weather)	**kjølig**	['çœli]
dangerous (adj)	**farlig**	['fɑːli]
dark (room)	**mørk**	['mœrk]
dead (not alive)	**død**	['dø]
dense (fog, smoke)	**tykk**	['tʏk]
destitute (extremely poor)	**utfattig**	['ʉt,fati]
different (not the same)	**ulike**	['ʉlikə]
difficult (decision)	**svær**	['svær]
difficult (problem, task)	**komplisert**	[kʊmpli'sɛːt]
dim, faint (light)	**svak**	['svak]
dirty (not clean)	**skitten**	['ʂitən]
distant (in space)	**fjern**	['fjæːŋ]
dry (clothoε, ɵtc.)	**tørr**	['tœr]
easy (not difficult)	**lett**	['let]
empty (glass, room)	**tom**	['tɔm]
even (e.g., ~ surface)	**jevn**	['jɛvn]
exact (amount)	**presis, eksakt**	[prɛ'sis], [ɛk'sɑkt]
excellent (adj)	**utmerket**	['ʉt,mærkət]
excessive (adj)	**overdreven**	['ɔvə,drevən]
expensive (adj)	**dyr**	['dyr]
exterior (adj)	**ytre**	['ytrə]
far (the ~ East)	**fjern**	['fjæːŋ]

fast (quick)	**hastig**	['hɑsti]
fatty (food)	**fet**	['fet]
fertile (land, soil)	**fruktbar**	['frʉktˌbɑr]
flat (~ panel display)	**flat**	['flɑt]
foreign (adj)	**utenlandsk**	['ʉtənˌlɑnsk]
fragile (china, glass)	**skjør**	['ʂør]
free (at no cost)	**gratis**	['grɑtis]
free (unrestricted)	**fri**	['fri]
fresh (~ water)	**fersk-**	['fæʂk-]
fresh (e.g., ~ bread)	**fersk**	['fæʂk]
frozen (food)	**frossen, dypfryst**	['frɔsən], ['dypˌfrʏst]
full (completely filled)	**full**	['fʉl]
gloomy (house, forecast)	**mørk**	['mœrk]
good (book, etc.)	**bra**	['brɑ]
good, kind (kindhearted)	**god**	['gʊ]
grateful (adj)	**takknemlig**	[tak'nɛmli]
happy (adj)	**lykkelig**	['lʏkəli]
hard (not soft)	**hard**	['hɑr]
heavy (in weight)	**tung**	['tʉŋ]
hostile (adj)	**fiendtlig**	['fjɛntli]
hot (adj)	**het, varm**	['het], ['vɑrm]
huge (adj)	**enorm**	[ɛ'nɔrm]
humid (adj)	**fuktig**	['fʉkti]
hungry (adj)	**sulten**	['sʉltən]
ill (sick, unwell)	**syk**	['syk]
immobile (adj)	**ubevegelig, urørlig**	[ʉbe'vɛgli], [ʉ'rø:ɭi]
important (adj)	**viktig**	['vikti]
impossible (adj)	**umulig**	[ʉ'mʉli]
incomprehensible	**uforståelig**	[ʉfɔ'ʂtɔəli]
indispensable (adj)	**nødvendig**	['nødˌvɛndi]
inexperienced (adj)	**uerfaren**	[ʉer'fɑrən]
insignificant (adj)	**ubetydelig**	[ʉbe'tydəli]
interior (adj)	**indre**	['indrə]
joint (~ decision)	**felles**	['fɛləs]
last (e.g., ~ week)	**forrige**	['fɔriə]
last (final)	**sist**	['sist]
left (e.g., ~ side)	**venstre**	['vɛnstrə]
legal (legitimate)	**lovlig**	['lovli]
light (in weight)	**lett**	['let]
light (pale color)	**lys**	['lys]
limited (adj)	**begrenset**	[be'grɛnsət]
liquid (fluid)	**flytende**	['flytnə]
long (e.g., ~ hair)	**lang**	['lɑŋ]

| loud (voice, etc.) | **høy** | ['høj] |
| low (voice) | **lav** | ['lɑv] |

251. Modifiers. Adjectives. Part 2

main (principal)	**hoved-**	['hɔvəd-]
matt, matte	**matt**	['mɑt]
meticulous (job)	**nøyaktig**	['nøjakti]
mysterious (adj)	**mystisk**	['mʏstisk]
narrow (street, etc.)	**smal**	['smɑl]

native (~ country)	**hjem-**	['jɛm-]
nearby (adj)	**nær**	['nær]
nearsighted (adj)	**nærsynt**	['næˌsʏnt]
needed (necessary)	**nødvendig**	['nødˌvɛndi]
negative (~ response)	**negativ**	['negɑˌtiv]

neighboring (adj)	**nabo-**	['nɑbʊ-]
nervous (adj)	**nervøs**	[nær'vøs]
new (adj)	**ny**	['ny]
next (e.g., ~ week)	**neste**	['nɛstə]

nice (kind)	**snill**	['snil]
nice (voice)	**trivelig, behagelig**	['trivli], [be'hɑgli]
normal (adj)	**normal**	[nɔr'mɑl]
not big (adj)	**liten, ikke stor**	['litən], [ˌikə 'stʊr]
not difficult (adj)	**lett**	['let]

obligatory (adj)	**obligatorisk**	[ɔbligɑ'tʊrisk]
old (house)	**gammel**	['gɑməl]
open (adj)	**åpen**	['ɔpən]
opposite (adj)	**motsatt**	['mʊtˌsɑt]

ordinary (usual)	**vanlig**	['vɑnli]
original (unusual)	**original**	[ɔrigi'nɑl]
past (recent)	**forrige**	['fɔriə]
permanent (adj)	**fast, permanent**	['fɑst], ['pɛrmɑˌnɛnt]
personal (adj)	**personlig**	[pæ'ʂʊnli]

polite (adj)	**høflig**	[ˈhøfll]
poor (not rich)	**fattig**	['fɑti]
possible (adj)	**mulig**	['mʉli]
present (current)	**nåværende**	['nɔˌværenə]
previous (adj)	**foregående**	['fɔreˌgoːŋə]

principal (main)	**hoved-, prinsipal**	['hɔvəd-], ['prinsiˌpɑl]
private (~ jet)	**privat**	[pri'vɑt]
probable (adj)	**sannsynlig**	[sɑn'sʏnli]
prolonged (e.g., ~ applause)	**langvarig**	['lɑŋˌvɑri]

public (open to all)	**offentlig**	['ɔfentli]
punctual (person)	**punktlig**	['pʉnktli]
quiet (tranquil)	**rolig**	['rʊli]
rare (adj)	**sjelden**	['ʂɛlən]
raw (uncooked)	**rå**	['rɔ]
right (not left)	**høyre**	['højrə]
right, correct (adj)	**riktig**	['rikti]
ripe (fruit)	**moden**	['mʊdən]
risky (adj)	**risikabel**	[risi'kabəl]
sad (~ look)	**trist**	['trist]
sad (depressing)	**sørgmodig**	[sør'mʊdi]
safe (not dangerous)	**sikker**	['sikər]
salty (food)	**salt**	['salt]
satisfied (customer)	**fornøyd, tilfreds**	[fɔr'nøjd], [til'frɛds]
second hand (adj)	**brukt, secondhand**	['brʉkt], ['sekɔnˌhɛŋ]
shallow (water)	**grunn**	['grʉn]
sharp (blade, etc.)	**skarp**	['skarp]
short (in length)	**kort**	['kʊːt]
short, short-lived (adj)	**kortvarig**	['kʊːtˌvari]
significant (notable)	**betydelig**	[be'tydəli]
similar (adj)	**lik**	['lik]
simple (easy)	**enkel**	['ɛnkəl]
skinny	**benete, mager**	['benetə], ['magər]
small (in size)	**liten**	['litən]
smooth (surface)	**glatt**	['glat]
soft (~ toys)	**bløt**	['bløt]
solid (~ wall)	**solid, holdbar**	[sʊ'lid], ['hɔlˌbar]
sour (flavor, taste)	**sur**	['sʉr]
spacious (house, etc.)	**rommelig**	['rʊmeli]
special (adj)	**spesial**	[spesi'al]
straight (line, road)	**rett**	['rɛt]
strong (person)	**sterk**	['stærk]
stupid (foolish)	**dum**	['dʉm]
suitable (e.g., ~ for drinking)	**egnet**	['æjnət]
sunny (day)	**solrik**	['sʊlˌrik]
superb, perfect (adj)	**utmerket**	['ʉtˌmærkət]
swarthy (adj)	**mørkhudet**	['mœrkˌhʉdət]
sweet (sugary)	**søt**	['søt]
tan (adj)	**solbrent**	['sʊlˌbrɛnt]
tasty (delicious)	**lekker**	['lekər]
tender (affectionate)	**øm**	['øm]
the highest (adj)	**høyest**	['højɛst]
the most important	**viktigste**	['viktigstə]

the nearest	**nærmeste**	['nærmɛstə]
the same, equal (adj)	**samme, lik**	['samə], ['lik]
thick (e.g., ~ fog)	**tykk**	['tʏk]
thick (wall, slice)	**tykk**	['tʏk]

thin (person)	**slank, tynn**	['ʂlank], ['tʏn]
tight (~ shoes)	**trange**	['traŋə]
tired (exhausted)	**trett**	['trɛt]
tiring (adj)	**trøttende**	['trœtɛnə]

transparent (adj)	**transparent**	['transpaˌraŋ]
unclear (adj)	**uklar**	['ʉˌklar]
unique (exceptional)	**unik**	[ʉ'nik]
various (adj)	**forskjellig**	[fɔ'ʂɛli]

warm (moderately hot)	**varm**	['varm]
wet (e.g., ~ clothes)	**våt**	['vɔt]
whole (entire, complete)	**hel**	['hel]
wide (e.g., ~ road)	**bred**	['bre]
young (adj)	**ung**	['ʉŋ]

MAIN 500 VERBS

252. Verbs A-C

to accompany (vt)	å følge	[ɔ 'følə]
to accuse (vt)	å anklage	[ɔ 'anˌklagə]
to acknowledge (admit)	å erkjenne	[ɔ ær'çɛnə]
to act (take action)	å handle	[ɔ 'handlə]
to add (supplement)	å tilføye	[ɔ 'tilˌføjə]
to address (speak to)	å tiltale	[ɔ 'tilˌtalə]
to admire (vi)	å beundre	[ɔ be'ʉndrə]
to advertise (vt)	å reklamere	[ɔ rɛkla'merə]
to advise (vt)	å råde	[ɔ 'roːdə]
to affirm (assert)	å påstå	[ɔ 'pɔˌstɔ]
to agree (say yes)	å samtykke	[ɔ 'samˌtʏkə]
to aim (to point a weapon)	å sikte på ...	[ɔ 'siktə pɔ ...]
to allow (sb to do sth)	å tillate	[ɔ 'tiˌlatə]
to amputate (vt)	å amputere	[ɔ ampʉ'terə]
to answer (vi, vt)	å svare	[ɔ 'svarə]
to apologize (vi)	å unnskylde seg	[ɔ 'ʉnˌsylə sæj]
to appear (come into view)	å dukke opp	[ɔ 'dʉkə ɔp]
to applaud (vi, vt)	å applaudere	[ɔ aplaʉ'derə]
to appoint (assign)	å utnevne	[ɔ 'ʉtˌnɛvnə]
to approach (come closer)	å nærme seg	[ɔ 'nærmə sæj]
to arrive (ab. train)	å ankomme	[ɔ 'anˌkɔmə]
to ask (~ sb to do sth)	å be	[ɔ 'be]
to aspire to ...	å aspirere	[ɔ aspi'rerə]
to assist (help)	å assistere	[ɔ asi'sterə]
to attack (mil.)	å angripe	[ɔ 'anˌgripə]
to attain (objectives)	å oppnå	[ɔ 'ɔpnɔ]
to avenge (get revenge)	å hevne	[ɔ 'hɛvnə]
to avoid (danger, task)	å unngå	[ɔ 'ʉŋˌgɔ]
to award (give medal to)	å belønne	[ɔ be'lœnə]
to battle (vi)	å kjempe	[ɔ 'çɛmpə]
to be (vi)	å være	[ɔ 'værə]
to be a cause of ...	å forårsake	[ɔ forɔː'ʂakə]
to be afraid	å frykte	[ɔ 'frʏktə]
to be angry (with ...)	å være vred på ...	[ɔ 'værə vred pɔ ...]

to be at war	å være i krig	[ɔ 'væːrə i ˌkrig]
to be based (on …)	å være basert på …	[ɔ 'væːrə bɑ'sɛːʈ pɔ …]
to be bored	å kjede seg	[ɔ 'çedə sæj]
to be convinced	å være overbevist	[ɔ 'væːrə 'ɔvərbeˌvist]
to be enough	å være nok	[ɔ 'væːrə ˌnɔk]
to be envious	å misunne	[ɔ 'misˌʉnə]
to be indignant	å bli indignert	[ɔ 'bli indi'gnɛːʈ]
to be interested in …	å interessere seg	[ɔ intəre'serə sæj]
to be lost in thought	å gruble	[ɔ 'grʉblə]
to be lying (~ on the table)	å ligge	[ɔ 'ligə]
to be needed	å være behøv	[ɔ 'væːrə bə'høv]
to be perplexed (puzzled)	å være forvirret	[ɔ 'væːrə for'virət]
to be preserved	å bevares	[ɔ be'vɑrəs]
to be required	å være nødvendig	[ɔ 'væːrə 'nødˌvɛndi]
to be surprised	å bli forundret	[ɔ 'bli fo'rʉndrət]
to be worried	å bekymre seg	[ɔ be'çymrə sæj]
to beat (to hit)	å slå	[ɔ ˌʂlɔ]
to become (e.g., ~ old)	å bli	[ɔ 'bli]
to behave (vi)	å oppføre seg	[ɔ 'ɔpˌførə sæj]
to believe (think)	å tro	[ɔ 'trʉ]
to belong to …	å tilhøre …	[ɔ 'tilˌhørə …]
to berth (moor)	å fortøye	[ɔ fɔ:'ʈøjə]
to blind (other drivers)	å blende	[ɔ 'blenə]
to blow (wind)	å blåse	[ɔ 'blo:sə]
to blush (vi)	å rødme	[ɔ 'rødmə]
to boast (vi)	å prale	[ɔ 'prɑlə]
to borrow (money)	å låne	[ɔ 'lo:nə]
to break (branch, toy, etc.)	å bryte	[ɔ 'brytə]
to breathe (vi)	å ånde	[ɔ 'ɔŋdə]
to bring (sth)	å bringe	[ɔ 'briŋə]
to burn (paper, logs)	å brenne	[ɔ 'brɛnə]
to buy (purchase)	å kjøpe	[ɔ 'çœːpə]
to call (~ for help)	å tilkalle	[ɔ 'tilˌkalə]
to call (yell for sb)	å kalle	[ɔ 'kalə]
to calm down (vt)	å berolige	[ɔ bə'rʉliə]
can (v aux)	å kunne	[ɔ 'kʉnə]
to cancel (call off)	å avlyse, å annullere	[ɔ 'avˌlysə], [ɔ anʉ'lerə]
to cast off (of a boat or ship)	å kaste loss	[ɔ 'kastə lɔs]
to catch (e.g., ~ a ball)	å fange	[ɔ 'faŋə]
to change (~ one's opinion)	å endre	[ɔ 'ɛndrə]
to change (exchange)	å veksle	[ɔ 'vɛkslə]
to charm (vt)	å sjarmere	[ɔ 'ʂarˌmerə]
to choose (select)	å velge	[ɔ 'vɛlgə]

to chop off (with an ax)	å hugge av	[ɔ 'hʉgə ɑ:]
to clean	å rengjøre	[ɔ rɛn'jørə]
(e.g., kettle from scale)		
to clean (shoes, etc.)	å rense	[ɔ 'rɛnsə]

to clean up (tidy)	å rydde	[ɔ 'rʏdə]
to close (vt)	å lukke	[ɔ 'lʉkə]
to comb one's hair	å kamme	[ɔ 'kamə]
to come down (the stairs)	å gå ned	[ɔ 'gɔ ne]

to come out (book)	å komme ut	[ɔ 'kɔmə ʉt]
to compare (vt)	å sammenlikne	[ɔ 'samənˌliknə]
to compensate (vt)	å kompensere	[ɔ kʉmpen'serə]
to compete (vi)	å konkurrere	[ɔ kʉnkʉ'rerə]

to compile (~ a list)	å sammenstille	[ɔ 'samənˌstilə]
to complain (vi, vt)	å klage	[ɔ 'klagə]
to complicate (vt)	å komplisere	[ɔ kʉmpli'serə]
to compose (music, etc.)	å komponere	[ɔ kʉmpʉ'nerə]

to compromise (reputation)	å kompromittere	[ɔ kʉmprʉmi'terə]
to concentrate (vi)	å konsentrere seg	[ɔ kʉnsen'trerə sæj]
to confess (criminal)	å tilstå	[ɔ 'tilˌstɔ]
to confuse (mix up)	å forveksle	[ɔ fɔr'vɛkʂlə]

to congratulate (vt)	å gratulere	[ɔ gratʉ'lerə]
to consult (doctor, expert)	å konsultere	[ɔ kʉnsʉl'terə]
to continue (~ to do sth)	å fortsette	[ɔ 'fɔrtˌsɛtə]
to control (vt)	å kontrollere	[ɔ kʉntrɔ'lerə]

to convince (vt)	å overbevise	[ɔ 'ɔvərbeˌvisə]
to cooperate (vi)	å samarbeide	[ɔ 'samarˌbæjdə]
to coordinate (vt)	å koordinere	[ɔ kɔːɖi'nerə]
to correct (an error)	å rette	[ɔ 'rɛtə]

to cost (vt)	å koste	[ɔ 'kɔstə]
to count (money, etc.)	å telle	[ɔ 'tɛlə]
to count on ...	å regne med ...	[ɔ 'rɛjnə me ...]
to crack (ceiling, wall)	å sprekke	[ɔ 'sprɛkə]

to create (vt)	å opprette	[ɔ 'ɔpˌrɛtə]
to crush,	å knuse	[ɔ 'knʉsə]
to squash (~ a bug)		
to cry (weep)	å gråte	[ɔ 'groːtə]
to cut off (with a knife)	å skjære av	[ɔ 'ʂæːrə ɑ:]

253. Verbs D-G

| to dare (~ to do sth) | å våge | [ɔ 'voːgə] |
| to date from ... | å datere seg | [ɔ dɑ'terə sæj] |

to deceive (vi, vt)	å fuske	[ɔ 'fʉskə]
to decide (~ to do sth)	å beslutte	[ɔ be'ʂlʉtə]
to decorate (tree, street)	å pryde	[ɔ 'prydə]
to dedicate (book, etc.)	å tilegne	[ɔ 'til,egnə]
to defend (a country, etc.)	å forsvare	[ɔ fɔ'ʂvarə]
to defend oneself	å forsvare seg	[ɔ fɔ'ʂvarə sæj]
to demand (request firmly)	å kreve	[ɔ 'krevə]
to denounce (vt)	å angi	[ɔ 'an,ji]
to deny (vt)	å fornekte	[ɔ fɔː'nɛktə]
to depend on ...	å avhenge av ...	[ɔ 'av,henə aː ...]
to deprive (vt)	å berøve	[ɔ be'røvə]
to deserve (vt)	å fortjene	[ɔ fɔ'tjenə]
to design (machine, etc.)	å prosjektere	[ɔ prʉʂɛk'terə]
to desire (want, wish)	å ønske	[ɔ 'ønskə]
to despise (vt)	å forakte	[ɔ fɔ'raktə]
to destroy (documents, etc.)	å ødelegge	[ɔ 'ødə,legə]
to differ (from sth)	å skille seg fra ...	[ɔ 'ʂilə sæj fra ...]
to dig (tunnel, etc.)	å grave	[ɔ 'gravə]
to direct (point the way)	å vise vei	[ɔ 'visə væj]
to disappear (vi)	å forsvinne	[ɔ fɔ'ʂvinə]
to discover (new land, etc.)	å oppdage	[ɔ 'ɔp,dagə]
to discuss (vt)	å diskutere	[ɔ diskʉ'terə]
to distribute (leaflets, etc.)	å dele ut	[ɔ 'delə ʉt]
to disturb (vt)	å forstyrre	[ɔ fɔ'ʂtʏrə]
to dive (vi)	å dykke	[ɔ 'dʏkə]
to divide (math)	å dividere	[ɔ divi'derə]
to do (vt)	å gjøre	[ɔ 'jørə]
to do the laundry	å vaske	[ɔ 'vaskə]
to double (increase)	å fordoble	[ɔ fɔr'dɔblə]
to doubt (have doubts)	å tvile	[ɔ 'tvilə]
to draw a conclusion	å konkludere	[ɔ kʉnklʉ'derə]
to dream (daydream)	å drømme	[ɔ 'drœmə]
to dream (in sleep)	å drømme	[ɔ 'drœmɔ]
to drink (vi, vt)	å drikke	[ɔ 'drikə]
to drive a car	å kjøre bil	[ɔ 'çœːrə ˌbil]
to drive away (scare away)	å jage bort	[ɔ 'jagə 'bʉːt]
to drop (let fall)	å tappe	[ɔ 'tapə]
to drown (ab. person)	å drukne	[ɔ 'drʉknə]
to dry (clothes, hair)	å tørke	[ɔ 'tœrkə]
to eat (vi, vt)	å spise	[ɔ 'spisə]
to eavesdrop (vi)	å tyvlytte	[ɔ 'tyv,lʏtə]

to emit (diffuse - odor, etc.)	å spre, å sprede	[ɔ 'spre], [ɔ 'spredə]
to enjoy oneself	å more seg	[ɔ 'mʊrə sæj]
to enter (on the list)	å skrive inn	[ɔ 'skrivə in]
to enter (room, house, etc.)	å komme inn	[ɔ 'kɔmə in]
to entertain (amuse)	å underholde	[ɔ 'ʉnər̩hɔlə]
to equip (fit out)	å utstyre	[ɔ 'ʉt̩styrə]
to examine (proposal)	å undersøke	[ɔ 'ʉnə̩søkə]
to exchange (sth)	å utveksle	[ɔ 'ʉt̩vɛkslə]
to excuse (forgive)	å unnskylde	[ɔ 'ʉn̩sylə]
to exist (vi)	å eksistere	[ɔ ɛksi'sterə]
to expect (anticipate)	å forvente	[ɔ fɔr'vɛntə]
to expect (foresee)	å forutse	[ɔ 'fɔrʉt̩sə]
to expel (from school, etc.)	å uteslutte	[ɔ 'ʉtə̩slʉtə]
to explain (vt)	å forklare	[ɔ fɔr'klɑrə]
to express (vt)	å uttrykke	[ɔ 'ʉt̩rʏkə]
to extinguish (a fire)	å slokke	[ɔ 'ʂløkə]
to fall in love (with ...)	å forelske seg i ...	[ɔ fɔ'rɛlskə sæj i ...]
to feed (provide food)	å mate	[ɔ 'mɑtə]
to fight (against the enemy)	å kjempe	[ɔ 'çɛmpə]
to fight (vi)	å slåss	[ɔ 'ʂlɔs]
to fill (glass, bottle)	å fylle	[ɔ 'fʏlə]
to find (~ lost items)	å finne	[ɔ 'finə]
to finish (vt)	å slutte	[ɔ 'ʂlʉtə]
to fish (angle)	å fiske	[ɔ 'fiskə]
to fit (ab. dress, etc.)	å passe	[ɔ 'pɑsə]
to flatter (vt)	å smigre	[ɔ 'smigrə]
to fly (bird, plane)	å fly	[ɔ 'fly]
to follow ... (come after)	å følge etter ...	[ɔ 'følə 'ɛtər ...]
to forbid (vt)	å forby	[ɔ fɔr'by]
to force (compel)	å tvinge	[ɔ 'tviŋə]
to forget (vi, vt)	å glemme	[ɔ 'glemə]
to forgive (pardon)	å tilgi	[ɔ 'til̩ji]
to form (constitute)	å danne, å forme	[ɔ 'dɑnə], [ɔ 'fɔrmə]
to get dirty (vi)	å skitne seg til	[ɔ 'ʂitnə sæj til]
to get infected (with ...)	å bli smittet	[ɔ 'bli 'smitət]
to get irritated	å bli irritert	[ɔ 'bli iri'tɛːt]
to get married	å gifte seg	[ɔ 'jiftə sæj]
to get rid of ...	å bli kvitt ...	[ɔ 'bli 'kvit ...]
to get tired	å bli trett	[ɔ 'bli 'trɛt]
to get up (arise from bed)	å stå opp	[ɔ 'stɔː ɔp]

to give (vt)	å gi	[ɔ ˈji]
to give a bath (to bath)	å bade	[ɔ ˈbɑdə]
to give a hug, to hug (vt)	å omfavne	[ɔ ˈɔmˌfɑvnə]
to give in (yield to)	å gi etter	[ɔ ˈji ˈɛtər]
to glimpse (vt)	å bemerke	[ɔ beˈmæːrkə]
to go (by car, etc.)	å kjøre	[ɔ ˈçœːrə]
to go (on foot)	å gå	[ɔ ˈgɔ]
to go for a swim	å bade	[ɔ ˈbɑdə]
to go out (for dinner, etc.)	å gå ut	[ɔ ˈgɔ ʉt]
to go to bed (go to sleep)	å gå til sengs	[ɔ ˈgɔ til ˈsɛŋs]
to greet (vt)	å hilse	[ɔ ˈhilsə]
to grow (plants)	å avle	[ɔ ˈɑvlə]
to guarantee (vt)	å garantere	[ɔ gɑrɑnˈterə]
to guess (the answer)	å gjette	[ɔ ˈjɛtə]

254. Verbs H-M

to hand out (distribute)	å dele ut	[ɔ ˈdelə ʉt]
to hang (curtains, etc.)	å henge	[ɔ ˈhɛŋə]
to have (vt)	å ha	[ɔ ˈhɑ]
to have a try	å forsøke	[ɔ fɔˈsøkə]
to have breakfast	å spise frokost	[ɔ ˈspisə ˌfrʉkɔst]
to have dinner	å spise middag	[ɔ ˈspisə ˈmiˌdɑ]
to have lunch	å spise lunsj	[ɔ ˈspisə ˌlʉnʃ]
to head (group, etc.)	å lede	[ɔ ˈledə]
to hear (vt)	å høre	[ɔ ˈhørə]
to heat (vt)	å varme	[ɔ ˈvɑrmə]
to help (vt)	å hjelpe	[ɔ ˈjɛlpə]
to hide (vt)	å gjemme	[ɔ ˈjɛmə]
to hire (e.g., ~ a boat)	å leie	[ɔ ˈlæjə]
to hire (staff)	å ansette	[ɔ ˈɑnˌsɛtə]
to hope (vi, vt)	å håpe	[ɔ ˈhoːpə]
to hunt (for food, sport)	å jage	[ɔ ˈjagə]
to hurry (vi)	å skynde seg	[ɔ ˈʃynə ɔɕj]
to imagine (to picture)	å forestille seg	[ɔ ˈfɔrəˌstilə sæj]
to imitate (vt)	å imitere	[ɔ imiˈterə]
to implore (vt)	å bønnefalle	[ɔ ˈbœnəˌfalə]
to import (vt)	å importere	[ɔ impɔːˈterə]
to increase (vi)	å øke	[ɔ ˈøkə]
to increase (vt)	å øke	[ɔ ˈøkə]
to infect (vt)	å smitte	[ɔ ˈsmitə]
to influence (vt)	å påvirke	[ɔ ˈpoˌvirkə]
to inform (e.g., ~ the police about)	å meddele	[ɔ ˈmɛdˌdelə]

to inform (vt)	å informere	[ɔ infor'merə]
to inherit (vt)	å arve	[ɔ 'arvə]
to inquire (about ...)	å få vite	[ɔ 'fɔ 'vitə]
to insert (put in)	å sette inn	[ɔ 'sɛtə in]
to insinuate (imply)	å insinuere	[ɔ insinʉ'erə]
to insist (vi, vt)	å insistere	[ɔ insi'sterə]
to inspire (vt)	å inspirere	[ɔ inspi'rerə]
to instruct (teach)	å instruere	[ɔ instrʉ'erə]
to insult (offend)	å fornærme	[ɔ fɔː'ŋærmə]
to interest (vt)	å interessere	[ɔ intəre'serə]
to intervene (vi)	å intervenere	[ɔ intərve'nerə]
to introduce (sb to sb)	å presentere	[ɔ presen'terə]
to invent (machine, etc.)	å oppfinne	[ɔ 'ɔp,finə]
to invite (vt)	å innby, å invitere	[ɔ 'inby], [ɔ invi'terə]
to iron (clothes)	å stryke	[ɔ 'strykə]
to irritate (annoy)	å irritere	[ɔ iri'terə]
to isolate (vt)	å isolere	[ɔ isʉ'lerə]
to join (political party, etc.)	å tilslutte seg ...	[ɔ 'til,slʉtə sæj ...]
to joke (be kidding)	å spøke	[ɔ 'spøkə]
to keep (old letters, etc.)	å beholde	[ɔ be'hɔlə]
to keep silent	å tie	[ɔ 'tie]
to kill (vt)	å døde, å myrde	[ɔ 'dødə], [ɔ 'mʏːɖə]
to knock (at the door)	å knakke	[ɔ 'knakə]
to know (sb)	å kjenne	[ɔ 'çɛnə]
to know (sth)	å vite	[ɔ 'vitə]
to laugh (vi)	å le, å skratte	[ɔ 'le], [ɔ 'skratə]
to launch (start up)	å starte	[ɔ 'staːʈə]
to leave (~ for Mexico)	å afrejse	[ɔ 'af,ræjsə]
to leave (forget sth)	å glemme	[ɔ 'glemə]
to leave (spouse)	å forlate, å etterlate	[ɔ fɔ'lɑtə], [ɔ ɛtə'lɑtə]
to liberate (city, etc.)	å befri	[ɔ be'fri]
to lie (~ on the floor)	å ligge	[ɔ 'ligə]
to lie (tell untruth)	å lyve	[ɔ 'lyvə]
to light (campfire, etc.)	å tenne	[ɔ 'tɛnə]
to light up (illuminate)	å belyse	[ɔ be'lysə]
to like (I like ...)	å like	[ɔ 'likə]
to limit (vt)	å begrense	[ɔ be'grɛnsə]
to listen (vi)	å lye, å lytte	[ɔ 'lye], [ɔ 'lʏtə]
to live (~ in France)	å bo	[ɔ 'bʊ]
to live (exist)	å leve	[ɔ 'levə]
to load (gun)	å lade	[ɔ 'lɑdə]
to load (vehicle, etc.)	å laste	[ɔ 'lɑstə]
to look (I'm just ~ing)	å se	[ɔ 'se]
to look for ... (search)	å søke ...	[ɔ 'søkə ...]

to look like (resemble)	å ligne, å likne	[ɔ 'linə], [ɔ 'liknə]
to lose (umbrella, etc.)	å miste	[ɔ 'mistə]
to love (e.g., ~ dancing)	å elske	[ɔ 'ɛlskə]
to love (sb)	å elske	[ɔ 'ɛlskə]
to lower (blind, head)	å heise ned	[ɔ 'hæjsə ne]
to make (~ dinner)	å lage	[ɔ 'lagə]
to make a mistake	å gjøre feil	[ɔ 'jørə ˌfæjl]
to make angry	å gjøre sint	[ɔ 'jørə ˌsint]
to make easier	å lette	[ɔ 'letə]
to make multiple copies	å kopiere	[ɔ kʊ'pjerə]
to make the acquaintance	å stifte bekjentskap med …	[ɔ 'stiftə be'çɛnˌskap me …]
to make use (of …)	å anvende	[ɔ 'anˌvɛnə]
to manage, to run	å styre, å lede	[ɔ 'styrə], [ɔ 'ledə]
to mark (make a mark)	å markere	[ɔ mar'kerə]
to mean (signify)	å bety	[ɔ 'bety]
to memorize (vt)	å memorere	[ɔ memʊ'rerə]
to mention (talk about)	å omtale, å nevne	[ɔ 'ɔmˌtalə], [ɔ 'nɛvnə]
to miss (school, etc.)	å skulke	[ɔ 'skʉlkə]
to mix (combine, blend)	å blande	[ɔ 'blanə]
to mock (make fun of)	å håne	[ɔ 'hoːnə]
to move (to shift)	å flytte	[ɔ 'flʏtə]
to multiply (math)	å multiplisere	[ɔ mʉltipli'serə]
must (v aux)	å måtte	[ɔ 'moːtə]

255. Verbs N-R

to name, to call (vt)	å kalle	[ɔ 'kalə]
to negotiate (vi)	å forhandle	[ɔ fɔr'handlə]
to note (write down)	å notere	[ɔ nʊ'terə]
to notice (see)	å bemerke	[ɔ be'mærkə]
to obey (vi, vt)	å underordne seg	[ɔ 'ʉnərˌɔrdnə sæj]
to object (vi, vt)	å innvende	[ɔ 'inˌvɛnə]
to observe (see)	å observere	[ɔ ɔbsɛr'verə]
to offend (vt)	å fornærme	[ɔ fɔːˈnɑɔrmɔ]
to omit (word, phrase)	å utelate	[ɔ 'ʉtəˌlatə]
to open (vt)	å åpne	[ɔ 'ɔpnə]
to order (in restaurant)	å bestille	[ɔ be'stilə]
to order (mil.)	å beordre	[ɔ be'ɔrdrə]
to organize (concert, party)	å arrangere	[ɔ araŋ'serə]
to overestimate (vt)	å overvurdere	[ɔ 'ɔvərvʉːˌderə]
to own (possess)	å besidde, å eie	[ɔ bɛ'sidə], [ɔ 'æje]
to participate (vi)	å delta	[ɔ 'dɛlta]

to pass through (by car, etc.)	å passere	[ɔ pɑ'serə]
to pay (vi, vt)	å betale	[ɔ be'tɑlə]
to peep, spy on	å kikke	[ɔ 'çikə]
to penetrate (vt)	å trenge inn	[ɔ 'trɛŋə in]
to permit (vt)	å tillate	[ɔ 'ti‚lɑtə]
to pick (flowers)	å plukke	[ɔ 'plʉkə]
to place (put, set)	å plassere	[ɔ plɑ'serə]
to plan (~ to do sth)	å planlegge	[ɔ 'plɑn‚legə]
to play (actor)	å spille	[ɔ 'spilə]
to play (children)	å leke	[ɔ 'lekə]
to point (~ the way)	å peke	[ɔ 'pekə]
to pour (liquid)	å helle opp	[ɔ 'hɛlə ɔp]
to pray (vi, vt)	å be	[ɔ 'be]
to prefer (vt)	å foretrekke	[ɔ 'fɔrə‚trɛkə]
to prepare (~ a plan)	å forberede	[ɔ 'fɔrbə‚redə]
to present (sb to sb)	å presentere	[ɔ presen'terə]
to preserve (peace, life)	å bevare	[ɔ be'vɑrə]
to prevail (vt)	å dominere	[ɔ dʉmi'nerə]
to progress (move forward)	å gå framover	[ɔ 'gɔ ‚frɑm'ɔvər]
to promise (vt)	å love	[ɔ 'lɔvə]
to pronounce (vt)	å uttale	[ɔ 'ʉt‚tɑlə]
to propose (vt)	å foreslå	[ɔ 'fɔrə‚slɔ]
to protect (e.g., ~ nature)	å beskytte	[ɔ be'sytə]
to protest (vi)	å protestere	[ɔ prʉte'sterə]
to prove (vt)	å bevise	[ɔ be'visə]
to provoke (vt)	å provosere	[ɔ prʉvʉ'serə]
to pull (~ the rope)	å trekke	[ɔ 'trɛkə]
to punish (vt)	å straffe	[ɔ 'strɑfə]
to push (~ the door)	å skubbe, å støte	[ɔ 'skʉbə], [ɔ 'støtə]
to put away (vt)	å stue unna	[ɔ 'stʉə 'ʉnɑ]
to put in order	å bringe orden	[ɔ 'briŋə 'ɔrdən]
to put, to place	å legge	[ɔ 'legə]
to quote (cite)	å sitere	[ɔ si'terə]
to reach (arrive at)	å nå	[ɔ 'nɔː]
to read (vi, vt)	å lese	[ɔ 'lesə]
to realize (a dream)	å realisere	[ɔ reɑli'serə]
to recognize (identify sb)	å gjenkjenne	[ɔ 'jen‚çɛnə]
to recommend (vt)	å anbefale	[ɔ 'ɑnbe‚fɑlə]
to recover (~ from flu)	å bli frisk	[ɔ 'bli 'frisk]
to redo (do again)	å gjøre om	[ɔ 'jørə ɔm]
to reduce (speed, etc.)	å minske	[ɔ 'minskə]

to refuse (~ sb)	å avslå	[ɔ 'ɑfˌslɔ]
to regret (be sorry)	å beklage	[ɔ be'klɑgə]
to reinforce (vt)	å styrke	[ɔ 'styrkə]
to remember (Do you ~ me?)	å huske	[ɔ 'hʉskə]

to remember (I can't ~ her name)	å huske	[ɔ 'hʉskə]
to remind of ...	å påminne	[ɔ 'poˌminə]
to remove (~ a stain)	å fjerne	[ɔ 'fjæːɳə]
to remove (~ an obstacle)	å fjerne	[ɔ 'fjæːɳə]

to rent (sth from sb)	å leie	[ɔ 'læjə]
to repair (mend)	å reparere	[ɔ repɑ'rerə]
to repeat (say again)	å gjenta	[ɔ 'jɛntɑ]
to report (make a report)	å rapportere	[ɔ rɑpɔ:'ʈerə]

to reproach (vt)	å bebreide	[ɔ be'bræjdə]
to reserve, to book	å reservere	[ɔ resɛr'verə]
to restrain (hold back)	å avholde	[ɔ 'ɑvˌhɔlə]
to return (come back)	å komme tilbake	[ɔ 'kɔmə til'bɑkə]

to risk, to take a risk	å risikere	[ɔ risi'kerə]
to rub out (erase)	å viske ut	[ɔ 'viskə ʉt]
to run (move fast)	å løpe	[ɔ 'løpə]
to rush (hurry sb)	å skynde	[ɔ 'ʂynə]

256. Verbs S-W

to satisfy (please)	å tilfredsstille	[ɔ 'tilfrɛdsˌstilə]
to save (rescue)	å redde	[ɔ 'rɛdə]
to say (~ thank you)	å si	[ɔ 'si]
to scold (vt)	å skjelle	[ɔ 'ʂɛːlə]

to scratch (with claws)	å klore	[ɔ 'klɔrə]
to select (to pick)	å velge ut	[ɔ 'vɛlgə ʉt]
to sell (goods)	å selge	[ɔ 'sɛlə]
to send (a letter)	å sende	[ɔ 'sɛnə]

to send back (vt)	å sende tilbake	[ɔ 'sɛnə til'bɑkə]
to sense (~ danger)	å kjenne	[ɔ 'çɛnə]
to sentence (vt)	å dømme	[ɔ 'dœmə]
to serve (in restaurant)	å betjene	[ɔ be'tjenə]

to settle (a conflict)	å løse	[ɔ 'løsə]
to shake (vt)	å riste	[ɔ 'ristə]
to shave (vi)	å barbere seg	[ɔ bɑr'berə sæj]
to shine (gleam)	å skinne	[ɔ 'ʂinə]
to shiver (with cold)	å skjelve	[ɔ 'ʂɛlvə]
to shoot (vi)	å skyte	[ɔ 'ʂytə]

| to shout (vi) | å skrike | [ɔ 'skrikə] |
| to show (to display) | å vise | [ɔ 'visə] |

to shudder (vi)	å gyse	[ɔ 'jisə]
to sigh (vi)	å sukke	[ɔ 'sɯkə]
to sign (document)	å underskrive	[ɔ 'ɯnəˌskrivə]
to signify (mean)	å bety	[ɔ 'bety]

to simplify (vt)	å forenkle	[ɔ fɔ'rɛnklə]
to sin (vi)	å synde	[ɔ 'synə]
to sit (be sitting)	å sitte	[ɔ 'sitə]
to sit down (vi)	å sette seg	[ɔ 'sɛtə sæj]

to smell (emit an odor)	å lukte	[ɔ 'lɯktə]
to smell (inhale the odor)	å lukte	[ɔ 'lɯktə]
to smile (vi)	å smile	[ɔ 'smilə]
to snap (vi, ab. rope)	å gå i stykker	[ɔ gɔ i 'stʏkər]
to solve (problem)	å løse	[ɔ 'løsə]

to sow (seed, crop)	å så	[ɔ 'sɔ]
to spill (liquid)	å spille	[ɔ 'spilə]
to spill out, scatter (flour, etc.)	å bli spilt	[ɔ 'bli 'spilt]
to spit (vi)	å spytte	[ɔ 'spʏtə]

to stand (toothache, cold)	å tåle	[ɔ 'tɔːlə]
to start (begin)	å begynne	[ɔ be'jinə]
to steal (money, etc.)	å stjele	[ɔ 'stjelə]
to stop (for pause, etc.)	å stoppe	[ɔ 'stɔpə]

to stop (please ~ calling me)	å slutte	[ɔ 'ʂlɯtə]
to stop talking	å slutte å snakke	[ɔ 'ʂlɯtə ɔ 'snakə]
to stroke (caress)	å stryke	[ɔ 'strykə]
to study (vt)	å studere	[ɔ stɯ'derə]

to suffer (feel pain)	å lide	[ɔ 'lidə]
to support (cause, idea)	å støtte	[ɔ 'stœtə]
to suppose (assume)	å anta, å formode	[ɔ 'anˌtɑ], [ɔ fɔr'mɯdə]
to surface (ab. submarine)	å dykke opp	[ɔ 'dʏkə ɔp]

to surprise (amaze)	å forundre	[ɔ fɔ'rɯndrə]
to suspect (vt)	å mistenke	[ɔ 'misˌtɛnkə]
to swim (vi)	å svømme	[ɔ 'svœmə]
to take (get hold of)	å ta	[ɔ 'tɑ]
to take a bath	å vaske seg	[ɔ 'vɑskə sæj]
to take a rest	å hvile	[ɔ 'vilə]
to take away (e.g., about waiter)	å fjerne	[ɔ 'fjæːɳə]
to take off (airplane)	å løfte	[ɔ 'lœftə]
to take off (painting, curtains, etc.)	å ta ned	[ɔ 'tɑ ne]

to take pictures	å fotografere	[ɔ fotɔgraˈferə]
to talk to …	å tale med …	[ɔ ˈtalə me …]
to teach (give lessons)	å undervise	[ɔ ˈʉnərˌvisə]

to tear off, to rip off (vt)	å rive av	[ɔ ˈrivə ɑː]
to tell (story, joke)	å fortelle	[ɔ fɔːˈʈɛlə]
to thank (vt)	å takke	[ɔ ˈtakə]
to think (believe)	å tro	[ɔ ˈtrʊ]

to think (vi, vt)	å tenke	[ɔ ˈtɛnkə]
to threaten (vt)	å true	[ɔ ˈtrʉə]
to throw (stone, etc.)	å kaste	[ɔ ˈkɑstə]
to tie to …	å binde fast	[ɔ ˈbinə ˈfast]

to tie up (prisoner)	å binde	[ɔ ˈbinə]
to tire (make tired)	å trette	[ɔ ˈtrɛtə]
to touch (one's arm, etc.)	å røre	[ɔ ˈrørə]
to tower (over …)	å rage over	[ɔ ˈragə ˈɔvər]

to train (animals)	å dressere	[ɔ drɛˈserə]
to train (sb)	å trene	[ɔ ˈtrenə]
to train (vi)	å trene	[ɔ ˈtrenə]
to transform (vt)	å transformere	[ɔ transfɔrˈmerə]

to translate (vt)	å oversette	[ɔ ˈɔvəˌsɛtə]
to treat (illness)	å behandle	[ɔ beˈhandlə]
to trust (vt)	å stole på	[ɔ ˈstʊlə pɔ]
to try (attempt)	å prøve	[ɔ ˈprøvə]

to turn (e.g., ~ left)	å svinge	[ɔ ˈsviŋə]
to turn away (vi)	å vende seg bort	[ɔ ˈvɛnə sæj bʊːʈ]
to turn off (the light)	å slokke	[ɔ ˈşlɔkə]
to turn on (computer, etc.)	å slå på	[ɔ ˈşlɔ pɔ]
to turn over (stone, etc.)	å vende	[ɔ ˈvɛnə]

to underestimate (vt)	å undervurdere	[ɔ ˈʉnərvʉːˌderə]
to underline (vt)	å understreke	[ɔ ˈʉnəˌstrekə]
to understand (vt)	å forstå	[ɔ fɔˈştɔ]
to undertake (vt)	å foreta	[ɔ ˈfɔrəˌta]

to unite (vt)	å forene	[ɔ fɔˈrenə]
to untie (vt)	å løse opp	[ɔ ˈlʉsə ɔp]
to use (phrase, word)	å anvende	[ɔ ˈanˌvɛnə]
to vaccinate (vt)	å vaksinere	[ɔ vaksiˈnerə]

to vote (vi)	å stemme	[ɔ ˈstɛmə]
to wait (vt)	å vente	[ɔ ˈvɛntə]
to wake (sb)	å vekke	[ɔ ˈvɛkə]
to want (wish, desire)	å ville	[ɔ ˈvilə]

| to warn (of the danger) | å advare | [ɔ ˈadˌvarə] |
| to wash (clean) | å vaske | [ɔ ˈvaskə] |

| to water (plants) | å vanne | [ɔ 'vɑnə] |
| to wave (the hand) | å vinke | [ɔ 'vinkə] |

to weigh (have weight)	å veie	[ɔ 'væjə]
to work (vi)	å arbeide	[ɔ 'ɑrˌbæjdə]
to worry (make anxious)	å bekymre, å uroe	[ɔ beˈçymrə], [ɔ 'ʉːrʊə]
to worry (vi)	å uroe seg	[ɔ 'ʉːrʊə sæj]

to wrap (parcel, etc.)	å pakke inn	[ɔ 'pɑkə in]
to wrestle (sport)	å bryte	[ɔ 'brytə]
to write (vt)	å skrive	[ɔ 'skrivə]
to write down	å skrive ned	[ɔ 'skrivə ne]

Made in the USA
Monee, IL
05 July 2023